CADOGAN GUIDES

"Cadogan Guides really need no introduction and are mini-encyclopaedic on the countries covered... they give the explorer, the intellectual or cultural buff – indeed any visitor – all they need to know to get the very best from their visit... it makes a good read too by the many inveterate armchair travellers."
—*The Book Journal*

"Rochelle Jaffe, owner and manager of Travel Books Unlimited in Bethesda, Maryland, attributes [Cadogan Guides'] popularity to both their good, clean-looking format and the fact that they include 'information about everything for everyone'.... These guides are one of the most exciting series available on European travel." —*American Bookseller* magazine

"The Cadogan Guide to Italy is the most massive, literate, and helpful guide to Italy in years."
—*International Travel News*, USA

"*Italy*, by Dana Facaros and Michael Pauls is an absolute gem of a travel book, humorous, informed, sympathetic, as irresistible as that land itself."
—Anthony Clare, Books of the Year, *The Sunday Times*, 1988–89

Other titles in the Cadogan Guide series:

AUSTRALIA
BALI
THE CARIBBEAN
GREEK ISLANDS
INDIA
IRELAND
ITALIAN ISLANDS
ITALY
NORTHWEST ITALY
MOROCCO
PORTUGAL
ROME
SCOTLAND
SPAIN
THAILAND & BURMA
TURKEY
TUSCANY & UMBRIA

Forthcoming:

ECUADOR,
THE GALAPAGOS
& COLOMBIA
MEXICO
NEW YORK
NEW ORLEANS
SOUTH ITALY
TUNISIA
VENICE

ABOUT THE AUTHORS

Travel writers Dana Facaros and Michael Pauls and their two children have left their semi-cat Piggy in Umbria, and have taken Michael's musical saw and Dana's indescribable boar mating call and the computer to France.

Dear Readers,
          Please, please help us to keep this book up to date. We would be delighted to receive any additional information or suggestions. Please write to us or fill in the form on the last page of this book. Writers of the best letters will be acknowledged in future editions, and will receive a free copy of the Cadogan Guide of their choice.

The Publisher

CADOGAN GUIDES

NORTHEAST ITALY

DANA FACAROS and MICHAEL PAULS

Illustrations by Pauline Pears

CADOGAN BOOKS
London, United Kingdom

THE GLOBE PEQUOT PRESS
Chester, Connecticut

Cadogan Books Ltd
16 Lower Marsh, London SE1

The Globe Pequot Press
138 West Main Street, Chester, Connecticut 06412

Cover design by Keith Pointing
Cover illustration by Povl Webb
Maps © Cadogan Books Ltd,
drawn by Thames Cartographic Services Ltd

Series Editors: Rachel Fielding and Paula Levey

First published in 1990

British Library Cataloguing in Publication Data
Facaros, Dana
Northeast Italy: Venetia, the Dolomites, Emilia–Romagna – (Cadogan guides).
1. Italy, Northeastern Italy – Visitors' guides.
I. Title   II. Pauls, Michael
914.5304929
ISBN 0–947754–22–9

Library of Congress Cataloging-in-Publication Data
Facaros, Dana
Northeast Italy / Dana Facaros and Michael Pauls: illustrations by Pauline Pears.
p.   cm.   – (Cadogan guides)
ISBN 0–87106–449–9
1. Italy, Northern – Description and travel – Guide-books.
I. Pauls, Michael.   II. Title.   III. Series.
DG416.F34   1990   914.5'304929–dc20   90–3086 CIP

Photoset in Ehrhardt on a Linotron 202
Printed and bound in Great Britain by Redwood Press Limited,
Melksham, Wiltshire

CONTENTS

LIST OF MAPS

ACKNOWLEDGEMENTS

We would particularly like to thank Michael Davidson and Brian Walsh, whose unfailing good humour helped us through the darkest corners of Italy, and who have contributed substantially to this book by updating all the practical information. We would like to thank the Italian National Tourist Office, and all the local and municipal tourist boards who so kindly answered all our questions that had answers and loaded us down with enough information to write several more volumes about Italy. Special thanks go to Paola Greco, in London, and the Terni tourist office for their kind help to Michael and Brian. Also we would like to extend our warmest gratitude to Mario, Fiorella, Alessandra and Sara who never minded having a couple of extra children in their happy home; to Anna and Tito Illuminati, who guided us through the intricacies of life in Rosciano and always let us use their phone; to Bruce Johnston, for his innumerable suggestions and his Deux Chevaux; to longtime residents Clare Pedrick, Anne, and Santimo, for their invaluable insights into the Italian miasma; to Carolyn Steiner and Chris Malumphy, who crossed the Atlantic to cheer us up; and especially to Rachel Fielding, who like Hercules in the Augean stables, makes us printable.

The publishers would particularly like to thank Dorothy Groves and Stephen and Meg Davies for respectively copy-editing, proof-reading and indexing.

PLEASE NOTE

INTRODUCTION

Italy, the Big Boot, or rather the world's Christmas stocking, is so rich and complex that many travellers avoid it altogether. Others, who take the plunge, risk becoming addicted to its charms and foibles, and yearning to return year after year. No one knows just how many people who start off as package tourists to Venice end up becoming students of Vitruvian proportions in Palladian architecture or of the fine points of Baroque gardens, or well-researched experts on where to find the best seafood antipasti within a 20-mile radius of their holiday villa.

This book covers one the most addictive corners of Italy, the Northeast and all of its confusingly hyphenated regions: the Veneto, Trentino-Alto Adige, Friuli-Venezia Giulia, and Emilia-Romagna—much of what used to be simply known as Cisalpine Gaul when Caesar crossed the Rubicon. From the pancake flats of the Po to the razor peaks of Rosengarten, it unfolds like the pieces in a kaleidoscope into an infinite variety of patterns: the autumnal landscapes painted by Giorgione, Bellini, and Titian, the wind-sculpted pinnacles of the Dolomites, the Renaissance cities of Shakespeare's imagination, the Roman ruins of Aquileia, Ghibbelline castles and sunlit vineyards, alpine meadows and creaking glaciers, Palladian villas, luminous mosaics straight out of the Dark Ages, soft green orchards, university halls encrusted with the escutcheons of mouldy scholars.

The kaleidoscope also reveals a fair amount of what used to be called progress—grisly sprawl, suburbia, and satanic industry; Northeast Italy is an immensely prosperous place. Hulking refineries stand even at the land entrance to Venice the Most Serene—Venice, where the things of this world were once loved more passionately than anywhere. But such worldliness has always been a two-edged sword. The secret to enjoying Venetia and Emilia-Romagna is to travel leisurely, as free from timetables and reservations as you possibly can. Watch the clouds drift over Lake Garda, spend an afternoon in a country trattoria, go miles out of your way to see an anonymous fresco in a Romanesque church, sail into the pearly silences of Venice's lagoon. Leave yourself open, take the time to tune in your senses, and with a little luck you may find your own version of Fellini's *Amacord* and peacocks in the snow.

Guide to the Guide

The three regions to the northeast, for centuries part of the Republic of Venice, are traditionally known all together as **Venetia**. The main attraction of the **Veneto**, the region east of Lake Garda, is of course Venice itself, one of the world's most extra-ordinary visions; but there are four other large and lovely cities—Padua, Verona, Vicenza, and Treviso—and a host of smaller jewels like Feltre, Ásolo, Conegliano, Monsélice, and Belluno. Magnificent villas, built for Venetian patricians, dot the land-scape, especially around the Brenta Canal between Padua and Venice, and in enchanting districts like the Euganean Hills near Padua, and Bassano del Grappa, Ásolo and Treviso in the foothills of the Dolomites. To the south lie the haunting flatlands of the river Po and its Delta.

Rising up in northern Venetia, **The Dolomites** are a majestic range of strange and fabulous peaks, a paradise for summer and winter sports. The Dolomites cross over two regions: the eastern half, still part of the Veneto, includes the famous Olympic resort of Cortina d'Ampezzo, while to the west is the partly autonomous region known as Trentino-Alto Adige. Trento, the capital of Trentino, is a fine old town associated with the great 16th-century Counter-Reformation council; nearby are the rugged Brenta Dolomites, valleys of apple orchards, castles, and vineyards. Alto Adige, on the Austrian border, is a bilingual region that prefers to be known as Süd Tirol—an intriguing mix of strudel and pasta, fairy-tale castles and resorts, vineyards and spas. Bolzano is its capital, but its most celebrated watering-hole, Merano, is better known. Much of the western portion of Alto Adige is occupied by Stelvio National Park, Italy's largest, with glaciers that permit year-round skiing.

East of Venice lies the third Venetia, **Friuli-Venezia Giulia**, occupying the corner between Austria and Yugoslavia, with the neoclassical city and seaport of Trieste. There are popular resorts on the coast like Grado and Lignano, pretty towns like Cividale del Friuli, with Italy's most remarkable Lombard art, and more Alps in the north that see few visitors. Friuli is famous for its white wines; its ethnic mix of Slavic, Germanic, and Friulian cultures give it a unique feel.

To the south lies **Emilia-Romagna**, another hyphenated region that almost crosses the entire peninsula, occupying the plain south of the Po and the northernmost section of the Apennines. Many people associate it with Italy's finest cuisine, but there are splendid cities to visit: the historic capital and medieval university town of Bologna; stately Parma, city of cheese, ham, and magnificent domes and paintings by Correggio; Modena, home of Ferraris, Lambrusco, and an amazing Romanesque cathedral; Busseto, the home of Verdi; Ferrara, the Renaissance city of the Este dynasty; Faenza, city of ceramics, and Ravenna, with dazzling Byzantine mosaics unique in the West. Here, too, the string of Adriatic resorts begins—with Rimini, scene of Fellini's *Amacord*, and the biggest and brashest of them all, yet secreting a Renaissance pearl in its heart. Just a short ride from Rimini, up in the mountains you'll find San Marino, the world's smallest and oldest republic, where tourists are more than welcome.

The Best of Northeast Italy

Art: see pages 50–64.

Bridges: Besides the hundreds in Venice, there's an unusual triple Trepponti bridge at **Comacchio**; battlemented medieval bridge, the Ponte Scaligero, in **Verona**; covered bridge, the Ponte degli Alpini, at **Bassano del Grappa**; 1620 Ponte S. Michele, **Vicenza**; medieval Ponte del Diavolo, **Cividale del Friuli**.

Castles and Fortifications: The northeast has some of Italy's most beautiful castles: a 12th-century one at **Brisighella**, and from the 13th-century the Scaliger castles at **Sirmione**, **Malcésine** (both on Lake Garda) and **Soave**. The countryside around Parma is dotted with remarkable medieval and Renaissance castles (especially Torrechiara). South of Padua, there are striking 13th-century walls and castles at **Este**, **Montagnana**, and **Monsélice**, and to the north at **Cittadella**, **Ásolo** and **Maróstica**. Near San Marino, **San Leo** has a perfect Hollywood Renaissance castle. **Bologna**, **Verona** and **Trento** have fine citadels in their centres. In the Dolomites rugged towers and castles guard the mountain valleys: one of the most interesting is the Castello di Sabbionara at **Avio** with fascinating 14th-century chivalric frescoes of knights, and the

Castel Tirolo near **Merano**, ancient home of the Counts of Tyrol. In Friuli you can walk in the walls of **Palmanova**, a 9-point radial planned fortress town of the Renaissance; while **Ferrara** has some of the best-preserved and longest city walls in Europe.

Cats and Dogs: Someone estimated there were about 10,000 lions in **Venice**, from the handsome creature on the column in Piazzetta San Marco to the ugliest, on a tomb in the church of San Giobbe. Nearly every town once under the paw of St Mark's lion has at least a few—the funniest are in **Chioggia** and **Feltre** but keep your eyes open for other candidates. Some of the best dogs are also in Venice: Carpaccio's little white dog in the Scuola di S. Giorgio, or Veronese's hounds, bystanders in his paintings in Venice's Accademia and the Ducal Palace, and in the Villa Bàrbaro at **Masèr**. In **Verona** look for the crowned dogs on the Scaliger tombs.

Caves: **Grotta del Gigante**, at Opicina, above Trieste; **Le Grotte del Calieròn**, near Vittorio Veneto

Curiosities: torture chamber and prisons, in the secret tour of the Palazzo Ducale, the 18th-century sea walls, the *murazzi*, and the Armenian polyglot press on S. Lazzaro Island, all in **Venice**; Europe's oldest astronomical clock and anatomy theatre in **Padua**; the drunken towers of **Bologna**; human chess game at **Maróstica**; the perspective stage of the Teatro Olimpico, **Vicenza**; loopy statues and Irredentist cafés in **Trieste**; the inexplicable Ipogeo Celtico at **Cividale del Friuli**; Gabriele D'Annunzio's villa at **Gardone Riviera**; 1298 Pharmacy of St John, **Parma**; the Ruritanian Republic of **San Marino**.

Gardens: Europe's oldest botanical garden, at **Padua**; also the pretty Giardino Botanico Hruska, at **Gardone Riviera** and alpine botanical garden at **Monte Bondone** (near Trento); classic Italian garden of Villa Barbarigo, at **Valsanzibio** in the Euganean Hills; 16th-century Giardini Giusti, **Verona**; Italian and English Sigurta Gardens, south of Lake Garda at **Valeggio**; Giardino Esperia, near **Sestola** in the Modenese Apennines.

Horses: One of Venice's medieval doges had a stable of four hundred horses dyed yellow, but these days the most memorable horseflesh forms the lower half of equestrian statues: there are, of course, the four ancient horses of St Mark's, and the fine horses under Donatello's *Gattamelata* in **Padua** and Verrocchio's *Colleoni* in **Venice**; in **Piacenza** two Farnese ride magnificent bronze steeds cast in 1620; **Verona**'s Cangrande della Scala rides the most comical; in **Padua**'s Palazzo della Ragione you can see a wooden one big enough to play the equine lead in a remake of the Trojan War; at the Castello Porto-Colleoni, in **Thiene** the walls are covered with horse portraits; real ones take the field in August at the European Trotting Championships, at **Cesena**.

Lakes: **Lake Garda**, largest and most spectacular of the Italian lakes; also the jigsaw-pretty **Lake Misurina** and **Lago Alleghe**, near Cortina; green **Lago di Braies**, near Monguelfo; **Lago di Tovel** and **Lake Toblino**, in the Brenta Dolomites, and lovely **Lago di Santa Croce** in the Alpago.

Landscapes: There are the obvious ones like the **Dolomites** and **Lake Garda**, and not-so-obvious places like the uncanny lagoons of **Venice** and **Grado** and the **Po Delta**; the green **Modenese Apennines**, laced with waterfalls; the grotto-pocked **Carso** near Trieste; the enchanting **Monti Lessini** north of Verona; the **Euganean Hills**, volcanic bubbles south of Padua; the lovely forests and lakes of the **Alpago** near Vittorio Veneto; the valleys of Trentino, especially the **Val di Non**.

Leaning Towers: Why go to Pisa? Some of Italy's craziest tilters are the Garisenda and Asinelli towers in **Bologna**, the civic towers of **Rovigo**, and the campaniles of S. Giorgio dei Greci and Santo Stefano in **Venice**, the Torre Pubblico **Ravenna**.

Natural Wonders: Underground Timavo river, **San Giovanni di Duino** (near Trieste); monstrously deep potholes and natural bridges in the **Monti Lessini**; Longomoso Pyramids—natural erosion pinnacles, near **Bolzano**; Parco Naturale di Sassi, by **Guiglia** (south of Modena).

Opera: You can take the Verdi tour at his birthplace **Roncole** and in **Busseto**, which puts on performances of his operas in its miniature version of La Scala. From September to May, you can find operas at La Fenice in **Venice**, and at the smaller houses in **Parma, Trieste, Bologna, Verona, Rovigo**, and **Modena** (the birthplace of Luciano Pavarotti, who comes back once a year to sing). In summer, the Arena in **Verona** hosts a major opera festival.

Outdoor Frescoes: also called *murales*, one of the delights of the region. **Treviso** is famous for them, and there are several good ones in **Trento**; the *Dance of Death* at **Pinzolo**; others are in **Cavalese**.

Pilgrimage sites: The most popular is the Basilica of St Anthony in **Padua**; others include the bizarre alpine Santuario di San Romedio, at **Sanzeno**; the Basilica of Monte Bérico, above **Vicenza**; the Sanctuary of the Madonna di San Luca, in **Bologna**, with its 4-km portico. **Venice** has more saintly odds and end than any city on the planet, but the relics of Santa Lucia in the church of San Geremia seem to be biggest attraction.

Spas: Feeling low? Go to **Grado**, where they'll bake you in sand; or **Merano**, where they'll ply you with grapes; or **Salsomaggiore**, with a beautiful Art Nouveau bath-house (now a congress centre) but where they'll still soak your arthritis in hot saline waters (or try nearby **Tabiano Bagni**, if you prefer sulphur springs). There are several spa towns in the **Euganean Hills**, where steaming hot radioactive water will blast away anything else that ails you; or little **Bagno di Romagna**, where they'll pack you in mud.

Tombs: Besides the beautiful tombs made for saints, doges, and signori, the northeast has more than its share of dead celebrities: **Dante** in Ravenna, **Petrarch** at Arquà Petrarca, **Igor Stravinsky, Monteverdi, Serge Diaghilev, and Ezra Pound** in Venice; **Eleonora Duse**, in Ásolo; **Gabriele D'Annunzio**, at Gardone Riviera; **Paganini** in Parma.

Unusual Museums: wrought iron in the Museo Rizzarda, **Feltre**; local museum in **Pieve di Cadore**, noted for its spectacles; the Museo Diocescano, with its *presepi*, or Christmas cribs, at **Bressanone**; Museo Civico, **Busseto**, full of Verdi memorabilia; **Parma**'s Glauco Lombardi Museum, devoted to the life of Empress Marie Louise; **Bologna**'s Anatomy Museum of Domestic Animals; Museum of Ladin culture, **Vigo di Fassa**; glass museum at **Murano**, lace musem at **Burano**, ceramics museum at **Faenza**, 'grapes in art' in **Conegliano**'s Civic Museum.

Villages and Small Towns: Medieval **Arquà Petrarca** south of Padua, and the walled town of **Castell'Arquato** south of Piacenza; **Feltre**, a well-preserved 16th-century town; **Brisighella**, with a castle and arcaded muleteers' road; **Conegliano** and **Ásolo**, in the north Veneto; ancient **Bressanone** in the Dolomites; **Muggia**, a Venetian fishing village on the Yugoslav border.

Villas: There are hundreds, but the top ones, for art and architecture, are: Palladio and Veronese's Villa Bàrbaro at **Masèr**; Palladio's Villa Rotunda and the Tiepolo frescoes at Villa Valmarana, both in **Vicenza**; the 18th-century Villa Pisani, also with Tiepolo frescoes, at **Stra** and Palladio's **La Malcontenta** (both on the Brenta Canal); Pre-Palladian Villa Castello Porto-Colleoni, **Thiene**; Petrarch's last home at **Arquà Petrarca** (south of Padua), little changed since the 13th century.

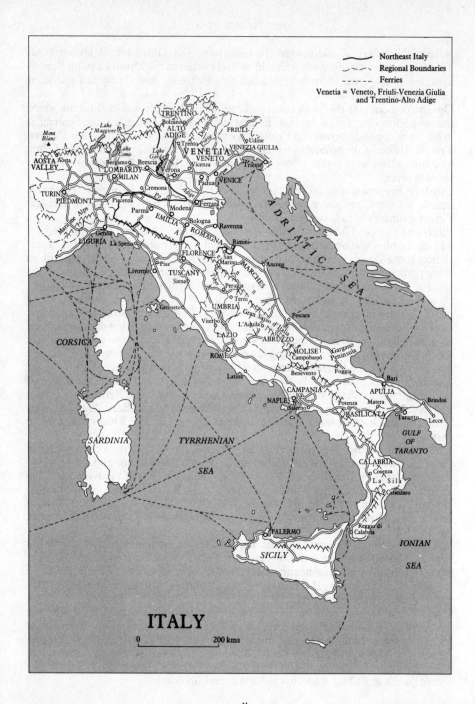

ITALY

0   200 kms

Part I

GENERAL INFORMATION

Winged Lion, Venice

Before You Go

A little preparation can make your trip many times more enjoyable (or at least less frustrating). Although this book was designed to be especially useful to frequent visitors who are ready to poke into some of Italy's nooks and crannies, it will also get you around the major sights if this is your first trip; study the Guide to the Guide (p. viii) and the list of festivals (p. 22) to get some idea of where you want to be and when. There are several tour operators who specialize in holidays to Italy. In the UK Citalia (tel (081) 686 5533 or (071) 434 3844) probably has the widest range. (See also p. 30 for Self-Catering Holidays and p. 20 for Special Interest Holidays.) You can pick up free hints, brochures, maps, and information from the Italian National Tourist Offices, at the following addresses; an especially useful booklet to request is the annually updated *Travellers' Handbook*, which has loads of good information and current prices.

UK: 1 Princes Street, London W1R 8AY (tel (071) 408 1254; telex 22402).
Eire: 47 Merrion Square, Dublin 2, Eire (tel (001) 766397; telex 31682).
USA:
630 Fifth Avenue, Suite 1565, New York, NY 10111 (tel (212) 245 4961; telex 236024).
500 N. Michigan Avenue, Chicago, Ill. 60611 (tel (312) 644 0990/1; telex 0255160).
360 Post Street, Suite 801, San Francisco, California 94108 (tel (415) 392 6206; telex 67623).

1

Canada: Store 56, Plaza 3, Place Ville Marie, Montreal, Quebec (tel (514) 866 7667; telex 525607).

Once you know where you want to go, you can pick up more detailed information by writing directly to any of the city or provincial tourist offices. These are usually very helpful in sending out lists of flats, villas, or farmhouses to hire, or at least lists of agents who handle the properties.

Getting to Northeast Italy

By Air

By Regular Scheduled Flights
There are direct flights from London to Venice and Bologna, and airports in Verona, Trieste and Rimini which you can reach by charters or by way of Milan and Rome. The real challenge is finding a bargain, especially in the high season (mid-May–mid-September); the trick is to start hunting around a few months in advance, or if you're a gambler, at the last minute.

There are advantages in paying out for a normal fare, mainly that it does not impose any restrictions on when you go or return; most are valid for a year. To sweeten the deal, Alitalia in particular often has promotional perks like rental cars (Jetdrive), or discounts on domestic flights within Italy, on hotels, or on tours. Ask your travel agent. Children under the age of two travel for 10 per cent of the adult fare on British Airways flights; Alitalia have a nominal charge of £20. Children between 2 and 12 travel for half fare, and bona fide students with proof of age and school attendance between the ages of 12 and 25 receive a 25 per cent discount on British Airways flights, and a 20 per cent discount on Alitalia.

The same carriers listed above have a variety of discounts for those who book in advance or are able to decide their departure and return dates in advance. If you're travelling from Europe, you can save quite a tidy sum by paying for your ticket when you make your reservations (Eurobudget); an extra advantage is that the return date is left open. Travellers from anywhere can save money by downing a little alphabet soup—PEX, APEX, and SUPERPEX, which like Eurobudget require reservations and payment at the same time on return-only flights. PEX (or APEX) fares have fixed arrival and departure dates, and the stay in Italy must include at least one Saturday night; from North America the restrictions are at least a week's stay but not more than 90 days. SUPERPEX, the cheapest normal fares available, have the same requirements as PEX, but must be purchased at least 14 days (or sometimes 21 days in North America) in advance. Disadvantages of PEXing are that there are penalty fees if you change your flight dates. At the time of writing, the lowest APEX fare between London and Venice in the off-season is £185; the lowest mid-week SUPERPEX between New York and Venice (via Milan) in the off-season is $685.

Other advantages of taking a regular flight over a charter are an increase in reliability in dates and in punctuality, and you're not out of a wad of cash if you miss your flight. Also, if you live in neither London nor New York, they will often offer big discounts to get you from your home airport to the international one. If you live in the US boondocks,

2

you can dial some '800' numbers to check out prices on your own: Alitalia's number is 800 223 5730.

From the USA, you almost always have to go through New York, and can fly directly only to Rome and Milan. Fares from Canada are often much higher than they are from the States. Also, it's worthwhile checking on budget fares to London (especially if Virgin Atlantic stays around), Brussels, Paris, Frankfurt, or Amsterdam; these routes are more competitive than the Italian ones, and you may save money by either flying or riding the rails to Italy from there.

Charter Flights

These aren't as much of a bargain to Italy as they are to other Mediterranean destinations, though they're certainly worth looking into—check ads in the travel section of your newspaper (*Sunday Times* and *Time Out* are especially good) and your travel agent. From London, Pilgrim Air (44 Goodge St, tel (071) 637 5333) has regularly scheduled charters to Milan; from the US, CIEE has regular charters from New York to Rome (tel 800 223 7402). Other charter flights are usually booked by the big holiday companies. To find out about extra seats on these and on commercial flights, visit your local bucket shop (in the USA, call Access (tel 800 333 7280) or Air Hitch for similar services—check listings in the *Sunday New York Times*). Pickings are fairly easy in the off season, and tight in the summer months, but not impossible. You take your chances, but you can save some of your hard-earned dough. The cheapest charter fare at the time of writing from London to Venice is £120.

The problem with charters is that they are delayed more often than not, and since the same plane is usually commuting back and forth it can mean arriving at 3 am. Another disadvantage is that you have to accept the given dates, and if you miss your flight (bus and train strikes in Italy do make this a distinct possibility) there's no refund. Most travel agencies, however, offer traveller's insurance that includes at least a partial refund of your charter fare if strikes or illness keep you from the airport.

Students

Besides saving 25 per cent on regular flights, students under 26 have the choice of flying on special discount charters. From the US, CIEE (see above) is a good place to start looking. From Canada, contact Canadian Universities Travel Services, 44 St George St, Toronto, Ontario M55 2E4, tel (416) 979 2406. From London, check out STA Travel, 117 Euston Road, NW1 or 86 Old Brompton Rd, SW7, for telephone enquiries for European destinations ring (071) 937 9921; WST, 6 Wrights Lane W8 tel (071) 938 4362 or USIT, 52 Grosvenor Gardens, SW1, tel (071) 730 8518.

By Train

At the time of writing approximate single, second class fares to Northeast Italy from London are: Bologna £94 (25 hours); Desenzano (Lake Garda) £90 (23 hours); Merano £109 (28 hours); Padua £93 (25 hours); Parma £94 (24 hours); Rimini £97 (27 hours); Trieste £100 (29 hours); Venice £98 (25 hours); Verona £92 (25 hours). Prices do vary according to the route you take, i.e. whether you go via Belgium, via Switzerland or simply through France into Italy.

3

These trains require reservations and a couchette, and are a fairly painless way of getting there. Discounts are available for families travelling together, for children—free under age 4 and 40 per cent discount between the ages of 4 and 8. Under 26-ers, students or not, can save up to 40 per cent and over on second-class seats by purchasing Eurotrain tickets available in the UK from any student travel office in the UK, many high street travel agents or direct from Eurotrain tel (071) 730 3402. Eurotrain also has a kiosk at Victoria Station which is open from 8 am to 8 pm seven days a week. Eurotrain tickets are also available throughout Europe at student travel offices (CTS in Italy) in main railway stations. Any rail tickets purchased in Britain for Italy are valid for two months and allow any stopovers you care to make on the way.

Rail travel to Italy becomes an even more attractive option if you intend to purchase an Inter-Rail pass (in Europe), or a EurRail pass (from North America). Inter-Rail cards (about £155) are sold by British Rail to people under 26 and offer discounts of over 30 per cent in Britain and 30 or 50 per cent on Channel Ferries, and free rail passage on the Continent, and are valid for a month. Inter-Rail Senior cards offer similar discounts to people over 60. EurRail passes must be purchased before leaving for Europe, and are valid for anywhere from 15 days to 3 months of unlimited first-class travel. These passes are a good deal if you plan to do lots and lots of rail travel and can't be bothered to buy tickets, etc. They seem rather less rosy if your travelling is limited to Italy, where domestic rail tickets are one of the few bargains available. Within Italy itself there are several discount tickets available (see below, travelling within Italy), which you can inquire about at CIT Italian State railways offices before you leave home:

UK: 50 Conduit St, London, W1, tel (071) 434 3844
also at Wasteels Travel, 121 Wilton Rd, London SW1, tel (071) 834 7066 or at any branch of Thomas Cook Ltd
USA: 666 Fifth Ave, New York NY 10103, tel (212) 223 0230
There's also an 800 number you can call from anywhere: (800) 223 0230
Canada: 2055 Peel St, Suite 102, Montreal, Quebec H3A 1VA, tel (514) 845 9101

Of course, you can wallow in romantic splendour, Grand-Tour style, on the luxurious vintage **Venice Simplon-Orient-Express** from London to Venice via Paris, Zurich, St. Anton, Innsbruck and Verona. Fares (including sharing a double cabin and all gourmet meals) start at about £695 (February and March) and £745 (April to November). There are several packages available for tours en route to Venice. For more information contact the Venice Simplon-Orient-Express Tours Ltd, Suite 200, Hudson's Place, Victoria Station, London SW1V 1JL, tel (071) 928 6000.

By Coach

Not really to be recommended. Eurolines will take you from London Victoria's Coach Station to Milan, where you have to change for Verona or Venice (£76 single, £122 return) or Bologna (£80 single, £138 return). Contact National Express, Victoria Coach Station, London SW1, tel (071) 730 0202 for times and bookings.

By Car

Driving to Northeast Italy from London is a rather lengthy and expensive proposition, and if you're only staying for a short period figure your costs against Alitalia's or other airlines' fly-drive scheme. Depending on how you cross the Channel, it is a good two-day trip—about 1600 km from Calais to Venice. Ferry information is available from the Continental Car Ferry Centre, 52 Grosvenor Gardens, London SW1. You can avoid many of the costly motorway tolls by going from Dover to Calais, through France, to Basle, Switzerland, and then through the Gotthard Tunnel over the Alps; in the summer you can save the steep tunnel tolls by taking one of the passes. You can avoid some of the driving by putting your car on the train (although again balance the sizeable expense against the price of hiring a car for the period of your stay): Express Sleeper Cars run to Milan from Paris or Boulogne, and to Bologna from Boulogne. Services are drastically cut outside the summer months, however. For more information, contact the CIT offices listed above.

To bring your car into Italy, you need your car registration (log book), valid driving licence, and valid insurance (a Green Card is not necessary, but you'll need one if you go through Switzerland). Make sure everything is in excellent working order or your slightly bald tyre may enrich the coffers of the Swiss or Italian police—it's not uncommon to be stopped for no reason and have your car searched until the police find something to stick a fine on. Also beware that spare parts for non-Italian cars are difficult to come by, almost impossible for pre-1988 Japanese models. If you're coming to live in Italy, remember that cars with foreign plates are obliged to leave the country every six months for a hazily defined period of time.

Before leaving, you can save yourself about 10–15 per cent of expensive Italian petrol and motorway tolls by purchasing **Petrol Coupons**, issued to owners of GB-registered vehicles by London's CIT office (see above), at Wasteels Travel, 121 Wilton Rd, London SW1, tel (071) 834 7066, or at your local AA or RAC office (though ring them ahead to make sure they have the coupons in stock) or at the frontier from Italian Auto Club offices. Coupons are sold only in person to the car-owner with his or her passport and car registration, and cannot be paid for in Italian lire—prices are tagged to current exchange rates, and unused coupons may be refunded on your return. Along with the coupons and motorway vouchers, you get a *Carta Carburante* which entitles you to breakdown services provided by the Italian Auto Club (ACI) (offices in Northeast Italy, p. 13). At the time of writing motorway tunnel tolls are:

Mont Blanc Tunnel, from Chamonix (France) to Courmayeur: small car or motorcycle L15 000 single, L19 000 return. Medium-sized car (axle distance 2.31–2.63 m) L23 000 single, L29 000 return. Large cars (axle distance 2.64–3.30) or cars with caravans L31,000 single or 38,000 return.

Fréjus Tunnel, from Modane (France) to Bardonécchia: same as above except for large cars or cars with caravans (trailers) L28 000 single, L36 000 return.

Gran San Bernardo, from Bourg St Pierre (Switzerland) to Aosta: small car or motorcycle: L13 500 single, L19 000 return. Medium car L20 000 single, L28 000 return. Large car or car with caravan L27 000 single, L38 000 return.

Traveller's Insurance and Health

You can insure yourself for almost any possible mishap—cancelled flights, stolen or lost baggage, and health. While national health coverage in the UK and Canada takes care of their citizens while travelling, the US doesn't. Check your current policies to see if they cover you while abroad, and under what circumstances, and judge whether you need a special traveller's insurance policy. Travel agencies sell them, as well as insurance companies; they are not cheap.

Minor illnesses and problems that crop up in Italy can usually be handled free of charge in a public hospital clinic or *ambulatorio*. If you need minor aid, Italian pharmacists are highly trained and can probably diagnose your problem; look for a *Farmacia* (they all have a list in the window detailing which ones are open during the night and on holidays). Extreme cases should head for the *Pronto Soccorso* (First Aid services). The emergency number from anywhere in Italy is 113.

Most Italian doctors speak at least rudimentary English, but if you can't find one, contact your embassy or consulate for a list of English-speaking doctors.

What to Pack

You simply cannot overdress in Italy; whatever grand strides Italian designers have made on the international fashion merry-go-round, most of their clothes are purchased domestically, prices be damned. Now whether or not you want to try to keep up with the natives is your own affair and your own heavy suitcase—you may do well to compromise and just bring a couple of smart outfits for big nights out. It's not that the Italians are very formal; they simply like to dress up with a gorgeousness that adorns their cities just as much as those old Renaissance churches and palaces. The few places with dress codes are the major churches and basilicas (no shorts or sleeveless shirts), the casinos, and some of the smarter restaurants.

After agonizing over fashion, remember to pack small and light: trans-Atlantic airlines limit baggage by size (two pieces are free, up to 62 inches in height and width; in second-class you're allowed one of 62 inches and another up to 44 inches). Within Europe limits are by weight: 23 kilos (59 lbs) in second-class, 30 kilos (66 lbs) in first. You may well be penalized for anything bigger. If you're travelling mainly by train, you'll especially want to keep bags to a minimum: jamming big suitcases in overhead racks in a crowded compartment isn't much fun for anyone. Never take more than you can carry, but do bring the following: any prescription medicine you need, an extra pair of glasses or contact lenses if you wear them, a pocket knife and corkscrew (for picnics), a flashlight (for dark frescoed churches, caves, and crypts), a travel alarm (for those early trains) and a pocket Italian-English dictionary (for flirting and other emergencies; outside the main tourist centres you may well have trouble finding someone who speaks English). If you're a light sleeper, you may want to invest in ear plugs. Your electric appliances will work in Italy if you adapt and convert them to run on 220 AC with two round prongs on the plug. Of course, what you bring depends on when and where you go....

Climate

O Sole Mio notwithstanding, all of Italy isn't always sunny; it rains just as much in Rome every year as in London. **Summer** comes on humid and hot in much of the north, especially along the Po; the Alps and high Apennines stay fairly cool, though the valleys, between the peaks, can be little ovens, and while the coasts are often refreshed by breezes, Venice in its lagoon tends to swelter. You can probably get by without an umbrella, but take a light jacket for cool evenings. For average touring, August is probably the worst month to stump through Italy. Transport facilities are jammed to capacity, prices are at their highest, and the large cities are abandoned to hordes of tourists while the locals take to the beach.

Spring and **autumn** are the loveliest times to go. In spring the apple orchards around Trento, the cherry orchards of Treviso and Modena, rival the wild flowers of Italy's countryside and mountains; by May and June the gardens are at their peak. But the real season of the northeast is autumn, when the landscape around you matches the autumnal colours of Venetian art; the Po Delta and lagoon are at their most haunting, the sumac on Trieste's karst bursts into scarlet flames, the vineyards turn red and are heavy with grapes. The weather is mild, places aren't crowded, and you won't need your umbrella too much, at least until November. During the **winter** the happiest visitors are either on skis, in the opera house, or at the table eating wild mushrooms and *radicchio*. It's the best time to go if you want the churches and museums to yourself, or want to meet Italians, and get a dose of nostalgia in Venice. Beware, though, that it can rain and rain, and mountain valleys can lie for days under banks of fog and mist.

Average Temperatures in °C (°F)

	January	*April*	*July*	*October*
Bologna	2.5 (36)	13.8 (56)	26.0 (79)	15.2 (59)
Trieste	5.3 (41)	12.9 (55)	24.0 (75)	15.6 (60)
Venice	3.8 (39)	12.6 (54)	23.6 (74)	15.1 (59)
Lake Garda	4.0 (39)	13.2 (55)	23.7 (74)	14.7 (58)
Cortina d'Ampezzo	−2.3 (29)	5.2 (41)	15.8 (60)	7.6 (45)
Merano	2.8 (37)	11.6 (52)	20.2 (68)	8.4 (47)
Tarvisio	−3.5 (26)	7.1 (44)	18.3 (64)	9.0 (48)
Rimini	6.7 (44)	13.5 (56)	24.3 (75)	10.5 (51)

Average monthly rainfall in millimetres (inches)

	January	*April*	*July*	*October*
Bologna	44 (2)	57 (2)	18 (1)	47 (2)
Trieste	57 (2)	104 (4)	57 (2)	112 (4)
Venice	58 (2)	77 (3)	37 (1)	66 (3)
Lake Garda	31 (1)	62 (3)	81 (3)	89 (3)
Cortina d'Ampezzo	51 (2)	138 (5)	148 (6)	119 (4)
Merano	10 (½)	11 (½)	6 (0)	90 (4)
Tarvisio	79 (3)	202 (8)	138 (5)	169 (6)
Rimini	11 (1/2)	32 (1)	95 (4)	132 (5)

Passports and Customs Formalities

To get into Italy you need a valid passport or a British Visitor's Card. Nationals of the UK, Ireland, USA, Canada, and Australia do not need visas for stays up to three months. If you mean to stay longer than three months in Italy, get a visa from your Italian consulate or face the prospect of having to get a *Visa di Soggiorno* at the end of three months—possible only if you can prove a source of income and are willing to spend a couple of exasperating days at some provincial Questura office filling out forms.

According to Italian law, you must register with the police within three days of your arrival. If you check into a hotel this is done automatically. If you come to grief in the mesh of rules and forms, you can at least get someone to explain it to you in English by calling the Rome Police Office for visitors, tel (06) 4686, ext. 2858.

Italian Customs are usually benign, though how the frontier police manage to recruit such ugly, mean-looking characters to hold the submachine guns and drug-sniffing dogs from such a good-looking population is a mystery, but they'll let you be if you don't look suspicious and haven't brought along more than 150 cigarettes or 75 cigars, or not more than a litre of hard drink or three bottles of wine, a couple of cameras, a movie camera, 10 rolls of film for each, a tape-recorder, radio, phonograph, one canoe less than 5.5 m, sports equipment for personal use, and one TV (though you'll have to pay for a licence for it at Customs). Pets must be accompanied by a bilingual Certificate of Health from your local Veterinary Inspector. You can take the same items listed above home with you without hassle—except of course your British pet. US citizens may return with $400 worth of merchandise—keep your receipts. British subjects are permitted £200 worth of dutiable merchandise.

There are no limits to how much money you bring into Italy, although legally you may not transport more than L400 000 in Italian banknotes, though they rarely check.

On Arrival

Money

It's a good idea to bring some Italian lire with you when you arrive; unforeseen delays and unexpected public holidays may foul up your plans to change at a bank when you arrive. Travellers' cheques or Eurocheques remain the most secure way of financing your holiday in Italy; they are easy to change and insurance against unpleasant surprises. Credit cards (American Express, Diners Club, Mastercard, Access, Eurocard, Barclaycard, Visa) are usually only accepted in hotels, restaurants, and shops (but never at any petrol stations) frequented by foreign tourists—Italians themselves rarely use them— and it is not unknown for establishments to fiddle with the exchange rates and numbers on your bill once you've left. Use them with discretion.

There's been a lot of loose talk about knocking three noughts off the Italian lira, but it never seems to happen; as it is, everybody can be a 'millionaire'. It is also confusing to the vistor unaccustomed to dealing with rows of zeros, and more than once you'll think you're getting a great deal until you realize you've simply miscounted the zeros on the price tag. Some unscrupulous operators may try to take advantage of the confusion when you're changing money, so do be careful. Notes come in denominations of L100 000, L50 000, L10 000, L5000, L2000, and L1000; coins are L500, L200, L100, L50, L20, all the way down to the ridiculous and practically worthless aluminium coinage of L10, L5 and L1. Telephone tokens (*gettoni*) may be used as coins as well and are worth L200.

The easiest way to have money sent to you in Italy is for someone from home to get a bank to telex the amount to an Italian bank, and for you to go and pick it up.

Technically—and if you're really lucky—it shouldn't take more than a couple of days to arrive, but make sure the telex includes the number of your passport, ID card, or driver's licence, or the Italians may not give you your money. Save all the receipts of your currency exchanges.

Getting Around Within Italy

Italy has an excellent network of airports, railways, highways, and byways and you'll find getting around fairly easy—until one union or another takes it into its head to go on strike (to be fair, they rarely do it during the high holiday season). There's plenty of talk about passing a law to regulate strikes, but it won't happen soon, if ever. Instead, learn to recognize the word in Italian: *sciopero* (SHOW-per-o) and be prepared to do as the Romans do when you hear it—quiver with resignation. There's always a day or two's notice, and strikes usually last only 12 or 24 hours—just long enough to throw a spanner in the works if you have to catch a plane. Keep your ears open and watch for notices posted in the stations.

By Air

Domestic flights are handled by Alitalia, Itavia, and ATI, and come in most handy when you want to hop from north to south. There are certain flights, such as from Milan to Venice, where, if you count in the time it takes to get to and from the airports, check in, etc., as well as the flight itself, you may find a *Rapido* train only slightly slower and much less expensive.

Domestic flights are priced comparatively to other continental countries, but there are discounts available for night flights of up to 30 per cent, youth fares (12–26, 25 per cent discount), while younger children pay half the adult fare. Travelling by air becomes especially attractive if you're travelling as a family (husband, wife, children) when you can get a discount of up to 50 per cent. Each airport has a bus terminal in the city; ask about schedules when you purchase your ticket or face a hefty taxi fare.

By Train

Italy's national railway, the FS (*Ferrovie dello Stato*) is well run, inexpensive (though prices have recently risen, it is still cheap by British standards) and often a pleasure to ride. There are also several private rail lines around cities and in country districts. We have tried to list them all in this book. Some, you may find, won't accept Inter-Rail or EurRail passes. On the FS, some of the trains are sleek and high-tech, but much of the rolling stock hasn't been changed for fifty years. Possible FS unpleasantnesses you may encounter, besides a strike, are delays, crowding (especially at weekends and in the summer), and crime on overnight trains, where someone rifles your bags while you sleep. The crowding, at least, becomes much less of a problem if you reserve a seat in advance at the *Prenotazione* counter. The fee is small and can save you hours standing in some train corridor. On the upper echelon trains, reservations are mandatory. Do check when you purchase your ticket in advance that the date is correct; unlike in some countries, tickets are only valid the day they're purchased unless you specify otherwise. If you're coming back the same way in three days or less, save money with a *ritorno* (a one-way ticket is an *andata*). A number on your reservation slip will indicate in which car your seat is—find it before you board rather than after. The same goes for sleepers and couchettes on overnight trains, which must also be reserved in advance.

Tickets may be purchased not only in the stations, but at many travel agents in the city centres. The system is computerized and runs smoothly, at least until you try to get a reimbursement for an unused ticket (usually not worth the trouble). Be sure you ask which platform (*binario*) your train arrives at; the big permanent boards posted in the stations are not always correct. If you get on a train without a ticket you can buy one from the conductor, with an added 20 per cent penalty. You can also pay a conductor to move up to first class or get a couchette, if there are places available.

There is a fairly straightforward hierarchy of trains. At the bottom of the pyramid is the humble *Locale* (euphemistically known sometimes as an *Accelerato*), which often stops even where there's no station in sight; it can be excruciatingly slow. When you're checking the schedules, beware of what may look like the first train to your desti-nation—if it's a *Locale*, it will be the last to arrive. A *Diretto* stops far less, an *Expresso* just at the main towns. *Rapido* trains whoosh between the big cities and rarely deign to stop. On some of these reservations are necessary, and on some there are only first-class coaches. On all of them, however, you'll be asked to pay a supplement—some 30 per cent more than a regular fare. The real lords of the rails are the TEE (Trans-Europe Express) *Super-Rapido Italiano* trains, kilometre-eaters that will speed you to your destination as fast as trains can go. Italy has three lines all to itself: the *Vesuvio* (Milan, Bologna, Florence, Rome, Naples), the *Adriatico* (Milan, Rimini, Pésaro, Ancona, Pescara, Foggia, Bari), and the *Colosseum/Ambrosiano* (Milan, Bologna, Florence, Rome). For these there is a more costly supplement and only first-class luxury cars. Of course there are others travelling between Italy and northern Europe; ask at any travel agent for details.

The FS offers several passes. One which you should ideally arrange at a CIT office before arriving in Italy, is the 'Travel-at-Will' ticket (*Biglietto turistico libera circolazione*), available only to foreigners. This is a good deal only if you mean to do some very serious train riding on consecutive days; it does, however, allow you to ride the *Rapidos* without paying the supplement. Tickets are sold for 8, 15, 21, or 30-day periods, first or second class, with 50 per cent reduction for children under 12. At the time of writing an eight-day second-class ticket is around £65, first-class £102. A more flexible option is the 'Flexi Card' which allows unlimited travel for either 4 days within a 9-day period (second class £48, first class £70), 8 days within 21 (second class £66, first class £100) or 12 days within 30 (second class £86, first class £128) and you don't have to pay any supplements. Another ticket, the *Kilometrico*, gives you 3000 kilometres of travel, made on a maximum of 20 journeys and is valid for two months; one advantage is that it can be used by up to five people at the same time. However, supplements are payable on Intercity trains. Second-class tickets are currently £68, first-class £116. Other dis-counts, available only once you're in Italy, are 15 per cent on same-day return tickets and three-day returns (depending on the distance involved), and discounts for families of at least four travelling together. Senior citizens (men 65 and over, women 60) can also get a

Carta d'Argento ('silver card') for L10 000 entitling them to a 30 per cent reduction in fares. For young people under 26 a *Carta Verde* ('green card') entitles one to a 30 per cent discount (20 per cent in peak season—Easter and Christmas holidays and 25 June to 31 August).

Refreshments on routes of any great distance are provided by bar cars or trolleys; you can usually get sandwiches and coffee from vendors along the tracks at intermediary stops. Station bars often have a good variety of take-away travellers' fare; consider at least investing in a plastic bottle of mineral water, since there's no drinking water on the trains.

Besides trains and bars, Italy's stations offer other facilities. All have a *Deposito*, where you can leave your bags for hours or days for a small fee. The larger ones have porters (who charge L800–1000 per piece) and some even have luggage trolleys; major stations have an *Albergo Diurno* ('Day Hotel', where you can take a shower, get a shave and haircut, etc.), information offices, currency exchanges open at weekends (not at the most advantageous rates, however), hotel-finding and reservation services, kiosks with foreign papers, restaurants, etc. You can also arrange to have a rental car awaiting you at your destination—Avis, Hertz, Eurotrans, and Autoservizi Maggiore are the firms that provide this service.

Beyond that, some words need to be said about riding the rails on the most serendipitous national line in Europe. The FS may have its strikes and delays, its petty crime and bureaucratic inconveniences, but when you catch it on its better side it will treat you to a dose of the real Italy before you even reach your destination. If there's a choice, try for one of the older cars, depressingly grey outside but fitted with comfortably upholstered seats, Art Deco lamps, and old pictures of the towns and villages of the country. The washrooms are invariably clean and pleasant. Best of all, the FS is relatively reliable, and even if there has been some delay, you'll have an amenable station full of clocks to wait in; some of the station bars have astonishingly good food (some do not), but at any of them you may accept a well-brewed *cappuccino* and look blasé until the train comes in. Try to avoid travel on Friday evenings, when the major lines out of the big cities are packed. The FS is an honest crap shoot; you may have a train uncomfortably full of Italians (in which case stand by the doors, or impose on the salesmen and other parasites in first class, where the conductor will be happy to change your ticket). Now and then, you and your beloved will have a beautiful 1920s compartment all to yourselves for the night.

By Coach and Bus

Intercity bus travel is often quicker than train travel, but also a bit more expensive. The Italians aren't dumb; you will find regular bus connections only where there is no train to offer competition. Buses almost always depart from the vicinity of the train station, and tickets usually need to be purchased before you get on. In many regions they are the only means of public transport and are well used, with frequent schedules. If you can't get a ticket before the bus leaves, get on anyway and pretend you can't speak a word of Italian; the worst that can happen is that someone will make you pay for a ticket. Understand clearly that the base for all country bus lines will be the provincial capitals; we've done our best to explain the connections even for the most out-of-the-way routes.

City buses are the traveller's friend. Most cities label routes well; all charge flat fees for rides within the city limits and immediate suburbs, at the time of writing around L1000. Bus tickets must always be purchased before you get on, either at a tobacconists', a newspaper kiosk, in many bars, or from ticket machines near the main stops. Once you get on, you must 'obliterate' your ticket in the machines in the front or back of the bus; controllers stage random checks to make sure you've punched your ticket. Fines for cheaters are about L20 000, and the odds are about 12 to 1 against a check, so you may take your chances against how lucky you feel. If you're good-hearted, you'll buy a ticket and help some overburdened municipal transit line meet its annual deficit.

By Taxi

Taxis are about the same price as in London. The average meter starts at L2500, and adds L600 per kilometre. There's an extra charge for luggage and for trips to the airport; and rates go up after 10 pm and on holidays.

By Car

The advantages of driving in Italy generally outweigh the disadvantages. Before you bring your own car or hire one, consider the kind of holiday you're planning. If it's a tour of Italy's great art cities, you'd be best off not driving at all: parking is impossible, traffic impossible, deciphering one-way streets, signals, and signs impossible. Take public transport. In nearly every other case, however, a car gives you the freedom and possibility of making your way through Italy's lovely countryside. Purchase the excellent green-cover **maps** issued by the Italian Touring Club (obtainable in good Italian bookshops, or from Stanfords, 12 Long Acre, London WC2; or Rizzoli International Bookstore, 712 Fifth Avenue, New York).

Be prepared, however, to face not only the highest fuel costs in Europe (when everyone else lowered theirs with slumping international prices, Italy raised them) but also the Italians themselves behind the wheel, many of whom, from 21-year-old madcaps to elderly nuns, drive like idiots, taking particular delight in overtaking at blind curves on mountainous roads. No matter how fast you're going on the *autostrade* (Italy's toll motorways, official speed limit 130 km per hour) someone will pass you going twice as fast. Americans in particular should be wary about driving in Italy. If you're accustomed to the generally civilized rules of motoring that obtain in North America, Italy will be a big surprise. Italians, and their northern visitors, do not seem to care if someone kills them or not. Especially in the cities, rules do not exist, and if you expect them to stop riding your tail you'll have a long time to wait. Even the most cultured Italians become aggressive, murderous humanoids behind the wheel, and if you value your peace of mind you'll stick with public transportation.

If you've purchased petrol coupons (see 'Getting to Italy'), you'll find the petrol stations that accept them put out signs. Many stations close for lunch in the afternoon, and few stay open late at night, though you may find a 'self-service' where you feed a machine nice smooth L10 000 notes. Petrol stations in the cities also sell the discs you can put on your windscreen to park in the *Zona Disco* areas of a city. Autostrada tolls are high—to drive on the A1 from Milan to Rome, for example, will cost you around L40 000. The rest stops and petrol stations along the motorways are open 24 hours. Other roads—*superstrada* on down through the Italian grading system, are free of charge. The Italians are very good about signposting, and roads are almost all excellently maintained—some highways seem to be built of sheer bravura, suspended on cliffs, crossing valleys on enormous piers—feats of engineering that will remind you, more than almost anything else, that this is the land of the ancient Romans. Beware that you may be fined on the spot for speeding, a burnt-out headlamp, etc.; if you're especially unlucky you may be slapped with a *Super Muta*, a superfine, of L100 000 or more. You may even be fined for not having a portable triangle danger signal (pick one up at the frontier or from an ACI office for L1500).

The ACI (Automobile Club of Italy) is a good friend to the foreign motorist. Assistance number 116; English-speaking operators are on duty 24 hours to answer your questions—also use this number if you have an accident, need an ambulance, or simply have to find the nearest service station. If you need major repairs, the ACI can make sure the prices charged are according to their guidelines; if you have a Fuel Card (given when you purchase petrol coupons) you will be given a car to use while your car is being repaired; if you need a tow, your car will be taken to the nearest ACI garage. Provincial offices are:

Belluno: Piazza dei Martiri 46, tel (0437) 213 132
Bologna: Via Marzabotto 2, tel (051) 389 908
Bolzano: Corso Italia 19a, tel (0471) 280 003
Ferrara: Via Padova 17a, tel (0532) 52 723
Forlì: Corso Garibaldi 45, tel (0543) 32 313
Gorizia: Via Trieste 171, tel (0481)21 266
Modena: Viale Verdi 7, tel (059) 239 022
Padua: Viale degli Scrovegni 19, tel (049) 654 935
Parma: Via G. Cantelli 15, tel (0521) 366 71/2
Piacenza: Via Chiapponi 37, tel (0523) 35 344
Pordenone, Viale Dante 40, tel (0434) 208 965
Ravenna: Piazza mameli 4, tel (0544) 22 567
Reggio Emilia: Via Secchi 9, tel (0522) 35 744
Rimini: Via Roma 66/b, tel (0541)26 408
Rovigo: Piazza XX Settembre 9, tel (0425) 25 833
Trento: Via Pozzo 6, tel (0461) 25 072
Treviso: Piazza S. Pio X, tel (0422) 547 801
Trieste: Via Cumano 2, tel (040) 393 225
Udine: Viale Tricesimo 46, tel (0432) 482 565
Venice (Mestre): Via Ca' Marcello 67, tel (041) 531 0362
Verona: Via della Valverde 34, tel (045) 595 333
Vicenza: Viale Della Pace 258, tel (0444) 510 855

If driving your own car, your ordinary licence is valid in Italy if it is accompanied by a translation, although an International Driving Licence is more convenient to carry (and necessary for those who hire cars). Insurance is mandatory in Italy. A 'Green Card' will be sufficient for 40 to 45 days (you can also purchase 'Frontier Insurance' when you enter), but for longer stays an Italian insurance policy is required. If you are caught breaking the Italian highway code (note that the size of your car determines your speed limit), it is advisable to pay the fine for your *infrazione* to the policeman writing your ticket.

Hiring a Car

Hiring a car is fairly simple if not particularly cheap. Italian car rental firms are called *Autonoleggi*. There are both large international firms through which you can reserve a car in advance, and local agencies, which often have lower prices. Air or train travellers should check out possible discount packages.

Most companies will require a deposit amounting to the estimated cost of the hire, and there is 18 per cent VAT added to the final cost. At the time of writing, a 5-seat Fiat Panda costs around L64 000 a day. Petrol is generally twice as expensive as in the UK. Rates become more advantageous if you take the car for a week with unlimited mileage. If you need a car for more than three weeks, leasing is a more economic alternative. The National Tourist Office has a list of firms in Italy that hire caravans (trailers) and campers.

Hitch-hiking

It's legal to thumb a ride anywhere in Italy except on the *autostrade*. The problem is that in most rural places there isn't that much traffic, and you may have a long wait. Increase your chances by looking respectable and carrying a small suitcase instead of a huge backpack.

By Motorbike or Bicycle

The means of transport of choice for many Italians, motorbikes, mopeds, and Vespas can be a delightful way to see the country. You should only consider it, however, if you've ridden them before—Italy's hills and aggravating traffic make it no place to learn. Italians are keen cyclists as well, racing drivers up the steepest hills; if you're not training for the Tour de France, consider Italy's mountains and hills well before planning a bicycling tour—especially in the hot summer months. Bikes can be transported by train in Italy, either with you or within a couple of days—apply at the baggage office (*ufficio bagagli*). Renting either a motorbike or bicycle is difficult; some cities (especially in flat Emilia-Romagna) rent out bikes for urban use only. Depending on how long you're staying, you may find it sensible (especially if you're coming from North America) to buy a second-hand bike in Italy when you arrive, either in a bike shop or through the classified ad papers put out in nearly every city and region. Alternatively, if you bring your own bike, you'll have to check the airlines to see what their policies are on transporting them.

Embassies and Consulates

UK
Rome (embassy): Via XX Settembre 80a, tel (06) 475 5441
Venice: Palazzo Querini, Accademia, Dorsoduro 1051, tel (041) 522 7207
Eire
Rome: Largo Nazareno 3, tel (06) 678 2541
USA
Rome (embassy): Via Vittorio Veneto 121, tel (06) 4674
Milan (the nearest consulate): Piazza della Repubblica 32, tel (02) 652 841
Canada
Rome: Via Zara 30, tel (06) 854 825

Official Holidays

The Italians have cut down somewhat on their official national holidays, but note that every town has one or two local holidays of its own—usually the feast day of its patron saint. Official holidays, on timetables for transportation and museum opening hours, etc., are treated the same as Sundays.

1 January (New Year's Day—*Capodanno*)
6 January (Epiphany, better known to Italians as the day of *La Befana*—a kindly witch who brings the bambini the toys Santa Claus or *Babbo Natale* somehow forgot)
Easter Monday (usually pretty dull)
25 April (Liberation Day—even duller)
1 May (Labour Day—lots of parades, speeches, picnics, music and drinking)
15 August (Assumption, or *Ferragosta*—the biggest of them all—woe to the innocent traveller on the road or train!)
1 November (All Saints, or *Tutti Santi*—liveliest at the cemeteries)
8 December (Immaculate Conception of the Virgin Mary—a dull one)
Christmas and Boxing Day (*Santo Stefano*)

Time
Italy is one hour ahead of Greenwich Mean Time. From the last weekend of March to the end of September, Italian Summer Time (daylight saving time) puts the country ahead another hour, though moves are afoot to standardize time in Europe for 1992.

Opening Hours

Although it varies from region to region, most of Italy closes down at 1 pm until 3 or 4 pm to eat and properly digest the main meal of the day. Afternoon hours are from 4–7, often from 5–8 in the hot summer months. Bars are often the only places open during the early afternoon. Shops of all kinds are usually closed on Saturday afternoons, through Sunday, and Monday mornings as well—although grocery stores and supermarkets do open on Monday mornings. Banking hours in Italy are Monday to Friday 8:35–1:35 and 3–4, those these vary slightly from place to place.

Italy's **churches** have always been a prime target for art thieves and as a consequence are usually locked when there isn't a sacristan or caretaker to keep an eye on things. All churches, except for the really important cathedrals and basilicas, close in the afternoon at the same hours as the shops, and the little ones tend to stay closed. Always have a pocketful of coins to batten the light machines in churches, or what you came to see is bound to be hidden in ecclesiastical shadows. Don't do your visiting during services, and don't come to see paintings and statues in churches the week preceding Easter—you will probably find them covered with mourning shrouds.

Many of Italy's museums are magnificent, many are run with shameful neglect, and many have been closed for years for 'restoration' with slim prospects of re-opening in the near future. With two works of art per inhabitant, Italy has a hard time financing the preservation of its national heritage; in the big cities you would do well to inquire at the tourist office to find out exactly what is open and what is 'temporarily' closed before setting out on a wild goose chase across town.

15

We have listed the hours of the important sights and museums. In general, Monday and Sunday afternoons are dead periods for the sightseer—you may want to make that your travelling day. Places without hours usually open on request—but it is best to go before 1 pm. We have also designated which attractions charge admission; unless labelled 'expensive' you'll have to pay between L1000 and L4000 to get in. Expensive ones are more—most L5000. Citizens of Common Market countries under 18 and over 60 get in free, at least on principle.

Post Offices

The postal service in Italy is the least efficient and most expensive in Europe; if you're sending postcards back home you can count on arriving there before they do. If it's important that it arrive in a week or so, send your letter *Expresso* (Swift Air Mail) or *Raccomandata* (registered delivery), for a L2000 supplement fee. Stamps (*francobolli*) may also be purchased at tobacconists (look for a big black T on the sign), but you're bound to get differing opinions on your exact postage. Mail to the UK goes at the same rate as domestic Italian mail, but it's still twice as much to send a letter from Italy to Britain than vice versa. Air-mail letters to and from North America quite often take three or four weeks. This can be a nightmare if you're making hotel reservations and are sending a deposit—telex or telephoning ahead is far more secure if time is short.

Ask for mail to be sent to you in Italy either care of your hotel or addressed *Fermo Posta* (poste restante: general delivery) to a post office, or, if you're a card-holder, to an American Express Office. When you pick up your mail at the *Fermo Posta* window, bring your passport for identification. Make sure, in large cities, that your mail is sent to the proper post office, easiest is to the **Posta Centrale**.

The Italian postal code is most inscrutable in dealing with packages sent overseas. Packages have to be of a certain size, and under a certain weight to be sent in certain ways, and must have a flap open for inspection or be sealed with string and lead. You're best off taking it to a stationer's shop *cartolibreria* and paying L500 for them to wrap it—they usually know what the postal people are going to require.

Telegrams (sent from post offices) are expensive but the surest way to get your message out of Italy. You can save money by sending it as a night letter (22 words or less).

Telephones

Like many things in Italy, telephoning can be unduly complicated. In many places you'll still find the old token *gettoni* telephones, in which you must insert a token (or better yet, several) before dialling. *Gettoni* cost L200 and are often available in machines next to the telephones, or from bars, news-stands, or *tabacchi*. If more *gettoni* are required while you are speaking, you'll hear a beep, which means put in more *gettoni* quickly or you'll be cut off. For long-distance calls (any one in Italy with a different telephone code), put in as many as the telephone will take (about 10) and be ready to feed in more as you go along. Any unused *gettoni* will be refunded after your call if you push the return button. Other public phones will take either coins, phone cards, or *gettoni*.

For international calls, head either for a telephone office with booths (usually only in the larger cities and major train stations, operated by either SIP or ASST) or a bar with a telephone meter. If you want to reverse the charges (call collect) you must do it from an

16

office (tell them you want to telephone 'a erre' and fill out the little card). Rates are lower if you call at a weekend (after 2:30 pm on Saturday until 8 am Monday morning—unfortunately just when many provincial telephone offices are closed). Phoning long-distance from your hotel can mean big surcharges.

Direct-dial codes are: USA and Canada 001, UK 0044 (leaving out the '0' before the British area code). If you're calling Italy from abroad, the country code is 39, followed by the area prefix—omitting the first '0'.

Police Business

There is a fair amount of petty crime in Italy—purse snatchings, pickpocketing, minor thievery of the white collar kind (always check your change) and car break-ins and theft—but violent crime is rare. Nearly all mishaps can be avoided with adequate precautions. Scooter-borne purse-snatchers can be foiled if you stay on the inside of the pavement and keep a firm hold on your property; pickpockets most often strike in crowded buses and gatherings; don't carry too much cash or keep some of it in another place. Be extra careful in train stations, don't leave valuables in hotel rooms, and always park your car in garages, guarded lots, or on well-lit streets, with temptations like radios, cassettes, etc., out of sight. Purchasing small quantities of reefer, hashish, cocaine, and LSD is legal, although what a small quantity might be exactly is unspecified, so if the police don't like you to begin with, it will probably be enough to get you into big trouble.

Once the scourge of Italy, political terrorism has declined drastically in recent years, mainly thanks to special squads of the *Carabinieri*, the black-uniformed national police, technically part of the Italian army. Local matters are usually in the hands of the *Polizia Urbana*; the nattily dressed *Vigili Urbani* concern themselves with directing traffic, and handing out parking fines. If you need to summon any of them, dial 113.

Photography

Film and developing are much more expensive than they are in the US or UK. You are not allowed to take pictures in most museums and in some churches.

Lavatories

Frequent travellers have noted a steady improvement over the years in the cleanliness of Italy's public conveniences, although as ever you will only find them in places like train and bus stations and bars. Ask for the *bagno, toilette,* or *gabinetto*; in stations and the smarter bars and cafés, there are washroom attendants who expect a few hundred lire for keeping the place decent. You'll probably have to ask them for paper (*carta*). Don't confuse the Italian plurals: *Signori* (gents), *Signore* (ladies).

Women and Children

Italian men, with the heritage of Casanova, Don Giovanni, and Rudolph Valentino as their birthright, are very confident in their role as great Latin lovers, but the old horror stories of gangs following the innocent tourist maiden and pinching her behind are out of date. Most Italian men these days are exquisitely polite and flirt on a much more sophisticated level; still, women travelling alone may frequently receive undesired company, 'assistance', or whatever, from local swains (usually of the balding, middle-age-crisis variety): a firm '*no!*' or '*Vai via!*' (Scram!), repeated as often as necessary, will generally solve the problem, which can be greatly reduced if you avoid lonely streets and train stations after dark. Travelling with a companion of either sex will buffer you considerably against such nuisances.

Even though a declining birthrate and the legalization of abortion may hint otherwise, children are still the royalty of Italy, and are pampered, often obscenely spoiled, probably more fashionably dressed than you are, and never allowed to get dirty. Yet most of them somehow manage to be well-mannered little charmers. If you're bringing your own bambini to Italy, they'll receive a warm welcome everywhere. Many hotels offer advantageous rates for children and have play areas, and most of the larger cities have permanent **Luna Parks**, or funfairs. If a **circus** visits the town you're in, you're in for a treat; it will either be a sparkling showcase of daredevil skill or a poignant, family-run, modern version of Fellini's *La Strada*.

If you've brought the children, and are dubious about letting them take a dip with the algae in the Adriatic, there are other sources of small fry fun. Near Lake Garda you can spend a day at **Gardaland**, Italy's Disneyland, or ogle concrete brontosauri nearby at the **Dinosaur Park**, at Pescantina. Rimini is another hot spot on the average kid's map: at **Italia in Miniatura** they can roam through the monuments of Italy, all cut down to size; at **Fiabilandia** there's a Mississippi river boat, King Kong, etc; also giant water slides, dolphin shows, miniature golf, and more. And it's a rare child who doesn't love **Venice**: the boat rides, the views from the campanile, the pigeons, the glass furnaces at Murano, and the sheer fun of walking through a labyrinth without any traffic to watch out for.

Sports and Activities

If you're coming to Italy intending to practise your favourite sport, you'll find a warm welcome; Italians may not always be the best at a sport, but few people are more enthusiastic or willing to give a new sport a try, from baseball and rugby to hang-gliding and darts. Be warned, however, if you were considering an Italian beach holiday: pollution is a very serious problem along the coasts, both in the sea, and one might say, on land as well. Most of the shoreline is disappointingly flat and dull anyway, and it hasn't been improved by endless neat rows of parasols and lounge chairs full of people scientifically perfecting their tans. Few actually venture into the water, especially since the outbreak of algae; to swim off the fabled Venetian Lido can be Death in Venice. Most of the resort hotels have now added pools to their lists of amenities.

The most controversial sport in Italy is **hunting**, pitting thousands of avid enthusiasts against a burgeoning number of environmentalists, who have recently elected the first Greens to parliament; anti-hunting petitions garner thousands of signatures, and the opening day of the season is marked by huge protests. It is, indeed, rather painful to run into some macho Italian hunter returning from the field with a string of tiny birds around his belt; in many places they have been hunted so thoroughly that it's rare to hear a bird sing. Without their natural predators, pesky insects and poisonous snakes have become a problem in many rural areas. Boar hunting is also extremely popular. **Fishing** is more ecologically sound; many freshwater lakes and streams are stocked, and if you're more interested in fresh fish than the sport of it, there are innumerable trout farms where you can practically pick the fish up out of the water with your hands. Sea fishing, from the shore, from boats, or underwater (however, it is illegal to do so with an aqualung) is possible almost everywhere without a permit; to fish in fresh water you need to purchase a year's membership card for L5000 from the Federazione Italiana della Pesca Sportiva, which has an office in every province; they will inform you about local conditions and restrictions.

You can bring your **boat** to Italy for six months without any paperwork if you bring it by car; if you arrive by sea you must report to the Port Authority of your first port to show passports and receive your 'Costituto' which identifies you and allows you to purchase fuel tax free. Boats with engines require a number plate, and if they're over 3 horsepower you need insurance. If you want to leave your boat in Italy for an extended period, you must have a Navigation Licence; after a year you have to start paying taxes on it. All yachts must pay a daily berthing fee in Italian ports. For a list of ports which charter yachts, write to the National Tourist Office.

Many regions now offer **riding holidays**, as well as stables where you can hire a horse for a few hours; write to the provincial tourist or Agriturist offices (see below) for details. **Golfers** will find about 60 courses in Italy where they may try their skill and luck; for particulars on visitors to the clubs, their locations, opening seasons, etc., write directly to the courses in the Northeast:

Cansiglio (9 holes), 33034 **Vittorio Veneto**, tel (0438) 585 398
Asiago (9 holes), 36012 **Asiago**, tel (0424) 62 721
Lido di Venezia (18 holes), 30011 **Alberoni** (Venice), tel (041) 731 015
Villa Condulmer (18 holes), 31021 **Mogliano Veneto** (near Venice), tel (041) 457 062
Verona (18 holes), 37066 **Sommacampagna**, tel (045) 510 060
Padua (18 holes) 35050 **Valsanzibio di Galzignano**, tel (049) 528 078
Albarella (18 holes) 45010 **Isola di Albarella**, tel (0426) 67 124
Campo Carlo Magno (9 holes) 38084 **Madonna di Campiglio**, tel (0465) 41 003
Udine (9 holes), 33034 **Fagagna Villaverde**, tel (0432) 800 418
Trieste (9 holes) 34100 **Trieste**, tel (04) 226 159
Bologna (18 holes) 45010 **Chiesa Nuova di M.S. Pietro**, tel (051) 969 100

The **skiing** in the Dolomites is thrilling as well as aesthetic. Facilities are on a par with other countries and are usually less expensive. There are high and low ski seasons—prices are highest during the Christmas and New Year holidays, in part of February, and at Easter. Most resorts offer *Settimane Bianche* (White Weeks) packages, which include room and board and ski passes for surprisingly economical rates; they are easy to purchase at a travel agent once you arrive in Italy, or you can write ahead to a particular resort. We have included the major ones in the text; the National Tourist Office can supply particulars on other special ski holidays. Other winter sports—ice skating and bob-sledding in particular, are available at the larger resorts like Cortina. If you can't get enough skiing in the winter, you can do a summer slalom on the glaciers of Stelvio National Park.

Hiking and mountaineering become more and more popular among the Italians themselves every year, and the country has an excellent system of marked trails and alpine refuges. The Dolomites offer spectacular, unforgettable scenery that makes even the stiffest climb worth while. Many of the trails and refuges are kept up by local offices of the Italian Alpine Club (CAI), located in every province (even the flat ones, where they organize excursions into the hills). If you're taking some of the most popular trails in the summer (especially in the Dolomites and in Aosta), you would do well to write ahead to reserve beds in the refuges. The local tourist offices can put you in touch with the right people and organizations. Walking in the Alps is generally practicable between May and October, after most of the snows have melted; all the necessary gear—boots, packs, tents, etc.—are readily available in Italy but for more money than you'd pay at home. The CAI can put you in touch with Alpine guides or climbing groups if you're up to some real adventures, or write to the National Tourist organization for operators offering mountaineering holidays. Some resorts in the Alps have taken to offering *Settimane Verdi* (Green Weeks)—accommodation and activity packages for summer visitors similar to the skiers' White Weeks.

Courses for Foreigners and Special Interest Holidays

The Italian Institute, 39 Belgrave Square, London SW1X 8NX, tel (071) 235 1461 or 686 Park Avenue, New York NY 10021, tel (212) 397 9300 is the main source of information on courses for foreigners in Italy. Graduate students should also contact their nearest Italian consulate to find out about scholarships—apparently many go unused each year because no one knows about them.

Summer courses on Italian language and civilization are a popular choice. They are offered by Padua University at Bressanone; write to the Segreteria dei Corsi Estivi, Università di Padova. Milan University has a similar programme at Gargnano, by Lake Garda (write the Università degli Studi, Via del Perdono 7, Milano); Bologna University at the beach Babylon of Rimini (information from Gioventù Studiosa, Via Cairoli 69, Rimini); you can also take language holidays at Riva del Garda, (Euroscuola, Via Venezia 47, Loc. Varone, 38060 Riva del Garda, Trento).

More scholarly courses include classes in culture, music, and sea sciences at the Fondazione Giorgio Cini, San Giorgio Maggiore in Venice; the September International Seminar of Studies and Research on the Language of Music, at the Istituto Musicale Francesco Canneti, Piazza Matteotti, Vicenza; Palladian seminars (often in August), sponsored by the Centro Internazionale di Architettura A. Palladio: write Casella Postale 593, Vicenza; September courses for conductors sponsored by the Ente Autonomo Teatro Comunale, Piazza Rossini, in Bologna.

Art classes include summer courses in the History and Technique of Mosaics, offered by the Centro Internazionale Insegnamento del Mosaico (write to the AAST, Via San Vitale 2, Ravenna) and in April, classes on Byzantine art, at the Istituto di Antichità Ravennati, Via San Vitale 28, Ravenna. Venice's Università Internazionale dell'Arte has courses between October and April in stage design, art restoration, and the history of art at the Palazzo Fortuny, San Marco 3780, Venezia. **Special Interest holidays** are an increasingly popular way to see Northeast Italy. UK operators include:

ACROSS TRUST (handicapped tours of the Dolomites), Crown House, Morden, Surrey, tel (081) 540 3897

ALTERNATIVE TRAVEL GROUP (walking and mountaineering in the Dolomites, Verona, and Venice) 3 George St, Oxford, tel (0865) 251 195

ART IN EUROPE (art and architecture, language and music, wine and gastronomy tours in Venice and the Veneto), 78 Shaftesbury Way, Twickenham, Middx, tel (081) 898 9888

C.H.A. (walking and mountaineering in the Val Gardena, Alleghe and Braies in the Dolomites), Birch Heys, Cromwell Range, Manchester, tel (061) 225 1000

CHEQUERS (motor racing holidays at Imola), Newbridge House, Newbridge, Dover, Kent, tel (0304) 204 515

CITALIA (Kosher holidays at Rimini), Marco Polo House, 3–5 Lansdowne Rd, Croydon, Surrey, tel (081) 686 5533

ENTERPRISE HOLIDAYS (singles holidays at Rimini), Groundstar House, London Road, Crawley, tel (0293) 517 866

GRAND UK HOLIDAYS (senior citizens at Riva del Garda), 6 Exchange St, Norwich, tel (0603) 619 933

HENEBERY G.W. LTD (opera in Verona and Venice), Kareol, Islip, Oxford, tel (08675) 6341

HOURMONT TOURS (language, art, cookery, tennis, dinghy sailing and windsurfing at Jesolo), Brunel House, Newfoundland Rd, Bristol, tel (0272) 426 961

ITALVIAGGI (golf holidays on Venice's Lido) High Street, Gillingham, Dorset, tel (0747) 825 353

J. M. B. TRAVEL CONSULTANTS (special events in Bologna, Ravenna, Venice, and Verona) Rushwick, Worcester, tel (0905) 425 628

JUST MOTORING JUST TICKETS (racing at Imola), Lincoln Oaks, Ranelagh Grove, Broadstairs, tel (0843) 65160

LIRICA-PEGASUS HOLIDAYS (events in Verona and Ravenna), 24A Earls Court Gardens, London SW5, tel (0273) 304 910

MAGNUM (senior citizens at Limone sul Garda), 7 Westleigh Park, Blaby, Leicester, tel (0533) 777 123

MARINA HOLIDAYS (riding holidays in Stelvio National Park), 38 Endless St, Salisbury, Wilts, tel (0722) 332 121

MOSAIC ELITE (art in Venice, Ravenna, and Sirmione),73 South Audley St, London W1, tel (071) 493 3380

NADFAS TOURS (National Association of Decorative and Fine Arts Societies, art and architecture tours in Verona, Vicenza, Bologna, Ravenna, Ferrara, and Venice), 80–98 Beckenham Rd, Beckenham, Kent, tel (081) 658 2308

QUO VADIS (special events in Venice, Verona, Bologna, and Parma), 243 Euston Road, London NW1, tel (071) 387 6122

RENAISSANCE (painting holidays in Venice; Renaissance art tour), P.O. Box 67, Folkestone, Kent, tel (0303) 47931

SAGA HOLIDAYS (senior citizens at Riva and Garda), The Saga Building, Middelburg Square, Folkestone, Kent, tel (0303) 40000

SERENISSIMA AND HERITAGE TRAVEL (Garden and villa tours at Ásolo, Vicenza, and Bassano del Grappa; art in Venice), 21 Dorset Square, London, NW1 tel (071) 703 9841

SJA (art in Verona and Venice), 48 Cavendish Rd, London SW12, tel (081) 673 4849
SPECIALTOURS (art and architecture in Verona, Ravenna, Rimini, and Ferrara) 2 Chester Row, London SW1, tel (071) 730 2297
SWAN HELLENIC (Botany and wild flowers in the Dolomites, Venetian Lagoon, and Po Delta), 77 New Oxford St, London WC1, tel (071) 831 1515
VOYAGES JULES VERNE (Botany and wildflowers, and painting holidays in the Dolomites) 21 Dorset Square, London NW1, tel (071) 724 6624

Festivals

There are literally thousands of festivals answering to every description in Italy. Every *comune* has at least one or two, not only celebrating a patron saint; others are sponsored by the political parties (especially the Communists and Socialists), where everyone goes to meet their friends and enjoy the masses of cheap food. No matter where you are, look at the posters; Italy is swamped with culture, and most refreshingly unsnobbish or elitist about it all. On the other hand, don't expect anything approaching uninhibited gaiety. Italy is a rather staid place these days, and festivals are largely occasions to dress up and have a pleasant outdoor supper. If, at a festival, you should ever happen to notice Italians laughing too loudly, drinking too much, or singing extemporaneously, drop us a line; we would love to see it.

Below is a calendar of the most popular annual events; some of particular interest will be mentioned in the text. For many you'll have to check at the tourist office for precise dates, which change from year to year.

Calendar of Events

January

1	National Naif Painters' competition, in **Luzzara** (near Parma), followed by a month-long exhibit; parade of folk costumes and horse drawn sleighs, at **Ortisei** (Bolzano).
Jan–April	Operas at the Teatro Comunale Verdi, **Trieste**.
Jan–May	Operas, chamber concerts, and song recitals at the Teatro Regio, **Parma**; opera at La Fenice, **Venice**.
5–6	Night of the Bisò, **Faenza**, bonfires and mulled wine accompany the burning of the *niballo*, or scapegoat for last year's trouble; Feast of the *pignarui*, **Tarcento** (Udine), 14th-century costumes in a torchlit parade of the Three Kings, followed by bonfires on all the surrounding hills.
6	Mass of the Sword, **Cividale del Friuli**, where the priest wears a sword in memory of the 14th-century Patriarch; Taller Mass, at **Gemona del Friuli**, a re-enactment of ancient ceremony, in which the mayor presents a coin (taller) to the priest, symbolizing homage to the Church's authority.
Jan-Feb	Chamber music at the Conservatorio, **Parma**.

Jan–March	Chamber music at the Teatro Comunale, **Bologna**.
13	Sant'Ilario, **Parma**, with the eating of special shoe-shaped cookies.
3rd weekend	Dog-sled races, **Brunico** (Bolzano).

February

5	Madonna of fire, patron saint of **Forlì**.
Carnival	**Venice** is the place to see the most beautiful masks and costumes, and to attend big-name events as the Lagoon city strives to recreate the old magic; **Sappada** (Belluno) celebrates with three weeks of parades and traditional events featuring a personage called Rollate, dressed in furs and hood, and wearing a carved wooden mask. Carnival at **Modena** features the 18th-century 'Pavironica family', who poke fun at current events. On Carnival Friday (just before Ash Wednesday) **Verona** celebrates the *Bacanal del gnocco*, a parade with the king of gnocchi and a feast, all in 15th-century costume. Other traditional Carnival celebrations take place in **Arco** (Trento) and **Ora/Auer** (Bolzano).
5	Procession of Sant'Agata, **San Marino**, celebration of independence regained in 1740 after occupation begun by Cardinal Alberoni.
2nd week	Antiques fair, **Reggio Emilia**.

March

Mid-Lent	*Segavecchia*, at **Forlimpopoli**, ancient festival including the burning of a witch in effigy.
Second half	Wine fair, **Bolzano**.
19	*Lis cidulis*, at **Forni Avoltri** (Udine), in which burning logs of wood are rolled down the hillside; **Castell' Arquato** (Piacenza), celebrates San Giuseppe with a feast of local pastries called *tortelli*.
Easter Mon	Egg Festival, **Tredozio** (Forlì), egg contests, floats, and folk music; Festival of *piè fritta*, in **Fontanelice** (Bologna), eating of traditional, unleavened bread called *piadine*; parades in costume and horse races at **Merano**.
2nd week	*Isola del Tempo*, spring antiques-market, **Parma**.

April

First week	Usual time for children's book fair, **Bologna**.
3rd week	Cherry Blossom Festival, with horse races, bicycle tours, and exhibitions, in **Vignola**.

May

May–June	Symphony concerts at the Teatro Verdi, **Trieste**.

23

Ascension | *Sensa*, or re-enactment of the Doge's Wedding of the sea, **Venice**; similar event since the 15th century held in **Cervia** (Ravenna); Cross-kissing ceremony, at **Zuglio** (Udine), in which all the crosses from the countryside are decorated and brought to the church of S. Pietro.

4th Sun | Palio of San Giorgio, at **Ferrara**, 13th-century traditional horse race between the city's eight districts, with lots of costumes.

June

13 | Sant'Antonio, **Padua**, with procession of saint's relics and torchlight procession along the Bacchiglione.

3rd Sat–Sun | Oath of the Cavalieri and flag-tossing contest, at **Faenza**, where 'knights' vow to compete in Palio.

20 | Migration of the flocks, at **Senales** (Bolzano), in which the sheep cross the glaciers to the Giogo Alto, with picnics, etc.

20–26 | San Vigilio, folklore, music, and stealing of the polenta pot at **Trento**.

end June–Aug | Operetta festival, **Trieste**.

Last Sun | Palio del Niballo, at **Faenza**, in which horsemen try to strike target in hand of the *niballo*, or dummy.

End of June | Medieval festival at **Brisighella**; Mystfest—an international mystery festival, with films, at **Cattolica**; flower markets, **Bolzano**.

July

July–Aug | Grand opera at the Arena, and Shakespeare in the Roman theatre, **Verona**.

First weekend | Threshing festival, at **Noale** (Venice), country events and ancient crafts, and fireworks.

9 | Historical pageant, **Palmanova** (Udine).

14 | Festival of the *rustida*, outdoor fish feast, at **Cattolica**.

15–16 | Feast of the Redentore, **Venice**, celebrating the end of the 1576 plague, with a tremendous fireworks show followed by a procession over a bridge of boats on the Giudecca Canal.

mid July–first week of Oct | International artistic ceramics contest, **Faenza**.

August

First weekend | Palio and pageant at **Feltre**; Garibaldi festival at **Cesenatico** with games, music, and fireworks.

10 | San Lorenzo, **Cervia** (Ravenna), with sports and fireworks.

15 | Palio delle Contrade, at **Garda**, with fishing boat regatta and historical parade; songbird market, **Vittorio Veneto**; traditional festival at **Pievepelago**, south of Modena.

Mid-Aug–Sept | International piano competitions at **Bolzano**.

21	Traditional festival of Santa Augusta, **Vittorio Veneto**.
Last Sun	Songbird festival, **Sacile** (Pordenone).

September

First Sun	Historical regatta in costume and gondola races in **Venice**; Palio in **Montagnana**.
Second weekend	Human Chess game at **Maróstica** (Vicenza); autumn festival at **Tirolo** (Bolzano).
Second half	Grand prix horse races at **Merano**.
2nd Sun	Braciola festival, **Castel San Pietro Terme** (Bologna), with food, wine and folklore.
3rd Sun	Gran Prix de **Merano** horse race and lottery.
end Sept-Nov	Symphony concerts at the Teatro Verdi, **Trieste**.

October

First Sun	Feast of the Rosary, **Galzignano Terme** (Padua), procession in historical costume recalling the Battle of Lepanto, and a donkey race.
2nd Sun	Grape festival, **Merano**, local wines, costumes, and folklore events.
3rd Sun	Truffle festival, **Dovadola** (Forlì), truffle dishes, recipe contests, music and dancing; Chestnut festival at **Teolo** (Padua) and **Drena** (Trento).
20–29	Wine-tasting festival, **Ora** (Bolzano).

November

1	All Souls' Fair, traditional horse fair at **Galatea** (Forlì).
First week	Art and Antiques show, **Bolzano**.
19	*Fugarena*, **Terra del Sole** (Forlì), harvest festival reviving old country customs.
Mid month	Major horse fair in **Verona** (since 1908); DOC wine and food fair, **Vicenza**.
21	Feast of the Madonna della Salute, **Venice**, pilgrimage on bridge of boats over the Grand Canal, in thanksgiving for deliverance from plague in 1630.
Third week	Italy's biggest ornithological exhibition, **Reggio Emilia**.

December

Throughout month	Exhibition of *presepi* (Christmas cribs) in **Verona**.
First week	Fair of San Nicolò, traditional fair in **Trieste**.
5	Fair of San Nicolò, with a Christmas parade at **Vipiteno** (Bolzano).
First Sun	Olive fair, at **Brisighella**.
Second week	Regional handicrafts fair, **Pordenone**.
10–13	Santa Lucia toy fair, **Verona**.
2nd Sun	Radicchio Fair, in **Treviso**.

Shopping

'Made in Italy' of late has become a byword for style and quality, especially in fashion and leather, but also in home design, ceramics, kitchenware, jewellery, lace and linens, glassware and crystal, chocolates, bells, Christmas decorations (especially *presepi*, figures for Christmas cribs), hats, straw work, art books, engravings, handmade stationery, gold and silverware, bicycles, sports cars, woodworking (especially in the Alps), a hundred kinds of liqueurs, wine, aperitifs, coffee machines, gastronomic specialities, antique reproductions, as well as the antiques themselves. If you are looking for the latter and are spending a lot of money, be sure to demand a certificate of authenticity—reproductions can be very, very good. To get your antique or modern art purchases home, you will have to apply to the Export Department of the Italian Ministry of Education—a possible hassle. You will have to pay an export tax as well; your seller should know the details.

Venice, despite all its tourists, is the major shopping city in northeast Italy, although Bologna comes in a respectable second. Serious shoppers should come in January, when the major sales take place; Reggio Emilia and Parma even sponsor huge bargain fairs. Italians don't like department stores, though Venice-based *COIN* stores often have good buys on almost the latest fashions. *Standa* and *UPIM* are more like Woolworth's; they have good clothes selections, housewares, etc., and often supermarkets in their basements. A few stay open throughout the day, but most take the same break as other Italian shops—from 1 pm to 3 or 4 pm. Be sure to save your receipts for Customs on the way home. Shipping goods is a risky business unless you do it through a very reputable shop. Note well that the attraction of shopping in Italy is strictly limited to luxury items; for less expensive clothes and household items you'll always, always do better in Britain or America. Prices for clothes, even in street markets, are often ridiculously high. Cheaper goods are often very poor quality.

Good buys in the northeast tend to be the obvious ones. Glass and lace in Venice, Faenza (and Este) for ceramics, San Marino for postage stamps and duty-free goods; Grazziano Visconti (near Piacenza) for ornamental wrought iron; Maniago for cutlery; wood carvings, at Ortisei; Ferraris and Maseratis, in Modena.

Italian clothes are lovely, but if you have a large-boned Anglo-American build, you may find it hard to get a good fit, especially on trousers or skirts (Italians are a long-waisted, slim-hipped bunch). Men's shirts are sold by collar size only, and shoes are often narrower than the sizes at home.

Sizes

Women's Shirts/Dresses

UK	10	12	14	16	18
US	8	10	12	14	16
Italy	40	42	44	46	48

Sweaters

10	12	14	16
8	10	12	14
46	48	50	52

Women's Shoes

3	4	5	6	7	8
4	5	6	7	8	9
36	37	38	39	40	41

Men's Shirts

UK/US	14	14½	15	15½	16	16½	17	17½
Italy		36	37	38	39	40	41	42	43

Men's Suits

UK/US	36	38	40	42	44	46
Italy	46	48	50	52	54	56

Men's Shoes

UK	2	3	4	5	6	7	8	9	10	11	12
US	5	6	7	7½	8	9	10	10½	11	12	13
Italy	34	36	37	38	39	40	41	42	43	44	45

Weights and Measures

1 kilogramme (1000 g)—2.2 lb
1 etto (100 g)—¼ lb (approx)
1 litre—1.76 pints

1 lb—0.45 kg

1 pint—0.568 litres
1 quart—1.136 litres
1 Imperial gallon—4.546 litres
1 US gallon—3.785 litres

1 metre—39.37 inches
1 kilometre—0.621 miles

1 foot—0.3048 metres
1 mile—1.161 kilometres

Where to Stay

Hotels

Italy is endowed with hotels (*alberghi*) of every description, from the spectacular to the humble. These are rated by the government's tourism bureaucracy, from five stars at the luxurious top to one star at the bottom. The ratings take into account such things as a restaurant on the premises, plumbing, air conditioning, etc., but not character, style, or charm. Use the stars, which we include in this book, as a quick reference for prices and general amenities only. Another thing to remember about government ratings is that a hotel can stay at a lower rating than it has earned, so you may find a three-star hotel as comfortable as a four.

There's no inflation in Italy, if you believe the government; the prices simply keep increasing. With the vacation business booming, this curious paradox is well expressed in the prices of the country's hotels; every year costs rise by 6–8 per cent across the board, and are quickly catching up with northern Europe. **The prices listed in this book are for double rooms only.** For a single, count on paying two-thirds of a double; to add an extra bed in a double will add 35 per cent to the bill. Taxes and service charges are included in the given rate. Some establishments charge L10–25 000 for air conditioning. Also note that if rooms are listed without bath, it simply means the shower and lavatory are in the corridor. Prices are by law listed on the door of each room; any discrepancies could be reported to the local tourist office. Most rooms have two or three different rates, depending on the season. Costs are sometimes a third less if you travel in the district's low season. Some hotels, especially in resorts, close down altogether for several months

27

of the year. Reservations are indispensable in summer. The Italian Tourist Office annually publishes lists of hotels and pensions with their most recent rates and amenities, which are very helpful (although note that the Tourist Boards do not make reservations).

Breakfast is optional in most hotels, although in pensions it is mandatory. And you may as well expect to face half (breakfast and lunch or dinner) or full-board requirements in the hotels that can get away with it—seaside, lake, or mountain resorts in season, spas and country villa hotels. Otherwise, meal arrangements are optional. Although eating in the hotel restaurant can be a genuine gourmet experience, in the majority of cases hotel food is mass-produced and bland, just as it is anywhere else. As a general rule, expect to pay (in lire) in 1990:

Category Double	With bath
Luxury (*****)	L300–700 000
Class I (****)	L200–400 000
Class II (***)	L100–200 000
Class III (**)	L60–100 000
Class IV (*)	L40–60 000
Pension	L30–40 000

For rooms without bath, subtract 20–30 per cent. Many resort hotels in particular offer discounts for children and children's meals. A *camera matrimoniale* is a room with a double bed, a *camera doppia* has twin beds, a single is a *camera singola*. There are several hotel chains in Italy. CIGA (*Compagnia Grandi Alberghi*) has many of the most luxurious, many of them grand, turn-of-the-century establishments that have been exquisitely restored. Another plush chain, *Chateaux et Relais*, specializes in equally comfortable, but more intimate accommodation, often in historic buildings. Both chains pride themselves on their gourmet restaurants. Even the once fairly standard *Jolly Hotels*, Italy's oldest chain, are quickly up-grading. The petrol company AGIP operates most of the motels along the major motorways, and usually makes a decent effort to give them good restaurants; you can book AGIP motels at Quo Vadis Ltd, 243 Euston Road, London NW1 (tel (071) 388 7512). The National Tourist Office has a complete list of these and booking information for both motels and five- and four-star hotels and chains. If you want to stay in a different kind of accommodation, you'll have to book ahead on your own. Outside the high season this is generally unnecessary; otherwise, and especially if you have a certain place in mind, it is essential to book several months in advance or even earlier if possible, considering the sorry state of the Italian post. (While you're at it, remember to request a room with a view.) If your Italian is non-existent, the National Tourist Office's *Travellers' Handbook* has a sample letter and list of useful terms. Under Italian law, a booking is valid once a deposit has been paid. If you have to cancel your reservation, the hotel will keep the deposit unless another agreement has been reached. If you're coming in the summer without reservations, start ringing round for a place in the morning.

Facilities for the Handicapped
Hotel listings sometimes make a note of which establishments are suitable for the physically handicapped. There are also a number of tours that can make a holiday much smoother—a list is available from the National Tourist Office. RADAR publishes an

extremely useful book, *Holidays and Travel Abroad—A Guide for Disabled People*, available for £3.00 from their offices at 25 Mortimer St, London W1M 8AB, tel (071) 637 5400. Another useful book, *Access to the World: a Travel Guide for the Handicapped* by Louise Weiss, covers a wide range of topics with listings for individual countries. It's available for $14.95 from Facts on File, 460 Park Ave South, New York, NY 10016.

Inexpensive Accommodation

Bargains are few and far between in Italy. The cheapest kind of hotel is called an inn, or *locanda*; some provinces treat these as one-star hotels or list them separately (or not at all). The majority of inexpensive places will always be around the railway station, though in the large cities you'll often find it worth your while to seek out a more pleasant location in the historic centre. You're likely to find anything in a one-star Italian hotel. Often they will be practically perfect, sometimes almost luxurious; memorably bad experiences will be few, and largely limited to the major cities (around the train stations!).

Besides the youth hostels (see below), there are several city-run hostels, with dormitory-style rooms open to all. In cities like Rome, Venice, Assisi, Florence, and many others, religious institutions often rent out extra rooms. Monasteries in the country sometimes take guests as well; if you seek that kind of quiet experience, bring a letter of introduction from your local priest, pastor, etc. Women can make arrangements through the *Protezione della Giovane*, an organization dedicated to finding inexpensive and virtuous lodgings in convents, hostels, etc. They have desks in major railway stations, or you can contact them at their headquarters at Via Urbana 158, Rome, tel 460 056.

Youth and Student Hostels

Italy isn't exceptionally endowed with Youth Hostels (*Albergo per la Gioventù*), but they are usually pleasant and often in historic buildings. In the northeast the hostels are: Ekar, at **Asiago**; Guastalla-Po, at **Guastalla** (Reggio Emilia); at **Coli** (Piacenza); in **Venice**, the Adriatico at Jesolo Lido and the Venezia on the Giudecca; the Rocca degli Alberi at **Montagnana** (Padua); Cittadella at **Parma**; Meridiana, at **Ponte dell'Olio** (Piacenza); Dante, at **Ravenna**; Urland at **Rimini-Miramare**; Benacus, at **Riva del Garda**, on Lake Garda; Tergeste, at **Trieste Miramare**; and the Villa Francescatti, in **Verona**.

Anyone can stay in a youth hostel, and senior citizens are often given added discounts. Many youth hostels sell cards or you can pick up one in advance from:

US: American Youth Hostels, 1332 Eye St NW, Suite 800, Washington, DC, 20005
Canada: Canadian Hostelling Association, Place Vanier, Tower A, 333 River Rd, Ottawa, Ontario, K11 8H9
UK: Youth Hostels Association, 14 Southampton St, London WC2

Accommodation—a bunk bed in single-sex room and breakfast—costs around L10 000 per day. There is often a curfew, and you usually can't check in before 5 or 6 pm. You can book in advance by sending your arrival and departure dates along with the number of guests (by sex) to the individual hostel, including international postal coupons for the return reply. The worst time to use the hostels is the spring, when noisy Italian school groups use them for field trips.

There are two other organizations to help students find lodgings in Italy—the Centro Turistico Studentesco e Giovanile (CTS), which has offices in every Italian city of any size and can book cheap accommodation for you, in their own town or at your next stop. The Associazione Italiana per il Turismo e gli Scambi Universitari can obtain rooms for foreign university students all year round in university towns. Write to them at Via Palestro 11, Rome 00185, tel 475 5265.

Alpine Refuges
The Club Alpino Italiano operates a large percentage of the *Rifugi Alpini*, or mountain huts in both the Alps and Apennines. Facilities range from the basic to the grand; some are exclusively for hikers and mountain-climbers, while others may be reached by funivias, and are used by skiers in the winter and holidaymakers in the summer. Rates average L10 000 a night, but rise by 20 per cent between December and April. Write to the club at Via Foscolo 3, Milan, tel (02) 802 554 for a list of huts, their opening dates, and booking information.

Self Catering Holidays: Villas, Flats, and Farmhouses

Self-catering holiday accommodation is *the* way to beat the high costs of Italy, especially if you're travelling with the family or with a group of friends. Most of the options available from the UK in the northeast are flats along the Adriatic or Lake Garda, and a few in Venice. Look for ads in major Sunday papers, or if you have your heart set on a particular region, write ahead to its tourist office for a list of local agencies and individuals. These ought to provide photos of the accommodation to give you an idea of what to expect. Maid service is included in the more glamorous villas, while for others be sure to inquire about sheets and towels. Prices vary widely: you can spend L2 000 000 a week, or L100 000. In general minimum lets are for two weeks. Rental prices usually include insurance, water, and electricity. For a genuine country experience, contact Agriturist (offices listed below).

Don't be surprised if upon arrival the owner 'denounces' (*denunziare*) you to the police; according to Italian law, all visitors must be registered upon arrival. Common problems are water shortages, unruly insects and low kilowatts (often you can't have your hot water heater and oven on at the same time). Many of the companies listed below offer, in addition to homes, savings on charter flights, ferry crossings or fly-drive schemes to sweeten the deal. Try to book as far in advance as possible for the summer season.

Villa and Flat Agencies
BEACHCOMBER (**Cattolica, Lido di Jesolo**), International House, Finkle St, Selby, N. Yorks, tel (0757) 707 070
CHAPTER (**Venice, Castelrotto on Lake Garda, Arquà**), 126 St John's Wood High Street, London NW8, tel (071) 586 9451
CITALIA (**Caorle, Cattolica, Riccione, Rimini, Sottomarina, Venice**), Marco Polo House 3–5, Lansdowne Road, Croydon CR9 9EQ tel (081) 686 5336
EUROVILLAS (**Gargnano, Prabione, Tignale, Tremosine**, all on Lake Garda), 36 East St, Coggeshall, Essex, tel (0376) 61165
INTERHOME (**Venice, Limone sul Garda, Riva di Garda, Sirmione, Cattolica,**

Lido Adriano, Lido di Spina, Lignano, Riccione, Sottomarina), 383 Richmond Rd, Twickenham, tel (081) 891 1294
MAGIC OF ITALY (Verona, Gardone), 47 Shepherds Bush Green, London W12, tel (081) 743 9555
TOURAUTO HOLIDAYS (Torbole, Sirmione, Peschiera, Lazise, Lido Adriano, Lido di Comacchio, Lido di Jesolo, Riccione, Sottomarina), Bridge House, Ware, Herts, tel (0920) 3050
VENETIAN APARTMENTS (Venice), 1a Warrington Rd, Richmond, Surrey, tel (081) 948 6950
VILLAS ITALIA (Venice, Riva del Garda, Limone sul Garda, Torbole, Lido di Jesolo, Lido delle Nazioni, Lido di Spina, Riccione, San Ginesio, Venice), 227 Shepherds Bush Rd, London W6, tel (081) 748 8668.

Besides these, every province has a certain number of farmhouses and rural accommodation available through its local Agriturist office. These are often extremely reasonably priced, and often include extras like chickens, rabbits, horses, and cheap homegrown produce and wine, often on working farms with families. Prices range from L4–9000 per person a night; write ahead to the following provincial offices:

VENETO
Via Zuppani 5, 32100 **Belluno**, tel (0437) 213 196
C. Monteverdi 15, 30174 **Mestre**,tel (041) 987 400
Piazza Martiri Libertà 9, 35137 **Padua**, tel (049) 661 655
Piazza Duomo 2, 45100 **Rovigo**, tel (0425) 28 823
Viale Cadorna 10, 31100 **Treviso**, tel (0422) 548 266
Via Locatelli 3, 37122 **Verona**, tel (045) 594 707
Viale Trento 193, **Vicenza**, tel (0444) 960 685

FRIULI-VENEZIA GIULIA
Via Angiolina 20, 34170 **Gorizia**, tel (0481) 84 429
Via Dante 27, 33170 **Pordenone**, tel (0434) 22 672
Fraz. Padriciano 176, 34012 **Trieste**, tel (040) 226 449
Via D. Moro 18, 33100 **Udine**, tel (0432) 504 027

TRENTINO
Via Brennero 23, 38100 **Trento**, tel (0461) 824 211

ALTO ADIGE
Via Brennero 7/a, 39100 **Bolzano**, tel (0471) 972 145

EMILIA ROMAGNA
Via Castiglione 24, 40124 **Bologna**, tel (051) 233 991
Contrada della Rosa 18, 44100 **Ferrara**, tel (0532) 32 173
Piazza A. Saffi 43, 47100 **Forlì**, tel (0543) 33 466
Via Diena 7, 41100 **Modena**, tel (059) 311 221
Piazzale Barezzi 3, 43100 **Parma**, tel (0521) 282 546
Via Mazzini 14, 29100 **Piacenza**, tel (0523) 20 271
Via M. d'Azeglio 38, 48100 **Ravenna**, tel (0544) 22 002
Via Guidelli 10, 42100, **Reggio Emilia**, tel (0522) 39 241

Camping

Most of the official camp sites are near the sea, but there are also quite a few in the mountains and near the lakes, and usually one within commuting distance of major tourist centres. A complete list with full details for all of Italy is published annually in the Italian Touring Club's *Campeggi e Villaggi Turistici*, available in Italian bookshops for L22 000, or you can obtain an abbreviated list free from the Centro Internazionale Prenotazioni Federcampeggio, Casella Postale 23, 50042, Calenzano (Firenze); request their booking forms as well to reserve a place—essential in the summer months when the tents and caravans (campers) are packed cheek to cheek. Camping fees vary according to the camp ground's facilities, roughly L5000 per person (less for children); L5000–15 000 per tent or caravan; and L4000 per car. Camping outside official sites is kosher if you ask the landowner's permission first.

Camper and Caravan Hire

Automobil Club, Corso Italia 19/a, **Bolzano**, tel (0471) 30 003
Campring, Via U. Bassi 1/g, **Bologna**, tel (051) 223 529
Camper Modena, Via Emilia Est 1418, **Modena**, tel (059) 371 251
Camper Trieste, Strada Basovizza 6, **Trieste**, tel (040) 567 956
Camper Tur, Via Dante 40, **Pordenone**, tel (0434) 208 965
Camper Vacanze, **Trento**, tel (0461) 912 608
Caravan CC. Via Moano 88, **Torre Del Moro di Cesena**, tel (0547) 331 990
Essebi, Via G. Galilei 2, **Bolzano**, tel (0471) 42 199
Intercaravan di Tomaello, Piazza 27 Ottobre 63, **Mestre** (Venice), tel (041) 950 331
Mever, Via dell'Artigianato 27, **Verona**, tel (045) 508 071
Motor Home Italia, Corso Milano 43a, **Verona**, tel (045) 568 544
Presticamper, Via Machiavelli 11, **Mogliano Veneto** (Treviso), tel (041) 451 481

Buying a House

Rural real estate is one of Italy's great buys, and the recommended way to do it is to buy a run-down property and restore it to your own needs and taste. But beware the pitfalls.

One estate agent is constantly amazed that his English clients invariably express two major concerns about a property: drainage and the presence of a bidet in the bathroom, as if it were a tool of the devil! What they should be asking are questions about water supply, electricity, and road access—often big problems for that isolated, romantic farmhouse that has caught your eye. Another thing to remember before purchasing a home or land is that you need permission from the local *comune* to make any changes or improvements, and it's no good buying anything unless you're pretty sure the *comune* will consent (for a sizeable fee, of course) to let you convert the old cellar or stable into a spare bedroom. Another thing to remember is that though there are no annual rates (property tax) to pay, there's a 10 per cent IVA (VAT) to be paid on the purchase price for a house and 17 per cent on land, as well as a hefty Capital Gains Tax on selling price and profit to be paid by the seller. Italians tend to get round this by selling at one price and writing down another on the contract. But remember if you sell you'll be in the same bind.

Once you've agreed to buy, you pay a deposit (usually 25–30 per cent) and sign a *compromesso*, a document that states that if you back out, you lose your deposit, and if the seller changes his mind, he forfeits double the deposit to you (be sure your *compromesso* includes this feature, called *caparra confirmatoria*). Always transfer payment from home through a bank, taking care to get and save a certificate of the transaction so you can take the sum back out of Italy when you sell. After the *compromesso*, your affairs will be handled by a *notaio*, the public servant in charge of registering documents and taxes who works for both buyer and seller. If you want to make sure your interests are not overlooked, you can hire a *commercialista* (lawyer-accountant) who will handle your affairs with the *notaio*, including the final transfer deed (*rogito*), which completes the purchase at the local Land Registry. Upon signing, the balance of the purchase price generally becomes payable within a year. The next stage for most buyers, restoration, can be a nightmare if you aren't careful. Make sure the crew you hire is experienced and that you're pleased with the work elsewhere—don't hesitate to ask as many other people in your area as possible for advice. One book that offers some clues on the ins and outs of taxes, inheritance law, residency, gardening, etc., is *Living in Italy*, published by Robert Hale, London 1987.

Eating Out

In Italy, the three Ms (the Madonna, Mamma, and Mangiare) are still a force to be reckoned with, and in a country where millions of otherwise sane people spend much of their waking hours worrying about their digestion, standards both at home and in the restaurants are understandably high. Best of all for the travelling trencherman or woman, the Italians are equally manic when it comes to preserving regional traditions in the kitchen; if you are ever bored poring over a menu in northeast Italy, you've been nipped in the tastebuds.

When asked which region has the finest cuisine, most Italians will say Emilia-Romagna, homeland of favourite pasta dishes like lasagne, tortellini, tagliatelle, ravioli, *cappelletti* (often filled with pumpkin) and spaghetti bolognese (which becomes a new experience in a good Bolognese restaurant) as well as staples like parmesan cheese, Parma ham, balsamic vinegar, a hundred varieties of sausage, salami, and pig's trotter (*zampone*). The cherries from Vignola are some of Italy's best.

Each city of the Veneto has its own speciality: gnocchi in Verona; salt cod simmered in milk in Vicenza; *radicchio rosso* (red chicory) in Treviso; *bigoli* (thin spaghetti), liver and onions, and *risi e bisi* (risotto with peas) in Venice. Seafood is popular everywhere, from the humble anchovy to the regal Mediterranean lobster; asparagus appears in many dishes in spring, while porcini mushrooms rule the autumn menu. In the winter the locals, at least, replace the pasta course with *polenta* (a pudding or cake of maize flour), a brick-heavy substance to be approached with caution. The cradle of good cooking in the Veneto is up in the Alpago hills, above Vittorio Veneto, where each little hamlet has a superb restaurant or two.

Mountain cheeses, mushrooms, river trout, and apples are the glory of Trentino's kitchen; its most famous first course, hazardous to clerics, is *strangolapreti* ('priest-stranglers')—little golf balls of pasta and spinach; another, safer, speciality is *pappardelle al lepre*—ribbon noodles with hare sauce. Once you pass over the border into Alto Adige/Süd Tirol, language isn't the only thing that changes. Wine soups, Tyrolean ham (*speck*), Wienerschnitzel, sauerkraut, dumplings, Sachertortes and cheese and nut strudels are the typical dishes, but old Italian favourites like pizza and pasta are never far. Similar Austro-Hungarian traditions permeate the cuisine of northern Friuli-Venezia

Giulia, while the eastern borderlands are partial to the goulash, cabbage soups, bread and potato dumplings, heavenly sour cream and poppyseed cakes, and plummy fire waters (*slivovitz*) of neighbouring Slovenia. The centre, at San Daniele di Friuli, is the home of a cured ham that rivals the prosciutto of Parma.

Italian eating establishments open from noon to 3 or 4 pm and from 7 or 8 until 11 pm. They come in many forms—the *ristorante*, *trattoria*, *rosticceria*, *tavola calda* and *pizzeria*. Although traditionally a *trattoria* is a cheaper, simpler place than a *ristorante*, in reality they are often exactly the same, both in quality and price, the only difference being that a *ristorante* has more pretensions. Most restaurants display a menu outside so that you know what to expect, at least as regards the price.

The *rosticceria*, *tavola calda*, or *gastronomia* are quite similar, the latter now the more popular name for the counters of prepared hot and cold food, where you choose what looks good, eat, pay and go. Some of these are quite elaborate, while the modest ones don't even have chairs or stools. If you're used to eating a light lunch instead of a major Italian midday feast, they're the answer.

You can tell a good *pizzeria* by the traditional Neapolitan pizza oven at the back. *Pizzerie* are often combined with *trattorie*, as many Italians like to eat pizza for the first course (the *primo*) of a large meal. In these places, the service charge may be 20 per cent if you order just a pizza and beer. Service in *ristoranti* and *trattorie* is generally 15 per cent, and there is also a *coperto e pane* (cover and bread) charge of L2000 or so. Tipping is discretionary, but customary. Tax law in Italy orders restaurants and bars to give patrons a receipt (*scontrino*) for everything they eat or drink, which you are supposed to take out of the restaurant with you and carry for 300 metres in case the receipt police stage one of their rare ambushes.

Many places offer *prezzo fisso* (set price) or *menu turistico* meals—often a real bargain. Posh joints with gourmet pretensions sometimes offer a *menu degustazione*, a fixed menu of the chef's specialities, which can be a real treat and usually good value as well. Of course you can always order *alla carta* from the menu, which is divided into the following categories (a fuller list of items on the menu can be found in the language section at the end of this book).

Antipasti (hors d'oeuvres). These are often sumptuously displayed to tempt you the minute you walk in; common starters are seafoods, vegetables, salami, ham, olives, etc. Depending on the restaurant, you can choose these yourself or order them from the menu.

Minestre. Broth or minestrone soups, or pasta dishes. The latter come under the sub-heading of *Pasta Asciutta*. Many Italians skip the antipasti, which are often as dear as they are good, and go straight for the spaghetti, before tackling the second course, or *secondo*. Note that you will be expected to have both a pasta and a main dish to follow, which can be a sharp surprise to one's digestive system if not used to it.

Pesce. Fish, often according to availability, since it is always fresh.

Carne. Meat, which includes chicken, beef, lamb, veal and pork. With meat or fish, you eat a *contorno* (side dish) of your choice—often salad, vegetables or potatoes.

Dolce o Frutta. Sweet or fruit, the latter being more popular after a big meal. Common sweets are the famous Italian ice cream, exotic cakes or pastries.

Wine of course is the most popular accompaniment to dinner. *Vino locale* (house wine) is the cheapest and usually quite good, and this is what you'll get unless you order a specific label. Mineral water (*acqua minerale*) comes under as many labels as the wine, with or without added or natural carbonation (or *gas*, as the Italians call those little bubbles). Italian beer, always served cold, is average, and of course you can always order the ubiquitous Coca-Cola or Fanta. A small, black espresso coffee puts the final touch to an Italian meal.

Bars have little in common with American bars or English pubs, and can be anything from luxurious open-air cafés to dingy back-alley meeting places for the boys. All serve primarily coffee in the form of *espresso* (small, stormy and black), *cappuccino* (with milk and a sprinkling of chocolate, and drunk only before noon), or simply *caffè con latte* (coffee with milk), often served in a glass. Many people have breakfast at a bar, where you can help yourself to *cornetti* (croissants) or whatever other pastries are available. Here the problems begin when you have to pay and haven't the slightest idea of what your pastry was called.

Of course you can also get alcohol, soft drinks, mineral water, juices, etc. at a bar, at any time of the day from 7 am to midnight. Alcohol is cheap, as long as it's not imported. Standing at the bar is about a third cheaper than sitting at a table to be served. The *scontrino* is the receipt, and you may be asked to collect one from the *cassa* (cash desk) before being served, especially in the big cities.

Note: The prices quoted for restaurants in this book are averages for a meal of three courses and wine, per person. In many you can eat for less, depending on what you order, but beware of the extra charges—service, *coperto*, and tax—that can add up to 20 per cent to the bill.

Wine

Most Italian wines are named after the grape and the district they come from. If the label says D.O.C. (*Denominazione di Origine Controllata*) it means that the wine comes from a specially defined area and was produced according to a certain traditional method. Nearly every hill of Venetia is draped in vines, and together the three regions of the Veneto, Friuli-Venezia Giulia and Trentino-Alto Adige produce nearly half of all Italy's wines. Some of their names are already familiar, especially the red *Bardolino* and *Valpolicella* and white *Soave* of Verona. Some, like the dry bubbling white or rosé *Prosecco* of Conegliano, or the splendid array of white wines from Friuli (*Tokai, Pinot Bianco* and *Pinot Grigio*) and Trentino-Alto Adige (*Riesling, Silvaner Chardonnay, Pinot Grigio* and *Gewurztraminer*) still seem to be Italian secrets. Emilia-Romagna, on the other hand, is known for two unique red wines: foamy *Lambrusco* and powerful *Sangiovese*, the blood of Jove.

From Bassano and surroundings comes **grappa**, rough and macho Italian eau de vie, often drunk in black coffee after a meal. Other members of any Italian bar include *Campari*, the famous red bitter, drunk on its own or in cocktails; *Fernet Branca, Cynar* and *Averno*, popular aperitif/digestives; and liqueurs like *Strega*, the saffron witch potion from Benevento, apricot-flavoured *Amaretto*, cherry *Maraschino*, aniseed *Sambuca*, or the herby *Millefiori*, as well as any number of locally brewed elixirs.

Stronger drinks like whisky or gin are less expensive in Italy than at home; the majority of Italians rarely touch the stuff, despite intensive advertising. You can go into many a small town bar and order a drink—watch the bartender dust off the bottle, pour you a quadruple and inquire if it's enough, then ask a pittance for it.

Part II

HISTORY AND ART

Palazzo Dario, Venice

History

Some of the most creative cultures grow up in some of the messiest historical composts. The Mediterranean is a case in point, and Italy an extreme case, and its northeast as historically messy and creative as any place on this planet. Inhabited in neolithic times by a mix of Illyrians, Italics, and Celto-Ligurians, it stayed out of the headlines until about 1600 BC, when the **Terramare culture** appeared on the plains of Emilia, giving the peninsula the most densely populated and sophisticated society it had yet seen. All over Emilia, and into the Veneto, the Terramare people dug networks of canals for drainage and irrigation. They lived in neatly rectangular villages surrounded by moats, with regular street plans oddly identical to those of the new towns Romans would be building a millennium and a half later.

Between 1200 and 1000, the Terramare culture comes to an abrupt and untimely end; its territory, the most prosperous in Italy, became virtually abandoned. No one knows whether this came about because of war, economic disruption or migration (or all three), but its fate is symptomatic of the great upheavals plaguing the entire Mediterranean at this time, the onset of what could be called the first Dark Age. The fall of Troy occurred about 1180. The Mycenaean Greeks who conquered it were themselves in a state of collapse.

But just as the western Mediterranean was suffering the raids of the shadowy 'Sea Peoples', the Italian scene was undergoing major changes. New peoples appear, such as the **Venetii**, who gave their name to the modern Veneto, while another people known

36

only as the **Villanova culture** (after a village near Bologna, where its first traces were discovered) came to occupy much of central Italy; Villanovan chamber tombs with false domes and vaults were the forerunners of Etruscan and Roman models. By the 9th century, the archaeological record suggests an improvement in political and economic conditions. Well-defined nations for the first time leave their own names for the historical record, most importantly for our region, the Etruscans.

750–509 BC: Etruscans and Gauls

With their shadowy past and as yet undeciphered language, the Etruscans are one of the puzzles of ancient history. According to their own traditions, they arrived from western Anatolia about 900 BC, a pirate-aristocracy that imposed itself on the Villanova peoples of Tuscany. By the 8th century BC they were the strongest people in Italy; by the end of the 6th, the Etruscans ruled almost the entire northeast, with their largest city and base at **Felsina** (Bologna). From here they ran trading posts on the Adriatic, at Ravenna and Rimini, and founded the new town of **Spina** by the mouth of the Po.

The Etruscans, enriched by the mines of Tuscany, became the chief metal merchants of their day, and the middlemen of Greek art to the Celtic tribes over the Alps. Their occupation led logically to a concentration on markets and cities, ruled by a king until the late 6th century, with a strong urban aristocracy raking in the money from the mines and their rural landholdings. These are the Etruscans we see captured in stone, reclining atop thousands of sarcophagi recovered from ancient tombs. They look strangely modern, serene and smiling; as with much else in Etruscan art, they strike a chord of sympathy across the centuries. Worldly they certainly were, a society featuring naughty stage shows and dyed blondes; according to one report they made their house servants work in the buff. Among the most common Etruscan artefacts are cosmetics cases and mirrors. Women enjoyed approximate legal equality and considerable personal freedom, in marked contrast to their counterparts in Greece or anywhere else in this era. Rural serfs and the slaves in the mines may not have appreciated much of this.

Unfortunately, the Etruscans were as reticent about leaving inscriptions as the Romans were prolix. As a result, scholars have never translated the language entirely. Though an ancient tongue, with little resemblance to Indo-European descendants like Greek and Latin, the Etruscans bequeathed much of their alphabet and vocabulary to Rome. It is probable that some hundreds of words in common English use today have their origin in Etruscan, by way of Latin.

Two of those are *auspices* and *temple*, reminders of the less worldly side of the Etruscan psyche. For all their carousing, these jaded sophisticates may have been the most carefully pious nation of antiquity, polishing their superstitions to an art form. For an Etruscan nearly anything observed in nature could be taken as a sign or omen. Piacenza's Civic Museum has a famous bronze model of a sheep's liver, divided into sections with inscriptions to show apprentice *haruspices* (augurs) how to interpret the signs after a ritual sacrifice. The other important function of the *haruspex* was to take the auspices by observing the flight of birds, according to a complex system that divided the heavens into sections, each under the influence of one of the many gods in the Etruscan pantheon.

The Etruscans had hardly made themselves cosy on the Adriatic and rich plains of the Po when trouble began, in waves of **Gauls** who repeatedly invaded from over the Alps.

37

Bear in mind that in classical antiquity, the expression 'Italy' referred only to the peninsula proper, south of the Apennines and the Po. Everything between the Apeninnes and Alps was **Cisalpine Gaul**. Celtic peoples had roamed over parts of it for centuries, but a permanent occupation by the strongest, best-organized Celts from Gaul (or Bohemia) occurred only in the 6th or 5th century BC. Extremely talented in art and metalworking, they present the singular paradox of a nomadic people, caring little for the comforts of home, and everything for their freedom, yet culturally and technologically up to date. The Gauls invented one significant though overlooked military advance—horseshoes—and carried better swords than most of their foes.

The Etruscans had the misfortune to be their neighbours, and after their initial success in colonizing the lower Po valley in the 4th century BC, the Gauls kept the pressure on, capturing Felsina in 350 after a bitter struggle.

The Romans, Rise and Fall: 283 BC–475 AD

More rumblings came from the south as Rome gradually subjugated the rest of the Etruscans, Latins, and neighbouring tribes. The little republic with the military camp ethic was successful on all fronts, and a sack by marauding Gauls in 390 BC proved only a brief interruption in Rome's march to conquest. Their arch-enemies, the Samnites, formed an alliance with the Northern Etruscans and Celts, leading to a general Italian commotion in which the Romans beat everybody, annexing almost all of Italy by 283 BC.

All the while, the Romans had been diabolically clever in managing their new demesne, maintaining most of the tribes and cities as nominally independent states (like Verona, Trieste, Bologna, Adria, and Padua) while planting Latin colonies at important transport nodes (Aquileia, Trent, Reggio Emilia, Parma, and Ravenna). The great network of roads, like the arrow-straight **Via Aemilia** (187 BC) and the Via Romana, from Fano to Tergeste (Trieste), grew up with speed, and a truly united Italy seemed close to becoming a reality.

Northeast Italy was one of the sleepier corners, and the men it contributed (like the poet Catullus, architect-author Vitruvius, and the historian Livy) and the events it saw, like Julius Caesar crossing the Rubicon, or Augustus meeting Herod the Great in Aquileia, made their mark elsewhere. The 2nd century AD saw the emergence of the well-known north-south split in Italy. The south—the former lands of Magna Graecia—impoverished by the Roman Republic, now sank deeper into decline, ruined by foreign competition. In the north, especially in Cisalpine Gaul, a sounder, more stable economy led to the growth of new centres—Padua, Verona, and Ravenna the most prominent—beginning the economic divide that continues even today. On balance, though, both politically and economically Italy was becoming an increasingly less significant part of the empire. Of the 2nd-century emperors, fewer came from Italy than from Spain, Illyria, or Africa.

By the third century, the legions were no longer the formidable military machine of Augustus' day. In 256 the Franks and Alemanni invaded Gaul, and in 268 much of the east detached itself from the empire under the leadership of Odenathus of Palmyra. Somehow Rome recovered and prevailed, under dour soldier-emperors like Diocletian, who completely revamped the structure of the state and economy, replacing it with a gigantic bureaucracy. Taxes reached new heights as people's ability to pay them declined, and society became increasingly militarized. The biggest change was the division of the empire into halves, each ruled by a co-emperor called 'Augustus'; the western emperors after Diocletian usually kept their court at army headquarters in Milan, and Rome itself became a marble-veneered backwater.

The confused politics of the 4th century are dominated by **Constantine** (306–337), who ruled both halves of the empire, and favoured Christianity, by now the majority religion in the East but largely identified with the ruling classes and urban populations in Italy and the West. But even the new faith wasn't able to stay the disasters that began in 406. Visigoths, Franks, Vandals, Alans, and Suevi overran Gaul and Spain; Italy's turn came in 408, when Western Emperor Honorius, ruling from the new capital of **Ravenna**, had his brilliant general Stilicho (who himself happened to be a Vandal) murdered. A Visigothic invasion followed, including Alaric's sack of Rome in 410. St Augustine, probably echoing the thoughts of most Romans, wrote that the end of the world must be near. Rome should have been so lucky; judgement was postponed long enough for **Attila the Hun** to pass through Italy in 451, decimating the northeast but indirectly founding a new city of refugees called Venice.

So completely had things changed, it was scarcely possible to tell the Romans from the barbarians. By the 470s, the real ruler in Italy was a Gothic general named **Odoacer**, who led a half-Romanized Germanic army and thought of himself as the genuine heir of the Caesars. In 476, he decided to dispense with the lingering charade of the Western Empire, and had himself crowned King of Italy at Pavia.

476–1000: The Dark Ages

In Italy, the Dark Ages were never as dark as common belief would have it. One key to understanding the period is that the Roman cities never entirely disappeared. A few expired totally, like Aquileia and Altinum, but most of the rest shrank to provincial market centres, their theatres, arenas, and aqueducts abandoned. Amidst the confusion of Rome's fall, popes and monks and battling barons, Goths, Greeks and Lombards were weaving a strange cocoon for Roman Italy. From its silence, centuries later, would be born a new Italian people, suddenly bursting with talent and energy.

Odoacer's government was a peaceful parenthesis for Italy until Emperor Zeno, in 488, commissioned young King **Theodoric** of the Ostrogoths to invade, a ploy meant to take Ostrogoth pressure off Constantinople. Odoacer's army was waiting, but the Goths defeated them decisively near Verona. Most of the peninsula was speedily occupied, though Odoacer held out in impregnable Ravenna for another three years. At last Theodoric tricked him out with a promise to share Italy with him, then performed the traditional murder at what was supposed to be a reconciliation banquet.

Despite that black mark, Theodoric—a strapping fellow with long Asterix moustaches, typical of the half-cultured, half-barbaric protagonists of the Roman twilight—reorganized his new dominions with remarkable sophistication. Inheriting a civil service that had come down from Odoacer, and before him the Empire, Theodoric used it well to stabilize his realm. The Church was a harder nut to crack. In the disorders of the first barbarian invasions, the Roman pope and scores of local bishops had achieved a great degree of temporal power, filling the vacuum left by the collapse of the Roman system.

This temporal power gave the Church a diabolical incentive to oppose any strong government in Italy—especially one of heretical Arian Christians. Theodoric himself had no use for theological disputes, but his policy of religious tolerance proved as intolerable to the Church as his Arianism. Most of his subjects, at least, were thankful for it.

Theodoric's reign also witnessed the last small Renaissance of Latin letters. There was Cassiodorus, Theodoric's secretary, whose talents at practical politics helped Italy somewhat more than his bombastic prose; Symmachus, president of the Senate, historian, essayist, and the last great pagan; and Symmachus' brilliant son-in-law **Boethius**, Theodoric's chief minister, and author of the *Consolation of Philosophy*, a magnificent synthesis of classical culture and Christianity that won him consideration as one of the Fathers of the Church, and ensured him a tremendous influence throughout the Middle Ages.

Still, the old guard Romans regarded the Goths as usurpers; religious bigotry grew, and many looked towards Constantinople in hopes of a restoration of legitimate government. Embittered, Theodoric's increasingly paranoid behaviour (he had both Symmachus and Boethius executed) besmirched his record before he died in 526, leaving as heir a young grandson named Athalaric. The difficult job of regent fell to his mother, Amalasuntha; and when the teenaged Athalaric, with his good Gothic warrior's upbringing, drank himself to death, Amalasuntha was forced to marry her cousin Theodehad, who had her murdered. With no strong hand in control, the kingdom was ripe for mischief. There was no doubt in anyone's mind that the next move would come from Constantinople.

The Eastern Empire had just the right sort of emperor to take up the challenge: the great **Justinian**. Amalasuntha's murder in 536 gave him his excuse to invade Italy, in the person of his young and brilliant general Belisarius. The historical irony was profound; in the ancient homeland of the Roman Empire, Roman troops now came not as liberators, but as foreign, largely Greek-speaking conquerors. Belisarius, and his successor, the eunuch Narses, ultimately prevailed over the Goths in a series of terrible wars that lasted until 563, but the damage to an already stricken society and economy was incalculable.

Italy's total exhaustion was exposed only five years later, when the **Lombards**, a Germanic tribe who worked hard to earn the title of barbarians, overran the north. Although first sharing Italy with semi-independent Byzantine dukes, the remarkable new trading city of Venice, and the Exarchs (Byzantine Viceroys) of Ravenna, the Lombards saw their chance to go for the whole boot. Their greatest threat arose with the ruthless and crafty King Aistulf, who conquered almost all of the Byzantine Exarchate; in 753, even Ravenna fell into his hands. If the Lombards' final solution were to be averted, the popes would need help from outside. The logical people to ask were the Franks.

At the time, the popes had something to offer in return. For years, the Mayors of the Palace had wanted to supplant the Merovingian dynasty, but lacked the appearance of legitimacy that only the mystic pageantry of the papacy could provide. At the beginning of Aistulf's campaigns, Pope Zacharias quickly gave his blessing to the change of dynasties, and **Pepin** sent his army over the Alps, in 753 and 756, to foil Aistulf's designs. His unsuccessful attempt to tame Venice, which refused to take sides, helped set that city on its idiosyncratic track.

By 773 the conflict remained the same, though with a different cast of characters. The new Lombard king was Desiderius, the Frankish, his cordially hostile son-in-law, **Charlemagne**, who also invaded Italy twice, in 775 and 776, deposed his father-in-law and took the Iron Crown of Italy for himself. In 799, Pope Leo III set an imperial crown on his head, resuscitating not only the idea of empire, but of an empire that belonged to the successors of St Peter to dispose of as they wished. It changed the political face of Italy for ever, beginning the contorted *pas de deux* of pope and emperor that was to be the mainspring of Italian history throughout the Middle Ages.

With the disintegration of Charlemagne's empire, Italy reverted to a finely balanced anarchy. Altogether the 9th century was a bad time of endless wars of petty nobles and battling bishops in the north. The 10th century proved somewhat better—perhaps much better than the scanty chronicles of the time attest. Sailing, and trading over the sea, always lead to better technologies, new ideas, and economic growth, and in these respects the maritime cities like Venice had become the most advanced in Europe. By the 900s many cities were looking to their own resources, defending their interests against the Church and nobles alike.

A big break for the cities, and for Italy, came in 961 with the invasion of the German **Otto the Great**, at the request of the powerful Count of Tuscany at Canossa. He deposed the last feeble King of Italy, Berengar II, and was crowned Holy Roman Emperor in Rome the following year. Not that any of the Italians were happy to see him, but the strong government of Otto and his successors beat down the great nobles and allowed the growing cities to expand their power and influence. A new pattern was established; the Germanic Emperors would be meddling in Italian affairs for centuries, not powerful enough to establish total control, but at least usually able to keep out important rivals.

1000–1154: The Rise of the *Comuni*

Like the rest of Christendom, Italy looked ahead to the year 1000 fearing nothing but the worst—the old legends prophesied that this nice, round number would bring with it the end of the world. Perhaps only historical hindsight could see the sprouts of new life and growth that were appearing everywhere on Italian soil at this time, perhaps most remarkably symbolized by the building of St Mark's in Venice. In the towns, business was very good, and the political prospects even brighter. The first mention of a truly independent *comune* (a term used throughout this book, meaning a free city state; the best translation might be 'commonwealth') was in Milan, in 1024; before long *comuni* appeared in Ravenna, Verona, Padua, Treviso, and Bologna.

Throughout this period the papacy had declined greatly in power. In the 1050s, a remarkable monk named Hildebrand controlled papal policy, working behind the scenes to reassert the influence of the Church. When he became pope himself in 1073, **Gregory VII** immediately set himself in conflict with the emperors over the issue of investiture—whether the church or secular powers would appoint church officials. Fifty years of intermittent war followed, including the famous penance in the snow of Emperor Henry IV in **Canossa** (1077). The result was a big revival for the papacy, but more importantly the cities of the north used the opportunity to increase their influence, and in some cases achieve outright independence.

1154–1300: Guelphs and Ghibellines

While all this was happening, of course, the First Crusade (1097–1130) occupied the headlines, partially a result of the new militancy of the papacy begun by Gregory VII. For Italy, and especially for Venice, with plenty of boats to help ship Crusaders, the affair meant nothing but pure profit. Trade was booming everywhere, and the accumulation of money helped the Italians to create modern Europe's first banking system. It also financed the continued independence of the *comuni*, with a big enough surplus for building projects like the great cathedrals of Modena, Parma, and Ferrara, Verona's S. Zeno, and Padua's Palazzo della Ragione.

By the 12th century, far in advance of most of Europe, Italy had attained a prosperity unknown since Roman times. The classical past had never been forgotten. Free *comuni* in the north called their elected leaders 'consuls' or 'senators', and artists and architects turned ancient Roman styles into the Romanesque. Roman jurisprudence was revived by the Glossators of the **University of Bologna**, and their disciples travelled to the four corners of Europe; one of them founded the school of law at Oxford (1144).

Emperors and popes were still embroiled in the north. **Frederick I Barbarossa** of the Hohenstaufen, or Swabian dynasty, was strong enough back home in Germany, and he made it the cornerstone of his policy to reassert imperial power in Italy. Beginning in 1154, he crossed the Alps five times, molesting free cities that asked nothing more than the right to fight one another continually. He spread dismay among them, until a united front of cities called the Lombard League, stretching from Ravenna to Asti, joined Pope Alexander III (whom Frederick had exiled from Rome in favour of his antipope) to defeat him in 1176, forcing Frederick to recognize their freedoms and kiss and make up with Alexander in Venice. Frederick's greatest triumph in Italy came by arranging a marriage that left his grandson **Frederick II** not only emperor but King of Sicily, thus giving him a strong power base in Italy itself.

The second Frederick's career dominated Italian politics for thirty years (1220–50). With his brilliant court, in which Italian was used for the first time (alongside Arabic and Latin), his half-Muslim army, his processions of dancing girls, eunuchs, and elephants, he provided Europe with a spectacle the like of which it had never seen. The popes excommunicated him at least twice, while all Italy divided into factions: the **Guelphs**, under the leadership of the popes, supported religious orthodoxy, the liberty of the *comuni*, and the interests of their emerging merchant class. The **Ghibellines** stood for the emperor, state economic control, the interests of the rural nobles, and religious and intellectual tolerance.

When the Guelph *comuni* of Padua and Treviso rebelled, and fierce family feuds tore Verona apart (the germ of the Romeo and Juliet story), Frederick sent his lieutenant **Ezzelino da Romano** to restore order. Ezzelino soon made himself a tyrant and earned a reputation for such inhuman brutality that even today his very name is synonymous with horror. Frederick's other campaigns and diplomacy in the north met with very limited success; Parma revolted against him in 1248, and in 1249 Bologna crushed his forces at Fossalta, capturing his son Enzo.

Frederick died in 1250; but Ezzelino, pretending to fight for the Imperial side, continued to terrorize the Veneto, Friuli, and the Marches for his own purposes, becoming one of Italy's first, and certainly its most devilish *signori*. The popes preached a crusade against him and he was hunted down and killed in 1259.

To fight Frederick's son **Manfred**, Pope Urban IV set an ultimately disastrous precedent by inviting in **Charles of Anjou**, brother of the King of France. As protector of the Guelphs, Charles defeated Manfred (1266) and murdered the last of the Hohenstaufens, Conradin (1268). He held unchallenged sway over Italy until 1282, when the revolt of the Sicilian Vespers started the wars up again. By now, however, the terms Guelph and Ghibelline had ceased to have much meaning; men and cities changed sides as they found expedient, and the old parties began to seem like the black and white squares on a chessboard. If your neighbour and enemy were Guelph, you became for the moment Ghibelline, and if he changed so would you.

Some real changes did come out of all this sound and fury. In 1208 Venice hit its all-time biggest jackpot when it diverted the Fourth Crusade to the sack of Constantinople, winning for itself a small empire of islands in the Adriatic and Levant. Other cities were falling under the rule of military *signori*, whose descendants would be styling themselves counts and dukes—the da Polenta of Ravenna, the Este of Ferrara, the da Carrara of Padua, the della Scala of Verona, the Malatesta of Rimini. Everywhere the freedom of the *comuni* was in jeopardy; after so much useless strife the temptation to submit to a strong leader often proved overwhelming. During Charles of Anjou's reign the popes extracted the price for their invitation. The **Papal State**, including much of central Italy (the Marches and Romagna) was established in 1278. Still, trade and money flowed as never before; cities built new cathedrals and incredible skyscraper skylines, with the tall tower-fortresses of the now urbanized nobles. Above all, it was a great age for culture. The time of Guelphs and Ghibellines was also the time of Dante (b. 1265) and Giotto (b. 1266).

1300–1550: Renaissance Italy

This paradoxical Italy continued into the 14th century, with a golden age of culture and an opulent economy alongside continuous war and turmoil. With no serious threats from any other foreign power, the myriad Italian states were able to menace each other joyfully without interference. By now most wars had become a sort of game, conducted on behalf of cities by bands of paid mercenaries, led by a hired captain called a *condottiere*, who were never allowed to enter the cities themelves. The arrangement suited everyone well. The soldiers had lovely horses and armour, and no real desire to do each other serious harm. The cities were usually free from grand ambitions; everyone was making too much money to want to wreck the system. Best of all, the worst schemers and troublemakers on the Italian stage were fortuitously removed from the scene. With the election of the French Pope Clement V in 1303, the papacy moved to Avignon, a puppet of the French king and temporarily without influence in Italian affairs.

By far the biggest event of the 14th century was the **Black Death** of 1347–48, in which it is estimated that Italy lost one-third of its population. The shock brought a rude halt to what had been four hundred years of almost continuous growth, though its effects did not prove a permanent setback for the economy. In fact, the plague's grim joke was that it actually made life better for most who survived; working people in the cities, no longer overcrowded, found their rents lower and their labour worth more, while in the country farmers were able to increase their profits by tilling only the best land.

By now the peninsula was split up by long-established, cohesive states pursuing different ends and often warring against each other. Italian statesmen well understood the idea of a balance of power long before political theorists invented the term, and, despite all the noise, most of them probably believed Italy was enjoying the best of all possible worlds. Foremost among the major states was **Venice**, the oldest and most glorious, with its oligarchic but singularly effective constitution, and its exotic career of trade and contacts with the East. The Venetians waged a series of wars against arch-rival Genoa, finally exhausting her after the War of Chioggia in 1379. Once serenely aloof from Italian politics, Venice then added to her sea realms a small land empire, by 1428 including Udine, Treviso, Verona, Padua, Vicenza, Brescia and Bergamo. One city she subdued but never captured was Adriatic rival Trieste, which in 1382 had come under the protection of the Austrian emperors. In the north the independent Bishop-Princes of Trent served to create a kind of demilitarized zone between Venice and the Counts of Tyrol. Refined independent courts in Ferrara, Modena, and Rimini managed to survive the rough seas of Italian politics; while Emilia-Romagna, as part of the the Papal States, fell into anarchy while the popes were in France (until 1378) and were woefully misgoverned when they came back.

Meanwhile, the Renaissance—the new art and scholarship that began in Florence in the 1400s from a solid foundation of medieval accomplishment—found a happy home in northeast Italy. Masters like Giotto, Donatello, Piero della Francesca, and Antonello da Messina came, leaving works that became seeds of the imagination for the region's artists. **Ferrara**, under the Este dukes, became a major cultural centre; **Ásolo**, under the exiled Queen of Cyprus, became a courtly ideal of Renaissance art and literature. While the university of Bologna continued to dominate in law schools, the University of Padua led in medicine.

1494–1529: The Wars of Italy

The Italians brought the trouble down on themselves, when Duke Lodovico of Milan invited the French King Charles VIII to cross the Alps and assert his claim to the throne of Milan's enemy, Naples. Charles did just that, and the failure of the combined Italian states to stop him (at the inconclusive Battle of Fornovo, 1495) showed just how helpless Italy was at the hands of emerging new nation-states like France or Spain. When the Spaniards saw how easy it was, they, too, marched in, and before long the German emperor and even the Swiss entered this new market for Italian real estate. The popes did as much as anyone to keep the pot boiling. Alexander VI and his son Cesare Borgia carried the war across central Italy in an attempt to found a new state for the Borgia family, and Julius II's madcap policy saw him unite the emperor and Italian states in the **League of Cambrai**, which soundly defeated Venice in 1508, sapping her strength just when Italy most needed her to fight the Turks. Julius egged on the Swiss, French and Spaniards in turn, before finally crying 'Out with the barbarians!' when it was already too late.

By 1516, with the French ruling Milan and the Spanish in control of the south, it seemed as if a settlement would be possible. The worst possible luck for Italy, however, came with the accession in Spain of the insatiable megalomaniac **Charles V** who bought himself the crown of the Holy Roman Empire in 1519, making him the most powerful ruler in Europe since Charlemagne. As soon as he had emptied Spain's treasury, driven her to revolt, and plunged Germany into civil war, he turned his attentions to Italy. The wars began anew, bloodier than anything Italy had seen for centuries, and in the end all Italy, save only Venice and the Veneto, was at the mercy of the Spaniards.

1529–1600: Italy in Chains

Two years after the dramatic 1527 Sack of Rome by Imperial troops and German mercenaries, Charles met Pope Clement VII in Bologna for his fateful coronation as Holy Roman Emperor (he was to be the last ever crowned by a pope) and to draw the map of Italy. Venice kept its territories, the pope made Ferrara a fief (and absorbed it into the Papal States in 1597) while the Este family got the Duchy of Modena and Reggio. The next pope, Paul III (Alexander Farnese) invented the **Duchy of Parma** for his son, and let loose the Inquisition.

Farnese's papacy marked the beginning of the bitter struggles of the **Counter-Reformation**. In Italy, the Spaniards found a perfect ally in the papacy. One had the difficult job of breaking the spirit of a nation that, though conquered, was still wealthy, culturally sophisticated and ready to resist; the other saw an opportunity to recapture by force the hearts and minds it had lost long before. Under the banner of combating Protestantism, they commenced a reign of terror. The job of re-educating Italy was put in the hands of the new Jesuit order; their schools and propaganda campaigns bore the pope's message deeply into the Italian mind, while their sumptuous new churches, spectacles and dramatic sermons helped re-define Catholicism.

Yet while all this was happening Renaissance artists attained a brilliance and virtuosity never seen before, just in time to embellish the scores of new churches, palaces, and villas of the mid-16th-century building boom. The **Council of Trent** (1545–63) provided long-needed reforms in the Church. The combined forces of Venice and Spain had turned back the Turkish threat at the **Battle of Lepanto** (1571), providing a tremendous boost in morale throughout Christendom.

1600–1796: The Age of Baroque

Palladio's country villas for the magnates of the Veneto are landmarks in architecture but also an early symptom of decay. The old mercantile economy was failing, and the wealthy began to invest their money unproductively in land instead of risking it in business. Despite Lepanto, Venice's position in the east continued to be eroded, damaged by the Portuguese discovery of the spice route to the Indies, by endless warfare with the Turks and Austrian-backed pirates, the Uskoks, in the north Adriatic. Yet when the chips were down, Venice had the spirit to stand up to Pope Paul V and his Spanish allies during the **Great Interdict** (1606), striking an irreversible blow to papal temporal authority while all Europe watched. It was her last starring role in European affairs, but the Venetians kept their heads and made their decadence remarkably serene and a great deal of fun.

Decline was not limited to Venice. After 1600 nearly everything started to go wrong for the Italians. The textiles and banking of the north, long the engines of the economy, both withered in the face of foreign competition; the popes soaked the Papal States for money to redecorate Rome. Bullied, humiliated and impoverished, 17th-century Italy tried hard to keep up its prominence in the arts and sciences. Galileo looked through telescopes, Monteverdi wrote the first operas, and hundreds of talented though uninspired artists cranked out pretty pictures to meet the continuing high demand. Baroque art—the florid, expensive, coloratura style that serves as a perfect symbol for the age itself, impressed everyone with the majesty of Church and State. Baroque impresarios managed the wonderful pageantry of Church holidays, state occasions and carnivals that kept the crowds amused; manners and clothing went decorously berserk.

By the 18th century, there were very few painters or scholars or scientists. There were no more heroic revolts either. Italy in this period hardly has any history at all; with Spain's increasing decadence, the great powers decided the futures of Italy's major states, and used the minor ones as a kind of overflow tank to hold surplus princes. This was the age of blundering spies and scamps like Casanova, of the glittering brilliance of Vivaldi, of Grand Tourists and Canaletto, and Bologna's great theatre designers and *trompe l'oeil* interior decorators.

1796–1830

Napoleon, (that greatest of Italian generals!) arrived in 1796 on behalf of the French revolutionary Directorate, sweeping away Austrians, Spaniards, and the Pope, replacing them with the 'Cisalpine Republic' and 'Kingdom of Illyria' in the north. Italy woke up with a start from its Baroque slumbers, and local patriots gaily joined the French cause. In 1799, however, while Napoleon was off in Egypt, the advance through Italy by an Austro-Russian army, aided by Nelson's fleet, restored the status quo.

In 1800 Napoleon returned in a campaign that saw the great victory at Marengo, which gave him the opportunity once more to reorganize Italian affairs as the nation's self-crowned king. Napoleonic rule lasted only until 1814, but in that time important public works were begun and laws, education and everything else reformed after the French model; immense Church properties were expropriated, and medieval relics everywhere put to rest—including the Venetian Republic, which Napoleon for some reason took a special delight in liquidating. The French, however, soon outstayed their welcome. Besides hauling much of Italy's artistic heritage off to the Louvre, implementing high war taxes and conscription (some 25,000 Italians died on the Russian front), and brutally repressing a number of local revolts, they systematically exploited Italy for the benefit of the Napoleonic elite and the crowds of speculators who came flocking over the Alps. When the Austrians and English came to chase all the little Napoleons out, no one was sad to see them go.

But the experience had given Italians a taste of the opportunities offered by the modern world, as well as a sense of national feeling that had been suppressed for centuries. The 1815 Congress of Vienna put the clock back to 1796; indeed the Habsburgs and Bourbons thought they could pretend the Napoleonic upheavals had never happened, and the political reaction in their territories was fierce. The only major change from the *ancien régime* was that Venice and its inland empire now belonged to Austria.

1848–1915: The Risorgimento and United Italy

Simmering discontent kindled into action across Italy in the revolutionary year of 1848. On 22 March, the fire spread to Venice. The Austrian authorities simply fled, and the Venetian Republic was back in business. Within a few days, a democratic assembly was elected; leadership passed to **Daniele Manin**, a lawyer who had distinguished himself in liberal struggles in Venice for a decade. A day after the events in Venice, King Carlo Alberto of Piedmont-Savoy declared war on Austria.

At first, the odds seemed to favour Piedmont, the strongest state and leading force in Italian unification. Austria's army was disorganized and outnumbered, and for the time being it could expect little help from Vienna. The Piedmontese won early victories, but under the timid leadership of the King they failed to follow them up. The Austrians fell back to the firm base of Austria's defences in Italy, the circuit of fortresses called the **Quadrilateral** (Peschiera, Verona, Mantua and Legnano, in the western Veneto). Here he won a resounding victory, at Custozza, on 25 July, that knocked Piedmont ingloriously out of the war.

Shutting out the disappointments of 1848, Venice put up a brave and determined resistance. Though blockaded by the Austrian fleet, the Venetians nevertheless had a large quantity of arms and men to complement the natural protection of their lagoon in withstanding a siege. The Austrians bombarded the city continuously from May of 1849. An outbreak of cholera, as much as a total absence of outside support, decided the issue. The city surrendered on 22 August.

Despite failure on a grand scale, at least the Italians knew they would get another chance. Unification was inevitable, but there were two irreconcilable contenders for the honour of accomplishing it. On one side, the democrats and radicals dreamed of a truly reborn, revolutionary Italy, and looked to the popular hero Garibaldi to deliver it; on the other, moderates wanted the Piedmontese to do the job, ensuring a stable future by making **Vittorio Emanuele II** King of Italy. Vittorio Emanuele's minister, the polished, clever **Count Camillo Cavour**, spent the 1850s getting Piedmont into shape for the struggle, building its economy and army, participating in the Crimean War to earn diplomatic support, and plotting with the French for an alliance against Austria.

War came in 1859, just as a rebellion chased the pope's troops out of Bologna. The French and Piedmontese defeated Austria in two inconclusive, extremely bloody battles, at **Magenta** and **Solferino**. Piedmont annexed Lombardy and the Marches, and the armistice of 1850 was arranged so that France picked up Nice and Savoy, while Tuscany, Emilia-Romagna, and the duchies of Parma and Modena went to Piedmont. These gains were increased in the next two years, when Garibaldi and his Thousand picked up Sicily and the south.

With Austria still in control of Venetia, most Italians felt that the first duty of the nation was to complete the work of unification. The logical place to look for an ally against Austria was with Bismarck and Prussia, then preparing for the climax of their own nation's struggle for unification. In April 1866, Italy and Prussia signed a treaty, proposing Venetia as reward for Italian aid in the coming war with Austria. That war was not long in coming. Hostilities began in June, and before the year was out the Italians had been decisively defeated on land, at Custozza (again) and on sea, at Lissa. Fortunately for them, von Moltke's Prussian army was causing even greater embarrassments to the Austrians up north. Venice and its hinterlands joined Italy—a gift from Prussia.

Despite popular feeling, and its conquest by Garibaldi, Trentino remained a part of Austria, as did Friuli-Venezia Giulia. In these regions secret revolutionary committees for unity with Italy soon gave politics a new word: **Irredentism**, from *irredenta* or 'unredeemed'. Unfortunately the price of their 'redemption' as part of Italy was to cost the country dear—its entrance into World War I.

After 1900, with the rise of a strong socialist movement, strikes, riots, and police repression often occupied centre stage in Italian politics. But at the same time new industries, at least in the north, made the country a fully integral part of the European economy. The fifteen years before the war, prosperous and contented ones for many Italians, came to be known by the slightly derogatory term *Italietta*, the 'little Italy' of modest bourgeois happiness, an age of sweet Puccini operas, the first motorcars, blooming 'Liberty'-style architecture, and Sunday afternoons on the beach.

1915–1945: War, Fascism, and War

Besides the hope of gaining Trentino, Trieste, and beyond it, Istria, Italy's entrance into World War I was influenced by a certain segment of the intelligentsia who found *Italietta* boring and disgraceful: followers of the artistic Futurists and the perverse, idolized poet **Gabriele D'Annunzio**. These helped Italy leap blindly into the war in 1915. The northeast saw the bulk of the fighting—especially along the Piave and Isonzo rivers, and at Monte Grappa. Italian armies fought with their accustomed flair, masterminding an utter catastrophe at **Caporetto** (October 1917) that any other nation but Austria would have parlayed into a total victory. No thanks to their incompetent generals, the poorly armed and equipped Italians somehow held firm for another year, until the total exhaustion of Austria allowed them to prevail (the *Vittorio Veneto* you see so many streets named after), capturing some 600,000 prisoners in November 1918.

In return for 650,000 dead, a million casualties, severe privation on the home front, and a war debt higher than anyone could count, Italy received Trieste, Gorizia, and the South Tyrol up to the natural frontier of the Brenner Pass, where many German-speakers who suddenly found themselves Italian began a new Irredentist movement, yearning to reunite with Austria. It lingers fitfully today.

Italians, who had expected much more, felt they had been cheated, and nationalist sentiment increased, especially when D'Annunzio led a band of freebooters to seize the half-Italian city of Fiume in September 1919, after the peace conferences had promised it to Yugoslavia. The Italian economy was a shambles, and, at least in the north, revolution was in the air. The troubles had encouraged extremists of both right and left, and many Italians became convinced that the liberal state was finished.

Enter **Benito Mussolini**, a professional intriguer with bad manners and no fixed principles. Before the War he had found his real talent as editor of the Socialist Party paper *Avanti!*—the best it ever had, tripling the circulation in a year. When he decided that what Italy really needed was war, he left to found a new paper, and contributed mightily to the jingoist agitation of 1915. In the post-War confusion, he found his opportunity. A little bit at a time, he developed the idea of **fascism**, at first less a philosophy than an astute use of mass propaganda and a sense of design. With a little discreet money supplied by frightened industrialists, Mussolini had no trouble finding recruits for his black-shirted gangs, who had their first successes bashing Slavs in Trieste and working as a sort of private police for landowners in stoutly socialist Emilia-Romagna.

The basic principle, combining left- and right-wing extremism into something the ruling classes could live with, proved attractive to many Italians, and a series of weak governments chose to stand by while the fascist *squadre* cast their shadow over more and more of Italy. Mussolini's accession to power was the result of an improbable gamble. In the particularly anarchic month of October 1922, he announced that his followers would march on Rome. King Vittorio Emanuele III refused to sign a decree of martial law to disperse them, and there was nothing to do but offer Mussolini the post of prime minister. At first, he governed Italy with undeniable competence. Order was restored, and the economy and foreign policy handled intelligently by non-fascist professionals. Mussolini increased his popularity by singling out especially obnoxious unions and corrupt leftist local governments for punishment. In the 1924 elections, despite the flagrant rigging and intimidation, the Fascists won only a slight majority.

Mussolini evolved a new economic philosophy, the 'corporate state', where labour and capital were supposed to live in harmony under syndicalist government control. But the longer fascism lasted, the more unreal it seemed, a patchwork government of Mussolini and his ageing cronies, magnified and rendered heroic by cinematic technique—stirring rhetoric before oceanic crowds, colourful pageantry, magnificent, larger-than-life post offices and railway stations built of travertine and marble, dashing aviators and winsome gymnasts from the fascist youth groups on parade. In a way it was the Baroque all over again, and Italians tried not to think about the consequences. In the words of one of Mussolini's favourite slogans, painted on walls all over Italy, 'Whoever stops is lost.'

Mussolini couldn't stop, and the only possibility for new diversions lay with the chance of conquest and empire. His invasion of Ethiopia and his meddling in the Spanish Civil War, both in 1936, compromised Italy into a close alliance with Nazi Germany. Mussolini's confidence and rhetoric never faltered as he led an entirely unprepared nation into the biggest war ever. The Allies invaded; the Germans poured in divisions to defend the peninsula. In 1943 they set Mussolini up in a puppet state called the Italian Social Republic at Salò, by Lake Garda. In September, the Badoglio government finally signed an armistice with the Allies, too late to keep the War from dragging on another year and a half, as the Germans made good use of Italy's difficult terrain to slow the Allied advance. Meanwhile Italy finally gave itself something to be proud of, a determined, resourceful Resistance that established free zones in many areas, and harassed the Germans with sabotage and strikes. The *partigiani* caught Mussolini in April 1945, while he was trying to escape to Switzerland; after shooting him and his mistress, they hung him by the toes from the roof of a petrol station in Milan.

1945–the Present

Post-War Italy *cinema-verità*—Rossellini's *Rome, Open City*, or de Sica's *Bicycle Thieves*—captures the atmosphere better than words ever could. In a period of serious hardships that older Italians still remember, the nation slowly picked itself up and returned things to normal. The eastern border with Yugoslavia was the most lingering problem in the north—Trieste, as the major bone of contention, was made a neutral zone from 1947 to 1954, when it was finally given to Italy in exchange for what bits of Istria it still controlled.

A referendum in June 1946 made Italy a republic, but only by a narrow margin. The first governments fell to the new Christian Democrat Party under Alcide di Gasperi; it has run the show ever since in coalitions with a preposterous band of smaller parties. The main opposition has been provided by the Communists, surely one of the most remarkable parties of modern European history. With the heritage of the only important socialist philosopher since Marx, Antonio Gramsci, and the democratic and broad-minded leaders Palmiere Togliatti and Enrico Berlinguer, Italian communism has become something unique in the world, with its stronghold and showcase in the well-run, prosperous cities of the Emilia-Romagna.

Italians, like everyone else, complain endlessly about their creaky, bureaucratic, monolithic governmental system, but at least it seems to be one perfectly adapted to the Italian psyche. No one knows how it works, though Italians often pretend to, but the general principle seems to be that everyone, left and right, has a certain share of the decision-making. The constant parade of collapsing and reforming governments, always led by a Christian Democrat (with the recent exception of Socialist Bettino Craxi) does not mean much, except as an echo of the real decisions which are being made in the back rooms. So far, it has worked well enough. The economic miracle that began in the 1950s continues today, and it has propelled the Italians into 6th place among the world's national economies. 'God made the world and Italy made everything in it,' was the slogan of the 60s.

The Italian economy has shown an unexpected capability for innovation; many Italians already talk about it as a new model for development. The northeast is perhaps the national showcase: Vicenza is the centre of Italy's 'Silicon Valley', Trieste a centre of physics and scientific research. Small firms, usually family-run like Benetton in Treviso and Ferrari and Maserati in Modena, employ a devoted work-force making something that is unique or at least better than foreign competition. Already luxury goods (fashion, cars, and everything else related to the cleverly promoted mystique of Italian design) are a mainstay, just as they were during the Renaissance and Middle Ages.

Art and Architecture and Where to Find it

Etruscan (8th–2nd centuries BC)

'There is a haunting quality in the Etruscan representations,' wrote D. H. Lawrence in *Etruscan Places*, 'they get into the imagination, and will not go out.' Nevertheless Etruscans rarely get their due. Many of the most significant archaeological discoveries have been made only this century. Though accomplished builders, their most important works were in wood, with painted terracotta decoration; only fragments have survived. Etruscan temples owed much to forms invented by the Greeks. Brightly coloured, with steep rooflines and projecting beams and rafters, their temples seem an odd cross between a Greek temple and an oriental pagoda. Of the streets, palaces and public buildings, very little is known. Etruscan architects saved their more lasting work for other things; remains of their stone bridges and drainage canals, some cut through solid rock, can still be seen.

In art, the Etruscans managed the trick of being at once strikingly original and blatantly imitative. For centuries, every advance and stylistic innovation imported from Athens or Corinth soon had to suffer comparison with the clever copies of Etruria's artistic magpies—black and red painted ceramics, Archaic style sculpture, followed in the 5th century by naturalistic bronze statues, and burial urns with relief scenes from Greek mythology. Their most creative work was in jewellery, with fantastically intricate gold and silver work that could scarcely be duplicated today, and especially in portrait sculpture. Here they excelled even the Greeks in depth and expressiveness; the hundreds of bronze and terracotta figures in Italy's museums—the gods, noble families, statesmen, comic caricatures and laughing children—are part of the Etruscan legend, an art that could only have been produced by a people that truly enjoyed life, and understood it well (good Etruscan collections are in the Museo Civico Archeologico, **Bologna**; Palazzo Lodovico il Moro, **Ferrara**, and Museo Civico, **Rimini**, though all the best is in Rome and Tuscany).

Roman Art (3rd century BC–5th century AD)

Roman art is a derivative of Etruscan and Greek models, but it showed a special talent for mosaics, portraiture, wall paintings, and glasswork; architecturally, the Italians were brilliant engineers, grand exponents of the arch and inventors of concrete. **Verona** is one of the best places in Italy to admire their ability to build both large and well, in the theatre, Porta dei Borsari, and especially the Arena, a pinkish oval that rivals the Colosseum in size and grandeur. Verona was the birthplace of Vitruvius, the only classical writer on architecture whose works have come down to us; in Verona he built an arch that survives.

Aquileia, once the most prominent city and port in Friuli, was one of the few Roman cities that died completely in the Dark Ages; its remains make up the most evocative archaeological site in the northeast, with Roman and palaeo-Christian mosaics and a fine museum; **Velleia**, a little Roman town south of Piacenza, has been recently excavated; the so-called 'Villa of Catullus' (actually a bath complex) at **Sirmione** on Lake Garda is one of Italy's most poetic ruins in a wonderful romantic setting. Other Roman odds and ends remain in **Padua** (tombs and an arena); **Rimini** (an arch, bridge, and good museum); **Trieste** (theatre, gate, museum). Other good collections of antiquities are in **Parma**, **Este**, and **Venice** (Museo Archeologico, including many Greek originals),

Dark and Early Middle Ages (5th–10th centuries)

Artistically, at least, the decline of Rome was a bonus for northeast Italy, especially when Emperor Honorius transferred the capital of the Western Empire to **Ravenna**. Though Roman sculpture and painting were already degraded, mosaics thrived, a decorative art patronized by the rich. It was a strange time; a 5th-century chronicle declares: 'Those who are alive perish from thirst, while corpses float in the water . . . priests practise usury and Syrians sing psalms . . . eunuchs learn the art of war and barbarian mercenaries study literature.'

The unique mosaics of Ravenna begin with the last Romans, continue under the Ostrogothic King Theodoric, and reach their height with the Byzantines, who brought artists from Constantinople to embellish their impressive building programmes. Their stiff, 'hieratic' portraiture, really an inheritance from decadent Rome, was to remain prominent in pictorial art until the 13th century; it is an art of highly stylized, spiritual beings who live in a gold-ground paradise, with no need of shadows or perspective or other such worldly tricks. Outside Ravenna, you can see good Ravenna-style mosaics at **Aquileia** and **Grado**, and at Torcello in **Venice**, where the style lingered long enough to create St Mark's, modelled directly on a church in Constantinople. In architecture, forms that originated in the time of Constantine prevailed—basilican churches, a form derived directly from Roman law courts—and octagonal (sometimes hexagonal) baptistries.

In the 7th–10th centuries, while Byzantine-trained artists made their ethereal almond-eyed creatures, the native population produced a style that had little use for Roman or Byzantine forms, known as **Lombard** or barbarian art. Instead of mosaics, their most remarkable talent was in architecture and sculpture, especially the latter. The churches of **Cividale del Friuli**, the capital of an ancient Lombard duchy, contain some of most remarkable sculptures and reliefs from the 8th century; others are in the Castelvecchio museum in **Verona**, another favourite Lombard town. Meanwhile, at the 7th-century monastery of **Bobbio**, Irish monks introduced not only literacy but their magnificent style of illumination.

Romanesque and Veneto-Byzantine (11th–12th centuries)

At this point, when an expansive society made new art possible, money and talent were found to build new cathedrals and town halls in the new Lombard Romanesque style, originating in Milan's church of Sant'Ambrogio, characterized by beautiful brickwork, blind arcading, bas-reliefs, and lofty campaniles. Some of the best examples are in Emilia-Romagna: the cathedrals at **Modena**, by master Lanfranco (1099), one of Italy's few fortified churches and decorated with striking reliefs; **Piacenza**, by an unknown master; **Parma**, with its exquisite Baptistry by Benedetto Antelami; **Ferrara**, by Wiligelmo and Nicolò; and the Santo Stefano complex in **Bolognà** (also see the reliefs by Wiligelmo at **Nonántola**).

Along the Adriatic and in the Veneto, **Venice** took over the artistic lead from Ravenna; the Veneto-Byzantine style, as it's called, is still heavily Byzantine; this is the great age of the magnificent mosaics and Pala d'Oro in St Mark's basilica. But Lombard influences also entered even into the heart of the lagoon, in the mighty brick Campanile of St Mark's (completed in 1173) as well as in SS. Maria e Donato in **Murano** and S. Sofia in **Padua**. Another mighty campanile, nine storeys high, was added to the 9th-century abbey and basilica of **Pomposa**.

Verona, near the Lombard-Venetian frontier, saw some major cross-fertilization of styles, in the Palazzo della Ragione (12th-century), the lower half of S. Fermo, S. Lorenzo, and most magnificently in San Zeno (1120–1138), a masterpiece of architecture and reliefs (by the same Nicolò who worked in Ferrara); its unique bronze doors, a kind of 'poor man's Bible', predate the church by a century.

This period also saw the erection of urban skyscrapers by the nobility, family fortresses and towers built when the *comuni* forced the barons to move into the towns. Larger cities once had hundreds of them; municipal authorities gradually succeeded in having most of them demolished. In the northeast **Bologna** has two of the tallest and crookedest, though **Rovigo** comes a close second.

Late Medieval and Early Renaissance (13th–14th centuries)

In many ways this was the most exciting and vigorous phase in Italian art, an age of discovery when the power of the artist was almost like that of a magician. Great imaginative leaps occurred in architecture, painting, and sculpture, especially in Tuscany—nor was it long before Tuscany masters introduced the new style to the northeast. In **Padua**'s Cappella degli Scrovegni (1308) Giotto taught local artists about forms in space, composition, and a new, more natural way to paint figures; his followers, most notably Altichiero and Menabuoi, applied his teachings in the city's baptistry and Oratorio di S. Giorgio. Tuscan students of 13th-century master sculptor Nicolo Pisano were called in to create the magnificent Arca in S. Domenico (**Bologna**), introducing a new realistic, classically inspired style to local sculptors, especially the dalle Masegne brothers.

Italian architects never really appreciated the lofty vertical **Gothic** style; trapped in their Roman sensibilities and snobbishness, they looked on it as barbaric. Still, they weren't entirely immune to its charms; witness Bonino's chivalric Scaliger tombs in **Verona** or the French Gothic S. Francesco in **Bologna**. **Venice**, richer than ever after the Sack of Constantinople, adapted Gothic in its half-oriental, flamboyant way, building scores of magnificent palaces like the Fondaco dei Turchi and the Ca' d'Oro on the Grand Canal, culminating in the incomparable Palazzo Ducale. Elsewhere, the Basilica of St Anthony in **Padua** is the rarest flower sown by Venetian Gothic. In painting, the colourful, fairy-tale style called International Gothic lingered in the northeast into the mid-15th century, with Gentile da Fabriano and Pisanello its major exponents; in Venice painters like Jacobello del Fiore and Paolo Veneziano continued to paint in a highly decorative, almost Byzantine style, perpetuated long into the 15th century by the Vivarinis. One unexpected jewel of the period is the anonymous, gorgeous fresco cycle of the Twelve Months, in **Trento**'s Castello di Buonconsiglio.

The Renaissance of the Quattrocento

All of these tendencies eventually gave way in the 15th century before the advanced styles of two great Veneto masters: **Andrea Mantegna** and **Giovanni Bellini**. Mantegna, trained in Padua, influenced generations of artists and sculptors with his strong interest in antiquity and powerful sculptural figures, while the long career of his brother-in-law Giovanni Bellini of Venice marked the transition in Venice from the Early to the High Renaissance. Giovanni's artist father Jacopo instilled a love of nature and the senses in his son, who was later influenced by the luminous oil painting techniques of the Sicilian Antonello da Messina (who visited Venice in 1475). The atmospheric light and rich, autumnal colours that are the hallmarks of Venetian painting were first explored by Giovanni Bellini, and his exquisite Madonnas are one of the delights of the Italian Renaissance. Other masters of the Venetian quattrocento include Giovanni's brother Gentile and **Vittore Carpaccio**, the great masters of narrative painting, the more rustic Cima da Conegliano, and Carlo Crivelli, a lover of clear detail—and cucumbers—who spent his later career in the Marches.

The great Donatello's prolonged stay in Padua was the major influence on local sculptors; the perfect harmony and classical calm of his great equestrian statue of Gattamelata was a formative influence on Venice's Lombardo and Bon families, as well as on Antonio Rizzo of Verona. The Lombardos and Bons also designed a fair share of Venice's best Renaissance churches and palaces, along with Mauro Codussi, who instilled a certain amount of Tuscan order and classicism into the Venetian imagination.

But Venice and Padua hardly had exclusive rights to 15th-century Renaissance art in the northeast: the sophisticated courts of **Ferrara** and **Rimini** patronized the best artists and architects of the day; Ferrara produced its own school of art, led by Tura, Cossa, and Roberti. Both cities are embellished with sublime examples of Renaissance architecture—the palaces in Ferrara and the Tempio Malatesta in Rimini.

The 16th Century: High Renaissance and Mannerism

The 16th century is often called the Golden Age of Venetian Art. While the rest of Italy followed the artists in Rome in learning drawing and anatomy, the Venetians went their own way, obsessed with the dramatic qualities of atmosphere. **Giorgione** of Castelfranco, a pupil of Bellini, was the seminal figure in this new manner; his *Tempest* in the Accademia is a remarkable study in brooding tension. Giorgione is also credited with inventing 'easel painting'—art that served neither Church nor State nor the vanity of a patron, but stood on its own for the pleasure of the viewer.

Giorgione's pupil, Tiziano Vecellio, or **Titian**, was another major transitional figure in Venetian art; while his early works are often confused with his master's, his later career is marked by dramatic, often spiralling compositions and striking tonal effects produced by large brushstrokes, or even fingerpainting. His contemporary, **Tintoretto**, took these Mannerist tendencies to unforgettable extremes, while the less emotional **Paolo Veronese**, originally of Verona, painted lavish canvases that are the culmination of all that Venice had to teach in decoration and illusionism.

The greatest architect, and one of the greatest sculptors in 16th-century Venice was **Jacopo Sansovino**, who adapted his training in Tuscany and Rome to create a distinctive Venetian style, richly decorated with sculpture and classical motifs that were to become two of the trademarks of the most influential architect of the Veneto, **Palladio**. Palladio's greatest talent was in adapting classical models to modern needs; his famous villas, and those of his followers, not only fit his client's need to look the part of a country-squire Roman patrician, but were also functional as working farm centres, affordable (hardly any real marble anywhere), and fit comfortably into the ordered Veneto landscape.

This was also a golden art century for **Parma** and **Bologna**. The former was endowed with the startling talent of **Correggio**, famous for the two amazing domes he painted, for his subtle chiaroscuro, derived from Leonardo da Vinci, and his sensuous mythologies; his Mannerist follower, Parmigianino, was a sophisticated draughtsman, whose elegance in comparison is rather cold and intellectual. In Bologna, where artists were known for their realism, a whole school of painters, led by the Carracci, caught the fancy of the popes and for a period dominated art in Counter-Reformation Rome with their easily digestible piety and saccharine mythologies.

Baroque (17th and 18th centuries)

As an art designed to induce temporal obedience and psychical oblivion, Baroque's effects are difficult to describe. On the whole, however, history saw that little of the most excessive brand of Baroque (i.e. as you see it in Rome) made it to the northeast; the Venetians kicked the Jesuits out early on, and the Spaniards had little influence in the Republic. In short, the 17th century saw more of the same Palladian villas, Venetian palaces, atmospheric painting, and decorated churches, but squared into Baroque. The age does provide some exceptions to the rule that in art, less is more: Longhena's magnificent church of the Salute in Venice or the uncanny paintings of Francesco Maffei of Vicenza, or some of the earlier canvases of **Guercino**, who followed Caravaggio in his early days and added a bit of spirit to the Bologna school, which continued and enhanced its reputation thanks to the pleasing brush of the 'Divine' Guido Reni.

Venice bloomed like Camille on her death bed, with a revival of painterly talent to ease its political decline in the 18th century; its charming, elegant style became the international fashion of its day, and was in high demand both in Venice and abroad. **Giambattista Tiepolo** and his son Giandomenico were the masters of a huge school of theatrical, buoyant ceiling art and narrative frescoes, while **Antonio Canaletto** and **Francesco Guardi** produced countless views of Venice that were the rage among travellers on the Grand Tour; even today the majority of their works are in Britain and France. **Pietro Longhi**, their contemporary, devoted himself to genre scenes that offer a delightful insight into the Venice of 200 years ago; **Rosalba Carriera's** pastel portraits were the rage of Europe's nobility. Meanwhile Venetian architect **Giorgio Massari** translated their rococo sensibility into stone, specializing in churches that doubled as concert halls.

Neoclassicism, Romanticism, and other isms (19th and 20th centuries)

Whatever artistic spirit remained at the end of the 18th century evaporated with Napoleon and remained evaporated for a long time. Although Europe's greatest neoclassical sculptor, **Antonio Canova**, hailed from Possagno in the northern Veneto, he left very few of his pseudo-Greeks and Romans in the region. Some fine opera houses and theatres were built, in Venice, Parma and Bologna, and the Habsburgs built an entire new neoclassical quarter for Trieste. Parma's spa, Salsomaggiore, was embellished with a touch of Art Nouveau, or Liberty style, as the Italians call it—as were the new grand hotels on Venice's Lido, in Rimini, and around Lake Garda. Good collections of 19th-century art can be seen in Piacenza's Ricci-Oddi Gallery, in Ferrara's Palazzini dei Cavalieri di Malta, in Venice's Palazzo Pésaro, and Trieste's Museo Revoltella.

Italians began to regain some of their artistic panache in the 20th century. Milan was the centre of Futurism, an artistic movement that made dynamism, movement, and modernity its creed, while Ferrara saw the birth of the 'Metaphysical' school of painting when two Futurists, **Giorgio de Chirico** and **Carlo Carrà**, met there during their military service (1916–18) and became enraptured with the Renaissance art in the Palazzo Schifanoia. A hallucinatory nostalgia, of mannikins in empty landscapes, is the hallmark of the school; **Giorgio Morandi**, the still-life painter, was their greatest follower.

Architecture in this century reached its admittedly low summit in the fascist period—Mussolini decorated Forlì with big public buildings, and Gabriele D'Annunzio built his tomb in Gardone Riviera in the same spirit. Fascist architecture often makes us smile, but as the only Italian school in the last two hundred years to achieve a consistent sense of design, it presents a challenge to all modern Italian architects—one they have so far been unable to meet.

In 1946 Renato Guttuso and Emile Vedova founded an avant-garde group in Venice, the *Fronte Nuova*, but without very noticeable improvement in the local art scene, then or now. But Venice does get its share of major international art in exhibitions at the Peggy Guggenheim museum, and at the Biennale (though the latter has lost some of its tone of late). Misplaced atavism prevented the contruction of Frank Lloyd Wright's palace on the Grand Canal (though when the same authorities vetoed a hospital designed by Corbusier, even Corbusier agreed they were right).

Besides the Peggy Guggenheim museum, there is a small amount of contemporary art scattered throughout the region—in the Galleria d'Arte Moderna in Bologna, the Museo Ciasa at Cortina, a museum devoted to the works of Futurist Fortunato Depero in Rovereto, works by the Mirko brothers in their hometown of Udine, a museum of contemporary naif painters in Luzzara (near Reggio Emilia), and a collection of contemporary ceramics in Faenza.

Artists' Directory

This includes the principal architects, painters, and sculptors of northeast Italy. The list is far from exhaustive, bound to exasperate partisans of some artists and do scant justice to the rest, but we've tried to include only the best and most representative works you'll find in the region.

Agostino di Duccio (1418–81), a precocious and talented Florentine sculptor who often seems to presage Art Deco; his best work is in Tempio Malatesta at **Rimini** (also Duomo, **Modena**).

Alberti, Leon Battista (1404–1472), architect, theorist, and writer. His greatest contribution was recycling the classical orders and principles of Vitruvius into Renaissance architecture (Tempio Malatesta, **Rimini**, also two churches in **Mantua**).

Altichiero (active 1369–84), Turone's pupil, but one of Giotto's most successful followers (Oratorio di S. Giorgio and Basilica di S. Antonio, **Padua**; S. Anastasia, **Verona**).

Antelami, Benedetto (1150–c. 1225), major figure in Italian Romanesque, the first sculptor-architect to design a building as a unified work of art: **Parma** Baptistry (also a relief in Parma Cathedral).

Antonello da Messina (c. 1430–79), a Sicilian painter who visited **Venice**. Antonello became one of the first Italians to perfect the Van Eyckian oil painting techniques of Flanders; his compelling mastery of light, shadows, and the simplification of forms was a major influence on the works of Giovanni Bellini (see the great but damaged *Pietà* in the Museo Correr).

Basaiti, Marco (1470–c.1530), student and collaborator of Alvise Vivarini (Accademia, **Venice**).

Baschenis, Simone (?, middle 16th century) precise, expressive Lombard Renaissance painter; undeservedly obscure, only because he left his best work in tiny Alpine villages (Dance of Death at **Pinzolo**, in the Dolomites, also at **Tuenno** in the Val di Non.

Bassano, Jacopo (da Ponte; 1510–92), paterfamilias of a clan of artists working mainly from **Bassano del Grappa**. Jacopo began by painting in the monumental Central Italian style, but is better known for cranking out a whole succession of religious night scenes in rustic barnyards. Son **Francesco** (1549–92) was his most skilled assistant and follower; the more prolific **Leandro** less so (*Return of Jacob*, in the Palazzo Ducale; works in **Vicenza**'s Museo Civico and **Bassano**, by Jacopo).

Bastiani, Lazzaro (c. 1420–1512), probably Carpaccio's master, and the painter responsible for the charming 'Baby Carpaccios' in **Venice**'s S. Alvise.

Bella, Gabriel (1730–99), Venice's charming naif painter of city scenes, a valuable source of information about the 18th century despite their ineptitude (Palazzo Querini-Stampalia, **Venice**).

Bellini, Gentile (1429–1507), elder son of Jacopo, famous for his meticulous depictions of Venetian ceremonies and narrative histories (*Procession of the Relic of the True Cross*, Accademia) and his portrait of Sultan Mehmet II, now in the National Gallery in London, painted during a sojourn in Istanbul. Unfortunately, his great histories painted for the Ducal Palace were lost in the fire.

Bellini, Giovanni (1435–1516), the greatest early Renaissance painter of Northern Italy, an innovator who kept experimenting even into his eighties, and greatly influenced (and was influenced by) his pupils, Giorgione and Titian. No artist before him painted with such sensitivity to light, atmosphere, colour, and nature; none since have approached the almost magical tenderness that makes his paintings transcendent (masterpieces in the Accademia, San Zaccaria, and the Frari in **Venice**; S. Corona, **Vicenza**).

Bellini, Jacopo (1400–70), pupil of Gentile da Fabriano, father of Giovanni and Gentile, father-in-law of Mantegna, all of whom were influenced by Jacopo's beautiful drawings from nature (in the Louvre and British Museum); in Venice his best works are his Madonnas, more natural and lifelike than others of his generation (Accademia, **Venice**).

Bibiena (Galli family) of Bologna, a dynasty of architects, engravers, and painters, best known for their theatres and scenographic work in the 17th and 18th centuries—Ferdinand (1657–1743) and his four sons were the chief figures, whose drawings of imaginary opera sets and theatres are among the most delightful creations of the period (Teatro Comunale, **Bologna**).

Bon, Bartolomeo (d. 1464), prolific Venetian sculptor and architect, who worked with his brother **Giovanni** to produce some of **Venice**'s most decorative work (Porta della Carta and statues of the Ducal Palace, Ca' d'Oro).

Bonino (c.1335–75), flamboyant Gothic sculptor from Campione (by Lake Lugano), the cradle of northern builders and sculptors; in **Verona** he carved most of the Scaliger tombs.

Bordone, Paris (1500–1571), student and imitator of Titian (**Venice**, Accademia; Duomo, **Treviso**).

Campagnola, Giulio (1482–1515), a Paduan follower of Giorgione, especially inspired by his landscapes (Scuola del Carmine, **Padua**).

Canaletto, Antonio (1697–1768), master of meticulous Venetian *vedute*, or views, but stay in England to see his paintings—there is but one in the Accademia, and two in the Ca' Rezzonico (both in **Venice**).

Canova, Antonio (1757–1821), born in **Possagno**, where he built a temple, Canova was Europe's neoclassical celebrity sculptor—the favourite of Napoleon and Benjamin Franklin and everyone in between. Most of his work went elsewhere, but Possagno has a museum of casts.

Caroto, G. F. (1480–1555), not the greatest Veronese artist, the Big Carrot is best known for his painting of a child in the Castelvecchio; also works in S. Fermo, both in **Verona**.

Carpaccio, Vittore (c. 1465–1525), the most charming of Venetian artists, with fairy-tale paintings full of documentary details from his life and times (major cycles at Scuola di S. Giorgio Schiavone and the Accademia, **Venice**).

Carpi, Girolamo da (1501–56), painter from Ferrara greatly influenced by Giulio Romano and Parmigianino, though best known for his *Roman Sketchbook*, the largest collection of Renaissance drawings of antiquities (S. Salvatore, **Bologna**).

Carrà, Carlo (1881–1966), started out as a Futurist but changed gears in Ferrara with de Chirico (Peggy Guggenheim, **Venice**).

Carracci, Ludovico (1560–1609), founder of a school of Bolognese painting, with his cousins Agostino and Annibale, who went on to lead dazzling careers in Rome, introducing other Bolognese painters into the capital. Influenced by Correggio and Titian, the Carracci, especially Annibale, became the model for later Baroque and Academic artists (Pinacoteca Nazionale in **Bologna**; Galleria Estense, **Modena**).

Carriera, Rosalba (1675–1757), a Venetian portraitist and miniaturist, was perhaps the first woman to make a good living as an artist; her soft, pastel portraits were the rage of the powdered wig set not only in Venice, but in Paris and Vienna (**Venice**, Accademia and Ca' Rezzonico).

Castagno, Andrea del (1423–1457), a Tuscan master of striking form and composition, who visited **Venice** in 1445 and left the city food for thought in St Mark's and S. Zaccaria.

Chini, Galileo (1873–1956), master of Italian Art Nouveau, or Liberty Style; designed the Throne Room of the King of Siam and, in our area, the Palazzo dei Congressi, **Salsomaggiore**.

Chirico, Giorgio de (1888–1978), a Greek-Italian who was one of the founding fathers of the Metaphysical School in Ferrara (1916–1918), best known for his uncanny urban landscapes dotted with classical odds and ends and mannikins (Peggy Guggenheim, **Venice**).

Cima da Conegliano, Giovanni Battista (1459–1518), whose luminous autumnal colours and landscapes were inspired by Bellini—as Bellini was inspired by several of his compositions (Madonna del Orto and Accademia in **Venice**; Duomo, **Conegliano**).

Codussi, Mauro (c. 1420–1504), architect from Bergamo, who worked mainly in Venice; a genius at synthesizing traditional Venetian styles with the classical forms of the Renaissance (S. Michele, S. Zaccaria, staircase at the Scuola di S. Giovanni Evangelista, Palazzo Vendramin-Calergi, all in **Venice**).

Correggio, Antonio Allegri (1494–1534), of Parma, who took Leonardo's *sfumato* technique to new heights of subtlety; his amazing frescoes in the domes of the Cathedral

58

and S. Giovanni Evangelista in **Parma** were revolutionary in their day, anticipating the Baroque (also the Galleria Estense, **Modena**).

Cossa, Francesco del (c.1438–1477), one of the Big Three in Renaissance Ferrara; painter of the charming springtime frescoes of the months in the Palazzo Schifanoia, **Ferrara**; also Pinacoteca, **Bologna**.

Costa, Lorenzo (1460–1535) one of the gentler painters to come out of Ferrara; followed Isabella d'Este to Mantua (Palazzo dei Diamanti, **Ferrara**; Pinacoteca and S. Giovanni in Monte, **Bologna**).

Crivelli, Carlo (c.1435–1495), meticulous Venetian painter enamoured of luminous, almost 3-D perspective, crystalline forms, garlands, and cucumbers; he spent most of his time in the Marches (Accademia, **Venice**).

Depero, Fortunato (1892–1960), a Futurist who moved to a colourful poster-like style (Museo Depero, **Rovereto**).

De Pisis, Filippo (1896–1956), a neo-Impressionist from Ferrara who spent a long period in Venice (Peggy Guggenheim, **Venice**).

Donatello (1386–1466), of Florence, was the best Italian sculptor of the quattrocento, if not of all time, never equalled in technique, expressiveness, or imaginative content. He spent a long period in **Padua**, casting his Gattamelata statue and altar for the Basilica di S. Antonio; also a statue in the Frari, **Venice**.

Dossi, Dosso (Giovanni Luteri; c.1490–1542), chief artist at the Ferrara court, evocative painter with a more than a touch of Giorgione (Palazzo dei Diamanti, in **Ferrara**; Pinacoteca in **Rovigo**).

Falconetto, Giovanni Maria (1468–1534), a Veronese architect who built in a charming antiquarian style that inspired Palladio, in **Padua** and **Luvigliano**.

Francesco di Giorgio, Martini (1439–1502), Tuscan architect, sculptor and painter of grace and symmetry (Carmini, **Venice**).

Francia (Francesco Raibolini; 1450–1517), a painter of Bologna highly influenced by Raphael (S. Giacomo Maggiore and Pinacoteca, **Bologna**).

Garofalo (Benvenuto Tisi; c.1481–1559), a Ferrarese pupil of Dosso Dossi and Raphael, who worked for a long period in Rome (Palazzo di Lodovico il Moro, **Ferrara**; Galleria Nazionale, **Parma**).

Giambono, Michele (c. 1420–1462), painter and mosaicist, one of the princes of Venetian retro; while everyone else moved on to the Renaissance, Giambono was still cranking out rich paintings in International Gothic (Accademia, altarpieces in St Mark's, **Venice**).

Giorgione (Giorgio da Castelfranco, c. 1478–1510), got his nickname 'Great George' not only for his height, but for the huge influence he had on Venetian painting. Although he barely lived past thirty and only several paintings are undisputedly by his hand, his poetic evocation of atmosphere and haunting, psychological ambiguity was echoed not only by Titian and Sebastiano del Piombo, his followers, but by his master Giovanni Bellini (paintings in the Accademia in **Venice** and **Castelfranco**).

Giotto di Bondone (c.1267–1337), was one of the most influential painters in Italian art, the first to break away from stylized Byzantine forms in favour of a more 'natural' and narrative style. Although most closely associated with Florence and Assisi, he painted his masterpiece in **Padua**: the Cappella degli Scrovegni.

Giovanni da Udine (1487–1562), master of stuccoes and grotesques; architect, and pupil of Raphael, who built the Torre dell'Orologio and fountain in Piazza Matteotti in his native **Udine**, but left everything else in Rome.

Giovanni da Verona (1457–1525), a Dominican friar and greatest marquetry artist of the century (S. Maria in Organo, **Verona**).

El Greco (Domenicos Theotokopoulos, 1541–1614), the most Mannerist of Mannerists, born in Crete and celebrated in Toledo, but spent his most formative period in Venice, studying Tintoretto and Jacopo Bassano (polyptych in the Galleria Estense, **Modena**; also Galleria Parmeggiani, **Reggio Emilia**).

Guardi, Francesco (1712–1793), younger brother of **Antonio**, with whom he often worked, making attributions sometimes difficult. Guardi's favourite subject was Venice, but his views, unlike Canaletto's, are suffused with light and atmosphere; some canvases approach Impressionism (Ca' d'Oro, Accademia, Angelo Raffaele, all in **Venice**).

Guariento (14th century), a Paduan follower of Giotto, whose greatest work, a massive fresco of Paradise in **Venice**'s Ducal Palace was lost in a fire, though fragments hint at what was lost.

Guercino (Francesco Barbieri, 1591–1666), Baroque painter from Cento, who went to the Carracci school of art, then dropped out to join Caravaggio's chiaroscuro camp—a master of composition, and a dabbler in the esoteric (best works in Rome, but also Cathedral dome, **Piacenza**, and pinacoteca and chapel, **Cento**).

Jacobello del Fiore (c.1370–1439), Venetian master of Gothic International, fond of raised gold embossing (Accademia, **Venice**).

Jappelli, Giuseppe (1783–1852), Paduan neoclassical architect; designed the Caffè Pedrocchi and several other buildings around **Padua**.

La Corte, Juste (1627–1679), Flemish sculptor who spent many years in **Venice**, responsible for the theatrical plague altarpiece in the Salute.

Lanfranco (11th–early 12th century), master builder (*mirabilis artifex*) of the Duomo in **Modena**.

Liberale da Verona (c.1445–1529), genteel painter of frescoes (Duomo, Castelvecchio, S. Fermo, all in **Verona**).

Lombardo, Pietro (c.1435–1515), founder of Venice's greatest family of sculptors and architects, strongly influenced by the Tuscan Renaissance (SS. Giovanni e Paolo, S. Giobbe, S. Francesco della Vigna, and S. Maria dei Miracoli, **Venice**).

Lombardo, Tullio (c. 1455–1516), son of Pietro, with whom he often worked; Tullio was an exquisite marble sculptor, best known for his tombs (**Venice**'s SS. Giovanni e Paolo and classical reliefs (Basilica of S. Antonio, **Padua**, which also has a relief by his brother **Antonio Lombardo** (c. 1458–c.1516)). Antonio was a major figure in the Venetian High Renaissance, though most of his works are now in Leningrad's Hermitage.

Longhena, Baldassare (1598–1682), Venetian architect, a student of Scamozzi, whose best work was one of his first: the church of the Salute (also Ca' Pesaro, both in **Venice**).

Longhi, Pietro (1702–1785), there weren't photographers in 18th-century Venice, but there was Pietro Longhi to dutifully portray society's foibles (Ca' Rezzonico, Accademia, Querini-Stampalia, all in **Venice**).

Lorenzo Veneziano (active 1356–1379), disciple of Paolo Veneziano (no relation) and painter in a luxuriant, golden International Gothic style (Duomo, **Vicenza**; Accademia, **Venice**).

Lotto, Lorenzo (c. 1480–1556), a native Venetian and pupil of Giovanni Bellini, best known for intense portraits that seem to catch their sitters off guard, capturing his own restless energy on canvas; was run out of Venice by Titian and Aretino (Accademia, **Venice**; Santa Cristina at **Quinto**; and S. Nicolò, **Treviso**.

Maffei, Francesco (c.1600–60), of Vicenza, dissonant and unorthodox Baroque painter, whose nervous brush brought out the dark side of the age of curlicues (Museo Civico and Oratorio di S. Nicola, **Vicenza**; Castelvecchio, **Verona**).

Mansueti, Giovanni (c. 1465–1527), underrated student of Giovanni Bellini and a talented painter of narrative histories (Accademia, **Venice**; Museo Civico, **Vicenza**).

Mantegna, Andrea (c. 1420–1506), a remarkable painter and engraver born near Padua, whose interest in antiquity, sculptural forms as hard as coral, and unusual perspectives dominated art in the Veneto until the rise of his brother-in-law Giovanni Bellini (Eremitani church, **Padua**; S. Zeno, **Verona**; Accademia, **Venice**).

Masegne, 14th-century Venetian family of architects and sculptors (S. Marco, **Venice**; S. Francesco, **Bologna**).

Massari, Giorgio (1687–1766), Venetian architect who collaborated with G.B. Tiepolo and Vivaldi (La Pietà, Gesuati, both in **Venice**).

Menabuoi, Giusto de' (d. 1397), a Florentine painter who followed Giotto to **Padua**, where his masterpiece is the Baptistry interior (also a few frescoes in the Palazzo della Ragione).

Montagna, Bartolomeo (1450–1523), a painter inspired by Antonello da Messina and founder of the Vicentine school (Monte Bérico, Museo Civico, **Vicenza**).

Morandi, Giorgio (1890–1964), an heir of the Metaphysical school, naturally austere, whose still-life paintings invite a subtle meditation on form (Galleria d'Arte Moderna, **Bologna**).

Morto da Feltre (Lorenzo Luzzo, 1467–1512), the Dead Man got his name from his pale complexion, but painted with Giorgione's colours and a bit of his panache, too (Museo Civico, **Feltre**).

Nicolò (12th century), master sculptor, a follower of Wiligelmo, responsible for the magnificent façades of **Ferrara** cathedral and S. Zeno, **Verona**.

Nicolò dell'Arca (1440–1494), an itinerant sculptor from Bari, a specialist in terracotta who did his finest work in **Bologna**: Palazzo Comunale, S. Domenico, and most movingly, S. Maria della Vita.

Palladio (Andrea di Pietro della Gondola, 1508–80), the Veneto's most influential architect, not only for his buildings, but for his books and drawings that re-interpreted Roman architecture to fit the needs of the day (major buildings in **Vicenza, Venice**, **Masèr**, and the villa at **La Malcontenta**).

Palma Giovane (1544–1628), the most prolific painter of his day in Venice, was the great-nephew of Palma Vecchio and a follower of Tintoretto, specializing in large but usually vapid narrative paintings (every church in **Venice** seems to have at least one).

Palma Vecchio (Jacopo Negretti, c. 1480–1528), a student of Giovanni Bellini who successfully adopted the new sensuous style of Giorgione, and is best known for his beautiful paintings of women—both courtesans and saints (S. Maria Formosa, **Venice**; S. Stefano, **Vicenza**; Galleria Estense, **Modena**).

Paolo Veneziano (c.1290–1360), the leading Venetian painter of the day, a powerful Byzantine influence in Venetian art that would linger longer in the lagoon than elsewhere (**Venice**, Accademia; **Padua**, Museo Civico).

Parmigianino (Francesco Mazzola, 1503–40), of Parma, a most exquisite Mannerist; Correggio's sensuality re-interpreted with cool fascination (Galleria Nazionale, **Parma**, Pinacoteca Nazionale, **Bologna**).

Piazzetta, Giambattista (1683–1754), Venetian Baroque painter *extraordinaire*, who went to dramatic extremes in his use of light and dark (Accademia and SS. Giovanni e Paolo, **Venice**).

Pisanello, Antonio Pisano (c. 1415–c.1455), originator of the Renaissance medal and one of the leading painters of the Gothic International school in Italy (Castelvecchio and S. Anastasia, **Verona**; medals in Ca' d'Oro, **Venice**).

Pordenone (Giovanni de' Sacchis, 1484–1539), Titian's main rival in Venice, with a more monumental, Roman style combined with quick brushstrokes (Madonna di Campagna, **Piacenza**; S. Giovanni Elemosinario, **Venice**).

Quercia, Iacopo della (1374–1438), the greatest Sienese sculptor, Gothic in his resistance to scientific perspective but charmed by antique models (S. Petronio, **Bologna**; Cathedral Museum, **Ferrara**).

Raphael (Raffaello Sanzio, 1483–1520), the son of a mediocre painter of Urbino who went on to become the darling of the High Renaissance; grace and elegance often overshadow the content (Pinacoteca, **Bologna**).

Reni, Guido (1575–1642), once known as 'the Divine Guido', this Bolognese painter and follower of the Carracci has taken a rather sharp drop in popularity of late; but when he cuts the sentimentality and facile piety he's not too bad (Galleria Estense, **Modena**; Pinacoteca, **Bologna**).

Ricci, Sebastiano (1659–1734), widely-travelled Venetian painter inspired by the scenographic monumentality of Roman Baroque (Museo Civico, **Vicenza**, S. Pietro, **Belluno**).

Riccio (Andrea Briosco, c. 1470–1532), High Renaissance sculptor and architect, famous for his intricate bronze work and statuettes (**Padua**, S. Antonio and S. Giustina).

Rizzo, Antonio (c.1445–1498), pure Renaissance sculptor and architect from Verona, who worked in **Venice** (Tron monument, Frari, courtyard of the Palazzo Ducale) and **Verona** (Torriani tombs in S. Fermo).

Roberti, Ercole de' (c.1450–1496), court painter in Ferrara, with the mystic quality of Giovanni Bellini; unfortunately most of his works have been lost (but Palazzo di Schifanoia, **Ferrara**, Pinacoteca Nazionale, **Bologna**).

Sammicheli, Michele (1484–1559), refined Venetian Renaissance architect, though best known for his fortifications (**Padua**; also palaces in **Treviso**; S. Bernardino, and Palazzo Bevilacqua, **Verona**; Palazzo Grimani, **Venice**).

Sansovino, Jacopo (Jacopo Tatti, 1486–1570), sculptor and architect who took his name from his Tuscan master, sculptor Andrea Sansovino. Jacopo fled the Sack of Rome in 1527 and came to Venice, where he became the chief architect to the Procurators of St Mark's and a good friend of Titian and Aretino, who promoted his career. Sansovino used his Tuscan and Roman periods to create a new decorative Venetian High Renaissance style—the rhythmic use of columns, arches, loggias, and reliefs, with sculpture playing an integral role in the building (major works in **Venice**, where he rebuilt St Mark's Square, sculptures in the Ducal Palace; reliefs in S. Antonio, **Padua**, also Museo Civico, **Vicenza**).

Scamozzi, Vincenzo (1552–1616), architect from Vicenza who became Palladio's closest follower, taking his ideas to classicizing extremes (perspective stage of the Teatro Olimpico, **Vicenza**; Procuratie Nuove, **Venice**; charming Rocca Pisani, at **Lonigo**; Via Sacra, **Monsélice**).

Sebastiano del Piombo (1485–1547), a pupil of Giorgione, and a rich autumnal colourist. Sebastiano went to Rome when Giorgione died, and became the chief notary of the Vatican (hence his nickname, for the leaden seals that still haunt the Posta Italiana); also painter after Raphael until he made enough money to stop painting altogether (S. Giovanni Crisostomo, **Venice**; Galleria Nazionale, **Parma**).

Squarcione, Francesco (c.1394–1474), a Paduan tailor who became a self-taught painter, one of the first antique dealers, and teacher of Mantegna; not much of his work survives.

Tiepolo, Giambattista (1691–1770), Venice's greatest Baroque interior decorator; a pupil of Piazzetta, though he had little use for chiaroscuro. Tiepolo's subjects, many mythological, live in the delightful warm afterglow of Venice's decline (Palazzo Labia, Scuola dei Carmini, and Gesuati, **Venice**; Villa Valmarana, **Vicenza**; Oratorio della Purità, **Udine**; Villa Pisani, **Stra**).

Tiepolo, Giandomenico (1727–1804), son of Giambattista, with whom he frescoed Villa Valmarana. Little interested in his father's grand, heroic manner, Giandomenico's work is more introspective and often wistful, especially his masquerades (Ca' Rezzonico, S. Polo, **Venice**; parish church, **Desenzano del Garda**).

Tintoretto (Jacopo Robusti, 1518–94), was given his name 'little dyer' because of his father's profession. A proud, ill-tempered workaholic, his ideal was to combine Michelangelo's drawing with the colouring of Titian, but his most amazing talent was in his visionary, unrestrained and totally original composition (Scuola di S. Rocco series; the world's largest painting, in the Palazzo Ducale; Accademia and S. Giorgio Maggiore, all in **Venice**).

Titian (Tiziano Vecellio, c.1480s–1576), came from Pieve di Cadore in the Dolomites to become 16th-century Venice's most popular painter, the favourite of princes, popes, and Emperor Charles V. At first a pupil of Giovanni Bellini, he left his workshop to paint like Giorgione, so much so that today many of his early works have often been attributed to Giorgione. Titian made his reputation with the monumental altarpiece in **Venice**'s Frari, a bold handling of form and colour which would prove the major influence on Tintoretto and Veronese and countless others. Although Titian spent most of his life in Venice, his international reputation saw most of his canvases scattered around the courts of Europe: besides the Frari altarpieces, Venice keeps a few of his works in S. Salvatore, the Accademia, the Salute; also the cathedrals of **Treviso** and **Verona**.

Tomaso da Modena (1325–1376), delightful 14th-century painter, a follower of Giotto who worked for a long period in **Treviso** (church and seminary of S. Nicolò, also S. Caterina).

Tura, Cosmè (c. 1430–1490), of the Ferrara school, whose singularly intense craggy, and weirdly tortured style is immediately recognizable and for many, an acquired taste (Palazzo Schifanoia and Museo del Duomo, **Ferrara**; Museo Correr, **Venice**).

Turone (active in the 1360s), Veronese master influenced by German miniaturists, teacher of Altichiero (Castelvecchio and S. Anastasia, **Verona**).

Veronese (Paolo Caliari, 1528–88), the most sumptuous and ravishingly decorative painter of the High Renaissance, fond of striking illusionism, shimmering colours, and curious perspectives set in pale Palladian architectural fancies (Villa Bàrbaro at **Masèr**; Accademia, Ducal Palace, and S. Sebastiano, **Venice**).

Verrocchio, Andrea del (1435–88), painter, sculptor, and alchemist, a follower of Donatello and teacher of Leonardo da Vinci, Verrocchio was considered the greatest bronze sculptor of the day, and was hired by **Venice** to create the dynamic equestrian statue of Colleoni.

Vitale da Bologna (active 1330–1359), a disarming and guileless fellow who set the tone for Bolognese painting, celebrated in part for the lack of mental effort it requires from the beholder (Museo del Duomo, **Udine**, Pinacoteca, **Bologna**).

Vittoria, Alessandro (1525–1608), Venetian sculptor, a student of Sansovino famous for his bronze statuettes and portrait busts (S. Francesco della Vigna, Frari, Ca' d'Oro, **Venice**).

Vivarini, 15th-century family of painters from Murano, the chief rivals of the Bellini dynasty; noted for their rich, decorative style. **Antonio** (c.1415–1476/84) collaborated with Giovanni d'Alemagna to paint altarpieces (S. Giobbe, **Venice**); brother **Bartolomeo** (1432–1499) played an influential role in Venetian art his use of colour and rhythm (S. Maria Formosa, Frari, **Venice**); **Alvise** (1446–1503), son of Antonio, was influenced by Antonello da Messina (Frari, S. Giovanni in Brágora, **Venice**).

Wiligelmo (12th century), a talented sculptor—one of the first whose name has come down to us—who began by working with Master Lanfranco on the reliefs of **Modena** cathedral; also worked in **Nonàntola**. His workshop decorated **Piacenza** cathedral; his principal follower was Master Nicolò.

Zelotti, Giambattista, a collaborater of Veronese who became one of Palladio's chief interior decorators (Villa Godi Malinverni, **Lonedo di Lugo**, Villa Emo, **Fanzolo**).

Zoppo, Marco (1433–1478), a Bolognese painter who, like Mantegna, was adopted by Squarcione, but left the Paduan fold to paint in the even more rigid style of Cosmè Tura (Pinacoteca Nazionale, **Bologna**).

VENETIA

Venetia, sometimes known as the Three Venetias, is one of Italy's ripest showpieces and most bodacious holiday playgrounds, bursting at the seams with brilliant art, palaces, villas, and beautiful cities. To these add some of Europe's most ravishing mountains, Alpine lakes, and sophisticated winter sports facilities; add a few of Italy's most famous wines, delicious seafood, and a very noticeable cultural diversity and richness. If you want to limit your holiday to a certain region of Italy, Venetia makes an exciting choice, though its very popularity can make it a trying and much more expensive one in the peak season of July and August. Late May–June and late September–October are the ideal periods to hike in the mountains or dispute with a gondolier.

Venetia encompasses roughly the region controlled by Venice from the 15th century until the conquest of Napoleon. It includes three modern Italian regions: the Veneto (Venice, Padua, Vicenza, Rovigo, Verona, Treviso and Belluno provinces), and the autonomous regions of Trentino-Alto Adige (Trento and Bolzano provinces), and Friuli-Venezia Giulia (Trieste, Udine, Pordenone, and Gorizia)—stretching from the Po to the Dolomites, from Lake Garda to the border of Yugoslavia. In this book they have been divided into four sections: Venice, the Veneto, the Dolomites (northern Veneto and Trentino-Alto Adige) and Friuli-Venezia Giulia.

Itineraries

The Best of Venetia: a Circular Route in a Fortnight
Days 1–4: Highlights of Venice and the lagoon. Day 5: Padua in the morning, evening and overnight in Bassano del Grappa. Day 6: Masèr and Ásolo, in the afternoon to Vicenza, via Maróstica. Day 7: Vicenza, on to Verona in the afternoon. Days 8–9: Verona. Day 10: Scenic drive along Lake Garda to Trento. Day 11: To Bolzano and Cortina d'Ampezzo, down the Great Dolomite Road. Days 12–13: Around Cortina (Lake Misurina, Dobbiaco). Day 14: Return to Venice, via Pieve di Cadore and Conegliano.

The Palladian Villas: Five Days to and from Padua
Day 1: Burchiello excursion down Brenta canal to Venice (Villa Pisani, Villa Widmann Foscari, and La Malcontenta). Return to Padua by bus. Day 2: To the Euganean Hills (Villa Barbarigo and Arquà Petrarca) and Fratta Polésine, near Rovigo (Villa Badoer). Day 3: To Vicenza (Villa Rotonda, Villa Valmarana, Villa Cordellina-Lombardi). Day 4: North to Lonedo di Lugo (Villa Godi-Valmarana and Villa Piovene) and Thiene (Castello Colleoni), on to Bassano. Day 5: Masèr (Villa Bàrbaro), and if you're flush, an overnight stay in Ásolo's Villa Cipriani.

Outstanding Roman and Medieval Art and Architecture: 10 Days
For when you begin to be satiated with Renaissance beauty—Days 1–2: Venice (St

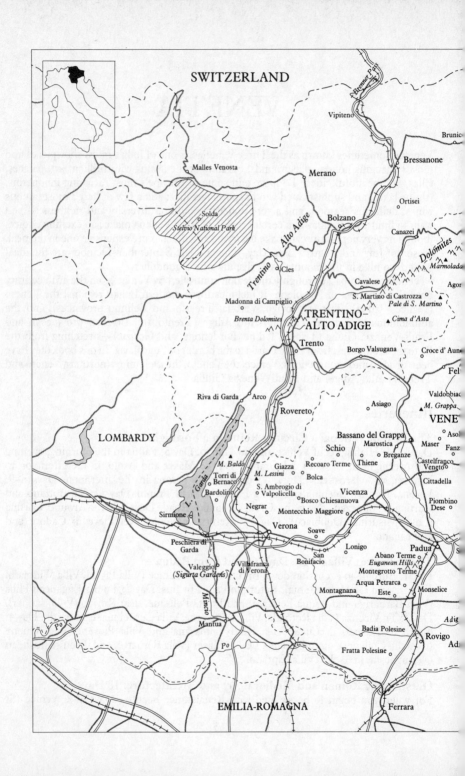

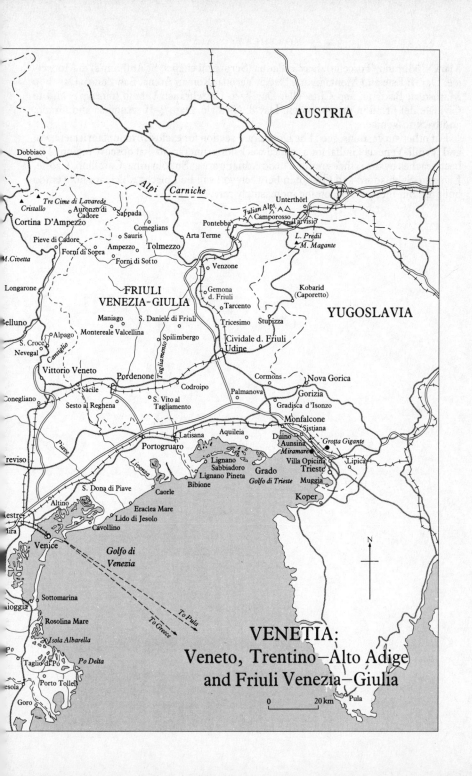

VENETIA:
Veneto, Trentino—Alto Adige
and Friuli Venezia—Giulia

Mark's, Murano, Torcello). Day 3: Padua (Scrovegni chapel, St Anthony's) to Monsél-ice. Day 4: Este and Montagnana. Day 5: Verona (Roman Arena, San Zeno). Day 6: to Maróstica, Bassano, and Cittadella. Day 7: to Castelfranco Veneto (morning) and to Cividale del Friuli in the afternoon. Day 8: Cividale. Days 9–10: Aquileia and Grado, and back to Venice.

For other suggestions, see 'The Dolomites' section for exclusive mountain itineraries, and 'Fruili-Venezia Giulia' for a special week-long itinerary in that obscure region. The best beaches by the rather grey and toxic Adriatic are at Sottomarina, Cavallino, Caorle, Lignano-Sabbiadoro and Grado; in between you will find places which are not yet too built up, but these are becoming increasingly rare.

Part III

VENICE (VENEZIA)

The Wedding Of The Sea Ceremony

Venice seduces, Venice irritates, but Venice rarely disappoints. She is a golden fairy-tale city floating on the sea, a lovely mermaid with agate eyes and the gift of eternal youth. On the surface she is little changed from the days when Goethe called her the 'market-place of the Morning and the Evening lands', when her amphibious citizens dazzled the world with their wealth and pageantry, their magnificent fleet, their half-Oriental doges, their crafty merchant princes, their splendid luminous art, their lack of scruples, their silken debauchery, and their long decline and fall into a seemingly endless carnival. One can easily imagine Julius Caesar bewildered by modern Rome, or Romeo and Juliet missing their rendezvous in the traffic of modern Verona, but Marco Polo, were he to return from Cathay today, could take a familiar gondola up the familiar Grand Canal to his house in the Rialto, astonished more by the motor boats than anything else. Credit for this unique preservation must go to the lagoon and the canals, the amniotic fluid of Venice's birth and the formaldehyde that has pickled her more thoroughly than many more venerable cities on the mainland, where Fiats and industry have not feared to tread.

For a thousand years Venice called herself the Serenissima Republic and at one point she ruled 'a quarter and a half' of the Roman Empire. The descent to an Italian provincial capital was steep, if gracefully bittersweet; and sensitive souls find gallons of melancholy, or, like Thomas Mann, even death, brewed into the city's canals that have nothing to do with the more flagrant microbes. In the winter, when the streets are silent, Venice can be so evocative that you have to kick the ghosts out of the way to pass down the narrower alleys. But most people (some million of them a year) show up in the summer, and like their ancestors, have a jolly good time. For Venice is a most experienced old siren in her boudoir of watery mirrors. International organizations pump in the funds to

69

keep her petticoats out of the water as well as smooth the worst of her wrinkles. Notices posted throughout the city acknowledge that she 'belongs to everybody', while with a wink and swivel of her fascinating hips she slides a knowing hand deep into your pocket. Venice has always lived for gold, and you can bet she wants yours—and you might just as well give it to her in return for the most enchanting, dream-like favours any city can grant.

WHEN TO GO

Venice is as much a character as a setting, and the same may be said of its weather. In no other city will you be so aware of the light; on a clear, fine day no place could be more limpid and clear, no water as crystal bright as the lagoon. The rosy dawn igniting the domes of St Mark's, the splash of an oar fading in the cool mist of a canal, the pearly twilit union of water and sky are among the city's oldest clichés.

If you seek solitude and romance with a capital R, go in January. Pack a warm coat, galoshes and an umbrella, and expect frequent fogs and mists. It may even snow—in 1987 you could even ski-jump down the Rialto bridge. But there are also plenty of radiant diamond days, brilliant, sunny and chill; any time after October you take your chances.

As spring approaches there is carnival, a game and beautiful (but so far lifeless) attempt to revive a piece of old Venice; Lent is fairly quiet, though in the undercurrent the Venetians are building up for their first major invasion of sightseers at Easter. By April the tourism industry is cranked up to full operational capacity; all the hotels, museums, and galleries have reopened, the gondolas are un-mothballed, the café tables have blossomed in the Piazza, the Casino has re-located to the Lido. In June even the Italians are considering a trip to the beach.

In July and August elbow room is at a premium. Peripheral camping grounds are packed, lines at the tourist office's room-finding service stretch longer and longer, and the police are kept busy reminding the hordes that there's no more sleeping out and no picnicking in St Mark's Square. The heat can be sweltering, the canals nastily pungent, the ancient city gasping under a flood of cameras, shorts, sunglasses and rucksacks. Scores head off to the Lido for relief; a sudden thunderstorm over the lagoon livens things up, as do the many festivals. In the autumn the city and the Venetians begin to unwind, the rains begin to fall, and you can watch them pack up the parasols and cabanas on the Lido with a wistful sigh.

History

Venice has always been so different, so improbable, that one can easily believe the legend that once upon a time the original inhabitants sprang up from the dew and mists on the muddy banks of their lagoon. Historians who don't believe in fairies prefer to think that Venice was born of adversity: the islands and treacherous shallows of the lagoon provided the citizens of the Veneto a refuge from Attila the Hun and the damning heresies sweeping the mainland. Twelve lagoon townships grew up between modern Chioggia and Grado; when Theodoric the Great's secretary visited them in 523 he wrote that they were 'scattered like sea-birds' nests over the face of the waters'.

In 697 the twelve townships united to elect their first duke, or doge. Fishing, trading, and their unique knowledge of the lagoon brought the Venetians their first prosperity, but their key position between the Byzantine Empire of the East and the 'barbarian' kings on the mainland made them a bone of contention. In 774, after the Frankish king Pepin the Short defeated the Lombards in the name of the pope, he turned his attention to the obstinate Venetians, hoping to add their islands to his new kingdom of Italy. The Venetians, until then undecided whether to support Rome or Constantinople, responded to the approach of Pepin's fleet from Ravenna by defiantly declaring for Byzantium and entrenching themselves on the islands of the Rialto. The shallows and queer humours of the lagoon confounded Pepin, and after suffering a defeat near the Lido he gave up. But there on the Rialto the city of Venice was born, and the subsequent treaty between Pepin's son Charlemagne and Emperor Nicephorus (810) recognized the city as a subject of Byzantium, with all-important trading concessions. The Venetians lacked only a dynamic spiritual protector; their frumpy, obscure St Theodore with his crocodile was undoubtedly too low in the celestial hierarchy to fulfil the destiny they had in mind. Supposedly the Venetian merchants who purloined the body of St Mark from Alexandria in 829 had secret orders from the doge; they got past Egyptian Customs by claiming that the Evangelist was a shipment of pickled pork.

Marriage to the Sea

As the East–West trade grew in importance, the Venetians designed their domestic and external policies to accommodate it. At home they required peace and stability, and by the beginning of the 11th century had squelched aristocratic notions of an hereditary dogeship by exiling the most prominent family; Venice would never have the despotic *signori* who plagued the rest of Italy.

The raids of Dalmatian pirates spurred the Venetians to fight their first war in 997, when the great Doge Pietro Orseolo captured the pirates' coastal strongholds. The Venetians were so pleased with this first victory that they celebrated the event with a splendidly arrogant ritual every Ascension Day, the *Sposalizio del Mar* or 'Marriage of the Sea', in which the Doge would sail out to the Lido in his sumptuous barge, the *Bucintoro*, and there cast a golden ring into the sea, proclaiming 'We wed thee, O sea, in sign of our true and perpetual dominion'.

Venice, because of her location and her mighty fleet, supplied transport for the first three Crusades, and in return received her first important trading concessions in the Middle East. Arch-rival Genoa became increasingly envious, and in 1171 persuaded the Byzantine Emperor to all but wipe out Constantinople's Venetian quarter. Rashly the Doge Vitale Michiel II attacked the Empire single-handedly and was so soundly defeated that the Great Council, the *Maggior Consiglio*, was brought into being to check the power of the doge and avert future calamities.

Vengeance stayed on the back burner until the next doge, the spry and cunning old Enrico Dandolo, was contracted to provide transport for the Fourth Crusade. When the Crusaders turned up without the Venetians' fee, Dandolo offered to forgo it in return for certain services: first, to reduce Venice's rebellious satellites in Dalmatia, and then, in 1204, to take Constantinople itself. Aged 90 and almost blind, Dandolo personally led the attack; Christendom was scandalized, but Venice had gained, not only a glittering hoard of loot, but three-eighths of Constantinople and 'a quarter and a half' of the Roman Empire—enough islands and ports to control the trade routes in the Adriatic, Aegean, Asia Minor and the Black Sea.

71

To ensure their dominance at home, the merchant princes limited membership in the *Maggior Consiglio* to themselves and their heirs (an event known in Venetian history as the *Serrata*), inscribing their names in the famous *Golden Book*. The doges were slowly reduced to honorary chairmen of the board: when a doge died, his wax effigy was subject to an 'Inquisition on the Defunct Doge' to determine what new oaths his successor should be made to swear to keep him powerless.

A Rocky 14th Century

First the people (1300) and then the snubbed patricians (the 1310 Tiepolo Conspiracy) unsuccessfully rose up against their disenfranchisement under the republic's government. The latter threat was serious enough for a committee of public safety to be formed to hunt down the conspirators, and in 1335 this committee became a permanent institution, the infamous Council of Ten. Because of its secrecy and speedy decisions, the Council of Ten took over much of Venice's government; in later years it was streamlined into a Council of Three. Membership was for one year and over the centuries the council (and especially its offshoot, the State Inquisition, set up in 1539) developed a reputation that fairly dripped with terror; its techniques—inviting private denunciations, torture, secret trials and executions, supported by a network of spies and informers—have often been compared to those of a modern police state, especially in the total anonymity of the governing officials.

Venice's patricians did everything to encourage their council's evil reputation, though in truth their unique system of government (which was to endure until 1797 without another revolt) was the most just and fair of the day, and would compare well with many modern states. Even the notorious Council of Three's powers were strictly limited; every position of power (except the dogeship) was temporary, and controlled by an almost paranoid system of checks and balances. And although at first glance the patricians of the Golden Book were the privileged class, their lives, from young manhood to the grave, were strictly ordered; their first duty was always to serve the state. The result was a government overwhelmingly popular with the governed—disenfranchised they may have been, but as John Julius Norwich summed it up in his monumental history of the Republic: 'Nowhere did men live more happily, nowhere did they enjoy more freedom from fear.'

Away from home the 14th century was marked by a fight to the death with Genoa over eastern trade routes. Events came to a head in 1379, when the Genoese, fresh from a victory over the great Venetian commander Vittor Pisani, captured Chioggia and waited for Venice to starve, boasting that they had come to 'bridle the horses of St Mark'.

As was their custom, the Venetians had imprisoned Pisani for his defeat (compassion was not a virtue in the Serenissima), but the republic was now in such a jam, with half of its fleet far away, that he was released to lead what remained of the navy. A brilliant commander, Pisani exploited his familiarity with the lagoon and in turn blockaded the Genoese in Chioggia. When the other half of Venice's fleet came dramatically racing home, the Genoese surrendered (June 1380) and never recovered their position in the East.

Fresh Prey on the Mainland

After the battle, Venice was determined never to feel hungry again, and set her sights on the mainland—not only for the sake of farmland, but to control her trade routes into the west that were increasingly harried and taxed by the *signori* of the Veneto. Opportunity came with the death of the Milanese duke Gian Galeazzo Visconti in 1402, when ownership of his possessions was contested by his neighbours. Venice snatched Padua, Bassano, Verona, and Belluno in the first round, and in 1454 added Treviso, Ravenna, Friuli, and Bergamo. In 1489 the republic reached its furthest extent when it was presented with Cyprus, a 'gift' from the king's widow, a Venetian noblewoman named Catherine Cornaro.

But just as Venice expanded, Fortune's wheel gave a creak and conspired to squeeze her back into her lagoon. The Ottoman Turks captured Constantinople in 1453, and although the Venetians tried to negotiate trading terms with the sultans (as they had previously done with the infidel Saracens, to the opprobrium of the West), they soon found themselves fighting and losing three centuries' worth of battles for their Eastern territories. Far graver to the merchants of Venice was Vasco da Gama's voyage around the Horn to India, blazing a cheaper and easier route to Venice's prime markets, breaking her ancient monopoly of Eastern luxuries.

On the mainland, Venice's rapid conquests had excited the fear and envy of Italy's potentates, who responded by forming the League of Cambrai (1508) with the sole aim of humbling the proud Venetians. They snatched her possessions after her defeat at Agnadello in 1509, but afterwards quarrelled, and before long all the territories they conquered voluntarily returned to Venice's more benign rule. But Venice never really recovered, and although her renowned Arsenal produced a warship a day and her captains helped the Spanish to win a glorious victory over the Turks at Lepanto (1571), she was increasingly forced to retreat.

A Most Leisurely Collapse

The odds were stacked against her, but in her golden days Venice had accumulated enough wealth and verve to cushion her fall. Her noble families retired into the country, consoling themselves in the classical calm of Palladio's villas, while the city was adorned with the solace of great masterpieces of Venice's golden age of art. Carnival, ever longer, ever more licentious was sanctioned by the state to bring in moneyed visitors like Lord Byron, who dubbed it 'the revel of the earth, the masque of Italy'. In the 1600s the city had 12,000 courtesans, many of them dressed as men to whet the Venetians' passion.

By the time of the French Revolution the Lion of St Mark had lost his remaining teeth, and Napoleon, declaring he would be 'an Attila for the Venetian state', took it with scarcely a whimper in 1797, neatly ending the story of the world's most enduring republic, in its 1000th year, in the reign of its 120th doge. Napoleon took the horses of St Mark to Paris as his trophy, and replaced the old *Pax tibi, Marce, Evangelista Meus* inscribed in the book the lion holds up on Venice's coat-of-arms with 'The Rights of Men and Citizens'. Reading it, a gondolier made the famous remark, 'At last he's turned the page'.

Napoleon unkindly bestowed Venice on Austria, whose main contribution was the railway causeway linking Venice irrevocably to the mainland (1846); twenty years later the former republic politically joined Italy as well. Luckily the city escaped damage in the two World Wars, despite heavy fighting in the environs; according to legend the Allies occupied it in a fleet of gondolas.

But Venice was soon to engage in its own private battle with the sea. From the beginning the city had manipulated nature's waterways for her own survival and defence, diverting a major outlet of the Po, the Brenta, the Piave, the Adige, and the Sile rivers to keep her lagoon from silting up; blocking off all but three outlets to the sea; and most famously, in 1782, completing the famous *murazzi*, the 4-kilometre-long, 6-metre-high sea walls to protect the lagoon. But on 4 November 1966 a combination of wind, torrential storms, high tides and giant waves breached the *murazzi*, wrecked the Lido and left Venice under record *acque alte* (high water) for twenty hours, with disastrous results to the city's architecture and art. The catastrophe galvanized the international community's efforts to save Venice. Even the Italian state, notorious for its indifference to Venice (historical grudges die slowly in Italy) passed a law in 1973 to preserve the city, and contributed to the construction of a new flood barricade similar to the one on the Thames.

The Face of Venice
The historic centre of Venice stands on 117 islets, divided by over 100 canals, spanned by some 400 bridges, each with steps that after a day's walking put enough kinks in your legs to make you want to pay any price asked for a café chair. The longest bridges are the 4.2 km rail and carriage causeways that link Venice to the mainland. The open sea is half that distance across the lagoon, beyond the protective reefs or *lidi* formed by centuries of river silt and the Adriatic current.

The Grand Canal, Venice's incomparable 'Champs Elysées' as the French call it, was originally the bed of a river that fed the lagoon. It snakes majestically through the heart of Venice; the other canals, its tributaries (called *rio*, singular, or *rii*, plural), were shallow channels meandering through the mud banks, and are nowhere as grand—some are merely glorified sewers. But they add up to 45 km of watery thoroughfares.

A warren of 2300 alleys, or *calli*, handle Venice's pedestrian-only traffic, and they come with a colourful bouquet of names—a *rio terrà* is a filled-in canal; a *piscina*, a filled-in pool; a *fondamenta* or *riva*, a quay; a *salizzada* is a street that was paved in the 17th century; a *ruga* is one lined with shops; a *sottoportico* passes under a building; a *lista* once led to an embassy. A Venetian square is a *campo*, recalling the days when they were open fields; the only square dignified with the title of 'piazza' is that of St Mark's, though the two smaller squares flanking the basilica are called *piazzette*, and there's one fume-filled *piazzale*, the dead end for buses and cars.

All of these *rii* and *calli* have been divided into six quarters, or *sestieri*, since Venice's earliest days: **San Marco** (by the piazza), **Castello** (by the Arsenale) and **Cannaregio** (by the Ghetto), all on the northeast bank of the Grand Canal; and **San Polo** (by the church), **Santa Croce** (near the Piazzale Roma), and **Dorsoduro**, the 'hard-back' by the Accademia, all on the southwest bank. Besides these, the modern *comune* of Venice includes the towns on the lagoon islands, the Lido, and the mainland townships of Mestre and Marghera, Italy's version of the Jersey Flats, where most Venetians live today. There is some concern that historic Venice (population around 75,000, down from 200,000 in its heyday) may soon become a city of second homes belonging to wealthy northern Italians and foreigners.

Dialect and Directions

To the uninitiated, Venetian dialect sounds like an Italian trying to speak Spanish with a numb mouth—and it turns up on the city's street signs. Your map may read 'SS. Giovanni e Paolo' but you should inquire for 'San Zanipolo'; 'San Giovanni Decollato' (decapitated John) is better known as 'San Zan Degola'. Still, despite the impossibility of giving comprehensible directions through the tangle of alleys (Venetians will invariably point you in the right direction, however, with a blithe *'sempre diritto!'*—'straight ahead!'), you can never get too lost in Venice. It only measures about 1.5 km by 3 km, and there are helpful yellow signs at major crossings, pointing the way to S. Marco, Rialto, and Accademia, or the Piazzale Roma and the Ferrovia if you despair and want to go home. When hunting for an address in Venice, make sure you're in the correct *sestiere*, as quite a few *calli* share names. Also, beware that houses in each *sestiere* are numbered consecutively in a system logical only to a postman from Mars; numbers up to 5000 are not unusual.

Architecture

At once isolated on her islands but deeply linked to the traditions of East and West, Venice developed her own charmingly bastard architecture, adopting only the most delightfully visual elements from each tradition, especially the Byzantines' fondness for colour, mosaics, rare marbles and exotic effects. Venetian Gothic is only slightly less elaborate, the style of the incomparable Palazzo Ducale and the Ca' d'Oro, with their ogival windows and finely wrought façades.

The Renaissance arrived relatively late, and in Venice its early phase is called Lombardesque, after the Lombard family (Pietro and sons Tullio and Antonio) who designed the best of it, including the small but flawless Santa Maria dei Miracoli and the rich Scuola di San Marco. Later Renaissance architects brought Venice into the mainstream of the classical revival, and graced it with the arcaded Piazza San Marco and Libreria of Sansovino, the San Michele and San Zaccaria of Mauro Codussi and two of Palladio's finest churches, which stand out in clear contrast to the exuberant jumble that surrounds them. To support all this on the soft mud banks, the Venetians drove piles of Istrian pine 5 m into the solid clay—over a million posts hold up the church of the Salute alone. If Venice tends to lean and sink (2–3 mm a year, according to the tourist office), it's due to erosion of these piles by the salty Adriatic, pollution, and the currents caused by the deep channels dredged into the lagoon for the large tankers sailing to Marghera, and the wash caused by motor-boat traffic. Or, as the Venetians explain, the city is a giant sponge.

Most Venetian houses are between four and six storeys high. On some you can see the wooden rooftop loggia, or *altane*, where Renaissance ladies were wont to idle, bleaching their hair in the sun; they wore broad-brimmed hats to protect their complexions, and spread their tresses through a hole cut in the crown. Others still wear their outlandish funnel-like chimney-pots, designed to keep sparks from starting fires.

GETTING TO AND AROUND VENICE

By Air

Venice's Marco Polo Airport is 13 km north of the city near the lagoon, and has regularly scheduled connections from London, New York (via Milan), Paris, Vienna, Nice,

Zurich, Frankfurt, Düsseldorf, Rome, Milan, Palermo, and Naples. For flight information, dial 661 262; the British Airways office is at Riva degli Schiavoni 4158, tel 528 5026. Alitalia is near S. Moisè at S. Marco 1463, tel 520 0355; TWA is nearby at S. Marco 1475, tel 520 3219.

The airport is linked with Venice by water-taxi (tel 964 084) the most expensive option (L75 000); or by *motoscafi* with San Marco (Zecca) roughly every hour and a half (L11 000 a person); or by bus with the Piazzale Roma (L4000). Buses depart for the airport an hour before each flight.

By Sea

Adriatic lines (Zattere 1412, tel 520 4322) has departures from June–September every 10 days for Split (15 hours) and Dubrovnik (24 hours). There are also 34 car-ferry journeys a year—roughly every 10 days to Piraeus (2 days), Heraklion, Crete (2½ days), and Alexandria, Egypt (3½ days).

By Train

Venice's Stazione Santa Lucia is the terminus of the *Venice Simplon-Orient Express* and numerous other less glamorous trains from the rest of Europe and Italy. There are especially frequent connections to Padua (½ hour), where the budget-conscious visitor may prefer to stay; also frequent trains from Milan (3½ hours), Bologna (2 hours), Florence (4 hours), Rome (8 hours), and Trieste (2½ hours). All trains from Santa Lucia stop in Mestre, where you may have to change for destinations like Udine or Ravenna. For rail information, tel 715 555; information and tickets are also available at the CIT office, Piazza S. Marco 4850, tel 528 5480.

Water-taxis, *vaporetti*, and gondolas (see below) wait in front of the station to sweep you off into the city. If you've brought more luggage than you can carry, one of Venice's famous/infamous porters (distinguished by their badges) will lug it to your choice of transport, and if you pay his fare on the water-taxi, will take it and you to your hotel (official price for one or two pieces of luggage is L7700 between any two points in the historic centre)—or you can track down a porter once you disembark at one of the main landings or Lido.

By Bus

Piazzale Roma is Venice's bus terminus; there are frequent city buses from here to Mestre, Chioggia, Marghera, and La Malcontenta; regional buses every half-hour to Padua and less frequently to other Veneto cities and Trieste. It has its own helpful tourist information office, tel 522 7404.

By Car

All roads to Venice end at the monstrous municipal parking towers in Piazzale Roma or its cheaper annexe, Tronchetto, where you can leave your car, for a daily arm and a leg. In the summer, where they're bursting at the seams, consider the Italian Auto Club's three alternative and less expensive car parks (open to non-members): **Fusina**, with a shady, year-round camp site, located at the mouth of the Brenta Canal south of Marghera; **S. Giuliano**, in Mestre near the causeway; and **Punta Sabbioni**, in between the Lido and Jesolo (reached by ferry boat 17 from Tronchetto). *Vaporetti* connect all three lots to historic Venice.

Around Venice: Vaporetti

Public transport in Venice means by water, and the huge *vaporetti*, or water-buses (or the sleeker, faster *motoscafi*) run by the ACTV, are the least expensive and most popular—try to avoid them during rush hour, when not a few tourists have been pushed overboard by the thundering horde. Each line has a number, and is priced according to speed and distance travelled (*diretto* is the fastest, *accelerato* slow, and a *traghetto* is a canal crossing). If you intend to hop on a boat at least six times in a given day, purchase a 24-hour **tourist pass** for L9000, valid for unlimited travel on all lines, or the 3-day pass for L17 000. Tickets should be purchased and validated at the landing stages, and as many of these don't always sell tickets it's best to stock up. Lines of interest to visitors are listed below; most run until midnight. Precise schedules are listed in the tourist office's free monthly guide, *Un Ospite di Venezia.*

Line 1 (L1750) runs from Tronchetto, Piazzale Roma and the Ferrovia (station), down the Grand Canal, to San Marco and the Lido, stopping everywhere; around the clock, every 10 min, although much less frequently after 9 pm. The entire journey takes one hour.

Line 2 (*diretto*: L2500) takes the short cut from Piazzale Roma, Tronchetto, and Ferrovia through the Rio Nuovo to Rialto, Accademia, San Marco and Lido. Every 10 min during the day, approximately once an hour at night.

Line 5 (*servizio circolare*, L1750) the circular route runs either to the left (*sinistra*) or right (*destra*), departing every 15 min. Main points of interest are the islands of Murano and San Michele, Fondamente Nuove, Campo della Tana (where you can take a peek inside the Arsenale), San Zaccaria, San Giorgio Maggiore, Redentore, Zattere, Piazzale Roma, Ferrovia, Ponte delle Guglie (Cannaregio Canal) and Madonna dell'Orto.

Line 5 barred (L1750) a summer-only line from Tronchetto, Piazzale Roma and the station to Murano.

Line 6 (L1750) is the large steamer from the Riva degli Schiavoni to Lido (every 20 min).

Line 8: (L1750) the motorists' friend, from S. Zaccaria, S. Giorgio Maggiore, Giudecca, and Zattere, to Tronchetto

Line 9 (L1200) from Zattere to Giudecca to Riva degli Schiavoni, every 15 min.

Line 11 (L3500)—the 'mixed' line begins at the Lido on a bus to Alberoni, from where you catch a boat for Pellestrina, then another boat for Chioggia—or vice versa (about every 2 hours).

Line 12 (L2500): Venice's Fondamente Nuove to Murano, Torcello, Burano, and Treporti (one an hour).

Line 14 (L2500): Riva degli Schiavoni to Lido and Punta Sabbioni (every hour).

Line 16 (L2500): Zattere–Fusina (summer only; every 50 min).

Line 17: Car ferry from Tronchetto (Piazzale Roma) to Lido and Punta Sabbioni (every 50 min).

Line 28 (L2500): summer only, Ferrovia, Piazzale Rome, S. Zaccaria, Lido/Casino (every 30 min).

Line 34 (L1700): San Marco, Giudecca, Tronchetto, Piazzale Roma, Ferrovia, Rialto, Accademia, and Lido (summer only, every 10 min).

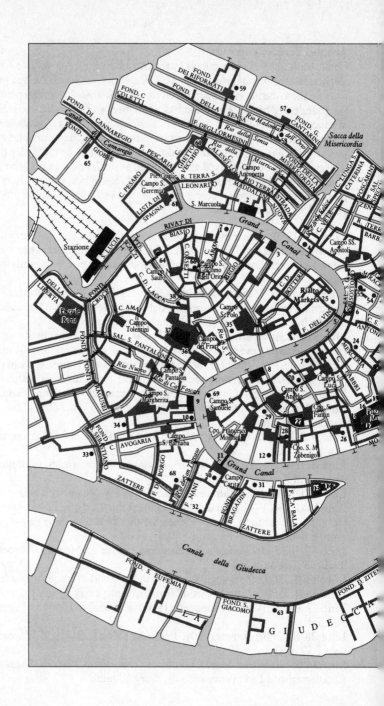

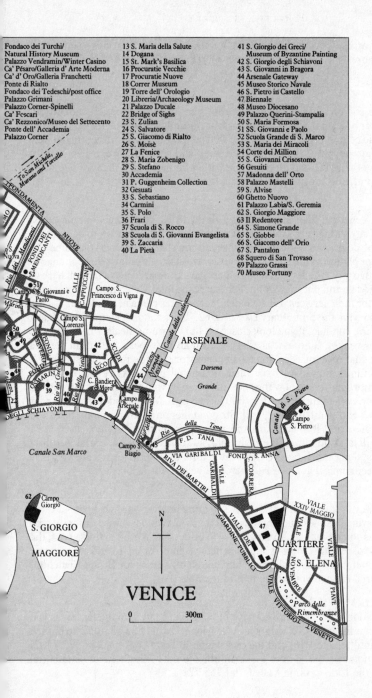

Fondaco dei Turchi/
Natural History Museum
Palazzo Vendramin/Winter Casino
Ca' Pésaro/Galleria d' Arte Moderna
Ca' d' Oro/Galleria Franchetti
Ponte di Rialto
Fondaco dei Tedeschi/post office
Palazzo Grimani
Palazzo Corner-Spinelli
Ca' Fescari
Ca' Rezzonico/Museo del Settecento
Ponte dell' Accademia
Palazzo Corner

13 S. Maria della Salute
14 Dogana
15 St. Mark's Basilica
16 Procuratie Vecchie
17 Procuratie Nuove
18 Correr Museum
19 Torre dell' Orologio
20 Libreria/Archaeology Museum
21 Palazzo Ducale
22 Bridge of Sighs
23 S. Zulian
24 S. Salvatore
25 S. Giacomo di Rialto
26 S. Moisè
27 La Fenice
28 S. Maria Zobenigo
29 S. Stefano
30 Accademia
31 P. Guggenheim Collection
32 Gesuati
33 S. Sebastiano
34 Carmini
35 S. Polo
36 Frari
37 Scuola di S. Rocco
38 Scuola di S. Giovanni Evangelista
39 S. Zaccaria
40 La Pietà

41 S. Giorgio dei Greci/
   Museum of Byzantine Painting
42 S. Giorgio degli Schiavoni
43 S. Giovanni in Bragora
44 Arsenale Gateway
45 Museo Storico Navale
46 S. Pietro in Castello
47 Biennale
48 Museo Diocesano
49 Palazzo Querini-Stampalia
50 S. Maria Formosa
51 SS. Giovanni e Paolo
52 Scuola Grande di S. Marco
53 S. Maria dei Miracoli
54 Corte dei Million
55 S. Giovanni Crisostomo
56 Gesuiti
57 Madonna dell' Orto
58 Palazzo Mastelli
59 S. Alvise
60 Ghetto Nuovo
61 Palazzo Labia/S. Geremia
62 S. Giorgio Maggiore
63 Il Redentore
64 S. Simone Grande
65 S. Giobbe
66 S. Giacomo dell' Orio
67 S. Pantalon
68 Squero di San Trovaso
69 Palazzo Grassi
70 Museo Fortuny

ARSENALE

Darsena
Grande

Canale San Marco

Campo S.
Francesco di Vigna

Campo S.
Lorenzo

Campo SS. Giovanni e
Paolo

Campo S.
Pietro

Campo
Arsenale

della Tana

F. D. TANA

Campo S.
Biagio

VIA GARIBALDI
RIVA DEI MARTIRI
FOND. S. ANNA

QUARTIERE
S. ELENA

VIALE
XXIV MAGGIO

VIALE IV
NOVEMBRE

Parco delle
Rimembranze

VIALE VITTORIO VENETO

Campo S.
Giorgio

S. GIORGIO
MAGGIORE

N

VENICE

0   300m

At San Marco you can also find a number of **excursion boats** to various points in the lagoon; they are more expensive than public transport but may be useful if you're pressed for time.

Water-Taxis

Stands are at the station, Piazzale Roma, Rialto, San Marco, Lido, and the airport. These jaunty motor boats can hold up to 20 passengers, and fares are set for destinations beyond the historic centre, or you may pay L85 000 per hour. Within the centre the base fare for up to four people is L20 000, the metre adding L350 every 15 seconds; additional passengers L2500, and there are surcharges for baggage, holiday or nocturnal service (after 10 pm), and for using a radio taxi (tel 523 2326).

Gondolas

Nothing is more 'Venetian' than the gondola, a sleek, stylish craft some 9 m long, first mentioned in the city's annals in 1094 and developed over the centuries to conform to the peculiarities of doge-land—it can glide through the shallowest canals, around the sharpest corners, or ply across the lagoon with an aura of stately mystique that commands all other boats to give way. Shelley and many others have compared it to a funeral bark or the soul ferry to Hades, and not a few gondoliers share the infernal Charon's expectation of a solid gold tip for their services. Like Model Ts, gondolas come in any colour as long as it's black, still obeying the Sumptuary Law of 1562. The gondolier stands in the back, on the *poppa*, and the gondola, if you look closely, is built asymmetrically to compensate for the shift in his weight. The bow is adorned with an iron 'beak' called the *ferro*, a mysterious device that resembles a Mongolian cleaver or obscure musical notation.

Hardly any gondolas nowadays have their traditional cabins, once notorious for clandestine and improper trysts; now they are quite frankly for tourists who can pay the official L50 000 for a 50-minute ride (L60 000 after 8 pm). Most gondolas can take six people, and before setting out, do agree with the gondolier on where you want to go and how much time you expect it to take, to avoid any unpleasantness later on.

You'll find gondola stands in all the main tourist areas, as well as several **gondola traghetti** services along the Grand Canal between its three bridges, where you may enjoy a brief but economical gondola ride across the canal for L300.

Hiring a boat

Perhaps the best way to spend a day in Venice is to bring or hire your own boat—a small motor boat or a rowing boat—though beware that the local versions have a different type of oar that requires some practice. You may have to be persistent even to find a boat; the Venetians are tired of rescuing tourists stranded in the lagoon. Easier to find are *motoscafi* with chauffeurs, operated by several firms. The tourist office (ask for Bruno Bianchini) in Piazza San Marco can tell you where to find them.

TOURIST INFORMATION

The main information office is in the corner of Piazza San Marco, to the far left as you face the square from the front of St Mark's (Ascensione 71c, tel 522 6356). The branch offices at the station (tel 715 016) and the bus station in Piazzale Roma (tel 522 7402) offer accommodation services. There's also an office on the Marghera autostrada (tel 921 638), and on the Lido at Gran Viale 6 (tel 765 721).

The post office and public telephones are in the Fóndaco dei Tedeschi, by the Rialto bridge; there's another post office at the foot of Piazza San Marco (Calle dell'Ascensione) and another at Piazzale Roma.

The Grand Canal

A ride down Venice's bustling and splendid main artery is most visitors' introduction to the city, and there's no better one. The Grand Canal has always been Venice's status address, and along its looping banks the aristocrats, or *Nobili Homini*, as they called themselves, built a hundred marble palaces with their front doors giving on to the water, framed by the peppermint-stick posts where they moored their watery carriages. The oldest palaces, dating back to the 12th century, reveal Byzantine influences, but most are either Venetian Gothic or Renaissance, or a combination of several periods and styles remodelled over the years.

Connoisseurs of palaces can purchase guides to the Grand Canal that give details of each structure, but in brief, the most acclaimed, heading from Piazzale Roma to the Piazza San Marco, are: the Veneto-Byzantine **Fóndaco dei Turchi** (on the right after the Station Bridge), formerly the Turkish warehouse, now the Natural History Museum (see p. 96); almost opposite, Mauro Codussi's Renaissance **Palazzo Vendramin**, where Richard Wagner died in 1883, now the winter home of the Casino. Back on the right bank, just after the San Stae landing, the Baroque **Palazzo Pésaro** by Longhena is adorned with masks. And then, on the left comes the loveliest of them all, the **Ca' d'Oro**, by its own landing-stage, with an elaborate florid Gothic façade, formerly etched in gold, now housing the Galleria Franchetti (see p. 100).

After the Ca' d'Oro Europe's most famous bridge, the **Ponte di Rialto**, swings into view. 'Rialto' recalls the days when the canal was the Rio Alto; originally it was spanned here by a bridge of boats, then by a 13th-century wooden bridge, and when that was on the verge of collapse, the republic held a competition for the design of a new stone structure. The winner, Antonio da Ponte, was the most audacious, proposing a single arch spanning 48 m; built in 1592, it has since defied the dire predictions of the day and still stands, even taking the additional weight of two rows of shops. The reliefs over the arch are of St Mark and St Theodore. To the right stretch the extensive **Rialto Wholesale Markets**, and on the left the **Fóndaco dei Tedeschi** (German Warehouse), once the busiest trading centre in Venice, where merchants from all over the north lived and traded. The building (now the post office) was remodelled in 1505 and adorned with exterior frescoes by Giorgione and Titian, of which only fragments survive in the Ca' d'Oro.

Beyond the Ponte di Rialto are two Renaissance masterpieces: across from the S. Silvestro landing, Sammicheli's 1556 **Palazzo Grimani**, now the Appeals Court, and Mauro Codussi's **Palazzo Corner-Spinelli** (1510) just before Sant'Angelo landing-stage. After the bend in the canal, the lovely Gothic **Ca' Foscari** was built in 1437 for Doge Francesco Foscari: two doors down, by its own landing-stage, is Longhena's 1667 **Ca' Rezzonico**, where Browning died. Further on the canal is spanned by the wooden **Ponte dell'Accademia**, built in 1932 to replace the ungainly iron 'English bridge'. On the left bank, before S. Maria del Giglio landing, the grand Renaissance **Palazzo Corner** (Ca' Grande) was built by Sansovino in 1550. On the right bank, Longhena's remarkable **Santa Maria della Salute** and the Customs House, or **Dogana di Mare**, crowned by a golden globe and weathervane of Fortune, guard the entrance of the Grand Canal. The next landing-stage is San Marco.

Piazza San Marco

Napoleon described this grand asymmetrical showpiece as 'Europe's finest drawing-room', and no matter how often you've seen it in pictures or in the flesh, its charm never fades. There are Venetians (and not all of them purveyors of souvenirs) who prefer it in the height of summer at its liveliest, when Babylonians of a hundred nationalities, but all wearing outlandish hats, outnumber even the pigeons, who are so overfed they can hardly waddle to the lilting notes of *Lara's Theme* or *Moon River* provided by the piazza's rival café bands. Others prefer it in the misty moonlight, when the familiar seems unreal under hazy, rosy streetlamps; or even when it lies under a few inches of water, criss-crossed by makeshift bridges of planks.

The piazza and its two flanking piazzette have looked essentially the same since 1810, when the 'Ala Napoleonica' was added to the west end, to close in Mauro Codussi's long, arcaded **Procuratie Vecchie** (1499) on the north side and Sansovino's **Procuratie Nuove** (1540) on the south. Both, originally used as the offices of the 'procurators' or caretakers of St Mark's, are now lined with jewellery and designer shops and two of Europe's best known cafés—the **Caffè Quadri** in the Procuratie Vecchie, the old favourite of the Austrians, and the pretty **Caffè Florian**, in the Procuratie Nuove, its decor unchanged since it opened its doors in 1720, although with coffees at L8000 a head the proprietors could easily afford to remodel it in solid gold.

St Mark's Basilica

This is the chief glory of the piazza and of all Venice—an exotic jewel in an incomparable setting. An ancient law decreed that all merchants trading in the East had to bring back from each of their voyages a new embellishment for St Mark's. The result is a glittering robbers' den, the only church in Christendom that would not look out of place in Xanadu.

Until 1807, when it became Venice's cathedral, the basilica was the private chapel of the doge, built to house the relics of St Mark after their 'pious theft' in 828, a deed sanctioned by a tidy piece of apocrypha that had the good Evangelist mooring his ship in the Rialto on the way from Aquileia to Rome, when an angel hailed him with the famous *'Pax tibi...'*, or 'Peace to you, Mark, my Evangelist. Here your body shall lie.'

The present structure was begun after a previous St Mark's burned in 976, and was modelled on Constantinople's former Church of the Apostles. Five rounded doorways, five upper arches, and five round Byzantine domes are the essentials of the exterior, all frosted with a sheen of coloured marbles, ancient columns and sculpture ('As if in ecstasy,' wrote Ruskin, 'the crests of the arches break into marbly foam...'). The spandrels of the arches glitter with the gaudy, Technicolor mosaics—the High Renaissance, dissatisfied with the 13th-century originals, saw fit to commission cartoons from several painters for the scenes, leaving intact only the *Translation of the Body of St Mark* on the extreme left, which includes the first historical depiction of the basilica itself.

Front and centre, seemingly ready to prance off the façade, the controversial copies of the bronze **horses of St Mark** masquerade well enough from a distance, no matter how purists rail. The 3rd- (or 2nd-) century BC originals (now in the Museo Marciano) were one of the most powerful symbols of the republic, part of a 'triumphal quadriga' that Constantine the Great took from Chios to grace the Hippodrome of his new city, only to be carried off in turn by the artful Doge Dandolo in the 1204 Sack of Constantinople.

The best mosaics, most of them 13th-century originals, cover the six domes of the **atrium**, or narthex, their old gold glimmering in the permanent twilight. A lozenge of red marble in the pavement marks the spot where the Emperor Barbarossa knelt and apologized to 'St Peter and his pope'—Alexander III, in 1177. This, a favourite subject of Venetian state art, is one of the few gold stars the republic ever earned with the papacy; mistrust and acrimony were far more common.

THE INTERIOR

The interior, in the form of a Greek cross, dazzles the eye with the intricate splendour of a thousand details. The domes and upper vaults are adorned with golden mosaics, the oldest dating back to the 11th century, though there have been several restorations since. Ancient columns of rare marbles, alabaster, porphyry and verd antique, sawn into slices of rich colour, line the lower walls; the 12th-century pavement is a magnificent geometric mosaic of marble, glass, and porphyry. Like a mosque, the central nave is covered with Eastern carpets.

The first door on the right leads to the **Baptistry** (currently closed for restoration) which is known for its 14th-century mosaics, portraying the life of John the Baptist, with a lovely Salome in red who could probably have had just as many heads as she pleased. The adjacent **Cappella Zen** was added in 1504 to house the tomb of a certain Cardinal Zen, who left the Republic his fortune on condition that he was buried in St Mark's; designed by Tullio Lombardo, it contains excellent bronze statues by his brother Antonio and medieval bas-reliefs and statuettes of prophets by the school of Antelami. In the right transept you can visit the **treasury** (open 9:30–5, Sun 2–closing time; adm), containing the loot from Constantinople that Napoleon overlooked—fairy-tale-like golden bowls and crystal goblets studded with huge coloured gems. In a chapel in the right transept, a lamp burns 'eternally' next to one pillar: after the 976 fire, it appeared that the body of St Mark had been lost, but in 1094 (after Bari beat Venice to the relics of St Nicolaus) the good Evangelist was made to stage a miraculous reappearance, popping his hand out of the pillar during Mass. St Mark is now said to buried in a crypt under the high altar, this adorned with the fabulous, glowing **Pala d'Oro** (same hours as Treasury; adm), a dazzling masterpiece of medieval gold and jewel work. The upper section may originally have been in the Church of the Pantocrator in Constantinople, and the lower section was commissioned in that same city by Doge Pietro Orseolo I in 976. Over the years the Venetians added their own scenes, and the Pala took its present form in 1345.

In the left transept the **Chapel of the Madonna of Nicopeia** shelters a much-venerated 10th-century icon, the *Protectress of Venice*, formerly carried into battle by the Byzantine Emperor. More fine mosaics are further to the left in the **Chapel of St Isidore** (whose body the Venetians kidnapped from Chios—and in the mosaic he seems happy to go, grinning like a chimp). The 1453 mosaics on the *Life of the Virgin* in the **Chapel of the Madonna dei Máscoli** (with the bilingual confessionals) are by Michele

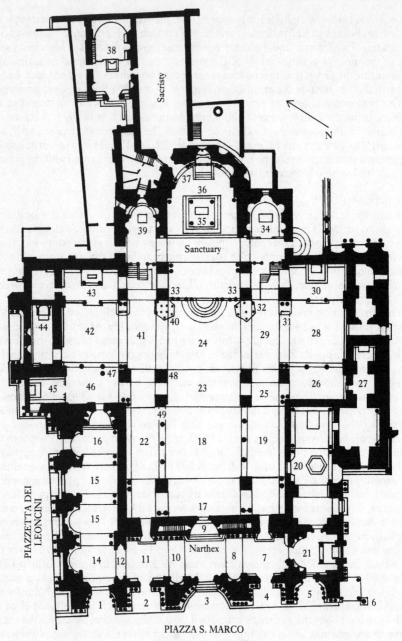

N

38

Sacristy

37
36
35
34
39

Sanctuary

43
33   33   30

44
32
42   41   40   31
24   29   28

47
48
45   46   23   25   26   27

49
16   22   18   19   20

15

15   17

PIAZZETTA DEI LEONCINI

14   12   11   10   9   8   7   21

Narthex

1   2   3   4   5   6

PIAZZA S. MARCO

Plan of St Mark's Basilica

Plan of St Mark's Basilica

Note how crooked it is! In the Middle Ages symmetry was synonymous with death. Numbers in *italics* refer to mosaics.

1 *Translation of the body of St Mark* (1270)
2 *Venice venerating the relics of St Mark* (1718)
3 Central Door, with magnificent 13th-century carvings in arches
4 *Venice welcoming the relics of St Mark* (1700s)
5 *Removal of St Mark's relics from Alexandria* (1700s)
6 Pietra del Bando, stone from which the Signoria's decrees were read
7 *Scenes from the Book of Genesis* (1200) and 6th-century Byzantine door of S. Clemente
8 *Noah and the Flood* (1200s), tomb of Doge Vitale Falier (d. 1096)
9 *Madonna and Saints* (1060s); red marble slab where Emperor Barbarossa submitted to Pope Alexander III (1177); stair up to the Loggia and Museo Marciano
10 *Death of Noah and the Tower of Babel* (1200s)
11 *Story of Abraham* (1230s)
12 *Story of SS. Alipius and Simon, and Justice* (1200s)
14 Tomb of Doge Bartolomeo Gradenigo (d. 1342)
15 *Story of Joseph*, remade in 19th century
16 Porta dei Fiori (1200s); Manzù's bust of Pope John XXIII
17 *Christ with the Virgin and St Mark* (13th century, over the door)
18 *Pentecost* dome (the earliest, 12th century)
19 on the wall: *Agony in the Garden* and *Madonna and Prophets* (13th century)
20 Baptistry, *Life of St John the Baptist* (14th century) and tomb of Doge Andrea Dandolo
21 Cappella Zen, by Tullio and Antonio Lombardo (1504–22)
22 on the wall: *Christ and Prophets* (13th century)
23 in arch, *Scenes of the Passion* (12th century)
24 Central Dome, the *Ascension* (12th century)
25 Tabernacle of the Madonna of the Kiss (12th century)
26 On wall: *Rediscovery of the Body of St Mark* (13th century)
27 Treasury
28 Dome of S. Leonardo; Gothic Rose Window (15th century)
29 In arch, *Scenes from the Life of Christ* (12th century)
30 Altar of the Sacrament; pilaster where St Mark's body was rediscovered, marked by marbles
31 Altar of St James (1462)
32 Pulpit where newly elected Doge was shown to the people; entrance to the Sanctuary
33 Rood screen (1394) by Jacopo di Marco Benato and Jacobello and Pier Paolo Dalle Masegne
34 Singing Gallery and Cappella di S. Lorenzo, sculptures by the Dalle Masegnes (14th century)
35 Dome, *Prophets foretell the Religion of Christ* (12th century); Baldacchino, with Eastern alabaster columns (6th century?)
36 Pala d'Oro (10th–14th century)
37 Sacristy Door, with reliefs by Sansovino (16th century)
38 Sacristy, with mosaics by Titian and Padovanino (16th century) and Church of St Theodore (15th century), once seat of the Inquisition, and now part of the Sacristy: both are rarely open
39 Singing Gallery and Cappella di S. Pietro (14th century) note the Byzantine capitals
40 Two medieval pulpits stacked together
41 *Miracles of Christ* (16th century)
42 Dome, with *Life of St John the Evangelist* (12th century)
43 Cappella della Madonna di Nicopeia (miraculous 12th-century icon)
44 Cappella di S. Isidoro (14th-century mosaics and tomb of the saint)
45 Cappella della Madonna degli Máscoli: *Life of the Virgin* by Andrea del Castagno, Michele Giambono, Jacopo Bellini
46 On wall: *Life of the Virgin* (13th century)
47 Finely carved Greek marble stoup (12th century)
48 Virgin of the Gun (13th century—rifle ex-voto from 1850s)
49 Il Capitello, altar topped with rare marble ciborium, with miraculous Byzantine Crucifixion panel

Giambono (left) and the Florentine Andrea del Castagno (right) one of the harbingers of the Renaissance in Venice.

Before leaving the atrium, climb the steep stair near the west door to the **Museo Marciano, Galleria and Loggia** (9:30–5, winter 10–4; adm), where you can walk through part of the former women's gallery in the basilica for a closer look at the dome mosaics; outside on the loggia you can inspect the replica horses and see how badly they compare with the excellently restored, gilded originals in the museum; the scratches on them are original, meant to catch the rays of the sun.

THE CAMPANILE
St Mark's bell tower, to those uninitiated in the cult of Venice, is an alien presence, a Presbyterian brick sentinel in the otherwise delicately wrought piazza. But it has always been there, at least since 912, and when it gently collapsed into a pile of rubble on 14 July 1902 the Venetians felt its lack so acutely they immediately began to construct an exact replica, only a few hundred tons lighter and stronger, completed in 1912. Just shy of 100 m, you can take the lift up for a bird's-eye vision of Venice and its lagoon (daily 10–7:30, winter 10–5:30; adm); from up here the city seems amazingly compact. Though you have to pay for the view, the republic's misbehaving priests had it for free, suspended in cages from the windows. Under the campanile, Sansovino's elegant **loggetta** adds a grace note to the brick belfry. Its marbles and sculptures glorifying Venice took it on the nose when the campanile fell on top of them, but they have been carefully restored.

The Correr Museum and Clock Tower
On the far end of the piazza from the basilica, in the Procuratie Nuove, the **Museo Correr** (open 10–4; Sun 9–12:30, closed Tues; adm) is Venice's attic of memories—the robes, ducal bonnets (a hard Phrygian cap called the *corno*) and old-maidish nightcaps the doges wore under them, the 20-inch heeled *zoccoli*, once the rage among Venetian noblewomen, and a copy of the statue of Marco Polo from the temple of 500 Genies in Canton. Upstairs is a fine collection of Venetian paintings, including two by Carpaccio, *Two Venetian Ladies* (an essay in total boredom) and the *Young Man in a Red Beret*, with his archetypal Venetian face; works by Jacopo Bellini and his sons, Gentile and Giovanni; Antonello da Messina's *La Pietà*, one of his best works; and the Boschesque *Temptation of St Anthony* by 'Il Civetta' (the little owl).

At the head of the Procuratie Vecchie two bronze wild men, called the 'Moors' sound the hours atop the clock tower, the **Torre dell'Orologio** (Mauro Codussi, 1499) built over the entrance to Venice's main shopping street, the Merceria. The old Italians were fond of elaborate astronomical clocks, but none is as beautiful as this, with its richly coloured enamelled and gilt face, its Madonna and obligatory lion: the Council of Ten supposedly blinded its makers to prevent them creating such a marvel for any other city. You can climb past its creaking works to the top and be deafened by its bell between 9–12 and 3–6 (closed Mon and Sun afternoons; adm, though at the time of writing closed for restoration). Two red lions, inevitably topped by several children, and the pigeons' drinking fountain stand in the nearby **Piazzetta Giovanni XXIII** (named after the beloved Venetian patriarch who became pope), flanking the basilica's north façade.

Piazzetta San Marco
On the south side of the basilica, the Piazzetta San Marco was the republic's foyer, where

ships would dock under the watchful eye of the doge. The view towards the lagoon is framed by two tall, Syrian granite columns, trophies brought to Venice in the 1170s. There were actually three, but in the unloading one slipped and fell in the lagoon and remains there to this day; the man who succeeded in righting the other two asked as his reward the right to set up gambling tables between the columns. The columns are even better known for the executions that took place between them—the worst traitors would be buried alive, leaving only their legs sticking above ground as a warning to others.

The Venetians had a knack for converting their booty into self-serving symbols: atop one of the columns several Roman statues were pieced together to form St Theodore with his crocodile (or dragon, or fish) while on the other stands an ancient Assyrian or Persian chimera-lion, under whose paw the Venetians adroitly slid a book, creating their symbol of St Mark.

Opposite the Ducal Palace stands the **Libreria**, begun in 1536 by Sansovino (finished by Scamozzi) and considered by Palladio to be the most beautiful building in the world, one especially notable for the play of light and shadow in its sculpted arcades. Sansovino, like most Renaissance architects, had been trained as a sculptor, and didn't always pay close attention to nitty-gritty details—the library was scarcely completed when its ceiling collapsed. The Council of Ten sent him to the slammer for his mistake, but released him when Titian pleaded his case. Ask at the Director's office to see the Library's magnificent main hall, with frescoes by Tintoretto and Veronese, and the elaborate grand stair by Vittoria. Sometimes the library's treasures are on display—a 1501 Grimani *breviary*, a masterwork of Flemish illuminators; early *codices* of Homer, the 1459 world map of Venice's Fra Mauro, the most accurate of the day, and Marco Polo's will.

Next door at no 17, Venice's **Archaeology Museum** (daily 9–2, Sun 9–1; adm) has just been remodelled and is one of the few in the city heated in the winter. It has an excellent collection of original Greek sculpture, including a lovely 5th-century BC *Persephone*, a violently erotic *Leda and the Swan* and ancient copies of the famous *Gallic Warriors of Pergamon*, all given to the city by Cardinal Grimani in 1523.

Next door, facing the basin of San Marco, stands another fine building by Sansovino, the 1547 **Zecca**, or Old Mint, which stamped out thousands of golden *zecchinos*,which gave English a new word: sequin.

The Palace of the Doges (Palazzo Ducale)

What St Mark's is to sacred architecture, the Doges' Palace is to the secular—unique and audacious, dreamlike in a half-light, an illuminated storybook of Venetian history and legend. Like the basilica, it was founded shortly after the city's consolidation on the Rialto, though it didn't begin to take its present form until 1309—with its delicate lower colonnade, its loggia of lacy Gothic tracery, and the massive top-heavy upper floor, like a cake held up by its own icing. Its weight is partly relieved by the diamond pattern of white Istrian stone and red Verona marble on the façade, which from a distance gives the palace its wholesome peaches-and-cream complexion. Less benign are the two reddish pillars in the loggia (on the Piazzetta façade), according to legend dyed by the blood of Venice's enemies, whose tortured corpses were strung out between them.

Some of Italy's finest medieval sculpture crowns the thirty-six columns of the lower colonnade, depicting a few sacred and many profane subjects—animals, guildsmen, Turks, and Venetians. Beautiful sculptural groups adorn the corners, most notably the

87

Judgement of Solomon (c. 1410, by Iacopo della Quercia) on the corner nearest the palace's entrance. This is the **Porta della Carta** (Paper Door), a florid Gothic symphony in stone by Giovanni and Bartolomeo Bon (1443); its name may derive from the clerks' desks that once stood near here. To the left of this, four porphyry 'Moors' from Byzantium huddle on the corner of St Mark's; according to legend, they were changed into stone for daring to break into the treasury, though scholars prefer to believe that they are four chummy Roman emperors, or **Tetrarchs**, organized by Diocletian.

Fires in 1574 and 1577 destroyed much of the palace, and at the time there were serious moves to knock it down and let Palladio start again à la High Renaissance. Fortunately, however, you can't teach an old doge new tricks, and the palace was rebuilt as it was with considerable Renaissance touches in the interior (open April–15 Oct 8:30–7, winter 8:30–1; adm expensive). Just within the Porta della Carta, don't miss Antonio Rizzo's delightful arcaded courtyard and his finely sculpted grand stairway, the **Scala dei Giganti**, named after its two Gargantuan statues of *Neptune* and *Mars* by Sansovino.

The palace is entered via another grand stairway, Sansovino's **Scala d'Oro**. The first floor, once the private apartments of the doge, is now used for frequent special exhibitions (separate admission), while the golden stairway continues up to the *Secondo Piano Nobile*, from where the Venetian state was governed. After the fire that destroyed its great frescoes, Veronese and Tintoretto were employed to decorate the newly remodelled chambers with mythological themes and scores of allegories and apotheoses of Venice—a smug, fleshy blonde in the eyes of these two. These paintings are the palace's chief glory, and helpful signboards in each room identify them. Some of the best works are in the first room, the **Anticollegio** (with Tintoretto's *Bacchus and Ariadne* and Veronese's *Rape of Europa*), and in the **Sala del Collegio**, its ceiling decorated with Veronese's *Venice Triumphant*. Tintoretto dominates in the **Sala del Senato**, a room where most of the important decisions were made, often based on the reports of Venice's ambassadors. The main work in the **Sala del Consiglio dei Dieci** is Veronese's ceiling, *Old Man in Eastern Costume with a Young Woman*. Under this the Council of Ten deliberated and pored over the accusations deposited in the *Bocche dei Leoni*—the lions' mouths, the insidious suggestion boxes spread over the city—there's one next door in the **Sala della Bussola**. Although no unsigned and unsupported accusations were considered (and false accusers were given the punishment of the crimes they reported) the procedure had such an evil reputation that when someone joked to Montesquieu that he was being watched by the Ten, he immediately packed his bags and left town.

From here steps descend to the old **Armoury** (Sala d'Armi) which houses a fine collection of medieval and Renaissance armour. Then it's back up again for the vast **Sala del Maggior Consiglio**, built in 1340 and capable of holding the 2500 patricians of the Great Council. Tintoretto's awesome, optimistically elbow-room only *Paradise*—the biggest oil painting in the world (7 m × 22 m)—faces Veronese's magnificent vertiginous *Apotheosis of Venice*. The frieze on the upper wall portrays the first 76 doges, except for the space that would have held the portrait of Marin Falier (1355) had he not led a conspiracy to take sole power; the dry inscription on the black veil notes that he was decapitated for treason. The portraits of the last 44 doges, each painted by a contemporary painter, continue around the **Sala dello Scrutinio**, where the votes for office were counted. Elections for doge were Byzantine and elaborate—and frequent; the Maggior onsiglio preferred to choose doges who were old and wouldn't last long enough to gain a following.

From here the arrows point you across the **Bridge of Sighs** (*Ponte dei Sospiri*) to the 17th-century **Palazzo delle Prigioni**, mostly used for petty offenders (the real rotters were dumped into uncomfortable *pozzi*, or 'wells' in the lower part of the Ducal Palace, while celebrities like Casanova got to stay up in the *Piombi* or 'leads' just under the roof, which you can visit in the fascinating 'Secret Itinerary').

DUCAL PALACE: THE SECRET ITINERARY

In 1984 the section of the palace where the real nitty-gritty business of state took place was restored and opened to the public. Because many of the rooms are tiny, the guided tour, or **Itinerari Segreti** is limited to 20 people, lasts an hour and a half and the only reason why more people don't know about it is because it's only in Italian. If you're still game, reserve a place (days in advance in the summer) on one of two daily tours with the secretary by the Golden Stair (tel 520 4287).

The tour begins at the shipshape wooden offices of the **Chancellery**, where Venice's acres of documents were processed, and includes the 18th-century **Hall of the Chancellery**, an elegant panelled room lined with cupboards for holding treaties, each bearing the arms of a chancellor. The rooms of the justice department, include the **Torture chamber** where the three *signori della notte dei criminali* (judges of the night criminals) would 'put to the question' their suspects, hanging them by the wrists by the rope still dangling in place. The two cells on either side of the rope were for prisoners whose turns were next, who, hearing the proceedings, might be encouraged to talk without the rigmarole. It all ended in the early 1700s, when Venice became the first state in Europe to abolish torture.

Next is the ornate **Sala dei Tre Capi**, the chamber of the three magistrates of the Council of Ten, who served as guardians of Venetian legality, and had to be present at all state meetings. As this chamber might be visited by some foreign dignitary or ambassador, it was given a lavish ceiling by Veronese, a luminous *Pietà* by the school of Antonello da Messina, and three paintings by Hieronymus Bosch: the peculiar *S. Libertà*, a crucified woman; *Paradise and Inferno*; and *St Jerome*, with the usual Boschian rogue's gallery of quaint little nightmares.

From here it's up to the notorious **Piombi**. In spite of their evil reputation, as prisons go they are downright cosy—wooden walls, neither too hot nor too cold, nor over-crowded. Casanova's cell is pointed out, and there's an elaborate explanation of his escape with the aid of a renegade monk through a hole in the roof, which you can read about in his memoirs. Near the end of the tour comes one of Venice's marvels: the **attic of the Sala del Maggior Consiglio**, where you can see exactly how the Arsenale's shipwrights made a vast ceiling float unsupported over the room below; built in 1567, it has yet to need any repairs.

San Marco to Rialto

The streets between the piazza and the market district of the Rialto are the busiest in Venice, especially the **Merceria**, which begins under the clock tower and is lined with some of the city's slickest and tackiest shops. It was down the Merceria that Bajamonte

Tiepolo led his rebels in 1310, when an old lady cried 'Death to tyrants!' from her window and hurled a brick at his standard-bearer, killing him on the spot, and causing such disarray that Tiepolo was forced to give up his attempted coup. It was a close call that the republic chose never to forget: the site (the first left after the clock tower) is marked by a stone relief of the heroine with her brick.

The Merceria continues to the church of **San Giuliano**, rebuilt in 1553 by Sansovino, with a façade marked by Sansovino's statue of its proud and scholarly benefactor. Sansovino also had a hand in **San Salvatore** in the next campo, adding the finishing touches to its noble Renaissance interior, a unique fusion of the basilica and central Greek cross. Sansovino also designed the *monument to Doge Francesco Venier* on the right wall, while nearby an 89-year-old Titian painted one of his more unusual works for this church, an *Annunciation*, which he signed with double emphasis *Titianus Fecit. Fecit* because his patrons refused to believe that he had painted it. The *Tomb of Caterina Cornaro*, ex-Queen of Cyprus (d. 1516) is in the right transept, while at the high altar, a fine 14th-century silver reredos is hidden by a bland Titian that you have to tip the sacristan to lift. Best of all, just left of the altar, is the *Supper at Emmaus*, attributed to Giovanni Bellini.

Humming, bustling **Campo San Bartolomeo**, next on the Merceria is graced by the **statue of Goldoni**, whose comedies in Venetian dialect still make the Venetians laugh; and by the look on his jolly face, he still finds their antics amusing. Follow the crowds up the **Ponte di Rialto** (see 'The Grand Canal'), the geographical heart of Venice, the principal node of its pedestrian and water traffic. The city's central markets have been here for a millennium, divided into sections for vegetables and for fish, and near the former you may pay your respects to Venice's oldest church, little **San Giacomo di Rialto**, founded in the 5th century and re-done in 1601, its façade dominated by a giant clock. In the same campo stands the famous medieval character, the hunchbacked **Gobbo di Rialto**, who supports the little stair and marble podium from which the laws of the republic were proclaimed to the Venetians. Just south, in Ruga Vecchia S. Giovanni, **S. Giovanni Elemosinario** contains Pordenone's best surviving altarpiece, a portait of Venice's first Patriarch, *S. Lorenzo Giustiniani*.

San Marco to the Accademia

Following the yellow signs from the piazza (start by the tourist office), the first campo belongs to Baroque **San Moisè**, with a staggering *opera buffa* façade of dirty ice cream; come between 3:30 and 7 pm to see the matching high altar. For more opera and less buffa, take a detour up Calle Veste (the second right after Campo San Moisè) to monumental Campo San Fantin and **La Fenice** (1792), one of Italy's most renowned theatres, and site of the premières of Verdi's *Rigoletto* and *La Traviata*. Venice has a venerable musical tradition; it was more tradition than music by the era of grand opera—though Lorenzo da Ponte, Mozart's great librettist, was a Venetian.

Back en route to the Accademia—in the next campo stands **Santa Maria Zobenigo** (or del Giglio), on which the Barbaro family stuck a fancy Baroque façade, not for God but for the glory of the Barbaros; the façade is famous for its total lack of religious significance. The signs lead next to the Campo Francesco Morosini (named after the doge who recaptured the Morea from the Turks, but who is known everywhere else as the man who blew the top off the Parthenon). One end is called **Campo Santo Stefano**, and is one of the most elegant squares in Venice. At one end, built directly over a canal, the Gothic church of **Santo Stefano** has, in a city of violently leaning towers, a campanile that deserves to be voted the one most likely to subside (most alarmingly viewed from the adjacent Campo Sant'Angelo). The interior, crowned by a striking wooden ship's keel roof, has beautiful wooden choir stalls (1488) and three late Tintorettos in the Sacristy.

For a possible detour at this point, take Calle Spezier from Campo S. Angelo, and turn left on Rio Terrà Mandola for the **Museo Fortuny** (9–7, closed Mon; adm), located in the former home and studio of artist-designer-jack-of-all-trades Mariano Fortuny (1871–1949); his famous silks, his deservedly not-so-famous paintings, hang in time-suspended langour. Nearly always there's a special exhibition on as well (usually photography).

The Accademia

The south end of Campo S. Stefano funnels into the Accademia bridge; and just over its wooden span lies S. Maria della Carità, a church rebuilt in 1451 by Bartolomeo Bon, and its adjacent convent by Palladio. Now both buildings house the **Gallerie dell'Accademia**, the grand cathedral of Venetian art, ablaze with light and colour; this is the best place in the world to study both the development of the school and some of its greatest masterpieces (open 9–2, holidays 9–1, closed Mon; adm).

The magnificent 15th-century wooden ceiling of **Room I**, the former refectory, has recently been restored, a fit setting for the Venetian-Gothic-Byzantine altarpieces by Jacobello del Fiore (*Allegory of Justice*) Paolo Veneziano (*Coronation of the Virgin*, rich in its quasi-Islamic patterns), and Lorenzo Veneziano (gorgeous, blonde *Annunciation* polyptych). Jacopo Alberegno's *Scenes from the Apocalypse* (1390) has the most original iconography, and the most smirking skeletons. On the left wall, note the *Coronation of the Virgin* (1450s), by Michele Giambono, set in a lush, claustrophobic scene of paradise.

The large altarpieces in **Room II** were all painted within the next generation: the most sublime, Giovanni Bellini's *Pala di S. Giobbe*, repeats in its setting the interior of S. Giobbe, where it was originally hung; on the left St Francis invites the viewer to contemplate the scene, accompanied by the timeless music of the angels at the Madonna's feet. Other fine altarpieces here are Carpaccio's surreal *Crucifixion and Apotheosis of 10,000 Martyrs on Mt Ararat*; Marco Basaiti's brilliantly-coloured *Vocation of the sons of Zebedu* (1510); and Cima da Conegliano's softer *Madonna of the Orange Tree*.

The next rooms, especially **Rooms IV** and **V**, are small but like gifts, contain the best things: Giovanni Bellini's tender, brown-eyed Madonnas, most poignantly the *Madonna with the Blessing Child*; father Jacopo Bellini's *Madonna and Child*, which look like icons next to his Giovanni's; Cosmè Tura's wiry yet lumpy *Madonna and Child*; Andrea Mantegna's *St George*, confident amid garlands of fruit; Piero della Francesca's youthful study in perspective, *St Jerome and Devotee*, brown, dry, and austere company for the Venetians.

Room V contains the gallery's most famous and mysterious painting: Giorgione's *The Tempest*, imprisoned behind reflective glass, near his *La Vecchia*, with the warning '*Col Tempo*' ('With Time') in her hand. These are two of the few paintings scholars accept as being indisputably by this artist, but how strange they are! It is said that Giorgione invented easel painting, serving neither Church, state, nor individual vanity, for the pleasure of the bored, purposeless patricians in Venice's decline, but the paintings seem to reflect rather than lighten their ennui and discontent.

In **Rooms VI–IX** belong to the High Renaissance with Palma Vecchio (*Holy Family with saints*), Paris Bordone (his masterpiece, *The Fisherman presenting St Mark's ring to the Doge*) and Lorenzo Lotto (*Gentleman in his Study*, caught off guard with his book and lizard). The climax comes in **Room X**, with Veronese's *Last Supper* (1573), set in a Palladian loggia with a ghostly white imaginary background, in violent contrast to the rollicking feast of Turks, hounds, midgets, Germans, and artist himself (in the front, next to the pillar on the left). The painting fell foul of the Inquisition, which took umbrage (especially at the Germans). Veronese was cross-examined, and in the end was ordered to make pious changes at his own expense; the artist, in true Venetian style, saved himself the trouble and expense by simply changing its name to *Christ in the House of Levi*.

Room X also has the painting that first made Tintoretto's reputation: *St Mark freeing the slave* (1548); in true Tintoretto-esque fashion, St Mark doesn't merely walk into the scene, but nosedives from the top of the canvas. Even more compelling is his *Translation of the body of St Mark*, on the subject of the 'pious theft' of the relics from Alexandria. The camel is nonplussed, but who are those pale figures on the left, fleeing in a row into a row of doorways, and who are those people sprawled on the ground? The eye is drawn past them all to a boiling orange and black sky.

The last great painting in Room X, *La Pietà*, was also Titian's last, which he was working on at the age of ninety-nine (probably for his own tomb) when felled by the plague. Dark and impressionistic and more moving than ten other Titians put together, it was left uncompleted at his death and, as the inscription states, finished by Palma Giovane.

Room XI has Tintoretto's *Madonna dei Camerlenghi* ('of the treasurers'), where prosperous Venetians bring the Virgin a sack of money. **Room XIII** is a long corridor murky with 17th-century landscapes; further on, **Room XVI** features mythological scenes gone a bit haywire, as in Giambattista Tiepolo's *Rape of Europa* with its bored bull and urinating cherub. The star of **Room XVIa** is Piazzetta's *Fortune Teller* (1740), the most surprising work to come from the Accademia's first director.

Room XVII contains more paintings from the 18th century, a time when Venice proved one of the few bright spots in Italian art. There are works by the brothers Guardi (*Fire at San Marcuolo*), a Canaletto with nuns, rosy pastel portraits by Rosalba Carriera. Pietro Longhi contributes his genre scenes, one called *L'Indovina*, with a fortune teller speaking through a tube.

In **Room XVIII** is the entrance to the upper level of the 15th-century church of the Carità (**Room XXIII**), which is usually closed, but if it's your lucky day, you can take in lovely paintings by Gentile Bellini and four triptychs from the workshop of his brother Giovanni. Their Vivarini rivals get their say here, as do Lazzaro Bastiani and Carlo Crivelli.

Room XX is given over to a series of delightful paintings from the Scuola di San Giovanni Evangelista, depicting the *Miracles of the True Cross*, a meticulous late 15th-century documentary of Venice itself: a view of the old Rialto bridge by Carpaccio; Gentile Bellini's dry, almost photographic view of Piazza San Marco; while Giovanni Mansueti contributes an inside look at a Venetian palace.

Room XXI is entirely devoted to Vittore Carpaccio's superb *Legend of St Ursula* series, painted 1490–96 for the ex-Scuola di Sant'Orsola and recently restored to its original fairy-tale colours. The grand and absurd tale of Ursula, daughter of King Maurus of Brittany, was so long ago and far away that Carpaccio had considerable scope in re-interpreting the events, moving the tale up to 15th-century Venice. After much confabbing by ambassadors, Ursula and her British fiancé depart for a pilgrimage to Rome in a 15th-century Venetian galley. But then Ursula, nicely tucked in her little bed, with her crown at the foot, has a dream of an angel foretelling her martyrdom. Undeterred, Ursula, her fiancé, and 11,000 virgins continue to Rome, and meet the Pope, then decide to travel to Cologne just when the Huns enter the scene and send all 11,002 to their heavenly reward.

Last of all, **Room XXIV**, part of the Scuola della Carità, preserves its original panelling and a fine Titian painted for this very room—the *Presentation of the Virgin* (1538), a charming scene set before the artist's native Cadore in the Dolomites, with the child Mary walking alone up the great flight of steps to the temple. Also painted for this room is a lovely triptych by Antonio Vivarini and Giovanni d'Alemagna.

Dorsoduro

The Accademia lies in the *sestiere* of Dorsoduro, which can also boast the second-most-visited art gallery in Venice, the bright and vibrant **Peggy Guggenheim Collection**, just down the Grand Canal from the Accademia in her 18th-century ranch-style (the top was never finished) palazzo (open April–Oct, 12–6, closed Tues; adm expensive but free on Sat from 6–9 pm). In her thirty years as a collector, until her death in 1979, Ms Guggenheim amassed an impressive quantity of brand-name 20th-century art, from nearly every modern movement—Bacon, Brancusi, Braque, Carrà, Calder, Chagall, Dali, De'Chirico, Duchamp, Dubuffet, Ernst (Peggy's ex-husband), Giacometti, Gris, Kandinsky, Klee, Magritte, Mirò, Moore, Mondrian, Picasso, Pollock, Rothko, Smith, and Peggy's daughter Peggine, vintage 1960s. On the terrace, overlooking the Grand Canal, don't miss Marino Marini's joyfully obscene *Angel of the Citadel*.

From here it's a five-minute stroll down to another masterpiece: Baldassare Longhena's white basilica of **Santa Maria della Salute** (1631–81), with its superb dome and jellyroll scrolls as big as roundabouts. The fifth Venetian church to be built in thanksgiving after plagues (Venice, a busy international port isolated in its lagoon, was particularly susceptible), 'St Mary of Health' is dramatically set near the entrance of the Grand Canal (open from 7–12 and 3–6). Longhena modelled his interior on the Byzantine church of San Vitale in Ravenna: an octagon encircled by an ambulatory, creating a striking visual play of arches. The high altar, by Juste La Corte, vividly portrays the Queen of Heaven dismissing hag-like plague, while the Sacristy (adm) contains the *Marriage at Cana* by Tintoretto and Titian's *St Mark enthroned between Saints* and three violent ceiling panels on Old Testament subjects.

Behind the Salute, the **Zattere**, facing the freighter-filled canal and island of Giudecca, leads to the church of the **Gesuati** built by Giorgio Massari as an echo of Palladio's Redentore church across the canal; inside it is decorated by Giambattista Tiepolo. For a more substantial feast, take the long stroll down the Fondamenta (or *vaporetti* Line 5 or 8, San Basilio) to Veronese's parish church of **San Sebastiano** off

Rio di San Basilio (open 9–12 and 3–6; Sun 12–1 and 3–6; fee for the lights). Assisted by his brother Benedetto Caliari, Veronese spent ten years decorating San Sebastiano—beginning in 1555 with the ceiling frescoes of the sacristy and ending with the magnificent ceiling, *The Story of Esther*, quintessential scenographic Veronese—as are the frescoes in the choir, though they have yet to be restored. Veronese himself is buried to the left of the altar.

From San Sebastiano you can head back towards the Grand Canal (Calle Avogaria and Lunga S. Barnaba), turning left on Calle Pazienza to visit the **Church of the Carmini**, its basilican interior lined with a unique collection of gilded wooden sculpture and statues that wouldn't look out of place in front of a cigar store; it also has lovely altar pieces by Cima da Conegliano and Lorenzo Lotto. Longhena's **Scuola Grande dei Carmini** next door contains one of Giambattista Tiepolo's best and brightest ceilings, *Virgin in Glory* (open 9–12, 3–6, closed Sun; adm).

The Carmini stands on the corner of the **Campo Santa Margherita**, one of Venice's most delightful campos and crossroads. Just to the north, across the wide Rio Nuovo, the church of **San Pantalon** has, for its ceiling, Italy's most outrageous example of *trompe-l'oeil* wizardry: Giovanni Antonio Fumiani's *Life of S. Pantalon*. What, you've never heard of Fumiani? After spending 1680–1704 on this 3-D wonder, he fell off the scaffolding and died (closed 11:30–4:30).

Campo S. Margherita is also near **Ca' Rezzonico** (Rio Terrà Canal down to the Traghetto S. Bernardo), now home to the **Museo del Settecento Veneziano** (open 10–4, holidays 9–12:30, closed Fri; adm). This is Venice's main shrine to its gilded 18th-century, with its wistful carnival frescoes by Giandomenico Tiepolo, period furniture and interiors, 34 paintings by Longhi (including *The Rhinoceros*, dutifully recorded next to a pile of rhino droppings), and a breathtaking view of the Grand Canal. One of the palaces you see opposite belonged to Doge Cristoforo Moro, whom the Venetians claim Shakespeare used as his model for Othello, confusing the doge's name with his race.

Sestieri of San Polo and Santa Croce

From the Ponte di Rialto, the yellow signs to the Piazzale Roma lead past the pretty Campo and church of **San Polo**, with a fine Gothic door by Bartolomeo Bon and inside, Giandomenico Tiepolo's *Stations of the Cross* in the Oratory of the Crucifix (7:30–12 and 4–7, Sun 8–12). Painted at the age of 20, Giandomenico's scenes have a precocious, almost photographic angle in their composition.

Church of the Frari
The signs will take you next to the giant brick Gothic Franciscan church of the **Frari**. Founded in 1250, not long after St Francis' death, it was rebuilt in 1330 and not completed until 1469. For Venice, the exterior is very severe; a hint of Gothic edging on the cornice, some carving by the doors, and Venice's second tallest campanile are its most memorable features. Open 9–12:30 and 3–6, the long cruciform interior is pinned together by wooden tie beams, adding an abstract quality to the aisle bays and ceiling.

Like the Dominican SS. Giovanni e Paolo on the other side of Venice, the Frari is crowded with tombs. On the back wall, the **Tomb of Pietro Bernardo** (d. 1538) is a late work by Tullio Lombardo; **Titian's Tomb** (second altar on the right) follows a venerable Italian tradition of giving its favourite artists the most inartistic tombs (Titian's is even worse than Michelangelo's): a massive 19th-century inanity. The third altar is graced by Vittoria's statue of *St Jerome*, said to be a likeness of Titian at the age of 93.

The **Monk's Choir** in the centre of the nave has a marble choir screen by Bartolomeo Bon and Pietro Lombardo, but even more impressive are its three tiers of monks' stalls, carved by Marco Cozzi. In the right transept are four diverse tombs: the **Tomb of Iacopo Marcello** (d. 1484), a fine piece of quirkiness attributed to Giovanni Buora; the hyper-florid Gothic terracotta **Tomb of Beato Pacifico** by Tuscans Nanni di Bartolo and Michele da Firenze; the marine **Memorial of Captain Benedetto Pésaro**, with reliefs of Ionian island fortresses and battle galleys; and the **Monument to Condottiere Paolo Savelli** (1405), his wooden equestrian statue quaintly stuck high up on a shelf. The door here leads to the **Sacristy**, with one of Giovanni Bellini's most compelling, inspired works, his 1488 *Triptych of the Madonna and Child, with SS. Nicholas, Peter, Mark, and Benedict*, still in its original frame, in the place Bellini intended it to be seen.

The first chapel in the **Choir** has an altarpiece by Bartolomeo Vivarini (*Madonna, Child and Saints*, 1482). The chapel nearest the High Altar belonged to the Florentines, who hired Donatello to make its rustic but gilded wooden *Statue of John the Baptist* in 1438, his earliest work in the Veneto, and like many of his Baptists in Florence, one who obviously lived on locusts.

What the Frari is most famous for, however, is Titian's enormous *Assumption of the Virgin* (1516–18) a sensation for its extraordinary colour and revolutionary spiralling composition. For all the hullabaloo, it must be the most overrated painting in Italy; after the Bellini in the Sacristy its virtues are mere virtuosity, and its big-eyed, heaven-gazing Virgin as spiritual and perspective as a Sunday school holy card. Sentimentality, especially on such a grand scale, rarely appears elsewhere in Venetian art or even in Titian's own works. One wonders what the artist thought about it in his old age.

In the chancel, to the left of the *Assumption*, is one of Venice's Renaissance gems, the **Tomb of Doge Nicolò Tron** (d. 1473) by Antonio Rizzo, serene and lovely with its Renaissance allegories; among the chapels to the left of the sanctuary, the third contains the grave of Claudio Monteverdi, the father of opera (1567–1643); the crowded altarpiece here is by Alvise Vivarini and Marco Basaiti. The fourth chapel, in the left transept, is usually locked, but through the grilleshines Bartolomeo Vivarini's crystal-clear painting of *St Mark enthroned with four saints*, and Sansovino's broken but beautiful marble *St John* on the font.

In the left aisle hangs Titian's *Madonna di Ca' Pésaro* (1519), a painting nearly as influential in its time as the *Assumption*; its diagonal composition would later be taken to extremes by Titian's pupil, Tintoretto. The next monument, the godawful **Tomb of Doge Giovanni Pésaro** (d. 1669), is supported by Moorish telamons, though the sculptor, a certain Melchiore Barthel, at least carved them pillows to lighten the load of decomposing bodies on top. Next, the **Tomb of Canova**, with a neoclassical pyramid, was designed by Canova as a tomb for Titian, but carved after his death as his own memorial, although only his heart is buried here.

Since the early 1800s, the adjacent monastery has housed the **State Archives of Venice**. The Republic left behind 70 km of files (about the distance from Venice to Vicenza) from the 9th century onwards; a hoard of paper occupying 300 rooms. Two or three times a year exhibitions are held here, based on archival material.

Scuola di San Rocco

Next to the Frari, the **Scuola di San Rocco** is one of Venice's numerous 'schools' or charitable confraternities. San Rocco, renowned for his juju against the Black Death, was so popular among the Venetians that they canonized him before the pope did, and his confraternity was one of the city's wealthiest. The school has a beautiful, lively façade by Scarpagnino, and inside it contains one of the wonders of Venice—or rather, fifty-four wonders—all painted by Tintoretto, who worked on the project from 1562 to 1585 without any assistance (open 9–1 and 3:30–6:30, winter 10–1; adm expensive).

Tintoretto always managed to look at old, conventional subjects from a fresh point of view; while other artists of the High Renaissance often composed their subjects with the epic vision of a Cecil B. de Mille, Tintoretto had the revolutionary eye of a 16th-century Orson Welles, creating audacious, dynamic 'sets', often working out his compositions in his little box-stages, with wax figures and unusual lighting effects. In the *scuola*, especially in the upper floor, he was at the peak of his career, and painted what is considered by some to be the finest painting cycle in existence. Vertigo is not an uncommon response—for an antidote, look at the funny carvings along the walls by Francesco Pianta. The greatest work in the cycle is the *Crucifixion*, where the event is the central drama of a busy human world. In the same room there are also several paintings on easels by Titian, and one of Christ that some attribute to Titian, some to Giorgione.

Just to the north, beyond the Campo San Stin, the **Scuola di San Giovanni Evangelista** deserves a look inside for its beautiful Renaissance courtyard and double-ramp stairway by Mauro Codussi (1498), noted for the rhythms of its domes and barrel vaults (open Mon–Fri, 9:30–12:30; ring). North of Campo San Stin, work your way through the maze to venerable 13th-century **San Giacomo dell'Orio**, with another beautiful ship's keel roof; inside, among its massive, squat Byzantine columns are paintings by Lotto, Veronese, and Palma Giovane, and a charming Romanesque statue of the Virgin with a spindle.

To really escape the crowds, walk north up Calle Larga to see the aborted sharks and huge prehistoric crocodile in the **Natural History Museum** (9–1, closed Mon; adm) in the Veneto-Byzantine **Fóndaco dei Turchi**, over-restored in 1858. Following the Grand Canal east, you'll eventually find Longhena's massive **Ca' Pésaro**, housing the **Galleria d'Arte Moderna** with a not very riveting collection of 19th-century paintings and gleanings from the Biennale exhibitions (open 10–4, Sun 9:30–12:30, adm).

San Marco to Castello

Starting at Piazzetta San Marco, the gracefully curving and ever-bustling **Riva degli Schiavoni** was named after the Slavs from Dalmatia, many of whom served as long-shoremen in Venice. A few steps behind the Doges' Palace is one of the city's finest Gothic palaces, now the famous **Hotel Danieli**, its name a corruption of the 'Dandolo' family who built it. On the quay stands a robust 1887 **Memorial to King Vittore Emmanuele II**, where two of Venice's 10,000 lions shelter, as often as not, members of Venice's equally numerous if smaller feline population between their paws.

From the Riva, Sottoportico San Zaccaria leads back to the lovely Gothic-Renaissance **San Zaccaria**, its beautiful façade with seashell motifs completed by Mauro Codussi in 1515 (open 10–12 and 4–6). The elegant interior is lit by the narrow windows of the ambulatory, a northern Gothic inspiration, crowned with cupolas (also by Codussi). In the second chapel on the left is Bellini's beautifully luminous *Madonna and Saints*; in the right aisle the **Chapel of Sant' Athanasio** (adm) contain three fine altarpieces by Antonio Vivarini and Giovanni d'Alemagna. The adjacent 9th-century **Cappella San Tarasio** (part of the original church) has faded frescoes by Andrea del Castagno, and a spooky flooded crypt with the tombs of Venice's earliest doges.

On the Riva itself, Giorgio Massari's **La Pietà** church served the girls' orphanage which the red-headed priest Vivaldi made famous during his years as its concert master and composer (1704–38). Rebuilt shortly after Vivaldi's departure, the church has an elegant oval interior and several acoustical innovations that the maestro suggested to Massari. Now used exclusively for concerts, it is sometimes open on Mon, Wed, and Fri mornings.

Due north of La Pietà is Venice's Greek Orthodox Church, the 16th-century **San Giorgio dei Greci**, with its campanile leaning alarmingly over the canal and beautiful golden iconostasis, with icons brought to Venice after the fall of Constantinople. The adjacent *scuola*, designed by Longhena, is now the **Museum of Byzantine Religious Painting** (open 9–12:30 and 2–6, Sun 9–12, closed Tues; adm). Run by the Hellenic Institute of Byzantine studies, it contains icons from the 16th and 18th centuries, many painted by Greek artists who fled the Turkish occupation and its ban on portraying images. In Venice the Greeks came into contact with the High Renaissance and created the Venetian-Cretan school of art, which nourished, most famously, El Greco.

Nearby, another minority, the Dalmatians, built the tiny **Scuola San Giorgio degli Schiavoni** (10–12:30, 3:30–6; holidays, morning only, closed Mon; adm), its interior decorated with the most beloved and charming canvases in all Venice, Carpaccio's magical paintings on the lives of the Dalmatian patron saints: Jerome (or Augustine) with his patient little white dog; George charging a petticoat-munching dragon in a landscape strewn with maidenly leftovers from lunch—and more. Some of the greatest works by Carpaccio's contemporaries, the Vivarinis and Cima da Conegliano, hold pride of place in **San Giovanni in Bragora** (in Campo Bandiera e Moro, between San Giorgio degli Schiavoni and the Riva); the best work, Cima's *Baptism of Christ*, is in the sanctuary.

The Arsenale

FromtheRiva, the Fondamenta dell'Arsenale leadsback tothetwin towers guarding the **Arsenale**. Founded in 1104, this first of all arsenals derived its name from the Venetian pronunciation of the Arabic *darsina'a*, or artisans' shop, and until the 17th century these were the greatest dockyards in the world, the very foundation of the republic's wealth and power. In its heyday the Arsenale had a payroll of 16,000 and produced a ship a day to fight the Turks. Dante visited this great industrial complex twice, and as Blake would later do with his Dark Satanic Mills, confined it to the *Inferno*. Today the Arsenale is occupied by the Italian military, but you can look at the **Great Gateway** next to the towers, Venice's 'first' Renaissance work constructed by Gambello in 1460. Around it are marble trophies from Greece—including two ancient lions Doge Francesco Morosini found in Piraeus, one with 11th-century runes faintly traced in its back in the name of Harold Hardrada, a member of the emperor's Varangian guard before being crowned king of Norway. Others, eroded into Paschal lambs, are from Delos; the one on the gate looks as if it had a poodle in its family tree.

Venice's glorious maritime history is the subject of the artefacts and many detailed models (used by Venice's shipwrights) in the **Museo Storico Navale**—most dazzling of all is the model of the doge's sumptuous barge, the *Bucintoro*; another room has beautiful models of ancient junks (open 9–1, Sat 9–12, closed holidays; adm). The museum is located near the beginning of Via Garibaldi; across the street lived two seafarers who contributed more to the history of Britain and Canada than that of Venice—Giovanni and Sebastiano Caboto.

Via Garibaldi and the Fondamenta S. Anna continue to the Isola di San Pietro, site of the unmemorable Palladian-style **San Pietro di Castello**, until 1807 Venice's cathedral, its lonely, distant site no small comment on the republic's attitude towards the papacy. The attractive, detached campanile is by Codussi; inside, a hoary marble throne once claimed to be St Peter's in Antioch until someone noticed the inscriptions from the Koran. To the south are the refreshing pines and planes of the **Public Gardens**, where the International Exhibition of Modern Art, known as the Biennale, takes place in the artsy pavilions (in even-numbered years). This, and the **Parco delle Rimembranze** further on, were given to this sometimes claustrophobic city of stone and water by Napoleon, who knocked down four extraneous churches to plant the trees. From here you can take Line 1 or 2 back to San Marco, or to the Lido.

San Marco to SS. Giovanni e Paolo

The calle around the back of San Marco and over the Rio di Palazzo leads to one of Venice's newest museums, the **Museo Diocesano** (10:30–12:30, free) in the Romanesque cloister of Sant'Apollonia, a safe harbour for church trappings and art salvaged from the city's churches. Through a web of alleys to the north there's more art in the 18th-century **Palazzo Querini-Stampalia** (10–2:45, closed Mondays; adm) with the best collection of Venetian 18th-century genre paintings, by the humourless Longhi and the charmingly inept Gabriele Bella. Other notable works are few: Giovanni Bellini's *Presentation at the Temple*, portraits by Palma Giovane, and a room is dedicated to minor 17th-century psychotics.

Santa Maria Formosa, in its charming campo just to the north, was rebuilt by Codussi, who made creative use of its original Greek-cross plan. The leering head near the bottom of its campanile is notorious as being the most hideous thing in Venice, while inside, Palma Vecchio's *Santa Barbara* is famed as the loveliest woman, modelled on the artist's own daughter. Another celebrated work, Bartolomeo Vivarini's *Madonna della Misericordia* of 1473, is in the first chapel; the people under the Virgin's protection earned it by paying for the painting.

The next campo to the north belongs to **Santi Giovanni e Paolo** (San Zanipolo), after St Mark's the most important church on the right bank. A great Gothic brick fane begun in 1246 by the Dominicans, no one could accuse it of being beautiful, despite its fine front doorway and impressive apse. The church (open 7–12:30 and 3:30–7:30) has long served as a kind of pantheon of doges; all their funerals were held here after the 1300s, and some 25 of them went no further, but lie in splendid Gothic and Renaissance tombs: the west wall, entirely occupied by the Mocenigo family, is dominated by the great **Tomb of Doge Pietro Mocenigo**, by Pietro Lombardo, assisted by his sons Tullio and Antonio (1476–81); it is decorated with statues of the Three Ages of Man and other warriors, with religion relegated to the tiny bit at the very top. An inscription proudly remarks that the tomb was paid for by his enemies (not willingly, mind you).

After the first altar in the right aisle, is the **monument to Bragadin**, the unfortunate captain who in 1571 was flayed alive by the Turkish pasha of Famagusta, after a long siege; his bust sits on an urn that holds his neatly folded skin. The adjacent chapel contains Giovanni Bellini's excellent polyptych of *St Vincent Ferrer*, a fire-eating subject portrayed by the gentlest of painters.

The stained glass in the right transept, the finest in Venice, was made in Murano in the 15th century, from cartoons by Bartolomeo Vivarini. Gothic windows light the polygonal **chancel**: on the right wall is the fine Gothic **tomb of Doge Michele Morosini** (d. 1382); on the left wall, the **tomb of Doge Andrea Vendramin**, a masterpiece by Tullio and Antonio Lombardo (1478).

The **Chapel of the Rosary**, off the left transept, was built to celebrate the victory at Lepanto. Burned in 1867, with all of its art, a fine ceiling by Veronese was added from a demolished church. More monuments line the left aisle, including two very fine works by Pietro Lombardo: his 1462 **Tomb of Doge Pasquale Malipiero** (the first monument) and **Tomb of Doge Nicolò Marcello**, this just to the right of a copy of Titian's *St Peter Martyr*, one of the works lost in the Chapel of the Rosary fire.

Adjacent to San Zanipolo, the **Scuola Grande di San Marco**, has one of the loveliest Renaissance façades in Italy, its fascinating *trompe l'oeil* lower half by Pietro and Tullio Lombardo, its upper floor by Mauro Codussi, finished in 1495. The *scuola* is now used as Venice's municipal hospital, but you can enter to see the lavish ceiling in the library.

Opposite stands Verrocchio's famous **Equestrian Statue of Bartolomeo Colleoni**, the Bergamask *condottiere* (1400–76) and Klaus Kinski look-alike who did so much for the republic's claims on the mainland. In his lifetime proud of his emblem of *coglioni* (testicles—a play on his name), Colleoni envied Donatello's statue of his predecessor Gattamelata (in Padua), and in his will he left the republic 100,000 ducats if it would erect a similar statue of him in front of St Mark's. Greedy for the money but unable to countenance a monument to an individual in their Piazza, the wily Venetians put the statue up in front of the *scuola* of St Mark.

Due east of SS. Giovanni e Paolo, **S. Francesco della Vigna** was designed by Sansovino, with a façade by Palladio (1572). Inside, the Giustiniani Chapel (left) has beautiful sculptures by Pietro Lombardo; to the right are three statues of saints by Vittoria.

Santa Maria dei Miracoli and Ca' d'Oro
From the Campo San Zanipolo, Larga G. Gallini leads to the perfect little Renaissance church, **Santa Maria dei Miracoli**, built by Pietro Lombardo in the 1480s and often compared to an exquisite jewel box, elegant, graceful, and glowing with a soft marble sheen, inside and out. Just to the south are the **Corte della Prima e della Seconda Milione**. The latter courtyard in particular looks much as it did when Marco Polo lived there; 'Million', his nickname in Venice, was derived from the million tales he brought back with him from Kubla Khan's China. Nearby, Codussi's **San Giovanni Crisostomo** (1504), is the master's last work, a small but seminal piece of Renaissance architecture that contains Giovanni Bellini's last altar painting (*SS. Jerome, Christopher, and Augustine*), as well as a beautiful high altarpiece by Sebastiano del Piombo.

Up the Grand Canal, signposted off the Strada Nuova (Via 28 Aprile), stands the enchanting Gothic **Ca' d'Oro** (1440), currently housing the **Galleria Franchetti** (9–2, Sun 9–1; adm). Among its celebrated works are Mantegna's stern *San Sebastiano*, Guardi's series of Venetian views, Titian's voluptuous *Venus*, an excellent collection of Renaissance bronzes and medallions (some by Pisanello), busts by Alessandro Vittoria, and a portrait of Sultan Mehmet II by Gentile Bellini (who did a stint in Istanbul, until the Sultan, wanting to provide him with models, sent him the head of a freshly decapitated slave as a present). Non-Venetian works include Dürer's *Deposition* and a fine *Crucifixion* by a follower of Van Eyck.

Due north, near the Fondamente Nuove, stands the church of the **Gesuiti**, a Baroque extravaganza that would make a fitting memorial for Liberace. This church, with its decor of white and green-grey marble draperies, was Titian's parish church, to which he contributed the *Martyrdom of St Lawrence*—the saint on a grill preferred by Titian's patron, Philip II of Spain.

Cannaregio

Crumbling, piquant Cannaregio (named after an old bamboo marsh) is the least visited *sestiere* in Venice, and here, perhaps, more than anywhere else in the city you can begin to feel what everyday life in Venice is like behind the tourist glitz—children playing tag on the bridges, old men in vests (undershirts) messing around in unglamorous, unpainted boats on murky canals, neighbourhood greasy spoons and bars, banners of laundry waving gaily overhead.

Northern Cannaregio was Tintoretto's home base, and he is buried in the beautiful Venetian Gothic **Madonna dell'Orto**, which also contains several of his jumbo masterpieces: the *Sacrifice of the Golden Calf*, in which Tintoretto painted himself bearing the idol—though he refrained from predicting his place in the *Last Judgement* which hangs opposite it. He also painted the highly original *Presentation of the Virgin in the Temple* in the south aisle, near one of Cima da Conegliano's greatest works, *St John the Baptist*. The first chapel near the door contains a Madonna by Giovanni Bellini (open 9:30–12 and 4:30–7, winter 3:30–5).

From the Campo Madonna dell'Orto, take a short walk down the Fondamenta Contarini, where, across the canal, in the wall of the eccentric **Palazzo Mastelli** you can see one of Venice's curiosities: an old, stone relief of a Moor confronting a camel. There are three more 'Moors' in the **Campo dei Mori**, just in front of the Madonna dell'Orto, believed to be three brothers and merchants, who posed in the then fashionable costumes of the Morea for their sculpture. A fourth one, with a metal nose like Tycho Brahe is formally known as Signore Antonio Rioba, and has long been the butt of many Venetian pranks. Another church in the area, **Sant'Alvise**, features a forceful *Calvary* by Giambattista Tiepolo and a set of charming tempera paintings that Ruskin called the 'Baby Carpaccios', but are actually attributed to Carpaccio's master, Lazzaro Bastiani.

Three *rii* to the south of Sant'Alvise is the **Ghetto**—*THE* Ghetto, that is, for, like 'Arsenal', it is a Venetian word: 'ghetto' derives from the word 'getto' meaning 'casting in metals', and there was an iron foundry here which preceded the Jewish quarter established in 1516. The name is poignantly apt, for in Hebrew 'ghetto' comes from the root for 'cut off'. And cut off its residents were in Venice, for the Ghetto is an island,

100

surrounded by a moat-like canal, and at night all Jews had to be within its windowless walls. Cramped for space, the houses were built tall, eerily presaging the ghetto tenements of centuries to come. But the Venetians did not invent the mentality behind the Ghetto even if they invented the name; Spanish Jews in the Middle Ages were segregated, as were the Jews in ancient Rome. Venetian law specifically protected Jewish citizens and forbade preachers to incite mobs against them—a common enough practice in the 16th century. Jewish refugees came to Venice from all over Europe, but though they were safe in Venice, they paid for it with high taxes and rents. When Napoleon threw open the gates of the Ghetto in 1797, it is said that the impoverished residents who remained were too weak to leave.

The island of the **Ghetto Nuovo**, the oldest section, is a melancholy place, its small campo often empty and forlorn. The ornate **Scuola Grande Tedesca** is the oldest of Venice's five synagogues (1528), and may be visited as part of the small **Jewish Community Museum** in the same building (10:30–1 and 2:30–5, closed Sat and Jewish holidays; adm).

Light years from the Ghetto in temperament, but only three minutes away on foot, the **Palazzo Labia** (by the 1580 **Ponte delle Guglie** and the garish lively Lista di Spagna, Venice's tourist highway) has a ballroom with Giambattista Tiepolo's lavish, sensuous *trompe l'oeil* frescoes on the life of Cleopatra. To visit, ring to make an appointment, tel 781 111. The adjacent campo is home to the 18th-century **San Geremia**, not much of a looker from the outside, but the last resting-place of the patroness of eyesight, Santa Lucia.

San Giorgio Maggiore and the Giudecca

The little islet of San Giorgio Maggiore, crowned by the **Church of San Giorgio** by Palladio, dominates the view of the lagoon from the Piazzetta San Marco (*vaporetto* Line 5). It's hard to imagine Venice without its pure white classical façade, hanging where it does, between the water and the sky, bathed by the light that varies it as magically as Monet's series on the Cathedral of Rouen. The equally classical white interior is relieved by Tintoretto's *Fall of Manna* and his celebrated *Last Supper* on the main altar, which is also notable for the fine carving on the Baroque choir stalls. A lift (10–12 and 2:30–6; adm) can whisk you to the top of the **campanile** for a remarkable view over Venice and the lagoon, and straight down into Palladio's stately cloister and refectory. The monastery is now the headquarters of the Giorgio Cini Foundation, dedicated to the arts and the sciences of the sea, and venue for frequent exhibitions; to visit, tel 528 9900 in advance.

La Giudecca (Line 5 or 8) consists of eight islands that curve gracefully like a Spanish *tilde* just south of Venice. Like Cannaregio, it's seldom visited by the throngs, though a few people wander over to see Palladio's best church, **Il Redentore**. In 1576, during a plague that slew 50,000, the doge and the senate vowed that if the plague ended, they would build a church and visit it in state once a year. In July a bridge of boats is constructed from the Zattere—still the most exciting event of the Venetian calendar. The church itself provides a fitting backdrop, with its classical façade, interlocking pediments, and interior designed after a Roman bath that suits the rest of the church.

ENTERTAINMENT

The tourist office's free booklet, *Un Ospite di Venezia*, contains an up-to-date calendar of current events, exhibitions, shows, films, and concerts in the city. Venice is one of Europe's top cities for exhibitions: major international shows have become the norm at the Palazzo Ducale and Palazzo Grassi, and high calibre art and photographic exhibitions frequently appear at the Palazzo Querini-Stampalia, Ca' Pésaro, Correr Museum, Museo Fortuny, Peggy Guggenheim Museum, and smaller ones in a host of churches.

Carnival Masks

Sadly, however, in a city made-to-order for nightlife and romance, the former 'revel of the earth' comes up so short that it drops off the charts. The locals make their evening stroll to Campo S. Bartolomeo, Riva degli Schiavoni, Piazza San Marco, or to their neighbourhood campo, for a chat with friends and an *aperitivo* before heading home to dinner and the dubious delights of Italian TV—the hotblooded may go to the clubs, discos, or bars in Mestre or Marghera. Visitors are left to become even poorer at the **Municipal Casino**, out on the Lido April–Oct, and other times at Palazzo Vendramin on the Grand Canal; hours are 3 pm–2 am, dress up and bring your passport. You may spend less more memorably on a moonlit gondola ride, or you can do as most people do—wander about. Venice is a different city at night, when the *bricole* lights in the lagoon are a fitting backdrop for a merking's birthday pageant. Main refuelling points are at one of the cafés in the Piazza San Marco or **Harry's Bar**, Calle Vallaresso, San Marco (especially if someone else is paying), or at Venice's celebrated old wine bar, **Enoteca Volta**, Calle Cavalli di San Marco 4081, with over two thousand Italian and foreign labels to choose from as well as an array of snacks; or try the icy fare at **Paolin**, in Campo S. Stefano, where pistachio ice cream is synonymous with divine.

Live jazz is regularly featured at **Da Codroma**, Fondamenta Briasti, in Dorsoduro; or at **Paradiso Perduto** at weekends (also inexpensive late-night dining, Fondamenta

Misericordia, Cannaregio). After midnight, there's the **Corner Pub** (till 2am), Calle della Chiesa, near the Guggenheim museum, Dorsoduro; **Vino Vino** (see below), or the adjacent, more up-market piano bar-night club, **Martini Scala Club**, next to La Fenice; or the equally up-market **Linea d'Ombra**, Zattere ai Saloni. In the summer there's a disco on the Lido: **Club 22**, Lungomare Marconi 22.

FESTIVALS

From December to May there's grand opera at **La Fenice** in Campo San Fantin, which also hosts concerts in the summer and a **Vivaldi Festival** in September. Late August–early September is marked by the **Venice International Film Festival**, followed on its heels by the **Festival of Contemporary Music**. Venice's most exciting festival, **Il Redentore** (see p. 101), takes place on the third Sunday of July, with fantastic fireworks and hundreds of boats. The first weekend of September sees a **regatta** in costume down the Grand Canal, which includes the traditional gondola race and enough pageantry to satisfy a doge. In 1988 Venice revived its ancient marriage to the sea ceremony, the *Sensa* (in May, on Ascension Day), but so far reports say it's more pompous than successful.

Venice's renowned **carnival** was revived in 1979 after several decades of dormancy, but has faced an uphill battle against the inherent Italian urge to make everything *bellissima*—at the expense of any serious carnival carousing and fun. Big-name celebrities perform at La Fenice, while in the streets and squares you can enjoy a variety of music, including Renaissance carnival madrigals, Commedia dell'Arte performances, but blessed little spontaneity. Posing in and taking photos of brilliant costumes and masks is what it's all about, and in response the art of making the masks has been revived in little workshops all over the city; even if you miss carnival a mask makes a good souvenir, either in inexpensive papier mâché (*carta pesta*) or in leather. Mask shops are hard to avoid, but for the real traditionally crafted McCoy, try **Giorgio Clanetti (Laboratorio Artigiano Maschere)**, on Barbaria delle Tole 6657, near SS. Giovanni e Paolo, Castello, or the master of them all **Emilio Massaro**, Calle Vitturi, by Campo Morosini, San Marco where you may watch them being made.

SHOPPING

Venice is a fertile field for shoppers, whether you're looking for tacky bric-à-brac to brighten up the den (just walk down the Lista di Spagna) or the latest in Italian design. A flea market appears periodically in Campo S. Maurizio, the principal antiques area. Most of the designer boutiques are located to the west of Piazza San Marco; fashion names like **Missoni**, Calle Vallaresso, S. Marco 1312, near Harry's Bar; **Elisabetta alla Fenice**, Campo San Fantin, San Marco 1996/1; **Krizia**, Calle delle Ostreghe, off Via XXII Marzo; **Laura Biagiotti**, Via XXII Marzo 2400a; **Trussardi**, on the Spadaria 695; **Gianni Versace**, Frezzeria 1722; the reasonably priced **Emporio Giorgio Armani**, Calle dei Fabbri 989; **Gianfranco Ferre**, Calle Largo di S. Marco 287. For fashions by maverick Italian and French designers, try **La Coupole**, Via XXII Marzo or Frezzeria 1674.

Most Venetians, however, buy their clothes at the **COIN** department store, a national chain based in the city (Rioterrà S. Leonardo, Cannaregio 5788). Fashionable second-hand clothes are the mainstay at **Aldo Strausse**, Campo S. Giustina, in Castello. **Emilio Ceccato**, Sottoportego di Rialto, S. Polo, is the place to buy gondoliers' shirts, jackets, and tight trousers. **Valli**, Merceria S. Zulian 783, S. Marco, not clothes, but designer silks and fabrics to create your own. Fortuny silk dresses were revived by **Fiorella Mancini**, Campo S. Stefano 2806, San Marco.

For posh shoes, **La Fenice**, Via XXII Marzo has a good selection by French and Italian designers; **Mario Valentino**, Ascensione 1255, has his own. The greatest name in Venetian leather is **Vogini**, Via XXII Marzo 1300. **Jesurum**, Ponte Canonica, S. Marco 4310, is a veritable cathedral of Venetian lace and linen, located in a 12th-century church just behind St Mark's basilica (though you'll pay less for lace at Burano).

Venice has a good collection of bookshops. **Fantoni**, Salizzada di S. Luca 4121, S. Marco, has a monumental display of monumental art books. **Il Libraio a San Barnaba**, Fondamenta Gherardini 2835/a, Dorsoduro, for Venice's best of books in English. **Sangiorgio**, Calle Larga XXII Marzo 2087, S. Marco, for books in English, especially about Venice. **Sansovino**, Bacino Orseolo 84 (just outside the Procuratie Vecchie), S. Marco, art and coffee-table books. **Serenissima**, Merceria dell'Orologia 739, S. Marco has a good selection of books about Venice in English. **Cartoleria Accademia**, Accademia 1052 on the Rio Terrà della Carità, Dorsoduro, is jam packed with paints, paper, easels, etc. for those who want to make their own souvenir of Venice.

Need an unusual gift? Try **La Scialuppa**, Calle Seconda dei Saoneri 2695, a little shop run by woodworker Gilberto Penzo, who carves beautiful *forcole*, or walnut gondola oar locks; or you can pick up a make-your-own little gondola kit, a replica of Venetian guild signs or a marine ex-voto, painted on wood. **Legatoria Piazzesi**, Santa Maria del Giglio 2511, San Marco, for beautiful marbled paper, papier mâché items, block prints etc. **Il Pastaio**, Calle del Varoteri 219, in the Rialto markets, sells bags of tagliatelle in a score of different colours, as does **Pastificio Artigiano**, Strada Nuova 4292, Cannaregio—*pasta al cacao* (chocolate pasta), or *pasta al limone* (lemon), or beetroot, garlic, mushroom, or curry.

WHERE TO STAY (tel prefix 041)

The rule of thumb in Venice is that in whatever class of hotel you lodge, expect it to cost at least a third more than it would on the mainland, even before the often outrageous charge for breakfast is added to the bill. Reservations are essential for Carnival, Christmas and New Year, Easter school holidays, and from June to October; many hotels close in the winter—those that stay open often send touts to the railway station to find clients, and with a bit of luck you can find a real bargain. The tourist office at the station has a free room-finding service; write to them for their list of agencies that rent self-catering flats in Venice and neighbouring resorts that you can reserve in advance.

Note: the prices given below are for doubles in the high season—which in Venice is from 15 March to 2 November, and from 12 December to 1 January. Singles, hard to find anywhere in Italy, are extremely difficult to scare up in Venice. If you arrive without reservations, start your room-hunt as early as possible—or stay in Padua, half an hour away by train. The tourist offices in the railway station and Piazzale Roma specialize in finding rooms, but again, if you intend to use their service try to arrive early before the crowds.

For pure luxury, no hotel in Venice can top the *****Hotel Cipriani**, at Giudecca 10, tel 520 7744 (UK reservations (071) 583 3050, US (800) 233 6800). This is the only hotel in the city with a swimming-pool (Olympic-sized and heated in the winter), as well as a lovely garden, tennis courts, sauna, and more to keep guests fit during their stay.

Rooms are modern and plush; suites are decorated in Venetian style. The Cipriani, built by the late Giuseppe Cipriani, founder of Harry's Bar, is so quiet and comfortable you may forget that Venice exists—though it's only 10 minutes away in the hotel's 24-hour private motor launch (L850 000, for the best doubles, down to 460 000; all rooms have views; closed 11 November–27 February). The restaurant, one of the best in Venice, features such delectables as fillet of sole Casanova and lobster rosettes (L120 000 and up). The *****Gritti Palace, 2467 Campo Santa Maria del Giglio, tel 794 611, once belonged to a 15th-century doge, Andrea Gritti, and now forms part of the CIGA chain. Across the Grand Canal from La Salute, the rooms are furnished with Venetian antiques and are all air-conditioned. Accommodation varies from elaborate, sumptuous suites facing the canal to small attic rooms with four-posters (L360 000–700 000). One of the delights of Venice is to dine on the Gritti's terrace at the **Club del Doge** (tel 522 6044), both for the food and the enchanting view (famous Venetian cuisine and exquisite scampi from L120 000).

Another CIGA hotel that formerly belonged to a doge, the *****Danieli (Riva degli Schiavoni 4196, tel 522 6480), can claim the most glorious location in Venice—on the basin of St Mark's, just a stone's throw behind the Doges' Palace. Although the unpleasant new wing still makes purists sniff, the decor is all oriental carpets, gilt mirrors, marbles, and a magnificent Gothic staircase (L380 000–600 000, depending on room). The rooftop restaurant, **Danieli Terrace** (tel 522 6480) features notable views, if not cuisine—avoid the 'international' entrées (L100 000 and up).

Tchaikovsky wrote his *Fourth Symphony* in the *****Londra Palace, Riva degli Schiavoni 4171, tel 520 0533. The elegant interior is relaxing, the lobby part English club, and the service better than you get at home—waterproof clothing and umbrellas for rainy days—and a member of the staff will even take you on a jogging tour of Venice. The hotel has an excellent restaurant, **Do Leoni** (tel 700 533) where you can have brunch or dinner. Delicious antipasto, *tagliatelle alla trota fumata* (smoked trout) and liver dishes in various forms—the American born maitre-d', Baronessa Sylvia von Block, can help you choose (L100 000). Its near neighbour, ****Hotel Metropole (Riva degli Schiavoni 4149, tel 520 5044) is a charmer, romantic (it even belongs to the Romantik chain) with its white and pink interior, wood-burning fire in the bar; the 64 rooms are furnished Venetian-style, and many overlook the lagoon (L220 000–330 000, 40–50 per cent discount from Nov to mid-March).

An old Venetian favourite, ***La Fenice et Des Artistes, Campiello della Fenice 1935, tel 523 2333, has the opera house as its neighbour, as well as elegant period furnishings that are also comfortable, terraces, and a secluded courtyard where you can linger over breakfast or a drink (L160 000, all with bath). Another charming little hotel, ***Hotel Flora, Calle Bergamaschi 2283a, tel 520 5844, is central—a block away from the Grand Canal, near Calle Larga XXII Marzo—but also quiet; it has one of Venice's most delightful gardens, with old stone fountains and climbing vines, where guests enjoy the hotel's breakfasts. When reserving, request one of the large, traditionally furnished rooms—others are more fit for midgets (L85 000–120 000 without bath, L120 000–145 000 with; prices much lower in the off season).

***Do Pozzi (Corte do Pozzi, S. Marco 2373, just off the Via XXII Marzo, tel 520 7855), often reminds people more of an Italian country inn than a Venetian hotel, with its pretty paved courtyard—and yet it's centrally located between the Grand Canal and

St Mark's. Bedrooms are spruce, bathrooms are very modern, and every room has air conditioning and a bar—and over half are singles (doubles L120 000–145 000; off season discounts). For a generous dollop of slightly faded charm, try the ***Accademia-Villa Maravegie**, Fondamenta Bollani 1058, in Dorsoduro, tel 521 0188. Located in a 17th-century villa just off the Grand Canal, with a shady garden along a small side canal, the Accademia has only 26 rooms, furnished with a menagerie of antiques, some of which look as if they had been left behind by the villa's previous occupant—the Russian Embassy. Only breakfast is served, but there's a friendly bar as well (L65 000–85 000 without bath, L100 000–130 000 with, less in the off season). Another moderate choice in a quiet area, **Mignon**, SS. Apostoli 4535 in Cannaregio, not far from the Ca' d'Oro, tel 523 7388, has a garden for tranquil breakfasts; rooms are adequate (L55–65 000 without bath, L68–80 000 with). An old Venetian home in Dorsoduro was converted by the Seguso family into the **Pensione Seguso** (Zattere al Gesuati, Dorsoduro 779, tel 522 2340). Rooms in the front overlook the bustling Giudecca canal, while side rooms have views of one of its 'tributaries'; inside, the Seguso has plenty of character, antiques, and there's a small terrace outside where you can have breakfast. Open March–Nov, half-board is mandatory but a Venetian bargain at the price: L120 000 per person in a bathless room, L140 000 in a room with bath.[ep]

Budget-minded travellers camp out by the thousands on Cavallino and at Fusina, or seek out the numerous *locandas* in Venice's alleyways. One of the best choices, if you reserve one of its seven rooms well in advance is the *Locanda Montin**, one of the last traditional old Venetian hostelries. Located in Dorsoduro, on the Fondamenta di Borgo 1147, tel 522 7151, bathless doubles are L50 000, and there's a superb restaurant at the back, though meals tend to cost as much as, if not more than, the rooms. Another seven-room wonder, *Casa Verardo**, Ruga Giuffa 4765 in Castello, tel 528 6127, is a classy locanda with friendly owners (L35 000), no private baths. *Locanda Sturion**, Calle del Sturion 679 in San Polo, tel 523 6243, is another excellent choice, the only bargain on the Grand Canal. Fine, large doubles go from L32 000–50 000, no private baths. *Silva**, on one of the prettiest little canals, between S. Zaccaria and S. Maria Formoso (Fondamenta Remedio 4423, Castello, tel 522 7643) is quiet though only a few minutes' walk from Piazza S. Marco; an aloof black cat presides over the breakfast room (L50 000, L60 000 with bath). Families are welcome at *Casa Messner**, very close to the Salute (Dorsoduro 237, tel 522 7443); recently remodelled rooms, Venice's best one-star showers and the worst coffee in Italy (L54 000 without bath, L75 000 with).

There's also a shiny bright **Youth Hostel**, on the Giudecca, overlooking the water (Fondamenta delle Zitelle 86, tel 523 8211; in the summer you should arrive by 3 pm to get a bed). IYHF cards required—L12 000 per head, breakfast included; L8000 meals also available.

EATING OUT
Venetian cuisine is based on fish, shellfish, and rice, often mixed together in a succulent seafood risotto. *Risi i bisi* (rice and peas) is perhaps the best known Venetian dish, often served with anchovy sauce, as is *bigoli*, the local vermicelli; for *secondo*, liver (*fegato alla veneziana*) with polenta (*tecia*) shares top billing with scampi, Sile eel, cuttlefish in its own ink (*seppie alla veneziana*), *fritto* (Adriatic mixed fry) and lobster (*aragosta*). Bitter red *radicchio* (chicory) is a favourite side-dish, and most restaurants feature excellent red

wines from the Veneto or whites from Friuli. Top it all off with a *tiramisù*, a traditional Venetian chilled dessert of chocolate, coffee, and cream.

Venice is famous for its bad restaurants, and the few really good ones tend to be astronomically expensive. Like her hotels, Venice's restaurants tend to be more expensive than the mainland norm (not altogether because they batten on tourists—transport and handling charges add 30 per cent to the cost of food). Even the moderate ones are liable to give you a nasty surprise at *conto* time with their excessive service and cover charges. The cheap ones, serving up 500 tourist menus a day to the international throng, are more filling than memorable (pizza is usually a safe bet). In the summer, be sure to make reservations to avoid disappointment.

There are several candidates for the best restaurant in Venice (several are in the hotels listed above), but one that makes nearly everyone's list is **Antico Martini**, near La Fenice in Campo San Fantin (tel 522 4121). All romance and elegance, it started out as a Turkish coffeehouse in the early 18th century but nowadays is better known for its excellent seafood and *pennette al pomodoro*. Excellent wine list; a full meal is around L110 000; its intimate piano-bar restaurant stays open until 2 am. For sheer variety of local and exotic dishes, prepared by a master chef, few restaurants in Italy can top **La Caravella**, Calle XXII Marzo, S. Marco 2397, an annexe to the Saturnia hotel (tel 708 901). Here, in this perfect reproduction of a dining hall in a 16th-century Venetian galley, you can try bouillabaisse, Turkish stuffed calamari, French onion soup, gazpacho, or the house's famous *bigoli*, followed by scampi in champagne or the delicious chicken in a paper bag (*en papillote*). The atmosphere is formal; meals with wine L90 000. For many Italians as well as foreigners, the **Trattoria Do Forni**, Calle dei Specchieri, S. Marco 468, tel 523 2148, is *the* place to eat. Its two dining rooms, one 'Orient Express'-style and the other rustic, are always filled with diners partaking of its excellent seafood antipasti, polenta, and well-prepared fish (L85 000).

Another, more moderately priced trattoria, **Corte Sconta** is off the beaten track in Calle del Pestrin, Castello 3886, tel 522 7024. Its fame rests solidly on its exquisite molluscs and crustacean dishes, served in a setting that's a breath of fresh air after the exposed beams and copper pots that dominate the typical Venetian restaurant decor. The Venetians claim the Corte Sconta is even better in the off season; be sure to order the house wine (L55 000). Another restaurant that marches to a different drummer is the tiny **Trattoria Vini da Arturo**, on the infamous Calle degli Assassini, S. Marco 3656 near La Fenice (tel 528 6974). It closes for half of August and on Sundays, when most restaurants are busiest, and it has not a speck of seafood on the menu. Instead, try the *tagliatelle al radicchio* and *stinco* (shin) *all'Amarone*, or Venice's best steaks; its *tiramisù* is famous (L55 000). **Antica Besseta**, Calle Salvio, Santa Croce 1395, tel 721 687, is a family-run citadel of Venetian homecooking, where you can experience an authentic *risi e bisi*, or *bigoli in salsa*, scampi, and the family's own wine for around L50 000.

For exceptional food and wine, however, Italian gourmets head out to Mestre to dine at least once at **Dall'Amelia**, Via Miranese 113, tel 913 951, which not only serves up delicious oysters and a divine *tortelli di branzino* (bass), but offers a choice of wine from one of Italy's most renowned cellars. Depending on what you order and drink, L60 000.

In a class by itself is the celebrated **Harry's Bar**, Via Vallaresso, San Marco 1323 (tel 523 6797), as much a Venetian institution as the Doges' Palace, though food has become secondary to its friendly, nostalgic atmosphere. The menu is short, beginning with the house cocktail (a Bellini, Tiziano, or Tiepolo—delectable fruit juices mixed with Prosecco), followed by antipasti (the *carpaccio* (raw beef) is especially good), risotto, baked lamb, liver, or scampi. Try to get one of the tables downstairs near the bar—upstairs is more formal (L90–100 000).

Moderate Restaurants

Well worth the trouble of getting lost several times en route, the excellent **Hostaria da Franz** is located in one of the quieter corners of the city on the Fondamenta San Isepo, Castello 754, tel 522 7505. Here the kitchen has yet to forget some of the advantages of the Austrian occupation—especially in the strudels and gnocchi. The house wine, a delicate Tocai, can't be bettered (L40 000). For a scrumptious seafood feast, it's worth buying a detailed map to find **La Furatola**, Calle Lunga S. Barnaba, Dorsoduro 2870, tel 520 8594; it's small, and closed for all of July and August, but the fish are jumping (or almost) as you select one that strikes your fancy (L35 000). Rather harder to find, behind the church of S. Cassiano at Santa Croce 2315, the **Antico Giardinetto da Erasmo** (tel 721 301), features delicious fresh seafood, in the form of antipasto or as a main course, cooked in a variety of styles. In good weather you can eat out in the little garden (closed July and August, L25 000). Also far from the maddening crowds on the Giudecca, is the fine old **Altanella** (Rio de Ponte Lungo 268, tel 522 7780), where the *risotto di pesce* and *fritto* are worth the trip (L25 000–30 000). At Cannaregio 5906, the intimate **Trattoria Tre Spiedi** offers a cosy atmosphere, *spaghetti alla veneziana* and *bracciola Bruno* for L35 000 (on Salizzada S. Canciano, near the Campiello F. Corner and the central post office).

There are several reasonably priced restaurants where even the budget-oppressed can shell out for a sit-down meal in Venice. **Vino Vino** is an economical new feature of the expensive Antico Martino (same address and phone), where you can eat a well-cooked filling main dish with a glass of good wine for L14 000 or even less. Dorsoduro's **Due Torre**, Campo S. Margherita 3408, tel 523 8126, offers a fine *spaghetti alle vongole* and *baccalà* (codfish) meal with wine for L20 000. For the same price you can dine on Venetian specialities at the **Trattoria della Donna Onesta**, Calle della Donna Onesta, Dorsoduro 3922, tel 522 9586. **Acciugheta da Fabiano**, Campo SS. Filippo e Giacomo, Castello, tel 522 4292, is one of the best cheap restaurants and bars near the piazza; L16 000, pizzas around L5000.

For pizza, no place comes near the variety served at **Alle Oche**, Calle del Tinto, behind the church of S. Giacomo dell'Orio (S. Croce 1552, tel 524 1161). In season get there early, except on Mon when it's closed (L8000). Another popular place for pizza, **Casa Mia**, Calle dell'Oca near Campo SS. Apostoli (Cannaregio 4430, tel 528 5590) is lively, and the pizzas aren't bad either (closed Tues, L8000).

The Lagoon and its Islands

Pearly and melting into the bright sky, iridescent blue, or murky green, a sheet of glass yellow and pink in the dawn, or just plain grey: Venice's lagoon is one of its wonders, a desolate, often melancholy and strange, often beautiful and seductive 'landscape' with a hundred personalities. It is 56 km long and averages about 8 km across, adding up to some 448 square km; half of it, the Laguna Morta ('Dead Lagoon') consists of mud flats

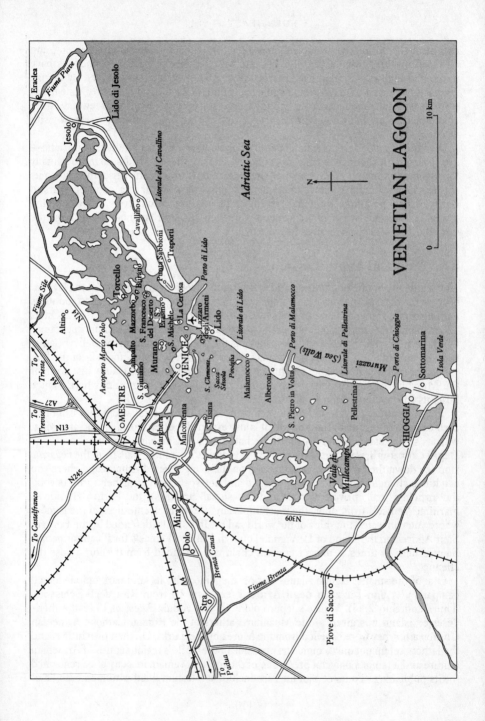

VENETIAN LAGOON

except in the spring, while the shallows of the Laguna Viva are always present, and cleansed by tides twice a day. To navigate this treacherous sea, the Venetians have developed highways of channels, marked by *bricole*—wooden posts topped by orange lamps—that keep their craft from running aground. Once the islands (thirty-nine in all) were densely inhabited, occupied by a town or a monastery. Now all but a few have been abandoned; many a tiny one, with its forlorn shell of a building, has been overgrown with weeds.

Weeds of a more desperate nature—algae, the curse of the post-industrial Adriatic—are threatening the lagoon and its economy, choking its fish and stinking out many tourists in the summer. This, on top of the toxins from industry and agriculture along its shores, makes a lethal mixture that local ecologists warn will take a hundred years to purify, if new pollution, by some miracle, stops pouring in tomorrow. It's a sobering thought, especially when many Venetians in their forties remember when even the Grand Canal was clean enough to swim in.

The Lido and South Lagoon

The Lido, one of the long spits of land that form the protective outer edge of the lagoon, is by far the most glamorous island of the lagoon, one that has given its name to countless bathing establishments, bars, amusement arcades and cinemas all over the world. On its 12 km of beach, the poets, potentates and plutocrats of the turn of the century spent their holidays in palatial hotels and villas, making the Lido the pinnacle of Belle Epoque fashion, so brilliantly evoked in Thomas Mann's *Death in Venice* and Visconti's film version of it. The story was set and filmed in the **Grand Hotel des Bains**, just north of the Mussolini-style **Municipal Casino** and the **Palazzo de Cinema**, where Venice hosts its International Film Festival.

The Lido is the playground of the Venetians and their visitors, where they can drive their cars, go riding, play tennis or golf; it is also expensive, often crowded, and annoying, with its sticky, status hierarchy of private bathing establishments. The free beach, the **Bagni Comunali**, is on the north part of the island, a 15-minute walk from the *vaporetto* stop (go down the Gran Viale and turn left on the Lungomare d'Annunzio), where you can hire a changing hut and enjoy fine sand and not-so-fine sea. Further north, beyond the airfield (small, private aircraft and occasional airshows), the Porto del Lido is maritime Venice's front door, the most important of the three entrances to the lagoon, where you can watch the ships of the world sail by. It is stoutly defended by the Forte di Sant'Andrea on the island of Le Vignole, built in 1543 by Venice's fortifications genius Sammicheli. In times of danger, a great chain was extended from the fort across the channel.

One of the smaller lagoon islands just off the Lido, with its landmark onion-domed campanile, is **San Lazzaro degli Armeni** (*vaporetto* 10 from Riva degli Schiavoni, Thurs and Sun 2:45). Venice's leper colony in the Middle Ages, in 1715 the then-deserted island was given to the Mechitar Fathers of the Roman Catholic Armenian Church after they were expelled from the Morea by the Turks. On their own little island the fathers set up not only a monastery but one of the world's major centres of Armenian culture and a famous polyglot press, one of the few that remain in a city once renowned for its publishing. Tours of San Lazzaro include a museum filled with memorabilia of

Lord Byron, who spent a winter visiting the fathers and bruising his brain with Armenian.

Buses/ferries (Line 11) from the Lido's *vaporetto* landing run all the way to Chioggia, passing through **Malamocco**, a tranquil fishing village named after one of the first lagoon townships (the original sank into the sea in the 11th century) and the small resort of **Alberoni**, home of the Lido Golf Course.

A ferry takes the bus across the Porto di Malamocca to an even thinner island reef, **Pellestrina**, with two sleepy villages, **S. Pietro in Volta** and **Pellestrina**, where you can see the impressive sea walls, the **Murazzi**, the last great public works project of the republic, constructed of huge, white Istrian blocks and built, as their plaque proudly states: 'Ausu Romano—Aere Veneto' ('With Roman audacity and Venetian money').

WHERE TO STAY   (tel prefix 041)

In 1907, the *******Excelsior** (Lungomare Marconi 41, tel 526 0201) was built on the Lido as the biggest and most luxurious resort hotel in the world. Stylistically it wavers between post-Gothic-Egyptian and neo-Moorish, and the interior is designed with a solemn flamboyance to match. Forget all the puffy clouds and cherubs in those Renaissance heavens—to the average upwardly mobile Italian of today, this is paradise. Come at the end of August to ogle the film stars (a CIGA hotel, open April to Oct; pool, beach, tennis, golf, private launch service to Venice, piano bar and nightclub. L350–600 000). CIGA has also snapped up the other *grande dame* on the Lido, the vast *******Hotel Des Bains** (Lungomare Marconi 17, tel 765 921), which preserves much of its Belle Epoque reveries in its great Liberty-style lobby, dining room, private cabanas, and garden designed for dalliance. There's an attractive sea-water swimming-pool, golf, tennis, and more (open April–Oct; L250–520 000).

More intimate and charming, the very, very popular ******Quattro Fontane** (Via 4 Fontane 16, tel 526 0227) was formerly the seaside villa of a Venetian family. Its white stucco exterior and green shutters and its cool walled-in courtyard are inviting and tranquil, the public and private rooms are sophisticated and decorated with antiques. (Open April–Sept; rooms are L180–200 000 without bath, and L260–300 000 with.) Another, less pretentious villa, the *****Pensione Villa Parco** (Via Rodi 1, tel 526 0015) is a block from the beach and has a fine little garden for a bit of privacy—and children are welcome (L55–68 000 without bath, L72–82 000 with bath).

Chioggia

Line 11 from the Lido (see above) or buses from Piazzale Roma will take you to Chioggia, the southernmost town on the lagoon. Chioggia is one of the most important fishing ports on the Adriatic, a kind of working-class Venice where the canals and streets are arrow straight; where the sails of the fishing fleet are painted with brightly coloured pictures and symbols; where the morning **fish market**, brimming with some of Neptune's most exotic and tastiest fry, is one of the wonders of Italy.

The Chioggians have a not entirely undeserved reputation for grumpiness, a temperament that is hardly improved when the uppity Venetians call their little lion up on its column in the Piazzetta Vigo the 'Cat of St Mark'. Goldoni was amused enough by it all to make the town the setting of one of his comedies, the *Baruffe Chizzotte*. And when you've had your fill of fish and the locals, you can stroll along the long bridge to Chioggia's resort island **Sottomarina**, or its more rural cousin **Isola Verde**, for a swim.

EATING OUT

There is, among the fish restaurants of Chioggia, an outstanding choice, both for the variety of seafood and price: the **Trattoria Buon Pesce**, Stradale Ponte Caneva 625, tel (041) 400 861 where you can start with *gnocchetti alla marinara* and follow it with oysters, crab or whatever the waiter suggests. The atmosphere is traditional; full meals begin at L25 000.

Islands in the North Lagoon

Most Venetian itineraries take in the islands of Murano, Burano, and Torcello, all easily reached by inexpensive public transport. Nearest is the cyprus-studded cemetery island, **San Michele** (Line 5), with its simple but elegant church of **San Michele in Isola** by Mauro Codussi (1469), his first known work, inspired by the Florentine Renaissance, albeit with a Venetian twist in the tri-lobed façade. Within is buried Fra Paolo Sarpi (d. 1623), Venice's most famous thinker, the philosopher who led the ideological battle against the pope during the Great Interdict of 1607, in a major duel of secular v. church authority. Venice, considering St Mark the equal of St Peter, had her priests say Mass despite the Interdict and eventually won the battle of wills, thanks mainly to Sarpi, who also wrote the famous *History of the Council of Trent*, discovered the contraction of the iris and helped Galileo build his first telescope.

In the cemetery you can visit the tombs of some of the many foreigners who preferred to face eternity from Venice, among them Ezra Pound, Serge Diaghilev, Frederick Rolfe (Baron Corvo) and Igor Stravinsky; signs point the way.

Murano

The island of Murano (see 'Getting Around') is synonymous with glass, the most celebrated of Venice's industries. The Venetians were the first in the Middle Ages to rediscover the secret of making crystal glass, and especially mirrors, and it was a secret they kept a monopoly on for centuries—helped by dark rumours that if a glassmaker let himself be coaxed abroad, the Council of Ten sent their assassins after him in hot pursuit.

However, those who remained in Venice were treated with kid gloves. Because of the danger of fire, all the forges in Venice were relocated to Murano in 1291, and the little island became a kind of republic within a republic—minting its own coins, policing itself, even developing its own nobility listed in its own Golden Book—aristocrats of glass, who built solid palaces along Murano's own Grand Canal. But glass-making declined like everything else in Venice, and only towards the end of the 19th century were the forges once more stoked up on Murano. Can you visit them? You betcha! In fact, a trip to the glass-blowers' is the single most touristy thing you can do in Venice. After watching the glass being made, there's the inevitable tour of the 'Museum Show Rooms'; these have the same atmosphere as a funeral parlour, all respect and solicitude, carpeting and hush-hush—not unfitting, for some of the blooming chandeliers, befruited mirrors, saccharine clowns, and poison-coloured chalices begin to make Death look good.

Yet among Murano's more mawkish and aberrant wares you can find some genuinely good stuff, and it's not even all repros of the classical past on display in the island's **Museo Vetrario** (10–4, Sun 9–12:30, closed Wed; adm) in the Renaissance Palazzo Giustinian. You can see glass that has survived both Roman times and 15th-century Venice, including the delightful 1470 Barovier *Marriage Cup*; some of the later glass goes to show that Murano's glass-blowers have long had a wayward streak (save your ticket for the new **Modern and Contemporary Glass** annexe, on the Fondamenta Manin, opposite Fondamenta Vetrai).

Nearby stands the primary reason to visit this rather dowdy island, the Veneto-Byzantine **Santi Maria e Donato**, a contemporary of St Mark's basilica, with a beautiful arcaded apse. Its floor is paved with a marvellous 12th-century mosaic, incorporating coloured pieces of ancient Murano glass, and on the wall there's a fine Byzantine mosaic of the Virgin. The relics of the other titular saint, Bishop Donato of Euboea, were part of yet another haul of the Venetian relic robbers, but in this case they outdid themselves, bringing home not only S. Donato's bones but those of the dragon the good bishop slew with a gob of spit; you can see them behind the altar.

A bridge over Murano's Grand Canal crosses to the Fondamenta dei Vetrai, the main glass bazaar and site of **San Pietro Martire**, a 15th-century church with a lovely Giovanni Bellini (*Madonna, Child, and saints*), an audience of Dominican saints frescoed in the nave and, in the sacristy, some elaborate 17th-century carvings of pagans and John the Baptist.

Burano

Burano (Line 12 from the Fondamente Nuove) is the Lego-land of the lagoon, where everything is in brightly coloured miniature—the canals, the bridges, the leaning tower, and the houses, painted with a Fauvist sensibility in the deepest of colours. Traditionally on Burano the men fish and the women make Venetian point, 'the most Italian of all lace work', beautiful, intricate and murder on the eyesight. All over Burano you can find samples on sale (as well as a lot that's machine-made or imported), or you can watch it being made at the **Scuola Merletti** in Piazza Galuppi (open 9–6, closed Tues; adm), though 'scuola' is misleading—no young woman in Burano wants to learn such an excruciating art. In the sacristy of the **Church of San Martino** (of the leaning campanile) look for Giambattista Tiepolo's *Crucifixion*, which Mary McCarthy aptly describes as 'a ghastly masquerade ball'.

From Burano you can hire a *sandola* (small gondola) to **San Francesco del Deserto**, some 20 minutes to the south. On this islet St Francis is said to have founded a monastery in 1220, on his return from the east. You can visit the friars from 9–11 and 3–5:30, but in true Franciscan fashion, it's not the buildings you'll remember, but the love of nature evident in the beautiful gardens.

WHERE TO STAY AND EATING OUT   (tel prefix 041)

There's one six-room *locanda* on Burano, the **Raspo de Ua**, Via Galuppi 560, tel 730 095; although it's simple, it offers the chance to know Burano after the tourists have gone. Doubles without bath are L52 000; telephone in advance. Burano is better known for its fish trattorias, especially the **Trattoria dei Pescatori**, Via Galuppi 371, tel 730 650, which has retained its simple decor while concentrating on a vast seafood menu, that depends on the catch (closed Mon; L45 000).

Torcello

Though fewer than a hundred people remain on Torcello (Line 12), this small island was once a serious rival to Venice herself. Its history tells how God ordered the bishop of Altinum (the old Roman town near Mestre) to take his flock away from the heretical Lombards into the lagoon. In its heyday Torcello had 20,000 inhabitants, palaces, a mercantile fleet and five townships; but malaria decimated the population, the Sile silted up Torcello's corner of the lagoon, and the rising star of Venice drew its citizens to the Rialto.

Torcello is a ghost island overgrown with weeds, its palaces either sunk into the marsh or quarried for their stone, its narrow paths all that remain of once bustling thorough-fares. One of these follows a canal from the landing-stage, past the picturesque Ponte del Diavolo to the grass-grown piazza and the main reason for visiting Torcello, its magnifi-cent Veneto-Byzantine cathedral, now simply **Santa Maria Assunta**. Serene by its lofty campanile, the church was founded in 639 and rebuilt in the same Ravenna basilica-style in 1008. The interior (10–12:30 and 2–4:30, summer 2–6:30; adm) has the best mosaics in Venice, all done by 11th-century Greek artists, from the wonderful floor, to the grand tragi-comic *Last Judgement* on the west wall, to the unsettling, heart-rending *Teotoco*, the stark, gold-ground mosaic of the thin, weeping Virgin portrayed as the 'bearer of God'. On the left side of the high altar, a bit of poking around will reveal some curious marble reliefs—a winged wheel among them.

Next to the cathedral is the restored 12th-century church of **Santa Fosca**, a Greek cross surrounded by an attractive portico, sheltering a serendipitously calm interior. Near here stands the ancient stone throne called the **Chair of Attila**; in the spring the basin in front of the cathedral is full of frogs. Across the square from the cathedral the old Palazzo del Consiglio now contains the small **Museo dell'Estuario** (10–12:30 and 2–5:30, closed Mon; adm) with a collection of archaeological finds and medieval artefacts from Torcello's former churches.

WHERE TO STAY AND EATING OUT

In season, a motor-boat leaves at 12:20 from the Danieli Hotel to transport lunch patrons to Torcello's **Locanda Cipriani**, a 'simple, rustic inn'. Actually, though the tables may be of wood, this is one of Venice's most renowned restaurants, and the great ebb and flow of tourists dissipates much of the rusticity as well. Be that as it may, you can feast rather grandly on a tasty seafood risotto or gnocchi, two of the chef's specialities (L90 000 and up). There are six very comfortable three-star rooms to rent as well (tel 730 150, L150 000); the *locanda* is open from mid-March–Nov. Otherwise, bring a picnic and pick up a drink at one of the few bars.

Cavallino and Jesolo

The Litorale del Cavallino, the 10-km peninsula that protects the northern part of the lagoon, was long known as a semi-wild place of beach, sand dunes and pine forests.

There's still some of that left, among the 28 camping grounds, hotels and restaurants. There are two ports on the *litorale*: **Punta Sabbioni** (Line 14 to the Lido and the Riva degli Schiavoni) and **Treporti** (Line 12 Torcello, Burano, Murano and Venice Fondamente Nuove). **Lido di Jesolo** is a far more developed and densely packed resort. Buses connect the Jesolo with Punta Sabbioni to coincide with the ferries.

Villas along the Brenta

In *The Merchant of Venice*, Portia, disguised as a young male lawyer, left her villa of Belmont on the Brenta Canal and proceeded down to Fusina to preserve Antonio's pound of flesh. For about the same price you can trace her route on the stately villa-lined Brenta in the modern version of the patricians' canal boat, the *Burchiello*, which makes the day-long excursion from the end of March to the end of Oct, Tues, Thurs, and Sat from Venice, and Wed, Fri, and Sun from Padua. The journey may be booked through any travel agent or CIT office abroad; the considerable price includes admission into the three villas open to the public, lunch, guide, and coach back to the city of origin. You can make the same excursion on your own, less romantically and far less expensively, along the road that follows the canal, by car or public bus from Piazzale Roma.

Often called an extension of the Grand Canal, the Brenta Canal was one of the choice locations among the Venetian patricians to go a-squiring in the country and still be within easy communication with the city; over seventy villas and palaces lie on or just off the waterway. The classical proportions and stately symmetry that are the hallmarks of Palladio were especially suited to the land and the Venetians' conceit, and his celebrated, temple-fronted 1560 Villa Foscari, better known as **La Malcontenta** was a major influence on all subsequent 17th- and 18th-century villa architecture. Viewed from the canal, the villa is a vision begging for a Scarlett O'Hara to sweep down the steps—not all that surprising, for Palladio's *Quattro Libri dell'Architettura* were Bibles for the 18th-century builders of America's old plantation homes, as well as for the important Palladian movement in Britain, led by Inigo Jones. (Located between Fusina and Oriago, La Malcontenta is open May–Oct on Tues, Sat, and the first Sun of each month from 9–12; adm expensive.)

Further up the canal lies the town of Mira Ponte, the site of the 18th-century **Villa Widmann-Foscari** (open 9–12 and 2–6, closed Mon; guided tours; adm expensive). If you only have time for one villa, don't make it this one—redone soon after its construction in the French Baroque style, the villa contains some sticks of its original furniture and bright, gaudy murals by two of Tiepolo's pupils. Mira's post office occupies the **Palazzo Foscarini**, Byron's address while working on sections of *Childe Harold*.

'If you've got it, flaunt it,' was the rule in Venice even into the 18th century, when one of the grandest villas in the entire Veneto region went up at **Stra**: the **Villa Nazionale (or Pisani)**, built by the fabulously wealthy Pisani banking family to celebrate the election of one of their own, Alvise Pisani, as doge. More of a royal palace than a country manor, it was completed in 1760, in time to be purchased by Napoleon for his viceroy Eugène Beauharnais; in 1934 it was chosen by Mussolini as a suitable stage for his historic first meeting with Hitler. Although most of the villa has been stripped of its decoration, the ballroom absolves most of the boredom with one of Giambattista Tiepolo's most shimmering frescoes, depicting (what else?) the *Apotheosis of the Pisani* *family* (open Tues–Sun 9–1; group tours; adm); its vast park (open to 6) contains the monumental stables and one of Italy's finest mazes.

EATING OUT   (tel prefix 041)

One of the traditional ways to round off an excursion along the Brenta Riviera is to dine on the lovely poplar-shaded veranda of the **Ristorante Nalin**, Via Novissimo 29, Mira, tel 420 083. The emphasis is on Venetian seafood, finely grilled; good Veneto wines as well (L40–60 000; closed Mon and Aug). Nearby, at *****Hotel Villa Margherita**, Via Nazionale 312, tel 420 879, you can live the life of a Venetian patrician, or simply stop off at the restaurant, where seafood reigns, prepared in a thousand different ways, accompanied by wines from Friuli's Collio region (L50–70 000, closed Wed and Jan; rooms L90–150 000).

a tropical habitat (March–Nov, 9:30–7; adm expensive). The other two spas—**Battaglia Terme** located in a small industrial town, and new, slick **Galzignano** were discovered after the Romans. Battaglia's villa-cum-castle, **Il Cataio**, was built in the 1570s and is noted for the elephant fountain in its garden. Near Galzignano, the tiny village of **Valsanzibio** has both a lovely 18-hole golf course and the lovely park and garden maze of the **Villa Barbarigo**, laid out in 1699 (open 15 March–31 Oct, 9–12 and 3–7, closed Sun and Mon mornings; adm).

Because of their unique conditions, the Euganean Hills are home to some interesting flora, highlighted in the natural park-botanical garden **Lieta Papafava da Carraresi**, located around **Teolo** (Livy's birthplace), on the jagged, western flank of the hills. Another fine villa, the **Villa dei Vescovi**, is over the hill to the east of Teolo in **Luvigliano**; designed in the early 16th century by Falconetto, it is a scenographic masterpiece that greatly influenced Palladio (open by request, tel (049) 521 1118; adm).

To the south on the N. 16 lies the prettiest village in the Euganean Hills, **Arquà Petrarca**. The world-weary Petrarch, accompanied by his daughter Francesca, chose Arquà as his last home; his villa, the charming **Casa del Petrarca**, given to him by the Carraresi, still preserves much of its 14th-century structure and furnishings. Later admirers added the frescoes illustrating his works, and you can browse over the autographs of some of the house's famous visitors. Even the delightful view has changed little since the days of the great poet (open 9:30–12:30 and 3:30–7:30 in the summer; 9:30–12:30 and 1:30–4:30 in the winter, closed Mon; adm). Petrarch died here in 1374 and is entombed in a simple marble sarcophagus near the church.

WHERE TO STAY AND EATING OUT (tel prefix 049)

All of the thermal establishments in the Euganean Hills have hot pools, gardens, and therapists on duty to shoot jets of water through your sinuses, but none can match the class and traditions of Abano Terme's ******Grand Hotel Orologio**, Viale delle Terme 66, tel 669 111, with an 1825 neoclassical façade by Japelli. In business for over two hundred years, the hotel offers an exotic variety of baths and mud treatments. So peaceful are its large park and verdant, landscaped pools that it attracts many guests who seek only tranquillity and supreme comfort, and don't mind paying around L250 000 a double a night for it (closed Dec–Feb). If you do mind, *****All'Alba**, Via Valerio Flacco 32, also in Abano, tel 669 244, is a comfortable hotel with all modern facilities and a pool; L80 000.

The health-filled environment of the spas is not the place to look for a good meal, though the local wines may tempt you to abuse your liver: there are seven white and red DOC *Colli Euganei* wines, all bearing the symbol of Gattamelata on the label. Save your appetite for Arquà Petrarca and the lovely **La Montanella**, Via Costa 33, tel (0429) 718 200, where you can enjoy not only the garden and view over the village itself, but an exquisite risotto and well prepared game dishes (L40 000; closed Thurs eve and Wed).

South of the Euganean Hills to the Po Delta

GETTING AROUND

For Monsélice (23 km), Este (32 km), Montagnana (52 km) and Rovigo (45 km) you can choose bus or train, both of which take about the same time, though with the train you may have to change at Monsélice.

TOURIST INFORMATION
Monsélice: Piazza Mazzini
Este: Piazza Maggiore, tel (0429) 3635
Montagnana: Piazza Trieste 3, tel (0429) 81 320

Monsélice

On the southern slopes of the Euganean Hills the natural volcanic citadel of **Monsélice** was first fortified by the Romans who gave it its name, *Mons silicis*. In its heyday it bristled with five concentric rings of walls and 30 towers, built by Frederick II's henchman, Ezzelino da Romano, to control the road linking Padua to Este; most fell victim to medieval Italy's biggest enemy—19th century town planners. Still, the citadel that remains is one of the finest and best restored in the northeast.

From the station, an iron bridge crosses the canal to the centre of town; just here you can see part of the outer ring of walls and the one surviving tower, the **Torre Civica** (1244). On the other side of this is Monsélice's arcaded **Piazza Mazzini**. From here, Via del Santuario leads up to the **Castello di Ezzelino/Ca' Marcello** (open for guided tours, April–Sept, Tues, Thurs, Sat at 9, 10:30, 3:30 and 5, Sun morning only; Oct–Nov same days, 9, 10:30, 2:30, and 4; adm). First built in the 11th century, it was expanded into a castle-residence by Ezzelino, and re-decorated by the Carraresi in the 14th century; and in this century, when it was on its last legs, it came down to industrialist and art patron Count Vittorio Cini, who restored it according to his charmingly romantic view of the Middle Ages. Furnishings were brought in to match the period and frescoes—medieval and Renaissance arms, antiques, tapestries, kitchen utensils.

Further up Via del Santuario passes the Baroque **Palazzo Nani-Mocenigo**, with its monumental pseudo-Roman stair, and the 13th-century **Duomo Vecchio**. This is next to the **Lion Gate**, the entrance to Vincenzo Scamozzi's unusual **Via Sacra delle Sette Chiese**, a private road leading up to his elegant **Villa Duodo** (grounds open mornings until noon, and Nov—Feb 1:30–7; Mar–May & Sept–Oct 1:30–7, summer 3:30–8). A condensed version of the seven churches of Rome, Scamozzi's six chapels and church of San Giorgio also offer a proportionately smaller indulgence. The villa itself is now a study centre in hydrology, while Ezzelino's **Rocca**, at Monsélice's highest point, has become a nesting area for endangered birds and is strictly off limits to featherless bipeds.

Este

Monsélice's old rival, **Este**, is only 9 km to the west; its name, from the ancient *Ateste*, was adapted by a noble, 11th-century Lombard family who conquered and ruled it before moving on to greater glory in Ferrara. Like Monsélice it was a hotly contested piece of real estate, as evidenced by the ruined walls and towers of the 1339 **Castello dei Carraresi**, now the public gardens. Within this, and made of material cannibalized from its walls, is the 16th-century Palazzo Mocenigo, home of the **Museo Nazionale Atestino** (open 9–1 and 3–6, Sun 9–2, closed Mon; adm), with one of northern Italy's finest pre-Roman collections: outstanding 5th–6th century BC bronze statuettes (a handsome Etruscan *Hercules*, in a pointy hat and sombre figures of devotees at the sanctuary of Reitia, the goddess of Caldevigo) and a charming 8th-century BC vase in the shape of a pig. Among the paintings, the star is Cima da Conegliano's *Madonna and Child*, recently moved in from a local church for safe keeping.

Behind the castle, **Villa De Kunkler** was Byron's residence 1817–18; here Shelley, his guest, penned 'Lines Written Among the Euganean Hills', after his little daughter Clara died. Among Este's churches, the only one of any note is the Baroque **Duomo** with an elliptical interior (1708), a large, sombre altarpiece by Giambattista Tiepolo (*Santa Tecla*).

Montagnana

Some 15 km west of Este lies **Montagnana**, famous for some of the best-preserved medieval fortifications in Italy, built by Ezzelino da Romano after he devastated the town in 1242. The walls extend for two kilometres, and are defended by 24 towers and battlemented gates—impressive but not very effective, as Venice lost and regained the town some thirteen times during the War of the Cambrai. The **Duomo**, in central Piazza Vittorio Emanuele, is a tardy Gothic bulk crowned by three tiny campanili, with a marble portal by Sansovino, a huge picture of the *Battle of Lepanto*, and an altarpiece by Veronese. Just outside of the Padua gate stands yet another **Villa Pisani**, this one a fine work by Palladio.

WHERE TO STAY AND EATING OUT   (tel prefix 0429)
In Este, the ****Beatrice d'Este**, Via Rimembranze 1, tel 36 81, is comfortable and centrally located near the castle (L46 000); for dinner, try the **Tavernetta da Piero Ceschi**, Piazza Trento 16, tel 2855, specializing in an unusual dish called *schisoto* (homemade bread baked with goose), as well as various game or seafood dishes, and snails (*lumache*) when available; L30 000. In Montagnana, the best place to stay is the **Ostello Rocca degli Alberi**, in the wonderful magnificent 14th-century Castello degli Alberi ('Tree Castle') at the Legnano Gate, 500 m from the station, tel 81 076; open April–mid-Oct, it may be your one chance to sleep in a medieval castle (L8 000 a head).

Little Mesopotamia

South of Monsélice, the region wedged between the Adige and the Po rivers, known as the Polésine or the 'Little Mesopotamia'. Like ancient Mesopotamia it has been blessed and cursed by its rivers, which make it fertile but often flood it; six complete cycles of creation and destruction have each rearranged the topography of Little Mesopotamia— miles of silt left its ancient capital and port Adria high and dry, and knocked the Etruscan port of Spina clean off the map. The main reason for a visit is to explore the Po Delta, a timeless horizontal landscape of water, dunes, and trees, of mists and light and colour that has inspired a native school of naif painting.

GETTING AROUND
The Palladian villa at Fratta Polésine can be reached by bus or train from Rovigo (direction: Trecenta). From Rovigo, there are trains or frequent buses along the SS443 to Adria. The train continues as far as Loreo, where you'll have to change to buses for the Adriatic resorts, and Delta towns like Porto Tolle; trains also run from Rovigo to Adria to

Chioggia (1 hour 20 min), or south to Ferrara (30 mins) and Bologna (1 hour). Rovigo's bus station is on the Piazzale G. Di Vittorio, tel 361 225; the railway station is on the Piazza Riconoscenza, tel 33 396. If you are driving, the A13 links Padua and Rovigo to Ferrara and Bologna; the 'Transpolesana' is the quickest route from Rovigo towards Verona.

TOURIST INFORMATION
Rovigo: Via J.H. Dunant 10, tel (0425) 361 481
Adria: Piazza Bocchi 6, tel (0426) 42 5554
Taglio di Po: SS. Roma 46, tel (0426) 660 531
Rosolina Mare: Piazza G. Albertin 16, tel (0426) 664 541

Rovigo

If the seven provincial capitals of the Veneto were Snow White's dwarfs, Rovigo would be 'Sleepy'. Still, it can claim two tilted towers, the **Torri Donà** in a park near the cathedral, built by the Bishop of Adria back in 954, and a rather splendid little opera house, the 1819 **Teatro Sociale** (season Sept–Dec), in Piazza Garibaldi. In Rovigo's finest square, arcaded Piazza V. Emanuele II, you can take in the **Pinacoteca dell'Accademia dei Concordi**, with a collection of minor paintings by major artists like Dosso Dossi, Giovanni Bellini, Lorenzo Lotto, and Palma Vecchio; the one that really stays with you, though, is a 17th-century *Cleopatra*, by Florentine Sebastiano Mazzoni, complete with a very realistic asp crawling along her langorous, moribund breast (10–12 and 4–6:30, Sat 10–12, closed Sun and afternoons in July and Aug). Signs lead to the octagonal **La Rotonda**, a 1594 church by Zamberlano, a pupil of Palladio, with a tower by Longhena and a ornate interior with a few canvases by Maffei.

From Rovigo it's 18 km southwest to **Fratta Polésine**, where you can visit Palladio's harmonious **Villa Badoer** built in 1570 with a classical temple façade. No furniture survives inside, but the original frescoes of pseudo-Roman grotesques by a Florentine painter named Giallo have recently been uncovered on the walls (open 10–12 and 3–5, closed Mon).

Adria

East on the N. 443 from Rovigo, lies **Adria**; the Venice of its day, Adria has but one canal to its name now. Colonized in the 6th century BC by the Greeks in the days when it stood on the shore of the sea that took its name, in the 5th and 4th centuries it came under Etruscan rule, when it knew its greatest prosperity; the Romans added it to their empire in the 2nd century BC. Nothing remains of all these former Adrias, thanks to the triumphant mud of the Adige and Po, except for the artefacts in the **Museo Archeologico Nazionale** on Via G. Badini 59 (open 9–1 and 3–6, till 7 in the summer; adm); they include Etruscan gold work and bronze, fragments of Attic vases, Roman glass, and the 4th-century BC **biga del Lucumone**, an iron chariot of Gaulish workmanship, entombed with its small horses.

The Po Delta

The Delta of the Po is a 400-square-mile wonderland of a thousand islets, dunes, reed banks, and pools, the realm of bitterns, coots, kingfishers, little egrets, herons, terns and visiting migratory fowl. Although a handful of resorts has mushroomed up along its sandy, pine-shaded shores—most prominently **Rosolina Mare** and **Isola Albarella** (owned by Crédit Suisse), they have behaved in an ecologically exemplary fashion, and co-exist with the delta's new status as a national park. Unfortunately the same cannot be said of the industries that line the 652-km length of the Po, at once Italy's greatest river and its greatest sewer.

The Po, as it nears the delta, splits into six major branches, each with its own character—the navigable canal-like Po di Levante; the contorted, lushly overgrown Po di Maistra; the majestic Po di Pila, which carries 60 per cent of the flow, has most of the fish farms and birds—best seen around **Rosapineta**. Dogged shepherds and their flocks, temporary shelters with great chimneys called *casone* and gypsy shanty towns dot the lonesome shores. If you can, visit the delta in spring, when the colours are fiery and transparent, or at the end of summer, when mists hover over the pools and dunes, tinted scarlet with salicornia and violet with sea lavender, and nature's alchemy changes the reeds and grasses to gold.

There are several full- or half-day boat cruises to choose from that explore the Delta, most of them departing from **Porto Tolle** or **Taglio di Po**; arrangements can also be made for major fishing outings. Contact: **Cacciatori Marino**, Via Varsavia 10, Porto Tolle, tel (0426) 81 508; **Società Barini e Vetri**, Ca' Vendramin, Taglio di Po, tel (0426) 88 019; **Filli Vicentini**, Via Ponte in Ferro 8, Corbola, tel (0426) 95 309. Alternatives include hiring a bicycle or canoe to explore under your own steam: the address is **Vittorio Cacciatori**, Via Bologna 1/2, Porto Tolle, tel (0426) 82 501; or letting a horse do all the work **Centro Equituristico Delta**, Via Calatafimi 13, Ca' Venier (across the Po di Venezia, and downstream from Porto Tolle), tel (0426) 82 290.

WHERE TO STAY AND EATING OUT
If you're passing through Rovigo at mealtime, you can eat well at the family-run **Tre Pini**, Via Porta Po 68, tel (0425) 27 111; the nondescript decor grows rosier as you eat your way through such delights as homemade tortellini and fresh salmon in champagne (L40 000; closed Sun and Aug). In the Delta, nothing fancy, either: *Renata, Via del Mare 21, Porto Tolle, tel (0426) 89 024, has rooms for L35 000; at Taglio di Po, there's the tonier **Tessarin, Piazza Venezia 4, tel (0426) 660 110, where rooms are L50 000. Both have restaurants, or try the fish, game dishes or pizza on the menu at **Al Cacciatore**, Via Roma 74, Porto Tolle, tel (0426) 89 000; L25 000, much less for just a pizza. The local style of cooking fish, especially Delta eels and wild duck in the autumn is the speciality at **Brodon**, a rustic restaurant at Ca' Dolfin, outside Porto Tolle, tel (0426) 84 021 (L35 000, closed Mon).

North of Padua

Some of the Veneto's best known sites are north of Padua, in the foothills of the Dolomites: Castelfranco, birthplace of Giorgione; Ásolo, where the Queen of Cyprus held her fabled Renaissance court; several outstanding villas, including Masèr, where Palladio and Veronese collaborated to create a unique work of art; Bassano del Grappa, with its covered bridge, and Maróstica, the medieval village where they play chess with human players.

Castelfranco, Ásolo, and Villa Masèr

GETTING AROUND

From Padua both buses and trains go to Bassano del Grappa (40 mins), via Castelfranco or Piazzola sul Brenta and Cittadella; coming from Vicenza you would change at Cittadella; from Venice, you'll have to change trains in Treviso for Cittadella and Castelfranco, or change buses there if you're aiming for Masèr, Ásolo, or Bassano. From Castelfranco there are trains or buses to Piombino Dese, and less frequent ones to Fanzolo. Note that buses (from Treviso, Bassano, or Padua) don't go into Ásolo, but drop passengers by the main road, where a minibus sooner or later collects them for a ride up the hill.

TOURIST INFORMATION

Cittadella: Galleria Garibaldi, tel (049) 597 0986
Castelfranco: Via Garibaldi 2, tel (0423) 495 000
Ásolo: Via Regina Cornaro, tel (0423)55 045; or Via S. Caterina 258, in the Villa De Mattia, tel (0423) 52 183.

Castelfranco and Cittadella

Piombino Dese, just off the main road from Padua to Castelfranco, is a must-detour for Palladio-philes, for its 1554 **Villa Cornaro**. One of Palladio's more monumental structures, it is fronted by a two-storey portico that was to prove irresistible to his imitators; the interior is frescoed with sleepy 18th-century biblical scenes (open May–15 Sept, Sat only 3:30–6; adm).

On the other hand, most people who come to **Castelfranco Veneto**, 9 km further north, come to pay homage to an earlier and more important genius. Giorgione was born here in 1478 and left behind one of the very few paintings undisputedly from his brush, the *Castelfranco Madonna* (1504), now hanging in the 18th-century **Duomo** (its original church was demolished). Although squirrelled away in a chapel behind a grille, the painting casts the same ineffable, dreamlike spell as the painter's *Tempest* in the Accademia. Fragments of allegorical frescoes by Veronese, from another demolished building, are in the sacristy.

Near the cathedral, the **Casa del Giorgione** (open 9–12:30, 3–6, closed winter mornings; free) is notable for a curious chiaroscura frieze attributed to Giorgione, of musical, scientific, and draughtsman's instruments, books, and portraits of philosophers; and a few elusive items vaguely related to this most elusive of painters.

Castelfranco itself is a fine, old brick-walled city built by the Trevisans in 1199 to counter the ambitions of their neighbouring Paduans; the Paduans, tit for tat, founded an egg-shaped frontier fortress 15 km to the west, **Cittadella**. Cittadella's most remarkable features are its fine, 13th-century walls and 16 towers, still in excellent condition. Near the south gate, or Porta Padova, stands the ominous **Torre di Malta**, where Ezzelino da Romano had his prison and torture chamber (cf. *Paradiso*, IX, 54), where he was accused of mutilating children and other atrocities; though as nearly every source to come down on Ezzelino is as Guelph as Dante, there could be a degree of blackballing exaggeration. The **Duomo** has Cittadella's finest painting: Jacopo Bassano's *Supper at Emmaus*, austerely coloured and austerely rustic in a way more Tuscan than Venetian.

There are two other impressive (and visitable) villas in the area. South of Cittadella, on the banks of the Brenta river in **Piazzola sul Brenta**, sprawls the **Villa Contarini**, with a 1500s core, and considerable later Baroqueing: one of its most impressive features is its long waterfront balustrade, so quintessentially Italian in its subtle, abstract, artificial effect. Inside, the frescoed rooms (especially the pretty Guitar Room) usually hold an exhibition of some kind (open summer 9–12 and 2–7:30, winter 9–12 and 2–6, closed Mon; adm). The second villa is in **Fanzolo**, five km to the northeast of Castelfranco: Palladio's lavish **Villa Emo**, decoratively frescoed with mythological subjects by Giambattista Zelotti (open Sat, Sun, and holidays, May–Sept 3–6, Oct–Apr 2–5; adm expensive).

Ásolo

In the hills above Masèr is the old walled town of **Ásolo**, the consolation prize given by Venice to Queen Caterina Cornaro after they demanded her abdication from the throne of Cyprus. With its arcaded streets and little palaces, its piazzas and gardens, Ásolo prettily fits the elegant legend of the days when it was ruled by Caterina's court, famous in the Renaissance for its refinement and cultivation of art and literature. Pietro Bembo used it as a setting for his dialogues on love, *Gli Asolani*. Giorgione is said to have strolled through its rose-gardens strumming his lute; the enforced idleness and pleasurable boredom in Ásolo might have inspired his invention of easel painting. In the last century, Ásolo was also a beloved retreat of Robert Browning (his last volume of poems was entitled *Asolando*; 'Pippa Passes' was set here as well), and of Eleonora Duse, who is buried in the local cemetery.

Bologna's poet, Giosuè Carducci, called Ásolo 'the town of a hundred horizons' as its tourist brochures gently remind you. Highest of these horizons is the **Rocca**, a citadel built over Roman foundations, with superb views to reward anyone who makes it all the way. Caterina Cornaro's **Castello** and remains of the garden where she lived in 'lace and poetry' is at the time of writing undergoing restoration. The **Duomo** on its lower edge of the main square has two paintings of the Assumption, one by Lorenzo Lotto and one by Jacopo Bassano; the 15th-century **Loggia del Capitano**, also in Piazza Maggiore, contains a museum of local works of art and memorabilia dedicated to Queen Caterina, La Duse and Browning (open 8–12 and 4–8, closed Mon; adm).

Masèr

Ásolo is a good base for visiting the best of all villas, the **Villa Bàrbaro** at **Masèr**, 7 km to the east (open Sat, Sun, and Mon 3–6, June–Sept and 2–5, Oct–May; adm). Built in 1568 for Daniele Bàrbaro, one of Venice's true 'Renaissance' men, a botanist, humanist scholar, Venice's diplomat in London, its official historian, and Patriarch of Aquileia, Masèr is a unique synthesis of two great talents—Palladio and Veronese, whose frescoes of its interior are one of the masterworks of his career. Bàrbaro and Palladio had worked together on an edition of Vitruvius and collaborated on the design of the villa: functional on the ground floor, and as serenely classical upstairs in the living quarters.

Palladio, it is said, taught Veronese about space and volume, and nowhere is this so evident as in these ravishing architectonic, *trompe l'oeil* frescoes, where the figures literally seem to inhabit the villa. While Bàrbaro suggested the scheme for the Olympian allegory in the main hall, it would seem that Veronese was left to follow his fancy elsewhere; there are portraits of the original owners, gazing from painted balconies; a very convincing dog sits beneath a ceiling of allegorical figures, dwarfs open the doors, painted windows offer views of totally convincing landscapes. The famous huntsman entering the imaginary door in the bedroom is Veronese's self-portrait, while the woman he gazes at on the other side of the house is believed to be his mistress. The elegant carvings inside the villa and the nymphaeum are by Alessandro Vittoria, who also did the sumptuous stuccoes in the serene circular **Tempietto**, a miniature Pantheon that Palladio added to the grounds in 1580, the year of his death.

WHERE TO STAY AND EATING OUT (tel prefix 0423)

One of the pleasures of visiting Castelfranco is dining at its celebrated restaurant, **Barbesin,** just above town on the Circonvallazione est, tel 490 446; its setting is as idyllic as the products of its kitchen, based entirely on fresh, seasonal ingredients; the veal with apples melts in your mouth (closed Wed eve, Thurs and Aug; L35 000). In the little town proper, **Ai Due Mori**, Vicolo Montebelluno, tel 497 174, specializes in local dishes at local prices: L20 000, closed Wed.

Ásolo has little in the way of lodging, but can claim one of Italy's most charming and romantic hotels, ******Villa Cipriani**, Via Canova 298, tel 55 444, dating from the 16th century, its floors covered with Persian carpets once owned by Eleanora Duse. The enchanting garden at the back is filled with roses and song birds; some of the hotel's 32 rooms are located in its garden houses (L240 000–300 000). The restaurant in the Cipriani family tradition, serves equally lovely (and expensive) meals in the L80 000 range. Other, less exalted places include ****Villa Bellavista**, Via Collato 5, tel 52 088, with pretty views and a little garden (L50 000 without bath, L64 000 with) and ***Due Mori**, Piazzetta Duse 29, tel 52 256 is much simpler, and much more affordable at L36 000 without bath (reserve). If you're in Ásolo just for the day, **Charly's One**, Via Roma 55, tel 52 201, offers some excellent versions of local and international specialities, and in the autumn, mushroom dishes. Delicious fish, English pub atmosphere and fair prices (L35 000; closed Fri). One of the oldest houses in Asolo is now the **Hosteria Ca' Derton**, Piazza D'Annunzio 11, tel 52 730, featuring traditional specialities to match the setting (L25 000). **Enacoteca M. Agnoletto**, in Via Browning, has a large variety of wines and snacks (closed Mon).

After visiting Palladio's villa at Masèr, you can dine in similar enchanting surroundings at **Da Bastian** (Via Cornuda, tel 565 400); famous pâté, risotto, tasty Venetian-style snails, and desserts (L30 000 and up; closed Wed eve, Thurs, and Aug).

Bassano del Grappa and Around

GETTING AROUND

Trains from Padua, Venice, or Trento will take you to Bassano. Bassano's bus station is in the Piazzale Trento, near the tourist office, tel 30 850, while the train station is at the top of Via Chilesotti (tel 25 034).

TOURIST INFORMATION
Bassano: Largo Corona d'Italia, tel (0424) 24 351 (be sure to ask for their monthly guide and events calendar, *Bassano Mese*).

Bassano del Grappa

Lying in the foothills of the Dolomites, where the Brenta River widens its flow down the plain, Bassano del Grappa is charming, picturesque, and relatively unspoilt. It produced a well-known family of 16th-century painters, the da Pontes, known by the adopted name Bassano. The 'Grappa' in the town's name comes from lofty Mt Grappa to the north, scene of terrible fighting in World War I (Bassano is surrounded with fascist-designed mass tombs and memorials); it is also synonymous with grappa, the firewater Italians use to spark up their post-prandial coffee.

From the station, it's a short walk to the centre of town, Piazza Garibaldi, which is dominated by the square, medieval **Torre Civica** and the old Gothic church of **San Francesco**. The cloister behind the church leads to the **Museo Civico** (open 10:30–12:30 and 3–6:30, closed Mon; adm), with paintings by members of the Bassano family, especially Jacopo (including his masterpiece, the Titianesque twilit *Baptism of St Lucia*); the strange prize goes to Alessandro Magnasco's *The Refectory*, depicting a crowd of wraith-like friars in a hall as big as Victoria Station, racing back into a sunset vanishing point. The museum also has casts and drawings by another local boy who made good, the neoclassical sculptor Antonio Canova (born in Possagno, see below); a room of Tito Gobbi memorabilia (another Bassano native), and a small archaelogical collection.

But it was Palladio who designed Bassano's landmark, the **Ponte degli Alpini**, the unique covered wooden bridge that spans the Brenta and links the two sides of town, and as such is a favourite gathering-place. First built in 1568, the bridge has been subsequently rebuilt several times to Palladio's original design. At the end of the bridge is Italy's oldest grappa distillery, Nardini, founded in 1779, and on the other side, the **Museo degli Alpini** at Taverna al Ponte, the sacred shrine of grappa (8–8, closed Mon).

A Grappa Digression

Although a lot of grappa comes from Bassano del Grappa, its name doesn't derive from the town or its mountain, but from *graspa*, or the residues left at the bottom of the wine vat after the must is removed; it can be drunk unaged and white, or aged in oak barrels, where it takes on a rich, amber shade. First mentioned in a 12th-century chronicle, grappa, or aquavitae 'the water of life', was chugged down as a miracle-working-concoction of earth and fire to dispel ill humours. In 1601 the Doge created a University Confraternity of Aqua Vitae to control quality; during World War I, Italy's Alpine soldiers adopted Bassano's enduring bridge as their symbol and grappa as their drink. One of their captains described it perfectly:

'Grappa is like a mule; it has no ancestors and no hope of descendants; it zigzags through you like a mule zigzags through the mountains; if you're tired you can hang on to it; if they shoot you can use it as a shield; if it's too sunny you can sleep under it; you can speak to it and it'll answer, cry and be consoled. And if you really have decided to die, it will take you off happily.'

These days the rough, trench quality of grappa appeals to few Italians; from 70 million litres guzzled in 1970, only 25 million were drunk in 1989. The Veneto with its 20 distilleries is a leading producer, and Bassano's a good place to seek out some of the better, harder to find labels that might make a grappa convert out of you: besides Nardini, look for names like Da Ponte, Folco Portinari, Jacopo de Poli, Maschio, Rino Dal Toso, or Carpenè Malvolti.

Up Monte Grappa

There are higher and mightier mountains, but few have been asked to absorb as much blood as Monte Grappa (1775 m). The road up passes through **Romano d'Ezzelino**, fief of the tyrants—the infamous Ezzelino was the third of the tribe, and when he was hunted down and slain, his family was massacred to make sure there would be no more. During World War I the battles between the Austro-Hungarians and the Italians were so vicious that the mountain is still scarred with memories, especially the Galleria Vittorio Emanuele III, a tunnel and artillery trench complex measuring 5 km. In 1935 Mussolini built an enormous, surreal five-ringed **Ossario di Cima Grappa**, an Italian-Austrian cemetery to hold the remains of 12,000 soldiers. Nine years later Nazi troops hunted down so many young partisans from Bassano hiding on the same mountain that the town was given a golden medal for heroism, now on the flank of the church of San Francesco in Piazza Garibaldi.

WHERE TO STAY AND EATING OUT (tel prefix 0424)

In the centre of Bassano, ****Hotel Belvedere, Piazzale Gen. Giardino 14, tel 29 845, has the best rooms in town, convenient if not quiet; request one in the back if you're a light sleeper (L80–110 000 with bath). Less expensive, on the north side of town near the castle, the *Locanda Castello, Via Bonamigo 20, tel 23 462, has pleasant rooms and nice beds for L34 000. In between, there's the **Vittoria, Viale Diaz 33, tel 22 300, doubles with bath L50 000.

Bassano is known for its restaurants, especially in the spring when asparagus is in season, or in the autumn when it's the turn of *porcini* mushrooms. Try them at the very elegant **Ristorante Belvedere**, Viale delle Fosse 1, tel 26 602, where you can enjoy other specialities such as risotto with shrimp and spinach, fish flavoured with fennel, and Venetian *tiramisù* for dessert (L40 000; closed Sun and last two weeks of Aug). Just outside of town on the road up to Mt Grappa, **Ca' Sette** (Via Cunizza da Romano 4, tel 25 005) is installed in a lovely settecento villa and offers more delicious asparagus specialities in season, and other dishes based on local mushrooms and red *radicchio*; in summer you may dine out in the garden (L40 000; closed Sun eve and Mon). Not far from the bridge, the **Trattoria Combattenti**, Via Gamba 22, tel 52 166 is Bassano's best bargain, with excellent *casalingua* meals of regional specialities for around L20 000; closed Sat.

Excursions from Bassano

GETTING AROUND

Buses from Bassano head west for Maróstica, Thiene (25 km, also reachable by train from Vicenza, and where you can change for the bus to Lonedo di Lugo); others go to Asiago (36 km), and frequently south to Vicenza; to the east, there are regular bus connections to Ásolo, Masèr, Treviso, and Possagno.

TOURIST INFORMATION
Maróstica: Castello Inferiore
Asiago: Piazza Carli 56, tel (0424) 62 661

Possagno

Buses leave Bassano every one or two hours for Possagno, a little town at the foot of Monte Grappa that in 1757 gave the world Antonio Canova, the ultimate neoclassical sculptor. In return, Canova gave Possagno what the town's own publicity calls 'one of the greatest monuments that man on earth has ever erected—in praise of God—to himself'. This is the **Tempio** (1819–1830), Parthenon on the front and Pantheon within, where all of Canova but his heart lies buried with his bronze Pietà (which he designed for someone else); he also painted the high altarpiece, which is almost as excruciating as Giovanni Demin's apostles that line the walls (open 8–12 and 2–5, till 7 pm in the summer).

After his death, all of Canova's clay models (*bozzetti*) and plaster casts were moved from his studio in Rome to the **Gipsoteca**, a wing added to his house—a complete collection that shows the means the sculptor used to reach his end: a bevy of highly finished goddesses, glistening, idealistic and glacial, whose cool smiles solaced their feverish age (9–12 and 2–5; May–Sept 9–1 and 3–6, closed Mon; adm).

West of Bassano: Maróstica

Maróstica, 7 km west of Bassano, is a storybook medieval town, with chivalric 13th-century walls, an upper **Castello Superiore** built by Ezzelino da Romano sprawled over the hill and a lower castle in the piazza, the **Castello Inferiore**, built by Cangrande della Scala. This castle, long-time residence of the Venetian governor and now the town hall, is the perfect setting for the event that put Maróstica on the map: the *Partita a Scacchi*, or the human chess match, which takes place in September in even-numbered years, on a 22-square-metre board painted in the Piazza del Castello. Townsfolk in 15th-century costume make the moves announced in Venetian dialect, re-enacting the 1454 contest for the hand of Lionora Parisio; her father, the podestà, had refused to let her two suitors fight the traditional duel for humanitarian reasons and suggested the chess match, even offering the loser the hand of his younger daughter. If you can't make the match, come on a Sunday afternoon to see the elaborate costumes and paraphernalia on display in the town hall. The other outstanding sight in town is the view from the Castello Superiore, but before starting the long walk up, make sure the castle bar is open.

Palladian Villas

Further west, in **Lonedo di Lugo** (or Lugo di Vicenza) near the town of Lugo (about 6 km north of Breganze), there are two important villas by Palladio. The **Villa Godi-Malinverni**, built in 1540, was his very first, with the central portion, usually the most prominent and decorated part of his villas, recessed behind two large wings. The interior is happily frescoed by Giambattisti Zelotti and assistants, and contains a fossil collection and museum of deservedly little-known Italian 19th-century painting (open March–Oct, Tues, Sat, Sun, and holidays from 2–6; Jun–Aug, same days but 3–7; adm expensive). The later and more neoclassically elegant **Villa Piovene** is a couple of doors up; its neat, equally neoclassical garden is open from 2:30–7; adm.

In **Thiene**, to the southwest of Lugo, the 1470 **Castello Colleoni di Thiene** is an attractive, pre-Palladio villa, from the days when defence was still more of a consideration than aping Romans; it is fortified with towers and battlements, yet decorated with fine Venetian Gothic windows. The frescoes within are from the busy brush of Zelotti, and there are some unusual jumbo paintings of the former residents of the 18th-century stables behind the villa—the family traditionally served in Venice's cavalry (open 15 March–15 Oct; closed Mon, guided tours from 9:30–1 and 3–6; adm). From here you can take a train to Vicenza.

Asiago
When the Venetians feel claustrophobic, they head up into the foothills of the Dolomites and relax at **Asiago**, north of Thiene and Bassano. Asiago is the chief town of the 'Seven Comuni of the Tableland', seven little towns on a rolling plateau, all pleasant summer and winter resorts known for their salubrious climate, white cheeses, laid-back skiing, and pretty walks. Most of Asiago had to be rebuilt after the devastating Battle of Asiago in 1916; the British dead lie in five surrounding cemeteries.

WHERE TO STAY AND EATING OUT
In Italy good food is never far. In Maróstica, your best bet is near the chessboard at **Pizzeria-Trattoria all'Alfiere**, Piazza Castello 16, tel (0424) 72 165 (L8 000 for a pizza, L20 000 for a meal). If you're visiting the villas in Lugo, you can have lunch in another one at nearby Breganze: **Al Cappello**, Via Marconi 4, tel (0445) 873 147. The kitchen has an Emilian bent (excellent and plentiful homemade pasta), and is especially known for its pigeon and local D.O.C. wine—but never on Sun, Mon, or in Aug (L35 000). In central Thiene, the old post house has been converted to the bright and charming **Roma**, Via Fogazzaro 8, tel (0445) 361 084; try the *crespelle* (crêpes) for starters (L35 000, closed Mon and July).

There's a wide choice of lodging at Asiago: the not overly-woodsy ****Villa Flora**, Via Col Rodeghiero 1, tel (0242) 462 674 (L50 000, with showers) or outside of town in the countryside, ***Kaberlaba**, Via Treviso 2 (at Kaberlaba), tel (0424) 462 157; most rooms have balconies (L42 000, with bath).

Vicenza

'The city of Palladio', prettily situated below the Monti Bérici, is an architectural pilgrimage shrine and knows it; where other Italians grouse about being a nation of museum curators, the prim and often grim Vicentini glory in it. Perhaps classical, monumental High Renaissance cities are better to visit than live in; there's little room for chance or fancy in their planned, symmetrical perfection, the intellectual product of a

VICENZA

0   400m
0   400yds

N

Giardino
Querini

CORSO S. MARCO

CORSO ARACOELIO

Porta S.
Croce

19

Ponte
Pusteria

PIAZZA XX
SETTEMBRE

VIA IV
NOVEMBRE

17

CORSO A. FOGAZZARO

C. PEDEMURO

18

PORTI

C. CANOVE

CONTRÀ

C. S.
CORONA

13

15

CORSO PORTA PADOVA

CORSO A.

CONTRÀ

16

C. PALLADIO

A.

12

14

PIAZZA
MATTEOTTI

CONTRA S. PIETRO

Porta
Padova

VIA L.
GALLIENO

20

RIALE
CORSO

21

PIAZZA
BIAVE

10

9

PIAZZA
DUOMO

7

Porta
Nova

Giardino
Salvi

6

Ponte
S. Michele

11

VIALE A. GIURIOLO

22

V. SS. FELICE

4

3

C.

PROTI

8

Porta S. Paolo

Porta
Castéllo

1

5

V.
LIOV

C.
S. QUANTO

Fiume Bacchiglione

E FORTUNATO

CONTRA MURA

CONTRA FASCINA

PALLAMIO

VIALE

DALMAZIA

C. S. TOMMASO

VIALE
ROMA

Porton del
Luzzo

Ponte
Furo

C. S. CATERINA

VIALE
MILANO

Porta
Lupia

Porta
Monte

2

VIALE VENEZIA

VIALE
RISORGIMENTO NAZIONALE

Fiume Retrone

VIALE DANTE

VIALE X GIUGNO

VIA M.
D'AZEGLIO

VIA S. BASTIANO

24

PIAZZA DELLA
VITTORIA

PORTICI DI MONTE BERICO

23

To La Rotunda

1. Tourist Office
2. Train and Bus Stations
3. Post Office
4. Telephones
5. Palazzo Da Porto-Breganze
6. Palazzo Bonin
7. Duomo
8. Casa Pigafetta
9. Basilica
10. Loggia del Capitanio
11. Oratorio di San Nicola
12. Palazzo da Schio/Palazzo Thiene
13. Santa Corona
14. Palazzo Chiericati/Museo Civico
15. Teatro Olimpico
16. Santo Stefano
17. Palazzo Regaù
18. Palazzo Colleoni Porto
19. Santa Maria d. Carmine
20. San Lorenzo
21. Palazzo Valmarana
22. SS. Felice e Fortunato
23. Basilica di Monte Berico
24. Villa Valmarana

gentry immersed in humanistic and classical thought (far better educated than those merchants and sailors in the lagoon, who ruled Vicenza during its heyday).

Although Vicenza was heavily damaged during the Second World War, restorers have tidied up most of the scars, everything is in its place, for these days the rouble rules in Vicenza; the city promotes itself as the 'Città d'Oro', the city of gold, for its huge goldworking industry that counts some 700 producers. The birthplace of the inventor of the silicon chip, Federico Faggin, it has developed electronic industries that allow it to call itself the 'Silicon Valley' of Italy; add machine tools, textiles, and shoes to this list, and you have the Veneto's, and one of Italy's, wealthiest cities.

PALLADIO

A Paduan by birth, Andrea di Pietro della Gondola (1508–80) received his classical nickname of Palladio in Vicenza, the city in which he began working as a stonecutter at the age of 16. His first major commission, che Basilica, so captured the hearts of the Vicentine ruling class that they commissioned him to build their urban and suburban palaces, the theatre for their Academy, and other public buildings. He was, for them, the perfect architect, able to flatter their 'aesthetics, lunatic cultural imaginings, and upper crust pride' as one Vicentine writer puts it, for very little money—mainly by using cheap brick coated with a marbly sheen of stucco.

Palladio owes his continuing reputation, not so much to his buildings, many of which were never completed, but to his books, especially *I Quattro Libri dell'Architettura* of which Sir Reginald Blomfield, in his *Studies in Architecture*, wrote pointedly, 'With the touch of pedantry that suited the times and invested his writings with a fallacious air of scholarship, he was the very man to summarize and classify, and to save future generations of architects the labour of thinking for themselves.' To modern eyes, many of Palladio's buildings seem only too familiar, a tribute to the wide following he has had in England and America from the 17th century on. If not the best, always remember that Palladio in many ways was the first. The centre for Palladian studies, the **Centro Internazionale di Architettura 'A. Palladio'**, housed upstairs in the Basilica, offers a popular architectural course in September; contact the tourist office for details.

GETTING AROUND

Vicenza is on the main railway line between Verona (45 mins) and Padua (35 mins); there is also a line up to Thiene (see 'North of Padua' above). The station is on the south end of town, at the end of Viale Roma (tel 324 396). From the station FTV buses (tel 544 333) depart for Bassano and Maróstica (see 'North of Padua' above), as well as Treviso, Padua, Asiago, etc; the tourist office has current timetables. Radio taxi tel 920 600. For serious villa exploration, hire a car at Maggiore, at the station, tel 545 962; AVIS, Viale Milano 88, tel 321 622; or at Scalabrin Fratelli, Contrà Vittorio Veneto 20, tel 321 868. If you're flush, Vola Vicenza, at the civic airport (tel 923 501), offers air tours over the city and villas of the countryside.

If you drive to Vicenza, parking is most convenient in the two large guarded lots, one at the west end of town by the Mercato Ortofrutticolo, and the other to the east, by the stadium, both linked to the centre by special bus service every 5 min. As in Venice, the street names are in dialect—instead of *'via'* look for *'contrà'*.

TOURIST INFORMATION
APT, Piazza Duomo 5, tel (0444) 544 122, open mornings only; AAST information office at Piazza Matteotti 12, tel 320 854. Ask about their free Palladio tour on Sunday mornings.

Porta Castello to the Piazza Signori

From the station, Viale Roma enters the city proper through the **Porta Castello**, marked by a powerful 11th-century tower. This dominates one end of Vicenza's long pedestrians-only **Corso Palladio**, a showcase of palaces of various eras; one of the first, Piazza Castello's **Palazzo da Porto Breganze** of the enormous columns, was designed by Palladio and partly built by his pupil Vincenzo Scamozzi before the very monumentality of the design defeated him. Scamozzi also built the less exciting **Palazzo Bonin** at no. 13 after his master's designs.

From the Piazza Castello, Contrà Vescovado leads to the **Duomo**, a Gothic temple with a diamond pattern façade, carefully pieced together after being flattened in the war. Inside, there's not much to look for apart from the polyptych by Lorenzo Veneziano (5th chapel on the right). Excavations in the cathedral crypt have reached the level of Roman Vicenza and revealed parts of the original 8th-century church, while in the square you can visit the **Cryptoporticus** (underground passageway) of a first century palace (Piazza Duomo 2, open Thurs and Sat 10–11:30).

Take Contrà Canneti and Contrà Porti east for the eclectic 1481 **Casa Pigafetta**, birthplace of Antonio Pigafetta, a local artistocrat who happened to be in Spain when Magellan was about to sail. Pigafetta talked Magellan into taking him on, and it was a good choice; he was one of the few to survive the first three-year-long journey around the world and wrote the definitive account of the voyage in 1525. On the parallel Contrà Garibaldi, there's a rare note of Vicentine whimsy in a bronze statue of children on a see-saw; straight past it lies Piazza dei Signori.

Piazza dei Signori

This large and kingly square is the heart and soul of Vicenza, its public forum in Roman times and today. In the 1540s, the Vicentines decided the piazza's crumbling old medieval Palazzo della Ragione would no longer do, and asked Italy's leading architects to find a way of propping up the sagging structure and giving it a facelift to match their new, Renaissance-humanist aspirations. Yet where such luminaries as Sansovino and Giulio Romano failed to convince the gentry, a young unknown, freshly-dubbed Palladio, succeeded and in 1549 began his work on the building now called the **Basilica** (which meant a hall of justice to the Romans, whom the locals were keen to emulate). Palladio kept at the Basilica on and off until his death, and the result is one of his masterpieces, one that perfectly fulfilled its aims, with two tiers of rounded arches interspersed with Doric and Ionic columns. Although the façade gives the appearance of monumental Roman regularity, in truth Palladio had to vary the sizes of the arches to compensate for the irregularities of the Gothic structure. The breadbox roof hides behind a pediment lined with life-size statues in the Roman mould, a hallmark of Palladio's later work; stare at them long enough and the urge to shoot them off like ducks in a penny arcade becomes almost irresistible. The great Gothic hall of the basilica is open 9:30–12 and 2:30–5, Sun 9–12, closed Mon).

For a look at what Palladio was disguising, go behind the basilica to the 16th-century **Piazza delle Erbe**, guarded by the pleasantly-named **Torre del Tormento**, the medieval prison. In the adjacent piazzetta stands a statue of Palladio, gazing at the Basilica (his favourite building) with finger on chin as if trying to figure out what he forgot.

The basilica shares the Piazza dei Signori with the needle-like **Torre di Piazza** (or Bissara, after the barons who raised it in the 12th century); in the 14th century the civic authorities tamed it with a mechanical clock and in 1444 added its headdress). Across the square is Palladio's **Loggia del Capitanio**, decorated in 1571 to celebrate the victory at Lepanto. If its grand columns and arches seem confined in too narrow a space, it's because the loggia was meant to extend several more bays. The neighbouring 16th-century **Monte di Pietà**, built in two sections, was frescoed in the 1900s with amazing Liberty-style pin-up girls, some still faintly surviving moral outrage, war damage, and Father Time. Two high columns at the entrance of the piazza support statues of the Redeemer and one of St Mark's more amicable lions.

From the columns, a right turn down Via S. Michele leads to the Retrone, one of Vicenza's two little rivers, spanned here by the pretty **Ponte S. Michele** (1620). Just on the other bank, the **Oratorio di Santa Nicola** is remarkable for the creepiest altarpiece in Italy, *La Trinità* by Vicenza's own 16th-century artist Francesco Maffei, whose tumultuously feverish brush infected some of the Oratorio's walls as well (July–Sept 9–12 and 3–6, though for digestion's sake, see it before rather than after lunch).

Contrà Porti and around

A left turn at the Piazza dei Signori's columns will return you to Corso Palladio and the city's prettiest Gothic palace, the 15th-century **Palazzo da Schio**, also known as the 'Ca' d'Oro' for its long-gone gilt decoration. It's enough to make the Palladian palaces, concentrated in the quarter just north of the Corso, seem as exciting as bank branches— the best are along the **Contrà Porti**, Vicenza's most dignified street (see Palladio's addition to **Palazzo Thiene**, on the corner of Contrà Porti and the Corso, all brick under its stone and plaster skin; his 1570s **Palazzo Barbaran Da Porto** at no. 11 and much earlier **Palazzo Da Porto Festa**, at no 21).

Just west, near the corner of Contrà Riale and Contrà Zanella stands Vicenza's mighty Gothic palace, **Casa Fontana**; across the street, the church of **Santo Stefano** contains one of Palma Vecchio's most beautiful paintings *Madonna with SS. George and Lucia*. More of Vicenza's finest art is just around the corner on the Contrà Santa Corona, in the chapels of the early Gothic church of **Santa Corona** (9:30–12:15 and 3:30–6): Veronese's 1573 *Adoration of the Magi* and Giovanni Bellini's *Baptism of Christ*, a late painting set in a rugged, very un-Venetian landscape. Under the Madonna hanging nearby is an accurate portrayal of Vicenza just before Palladio came on the scene.

More art is on display at the end of the Corso in Palladio's classic Palazzo Chiericati (1550–1650) now home of the **Museo Civico** (open 9:30–12:20 and 2:30–5, 10–12 Sun, closed Mon; adm; your *biglietto cumulativo* includes the Teatro Olimpico). On the ground floor are some of the original frescoes, with a hilarious ceiling by a certain

Brusasorci, who took it upon himself to portray, as accurately as possible, the naked sun god and his steeds in the position earthlings would see them at noon. The archaeological section has Vicenza's oldest goldwork—a lamina embossed with simple outlines of warriors from around 1500 BC. In the art wing there are fine works by Paolo Veneziano, Memling, the Vicentine Bartolomeo Montagna (a follower of Mantegna), Cima da Conegliano's *Madonna*, a lovely terracotta *Madonna col Bambino* by Sansovino, Tintoretto's *Miracle of St Augustine*, Van Dyck's *The Four Ages of Man*, and Jan Brueghel the Elder's *Madonna col Bambino*; there are also good works by Bassano and Veronese, and two major works by the irrepressible Francesco Maffei: *Glorification of Gaspare Zane* and *Glorification of the Inquisitor Alvise Foscarini*, and his wild and woolly sidekick, Giulio Carpioni.

Teatro Olimpico

Across the street from the museum, the Teatro Olimpico was Palladio's swansong and one of his most original and fascinating works, a unique masterpiece of the Italian Renaissance, said to be the oldest indoor theatre in Europe. Palladio himself was a member of the group of twenty-five literati and dilettantes who formed the high-minded Olympic Academy that built the theatre for their own plays and lectures. For the stage, Palladio as always went back to the ancient buildings he had seen during his sojourns in Rome and designed an elegant and permanent amphitheatre of wood and stucco, while his pupil Scamozzi added the amazing piazza and streets radiating out in the then popular Piazza del Popolo style in flawless, fake perspective—designed especially for the theatre's first production, Sophocles' *Oedipus Rex*, and meant to represent the city of Thebes. But here Thebes has become a pure ideal, a Renaissance dream city, so perfect that no one ever thought to change the set. If you come between April and October, you may be able to see a performance in this most historical of theatres: otherwise, it's open from 15 March–15 Oct 9:30–12:20 and 3–5:30, in winter 9:30–12:20 and 2–4:30, Sun 9:30–12:20; same ticket as Museo Civico (sometimes it may be closed for rehearsals).

Outside the historic centre

Vicenza has two fine parks—large and attractive **Parco Querini** to the north of Contrà Porti and over the bridge, and **Giardino Salvi**, just outside Piazza Castello on Corso SS. Felice e Fortunato. If you walk along this street away from the centre, you'll come in 10 minutes to Vicenza's oldest church, **SS. Felice e Fortunato**, built shortly after Constantine made Christianity the religion. Since then, it has taken its licks from barbarians and earthquakes, but has been un-restored as much as possible to its 4th-century appearance, especially its mosaics in the right aisle and palaeo-Christian martyrs' shrine.

If you have time on your hands, Vicenza has a pair of other churches along Corso Fogazzaro, running north from Corso Palladio: the first is 13th-century **San Lorenzo**, a large Franciscan church with a good marble portal, the second, further out, **Santa Maria del Carmine** is a Gothic church tarted up in the 19th century, with paintings by Jacopo Bassano, Veronese, and Montagna.

Monte Bérico and Villa Valmarana

Vicenza's holy hill, Monte Bérico, rises just to the south of the city. Buses make the ascent approximately every half-hour from the coach station, or you can walk up in half an hour from the centre (this area is not well signposted, so be sure to pick up the tourist office's map), through the 150-arch covered walkway, or **Portici**, built in the 18th century to shelter pilgrims climbing to the Baroque **Basilica di Monte Bérico** that crowns the hill. The basilica commemorates two apparitions of the Virgin in the 1420s, announcing the end of a plague that devastated Vicenza. It still does a busy pilgrim trade, and its well-polished, candle-flickering interior contains two fine paintings: *La Pietà* by Montagna, hanging near the altar, and the *Supper of St Gregory the Great* by Veronese, appropriately hung in the refectory in the cloister (down the steps to the left), and carefully pieced together after an Austrian soldier sliced it to shreds in 1848. The basilica is open from 7–6, till 7 in the summer; from the spacious piazza in front there are excellent views of the city.

From the basilica, it's only a 10-minute walk to **Villa Valmarana** (if you're walking, take Via M. D'Azeglio where the Portici bends, to Via S. Bastiano and continue straight). The villa is also called 'dei Nani' because of the statues of dwarfs in the garden, but the main reason to visit is its sumptuous decoration by Giambattista and Giandomenico Tiepolo, who frescoed its two parts, the *Palazzina* and the *Foresteria* (Guest House) with charming scenes from the *Iliad*, and from *Orlando Furioso* and other Renaissance poems; Giandomenico's intimate, ironical country scenes in the *Foresteria* mark his (and his generation's) divergence from his father's grand manner, though one wonders if Giambattista realized Baroque was dying right under his nose (open every afternoon except Sun from the 15 March–15 Nov, 2:30–5:30; May–Sept from 3–6; also 10–12 Thurs, Sat, and Sun; adm).

Villa Rotonda

Palladio designed his celebrated Villa Capra-Valmarana, better known as the **Villa Rotonda** for Cardinal Capra in 1551, but it wasn't completed until after his death by the faithful Scamozzi. Unlike the master's other villas, which, under their stuccoed, classical surfaces were really functional farmhouses, the Villa Rotonda was built for sheer delight, the occasional garden party, and though no one knew it at the time, as the perfect setting

Villa Rotonda

144

GETTING AROUND

There are two train stations near Lake Garda, at Desenzano and Peschiera, both of which are landings for the lake's hydrofoils (*aliscafi*) and steamers. Buses from Brescia, Trento, and Verona go to their respective shores; for Desenzano, the principal starting point for Lake Garda, there are buses from Brescia, Verona and Mantua, and two exits from the Serenissima Autostrada. Other bus lines run up and down the road that winds around the lake shores—a marvel of Italian engineering, called La Gardesana, Occidentale on the west and Orientale on the east. In summer, however, their scenic splendour sometimes pales before the sheer volume of holiday traffic.

All boat services on the lake are operated by *Navigazione sul Lago di Garda*, Piazza Matteotti 2, tel (030) 914 1321, where you can pick up a timetable; the tourist offices have them as well. The one car ferry crosses from Maderno to Torri; between Desenzano and Riva there are several hydrofoils a day, calling at various ports (2 hours) as well as the more frequent and leisurely steamers ($4^{1}/_{2}$ hours). Services are considerably reduced in the off-season. Full fare from Desenzano to Riva by steamer is L9500, on the hydrofoil L14 000. There are also regular afternoon cruises from July to mid-September from different points.

TOURIST INFORMATION

While Lake Garda's west shore belongs to the province of Brescia in Lombardy, its northern tip is in Trentino and its eastern shore is in Venetia in the province of Verona. Although this results not from a plan to divvy up the tourist dollar among regions, but from history (readers of Goethe will recall how the poet was nearly arrested as an Austrian spy while sketching a ruined fortress on the Veneto shore), each region parochially fails to acknowledge that Lake Garda exists beyond its own boundaries; their maps often leave the opposite shores blank, if they draw them in at all. Be sure to watch area codes when telephoning.

Desenzano del Garda: Piazza Matteotti 27, tel (030) 914 1510
Sirmione: Viale Marconi 2, tel (030) 916 114/916 245
Gardone Riviera: Corso Repubblica 35, tel (0365) 20 347
Saló: Lungolago Zanardelli 39, tel (0365) 21 423

Desenzano and Solferino

Desenzano del Garda, on a wide gulf dotted with beaches, is the lake's largest town and its main gateway (if you arrive by train, a bus will take you to the centre). Life is centred around its port cafés and a dramatic statue of Sant' Angela, foundress of the Ursuline Order. Originally a settlement of pile dwellings, Desenzano was a popular holiday resort of the Romans, and one of their **villas** has been excavated on Via Crocifisso, revealing colourful mosaics from the 4th century and artefacts now in the small museum on the site (open 9–4, till 5 in summer, closed Mon; adm). In Desenzano's 16th-century **church**, pride of place goes to an unusual 18th-century *Last Supper* by Giandomenico Tiepolo. A small antiques market takes place nearby the first weekend of each month.

Besides Lake Garda, Desenzano is the base for visiting the low war-scarred 'Risorgimento' hills to the south. The two most important battles occurred on the same day, 24 June 1859, in which Napoleon III defeated Emperor Franz Joseph at **Solferino** and

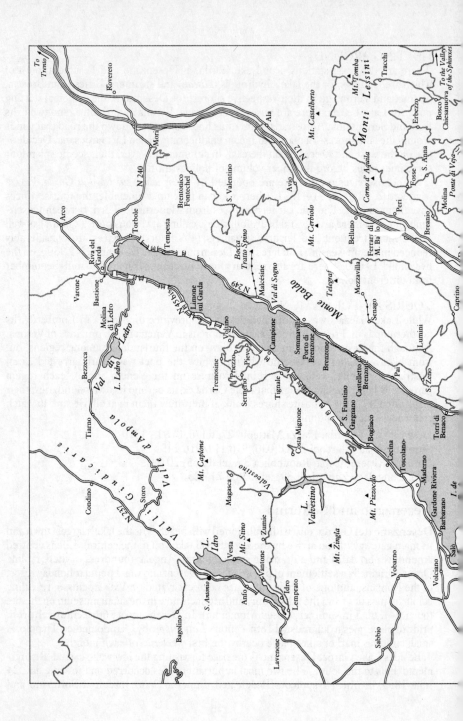

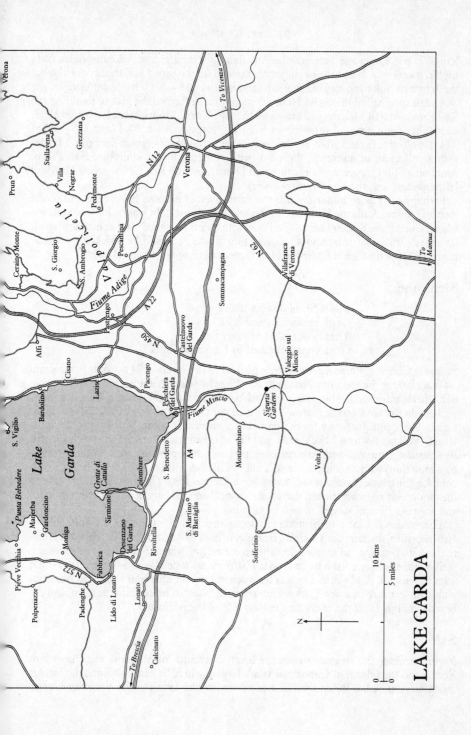

LAKE GARDA

King Vittorio Emanuele defeated the Austrian right wing at **San Martino della Battaglia**, 8 km away. It was the beginning of the end for the proud Habsburgs in Italy, but the Battle of Solferino had another consequence as well—the terrible suffering of the wounded so appalled the Swiss Henry Dunant that he formed the idea of founding the Red Cross. At San Martino you can climb the lofty **Torre Monumentale** erected 1893, containing paintings and mementoes from the battle (open 8:30–1 and 2–5, closed Tues). Solferino is marked by an old tower of the Scaligers of Verona, the **Spia d'Italia**, with a collection of uniforms; there's a battle museum by the church of **San Piero**, containing 7000 graves, and a memorial to Dunant and the Red Cross, erected in 1959 (all same hours as the San Martino tower).

Perhaps even more important was the battle averted in these hills at the end of the Roman empire. Attila the Hun, having devasted northeast Italy, was on his way to Rome when he met Pope St Leo I here. The Pope, with Saints Peter and Paul as his translators, informed Attila that if he should continue to Rome he would be stricken by a fatal nosebleed, upon which the terrible Hun turned aside, sparing central Italy.

Sirmione

> Sweet Sirmio! thou, the very eye
> Of all peninsulas and isles,
> That in our lakes of silver lie,
> Or sleep enwreathed by Neptune's smiles

So wrote Catullus, Rome's greatest lyric poet, born in Verona in 84 BC, only to die some 30 years later in the fever of a broken heart. When he wasn't haunting the Palatine home of his fickle mistress 'Lesbia', he is said to have visited the villa his family kept, like many well-to-do Romans, on the narrow 4-km-long peninsula of **Sirmione** that pierces Lake Garda like a pin. Just over 90 m across at its narrowest point, Sirmione is the most visually striking town on Lake Garda, and the principal attractions are the lovely **Grotte di Catullo**, entwined with ancient olive trees on the tip of the rocky promontory—romantic ruins with a capital R, though not of Catullus' villa, but of a great Roman bath complex (Sirmione is famous even today for its thermal spa). The views across the lake to the mountains are magnificent; there's also a small antiquarium on the site with mosaics and frescoes (9 until sunset, closed Mon; adm).

The medieval centre of Sirmione is dominated by one of the most memorable of Italian castles, the fairytale **Castello Scaligero**, built by Mastino I della Scala of Verona in the 13th century and surrounded almost entirely by water. There's not much to see inside, but fine views from its swallowtail battlements (open 9–1, 9–6 from April–Oct; adm expensive). Also worth a look is the ancient Romanesque **San Pietro in Mavino**, with 13th-century frescoes. Cars are not permitted over its bridge into the town, and the best swimming is off the rocks on the west side of the peninsula.

Saló

From Sirmione the steamer passes the lovely headlands of Manerba and Punta San Fermo and the **Island of Garda**, the lake's largest, where St Francis visited the former monastery; ruined, it formed the base of a monumental 19th-century Venetian-Gothic style palace, now owned by the Borghese princes, one of whom, Scipione, made the famous drive from Peking to Paris in the early days of the automobile. **Saló** (the Roman *Salodium*) enjoys one of the most privileged locations on the lake; it gave its name to Il Duce's last dismal stand, the puppet Republic of Saló of 1944, formed after the Nazis rescued him from his prison in an Abruzzo ski lodge. Saló has a number of fine buildings, including a late Gothic **Cathedral** with a Renaissance portal of 1509 and paintings within by Romanino, Moretto da Brescia, and a golden polyptych by Paolo Veneziano. **L'Ateneo**, in the Renaissance Palazzo Fantoni, contains a collection of 13th-century manuscripts and incunabula. North of Saló begins the **Brescia Riviera**, famous for its exceptional climate and exotic trees and flowers.

Gardone Riviera and D'Annunzio's Folly

Gardone Riviera, its shore marked by the tall, 1920s reconstruction of its **Torre di S. Marco**, has long been the most fashionable resort on the Brescia Riviera, if not on all of Lake Garda, ever since 1880 when a German scientist noted the almost uncanny consistency of its climate; profiting from its mildness is the loveliest sight in Gardone, **Giardino Botanico Hruska**, with imported tufa cliffs and artificial streams, and plants from Africa, the Alps, and the Mediterranean (open 8 am–7 pm, shorter hours in the winter; adm).

Above the garden it's a short walk to the equally uncanny **Il Vittoriale**, the last home of Gabriele D'Annunzio (1863–1938) (open from 9–12:30 and 2–5:30, except Mon; adm expensive. Try to arrive at 9 am to avoid the crowds and tour buses. There's an option of buying a ticket to the uninteresting museum and grounds only).

Gabriele D'Annunzio was a poor boy from the Abruzzo who became the greatest writer and poet of his generation, but not one who was convinced that the pen was mightier than the sword; a fervent right-wing nationalist, he was one of the chief warmongers urging Italy to intervene in World War I. Later he led his 'legionaries' in the famous unauthorized invasion of Fiume, which, though promised to Italy before its entrance into the First World War, was just being ceded to Yugoslavia. D'Annunzio instantly became a national hero, stirring up a diplomatic furore before coming home. For Mussolini the popular old jingoist was an acute embarrassment, and he decided to pension him off in 1925—in a luxurious Liberty-style villa designed by Gian Carlo Maroni, ostentatiously to give the debt-ridden poet a secure home in gratitude for his patriotism, but in reality to shut him up in a gilded cage. D'Annunzio dubbed the villa, formerly owned by a German family, 'Il Vittoriale' after Italy's victory over Austria in 1918 and proceeded to redecorate it and pull up its lovely garden to create an unrivalled arena of domestic kitsch.

Luigi Barzini describes D'Annunzio as 'perhaps more Italian than any other Italian' for his love of gesture, spectacle, and theatrical effect—what can you say about a man who would announce that he had once dined on roast baby? Yet for the Italians of his generation, no matter what their politics, he exerted a powerful influence in thought and fashion; he seemed a breath of fresh air, a new kind of 'superman', hard and passionate yet capable of writing exquisite, intoxicating verse; the spiritual father of the Futurists, ready to destroy the old bourgeois *Italia vile* of museum curators and parish priests and create in its stead a great modern power, the 'New Italy'. He lived a life of total exhibitionism, according to the old slogan of an American brewery, 'with all the gusto he could get'—extravagantly, decadently and beyond his means, the trend-setting aristocratic aesthete with his borzois, 'the Divine' Eleanora Duse and innumerable other loves (preferably duchesses). Apparently he thought the New Italians should all be as eccentric and clever, and he disdained the conformity and corporate state of the Fascists.

D'Annunzio made Il Vittoriale his personal monument and in his inexhaustible egotism knew that one day the gaping hordes would be tramping through, marvelling at his exquisite taste. Unfortunately the guides speak only Italian, so to fill in the gaps if you don't, the tour begins with what must be called a 'cool reception' room for guests D'Annunzio disliked, austere and formal compared to the comfy one for favourites. When Mussolini came to call he was entertained in the ice chamber; D'Annunzio, it is said, escorted Il Duce over to the mirror and made him read the inscription he had written above: 'Remember that you are of glass and I of steel.' Perhaps you can make it out if your eyes have had time to adjust to the gloom. Like Aubrey Beardsley and many of the characters played by Vincent Price, D'Annunzio hated the daylight and had the windows painted over, preferring low electric lamps.

The ornate organs in the music room and library were played by his young American wife, who gave up a promising musical career to play for his ears alone. His bathroom, with 2000 pieces of bric-à-brac, somehow manages to have space for the tub; the whole house is packed solid with a feather-duster's nightmare of art and junk. In his spare bedroom, adorned with leopard skins, you can see the cradle-coffin he liked to lie in to think cosmic thoughts about his mortality. He made the entrance to his study low so all would have to bow as they entered; here he kept a bust of La Duse, but covered, to keep her memory from distracting him. The dining room, with its bright movie-palace sheen, is one of the more delightful rooms. D'Annunzio didn't care much for it, and left his guests here to dine on their own with his pet tortoise, which he embalmed in bronze after the creature expired of indigestion, a subtle reminder of the dangers of overeating.

In the adjacent auditorium hangs the bi-plane D'Annunzio used to fly over Vienna in the war, while out in the garden the prow of the battleship *Puglia* from the Fiume adventure juts out mast and all in a copse of cypresses. Walk above this to the white travertine **Mausoleum** on its hill, baking and glaring in the bright sun like a kind of Stonehenge set up by an evil race from an alien galaxy. Within three concentric stone circles the sarcophagi of legionary captains respectfully pay court to the plain tomb of D'A himself, raised up on columns high above the others to be the closest to his dark star, all in jarring contrast to the mausoleum's enchanting views over the lake.

WHERE TO STAY AND EATING OUT

If you come to Garda in July or August without a reservation, it can mean big disappointment. For lower prices and more chance of a vacancy, try the small towns on the east shore; also check at the tourist offices for rooms in private homes. At least half-pension will be required in season at most hotels, and despite the mild climate most close after October or November until March.

Sirmione: For a total immersion in the peninsula's romance, the *******Villa Cortine**, Via Grotte 6, tel (030) 916 261, can't be surpassed, offering its guests perhaps the rarest amenity to be found in Sirmione—tranquillity. Its enchanting, century-old Italian garden occupies almost a third of the entire peninsula with its exotic flora, venerable trees, statues and fountains running down to the water's edge. The neoclassical villa itself was built by an Austrian general, and was converted into a hotel in 1954, preserving its frescoed ceilings and elegant furnishings. The rooms are plush, the atmosphere perhaps a bit too exclusive but ideal for a break from the real world, with private beach and dock, pool and tennis. Open March–Oct, full-board obligatory—L310–325 000 per person in a double with bath. Down a notch but still very, very comfortable, the ****Hotel Eden, Piazza Carducci 18, tel (030) 916 481, is housed in a medieval building in the centre of Sirmione, beautifully remodelled within with fine marbles and coordinated bedrooms with princely bathrooms, TV, and air conditioning; open March–Oct, no restaurant; L120 000 with breakfast. Although it's more attractive on the outside than in the rooms, the **Hotel Grifone, near the Scaliger castle on Via Bocchio 4, tel (030) 916 014, has a great location, and some rooms have lovely lake views; closed Nov–March (all rooms with bath, L55–60 000). It shares the weathered stone house with the more elegant Ristorante Grifone de Luciano, tel (030) 916 097, serving simple but delicious fish and more for around L40 000. Another fine place to dine with views that rival the food is the Piccolo Castello, Via Dante 9, tel (030) 916 138, facing the Scaliger castello, with fish and meat specialities from the grill (L35 000).

One of Italy's finest restaurants is near the peninsula at Lugana di Sirmione: the classy Vecchia Lugana, Via Lugana Vecchia, tel (030) 919 012, where the menu changes four times a year to adapt to the changing seasons and the food is exquisite, prepared with a light and wise touch—try the divine mousse of lake trout—L65 000, with wine (closed Mon eve, Tues, & Jan).

Saló: Although less glamorous than some of its neighbours, Saló has one of Lake Garda's loveliest hotels, the ****Laurin, Viale Landi 9, tel (0365) 22 022, an enchanting Liberty-style villa converted into a hotel in the 1960s, maintaining its elegant decor. The charming grounds include a swimming pool and beach access; all rooms have bath and TV; open Feb–mid-Dec; L140–162 000. For a good, reasonably priced and traditional meal, try the Trattoria alla Campagnola, Via Brunati 11, tel (0365) 22 153. Garden-fresh vegetables served with every dish, homemade pasta, and mushrooms in season (L30 000); closed Mon, Tues lunch, & Jan.

Gardone Riviera: Gardone Riviera and its suburb Fasano Riviera have competing de luxe Grand Hotels, both old pleasure domes. When Gardone's contender, the ****Grand Hotel, Via Zanardelli 72, tel (0365) 20 261, was built in 1881, its 180 rooms made it one of the largest resort hotels in Europe. It is still one of Garda's landmarks, and its countless chandeliers glitter as brightly as when Churchill stayed in 1948, still licking his wounds after taking a beating in the election. Almost all of the palatial air-conditioned rooms look on to the lake, where guests can luxuriate on the garden terraces, swim in the heated outdoor pool or off the private sandy beach. The dining room and delicious food match the quality of the rooms; closed mid-Oct to mid-April; L115–190 000. Fasano's ****Grand Hotel Fasano, Via Zanardelli 160, tel (0365) 21 051, was built in the mid 1800s as a Habsburg hunting palace and converted to a hotel at the turn of the century. Surrounded by a large park, the owners have furnished the hotel almost entirely with Belle Epoque furnishings; there are tennis courts, a heated pool, and private beach; the restaurant is one of Lake Garda's best. Open May–Sept, rooms are L90–166 000.

Another fine place to lodge in Fasano, the ****Villa del Sogno, Via Zanardelli 107, tel (0365) 20 228, was its creator's 'Dream Villa' of the 1920s—done in grand Renaissance style. Although not on the lake, it has a private beach five minutes' walk away and a pool in its flower-filled garden. Open April–Sept, rooms, all with bath, L110–160 000. Back in Gardone, the less expensive but lovely ***Villa Fiordaliso**, Via Zanardelli 132, tel (0365) 20 158, is a fine turn-of-the-century hotel, where the historically minded can request the suite where Mussolini and his mistress Claretta Petacci spent the last weeks of their lives. Located in a serene park, with a private beach, all seven rooms have bath and TV; it also boasts an elegant restaurant, open to the public, featuring classic Lombard and Garda dishes; specialities *insalata di coniglio all'aceto balsamico* (rabbit salad in balsamic vinegar) and lots of pasta dishes with vegetable sauces. Closed Nov–mid-Dec, rooms L90 000; meals L55 000 (closed Sun eve, Mon). The ***Bellevue**, Via Zanardelli 81, tel (0365) 20 235, is above the main road overlooking the lake, with a pretty garden sheltering it from the traffic. Rooms are modern, and all have private bath. Open April–10 Oct, L58 000. *Pensione Hohl**, Via dei Colli 4, tel (0365) 20 160, half-way up to Il Vittoriale, is another former villa in a pleasant garden. None of the rooms have baths but they're quiet and a steal in Gardone for L40 000.

Garda's West Shore: Gardone to Riva

TOURIST INFORMATION
Gargnano: Piazza Feltrinelli 2, tel (0365) 71 222
Toscolano-Maderno: Via Lungolago 18, tel (0365) 641 330
Limone: Via Comboni 15, tel (0365) 954 070
Riva: Giardini di Porta Orientale 8, tel (0464) 554 444
Arco: Viale delle Palme 1, tel (0464) 516 161

Toscolano-Maderno and Gargnano

The single *comune* of Toscolano-Maderno has one of the finest beaches on Lake Garda, a fine 9-hole golf course, the car ferry to Torri, and the distinction of having been the site of *Benacum*, the main Roman town on the lake. Toscolano had a famous printing press in the 15th century, and was the chief manufacturer of nails for Venice's galleys. Most of the Roman remains, however, have been incorporated into the fine 12th-century church of **Sant'Andrea** in Maderno, restored in the 16th century by St Charles Borromeo. **Gargnano** seems more of a regular town than a resort, though it was here, in a villa owned by the editor Feltrinelli (whose chain of bookstores are a blessing to the English-speaking traveller in Italy) that Mussolini ruled the Republic of Saló. The main sight in town is the 13th-century **Franciscan church and cloister**; in the latter the columns are adorned with carvings of citrus fruit, a reminder of the ancient tradition that the Franciscans were the first to cultivate citrus fruits in Europe.

North of Gargnano the lake narrows and the cliffs close into the shore; here La Gardesana road pierces tunnel after tunnel like a needle as it hems through some of the most striking scenery along the lake. An equally splendid detour is to turn off after Gargnano at **Campione**, a tiny hamlet huddled under the cliffs, along the old military road for **Tremosine**, atop a 300 m precipice that dives down sheer into the blue waters below; from the top there are views that take in the entire lake. The road from Tremosine rejoins the lake and La Gardesana at the next town along the lake, **Limone sul Garda**.

Although it seems obvious that Limone was named after its lemon groves, prominent in the neat rows of terraced white posts and trellises, scholars sullenly insist it was derived instead from the Latin *Limen*. Nor is it true that Limone was the first to grow lemons in Europe (the Arabs introduced them into Sicily and Spain), but none of that takes away from one of the liveliest resorts on the lake, with a beach over 3 km long.

Riva del Garda

After Limone the lake enters into the Trentino region and the charming town of Riva, snug under the amphitheatre of mountains. During the days of Austrian rule (1813–1918), Riva first blossomed as a resort, nicknamed the 'Southern Pearl on the Austro-Hungarian Riviera'. It is one of best bases for exploring both the lake and the Trentino mountains to the north.

The centre of town is the Piazza Tre Novembre with its plain, 13th-century **Torre Apponale**; just behind it, surrounded by a natural moat, stands the sombre grey bulk of the 12th-century castle, the **Rocca**, housing a civic museum with local archaeological finds from the prehistoric settlement at Lake Ledro and from Roman Riva (open 9–12 and 2:30–6; closed Mon). The early 17th-century church of the **Inviolata** was built by an unknown but imaginative Portuguese architect with a fine gilt and stucco Baroque interior. A funicular (or a steep path) makes the ascent to the Venetian watchtower, the 1508 **Bastione**.

There are a number of pleasant excursions from Riva, but one of the best is the closest, the **Cascata del Varone**, a lovely 87 m waterfall in a tight gorge only 3 km away, by the village of Varone. Another fine excursion is up over the exciting Ponale Road (N. 240) to green **Lake Ledro**, noted not only for its pretty setting, in wooded hills, but for the remains of a Bronze Age (1500 BC) settlement of *palafitte* lake dwellings, discovered in 1929; one has been reconstructed near the ancient piles around **Molina**, where there's also a museum, with pottery, axes, daggers, and amber jewellery recovered from the site. From here you can continue to Lake Idro, through the shadowy narrow gorge of the **Valle d'Ampola**. Another excursion is up to **Arco** (Roman *Arx*, 'stronghold'), a popular health resort in the days of the Austro-Hungarian Empire. Among the sights are a 16th-century palace, former property of the cultured Counts of Arco, who also built the castle crowning the town, set in clusters of cypresses—a half-hour's walk up, and worth it for the views. Arco has a fine collegiate church, **S. Maria Assunta**, designed by a follower of Palladio, and a botanical garden once owned by the Archduke.

WHERE TO STAY AND EATING OUT

Gargnano: In Gargnano's suburb, Villa di Gargano, ***Baia d'Oro**, Via Gamberera 13, tel (0365) 71 171, is a small but charming old hotel on the lakefront with an artistic inn-like atmosphere. It has a private beach, and picturesque terrace; all rooms have baths (open 20 March–Oct; L85 000). For a pure Victorian ambience, even if furnishings are replicas, reserve at the ***Hotel Giulia**, Viale Rimembranza tel (0365) 71 022; added attractions are its fine lake views, beach, and good food. (Open April–15 Oct, all rooms have bath; L78–90 000.) Eating out in Gargnano is a pleasure at the celebrated **La**

Tortuga, Via XXIV Maggio 5 (near the harbour), tel (0365) 71 251, a gourmet haven on Lake Garda featuring delicate dishes based on seasonal ingredients and fish from the lake, perfectly prepared; delicious vegetable soufflés, innovative meat courses, mouth-watering desserts and fresh fruit sorbets, grand wine and liquor lists. Closed Mon eve, Tues, & three weeks in July; reservations a must (around L75 000).

Limone: Prices here are not as astronomical as other resorts. The finest, ******Le Palme**, Via Porto 36, tel (0365) 954 681, is housed in a pretty Venetian villa, preserving much of its original charm with modern up-to-date amenities. Located in the old centre of Limone, and named after its two ancient palm trees, it has a fine terrace and tennis courts, though no beach. Open end of March–Oct, all 28 rooms have private baths; L70–80 000. Many of the lakeside choices here are large and ungainly, if inexpensive by Garda standards, but *****Sogno del Benaco**, Lungolago Marconi 7, tel (0365) 954 026, is of a more reasonable size and is open all year (L42 000).

Riva: When German intellectuals like Nietzsche or Günter Grass need a little rest and relaxation in Italy, they check in at the ******Hotel du Lac et du Parc**, Viale Rovereto 44, tel (0464) 520 202. Set in a large lakeside garden, the hotel is spacious, airy and tranquil, and the rooms all have bath and TV; and there are indoor and outdoor pools, a beach, sailing school, gym, sauna, and tennis. Closed Nov–March; L180–215 000. Right on the port in Riva's main square, the *****Hotel Sole**, Piazza III Novembre, tel (0464) 552 686, has plenty of atmosphere and a beautiful terrace; most rooms, which vary widely in size and quality, look out over the lake; most have private bath. Open all year round, L52–74 000 without bath, L68–110 000 with. A fine economy choice is the ***Villa Minerva**, Viale Roma 40, tel (0464) 553 031, not far from the centre and very pleasant—and popular. Open all year, L32–37 000 without bath, L45–50 000 with. The best place to eat around Riva is **Vecchia Riva**, Via Bastione 3, tel (0464) 555 061, where you can dig your fork into a spicy antipasta made of goose, and pasta dishes like *pennette con le code di scampi* or *farfalline al radicchio*, swordfish, smoked trout, or a number of meat dishes; L40 000, closed Tues.

In Arco: ***Hotel Garden**, Via Caproni 25, tel (0464) 516 379, is a modern hotel under the mountain, with a small pool (15 Mar–30 Oct), showers in each room, L40 000.

Riva to Peschiera: the East Shore

TOURIST INFORMATION
Torbole: Lungolago Verona, tel (0464) 505 177
Malcésine: Via Capitanato 1, tel (045) 740 0555
Garda: Lungolago Regina Adelaide 25, tel (045) 725 5194
Torri del Benaco: Viale F.lli Lavanda 10, tel (045) 722 5120
Bardolino: Piazza Matteotti 53, tel (045) 721 0078
Peschiera del Garda: Piazza Municipio, tel (045) 755 0381
Lazise: Via Fontana 14, tel (045) 758 0114

Torbole

The northern part of the east shore is dominated by the long ridge of **Monte Baldo**, rising up over **Torbole** at the mouth of the Sacra, the main river flowing into Lake

Garda. Torbole is a pleasant resort, where the winds especially favour sailing and wind surfing, but it's also famous in the annals of naval history. In 1437, during a war with the Visconti, the Venetians were faced with the difficulty of getting supplies to Brescia because the Milanese controlled Peschiera and the southern reaches of Lake Garda. A Greek sailor came up with the following suggestion: that the Venetians sail a fleet of provision-packed warships up the Adige to its furthest navigable point, then transport the vessels over Monte Baldo into Lake Garda. Anyone who has seen Herzog's film *Fitzcarraldo* will appreciate the difficulties involved, and the amazing fact that, under the command of Venice's great condotierre Gattamelata and aided by 2000 oxen, the 26 ships were launched at Torbole only 15 days after leaving the Adige. Yet after all that trouble the supplies never reached Brescia. The same trick, however, perhaps even suggested by the same Greek, enabled Mohammed II to bring his fleet into the upper harbour of Constantinople the following year, leading to the capture of the city.

Malcésine

South of Torbole and the forbidding sheer cliffs of the Monte de Nago hanging perilously over the lake (which nevertheless attract their share of human flies), the Gardesana Orientale passes into the Veneto at **Malcésine**, the loveliest town on the east shore. The Veronese, and later Venetians, have always taken care to protect this part of the coast, or the 'Riviera degli Olivi' as they've dubbed it, and the town is graced by the magnificent 13th-century **Scaliger castle**, rising up on a sheer rock over the water. The castle houses a small museum, but is especially worth visiting for the views from its tower (open April–Oct 9–8 pm; otherwise weekends and holidays only, 9–5; adm). It was while sketching this castle that Goethe was suspected of spying; Malcésine has since made up by erecting a bronze bust of the poet in a broad-rimmed hat.

Besides the Scaliger castle, there's the 16th-century **Palace of the Venetian Captains of the Lake** now the Municipio, in the centre of Malcésine's web of medieval streets. A cableway runs up to **Bocca Tratto Spino**, just below the highest peak of Monte Baldo, the Punta del Telegrafo (2201 m); its ski slopes are very popular with the Veronese, and its views are ravishing.

Torri del Benaco and Garda

Further south, past a stretch of shore silvery with olives, there are two pretty resort towns on either side of the promontory of San Vigilio. The first, **Torri del Benaco** (Roman *Castrum Turrium*) is defended by a 1383 **Scaliger castle**; in the church of **Santa Trinità** there are 14th-century Giottesque frescoes. The ferry boat crosses over from here for Maderno; the steamer continues around the lovely, cypress-tipped **Punta di San Vigilio** with its Renaissance **Villa Guarienti** by the great Venetian architect Sammicheli, the old church of San Vigilio, and a 16th-century tavern.

Between Punta di San Vigilio and the distinct soufflé-shaped headland called the Rocca lies **Garda**, which gave the lake its modern name. Although Garda was founded before the Romans (prehistoric graffiti and a necropolis have been found in its outskirts), it adopted the name the Lombards gave it, *Warthe*, 'the watch'. After Charlemagne defeated the Lombards Garda became a county, and in an ancient castle on the Rocca, of which only a few stones remain, the wicked Count Berenguer secretly held Queen Adelaide of Italy in 960, after he murdered her husband Lotario and she refused to wed his son. After a year she was discovered by a monk, who spent another year plotting her escape. She then received the protection of King Otto I of Germany, who defeated Berenguer, married the widowed queen, and thus became Holy Roman Emperor. Garda has many fine old palaces, villas, and narrow medieval lanes, and is the last really scenic spot on the lake.

East from Garda, the road climbs to **Caprino Veronese**, the capital of Monte Baldo, where you can visit **Palazzo Carlotti**, with a remarkable ceiling painted with grotesques. A winding road from here runs north along the entire eastern flank of Baldo, past **Ferrara di Monte Baldo**, set in a pretty green saddle of pasturelands, with the Monte Baldo botanical garden. The road carries on all the way north to Mori and the N. 240 to Torbole, without any little roads daring to cross the mighty mountain down to Garda's shore.

Bardolino and Peschiera

Bardolino's most important crop is familiar to any modern Bacchus, and more than a few Austrians and Germans pour into town from 15 Sept–15 Oct for a 'grape cure'. Between the vineyards rises a fine collection of 19th-century villas. It has two important churches: the 8th-century **San Zeno** and the 12th-century **San Severo** with frescoes. The next town, **Lazise**, was the main Venetian port, and by its harbour retains an ensemble of Venetian buildings as well as another fine Scaliger castle. Just east of here, in **Pastrengo**, there's the **Dinosaur Park** and **Garda Safari** for addicts of concrete brontosauri, with a zoo and reptilarium all rolled up in one, and an autosafari replete with Tibetan oxen, jaguars, tigers, and hippos, in a tropical garden setting.

Peschiera del Garda is an old military town on the railway from Verona, near the mouth of the River Mincio that drains Lake Garda. Its strategic position has caused it to be fortified since Roman times, though the imposing walls that you see today are 16th-century Venetian, reinforced by the Austrians when Peschiera was one of the corners of the Empire's 'Quadrilateral'. Today, like Desenzano, Peschiera is mainly a transit point to the lake, but its purifying plant still helps it to fulfil its ancient role as a defender, this time of the lake's ecology and fish population. Here, too, you can treat the children at **Gardaland**, Italy's largest and most popular amusement park (to the tune of 2 million visitors a year) with its Magic Mountain, Colorado boat ride, reproduction of the Valley of the Kings, the Amazon, electronic robots etc. etc. etc. for a perfect day of packaged fun.

The region south of Peschiera is known for its white wine *Custoza*, and for the pretty gardens and groves that line the Mincio River between Peschiera and the swampy lakes of Mantua. The greatest of these, the **Sigurtà Gardens** , were the 40-year project of 'Italy's Capability Brown'—500,000 square metres, containing 20 different Anglo-Italian gardens of flowering plants and trees, along seven km of porphyry paths. The Sigurtà Gardens are near **Valeggio**, an attractive town in its own right, with a castle and bridge built by the Visconti.

WHERE TO STAY AND EATING OUT (tel prefix 045)

The east shore of Garda is more family oriented, slower paced, and less expensive.

In Malcésine: Next to the lake and not far from the centre, the ***Excelsior Bay**, Lungolago, tel 740 0380, is a fine resort hotel with a pool and garden, and splendid views from the balconies of its rooms. Open end of March–end of Oct; L38–48 000 without bath, L50–68 000 with. Another good choice is the ***Malcésine**, Piazza Pallone 2, tel 740 0173, pleasantly situated in its garden with swimming terrace; nice rooms all with bath. Open 22 March–15 Oct; L45–65 000. **Hotel Panorama**, up at Val di Monte 9, tel 740 0171, has fine views over the lake, and a tennis court and swimming pools besides (L65 000, all with bath; open May–Sept).

In Torri del Benaco: The ***Gardesana**, Piazza Calderini 20, tel 722 5411, is the most comfortable hotel, right on the harbour with splendid views of lake and castle. Breakfast and meals are served on the harbour patio when the weather is good. All rooms have bath; L56–82 000.

Garda: ****Eurotel**, Via Marconi 18, tel 725 5107, is large, modern, and luxurious and again, good value compared with the west shore hotels. It has a fine garden and pool, and is open from 9 April–Oct; L56–92 000, according to season, all rooms with bath. The very stylish ****Regina Adelaide**, Via XX Settembre, tel 725 5013 has a golf course, frigo bars and TVs in each room (L60–110 000, all with bath). The ***Hotel du Parc**, Via Marconi 3, tel 725 5343, is a pleasant lakeside villa, open all year; all rooms with bath, L50–82 000.

Bardolino: One of the nicest lakeside hotels is the hot Italian pink **Riviera**, Via Lungolago Lenotti 12, tel 721 2600, with a beach and little garden of palm trees. There are cheaper, but not as attractive rooms in the annexe (L39–46 000 without bath, L30–60 000 with; open April–mid-Oct). You can dine well at **Aurora**, Via San Severo 18, tel 721 0038, near Bardolino's pretty Romanesque landmark. Specialities include the denizens of the lake, especially trout prepared in a variety of styles (L35–40 000; closed Mon & Nov).

Into the Dolomites: Treviso to Belluno

It hardly seems fair to Italy's other tourism organizations that Venetia should have both the country's most beautiful city and its most beautiful mountains as well. But it does mean that you can have a wonderfully varied holiday without having to spend much time on the road: Belluno is only an hour-and-a-half drive from Venice, and Cortina d'Ampezzo, the glamour puss of winter sports in the Dolomites, another hour-and-a-half further along.

Treviso

Treviso is one of the pleasant surprises of the Veneto. Famous in Italy for its cherries and Benettons, it is laced with little canals (or *canagi*) diverted from the river Sile, langorous with willow trees, and humming with more than a little discreet prosperity. Like Verona, it formed its character in the century preceding its domination by Venice (1389–1796), when it was ruled by the da Camino family and when its churches were embellished by

The Walls of Treviso

one of Giotto's greatest pupils, Tomaso da Modena, who did little outside of Treviso. Another unique and charming feature are the frescoed façades of its houses and palaces; attractive building stone was scarce, so it became the custom to cover the humble bricks with a layer of plaster and painted decoration—in the 1300s, with simple colours and patterns, and by the 1500s, with heroic mythologies and allegories. Although faded and fragmented since then—on Good Friday 1944 an air raid destroyed half of Treviso in five minutes—one of the delights of visiting the city is to pick out frescoes under the eaves, or hidden in the shadows of an arcade.

GETTING AROUND
Treviso's station is just south of the city walls, at the end of Via Roma, and the coach station is on the same street, only just within the walls. There are frequent buses and trains from Venice or Mestre to Treviso (½ hour); from Treviso you can pick up a bus for Masèr, Ásolo, and Bassano del Grappa, or a train for Castelfranco, Cittadella and Vicenza; other trains go east to Udine. The ACTT bus to Treviso's airport leaves from a stop across from the station.

TOURIST INFORMATION
Palazzo Scotti, Via Toniolo 41, tel (0422) 547 632; ask for their itinerary of frescoed houses.

Piazza dei Signori and Duomo
From the bus or train station, both located on Via Roma south of the centre, it's a 10-minute walk over the Sile along the Corso del Popolo and Via Venti Settembre to the **Piazza dei Signori**, the heart of Treviso. Here stands the city's only surviving *comunale* palace, the large brick **Palazzo dei Trecento**, though even it had to be mostly reconstructed after taking a bomb on the nose. Even more reconstructed is its towered neighbour, the **Palazzo del Podestà** (19th century).

172

Tucked behind the Palazzo dei Trecento and an iron door is the municipal pawn shop, or **Monte di Pietà**; on weekday mornings between 10 and 12 you can visit the recently restored **Sala dei Reggitori**, a rare survivor of 16th-century interior design, with walls of gilt leather, frescoed panels in their original place, and a lovely, painted, beamed ceiling. The other two rooms have paintings by Sebastiano Ricci and the Neapolitan Luca Giordano, which have the air of having been pawned long ago and never reclaimed. In the same irregular little square are two Romanesque churches, **Santa Lucia** with a chapel frescoed by Tomaso da Modena, and linked to it, **San Vito**, with damaged frescoes from the 1100s. From Piazza S. Vito, make a little detour down Via della Campana and along the canal of Via Buranelli, one of Treviso's prettiest spots.

Treviso's arcaded main street, **Calmaggiore**, leads from Piazza dei Signori to the **Duomo**, an oft-rebuilt church topped by a cluster of domes, founded in the 12th century; the adjacent but usually closed baptistry gives an idea of what the cathedral looked like before its many alterations. The artistic focus within is the **Cappella Malchiostro**, frescoed by Pordenone and his arch-enemy Titian; Vasari tells how Pordenone always painted with a sword at his hip in case Titian showed up (Titian is responsible for the *Annunciation*, and Pordenone the rest). Paris Bordone of Treviso is represented in the vestibule of the chapel, and elsewhere there are fine Renaissance tombs of local prelates, including one by Pietro Lombardo on the left side of the altar. The atmospheric **crypt** is a survivor of the original 12th-century cathedral.

Museo Civico and San Francesco

From the Piazza Duomo, Via Riccati meets the Borgo Cavour near the **Museo Civico** (9–12 and 2–5, closed Mon and Sun afternoons; adm). Its archaeological collection on the ground floor includes unusual 5th-century BC bronze discs from Montebelluna, a bronze winged penis, a favourite Etruscan motif, some Etruscan sarcophagi, and Gaulish swords, bent and buried with their warriors; a three-faced statue on display may have been an old symbol of Treviso. The upstairs is given over to paintings, all newly arranged but the net effect of all its acres of canvas is to set off the gems, all conveniently hung in the same room: Jacopo Bassano's *Crucifixion*, Titian's *Sperone Speroni*, a lushly coloured portrait, and best of all, Lorenzo Lotto's reflective *Portrait of the Guardian of S. Zanipolo*, a Dominican looking up from his writing.

Borgo Cavour exits the city through the great Venetian gate, the **Porta dei Santi Quaranta** (1517), encompassed by an impressive stretch of the ramparts. From here you can stroll along the top of the walls north towards the city's other great gate, Guglielmo Bergamasco's exotic white Istrian stone **Porta San Tomaso**, guarded by the lion of St Mark.

Back towards the centre on the Via Canova, the frescoed **Casa Trevigiana** is a reliquary of the city's architecture and decorative arts, containing bits and pieces salvaged from her ruins. Especially notable are the fire screens and other furnishings in wrought iron, a local craft since Renaissance times (but closed because of an endemic lack of funds).

San Francesco and Santa Caterina

The northeast quarter of Treviso is at times the smelliest, thanks to the lively and colourful **Fish Market** (Pescheria), built over a canal for hygienic reasons. From here,

Via S. Parisio leads north to the tall, brick Romanesque-Gothic **San Francesco**, a 13th-century church with a ship's keel roof, two frescoes by Tomaso da Modena—a giant *St Christopher* and a *Madonna and saints* to the left of the altar—as well as the tombs of Francesca Petrarco (Petrarch) and Pietro Alighieri, the children of Italy's two greatest poets, whose final meeting-place here in Treviso is only a coincidence. There are several frescoed houses in this area; from Via San Francesco follow Via Mazzoni, turning right in Via S. Agostino, to Piazza Matteotti and Via Stangade to see one of the best—**Casa Federici** (no. 12), decorated with scenes from the lovelorn lives of Cleopatra and Dido. Nearby, just around the corner from Piazza Matteotti, is **Santa Caterina**, a deconsecrated church where the powers that be have squirrelled away Tomaso da Modena's masterful *St Ursula cycle* of frescoes, which, though worn, show some of the same charm that Venice's Carpaccio would later bestow on the subject. Unfortunately you need to book at least a day ahead to see them: tel (0422) 51 337 or ask at the Museo Civico.

San Nicolò

Treviso's best church, the Dominican San Nicolò is located in one of the city's most charming quarters (southwest of the Piazza dei Signori; take Via A. Diaz from the Corso del Popolo). San Nicolò is the finer twin of San Francesco, with an attractive triple apse. The interior is a treasure-house of lovely frescoes—from a huge, luck-bringing *St Christopher* on the south wall to the charming pages by Lorenzo Lotto on the *Tomb of Agostino d'Onigo* sculpted in 1500 by Antonio Rizzo. Tomaso da Modena and his school painted the saints on the columns (*St Jerome* and *St Agnes* on the first column are by the master), a medieval conceit that symbolically made the saints part of the congregation. Even better are his candid frescoes of forty famous Dominicans in the chapter house of the adjacent **Seminario**; painted in 1352, the artist leápt ahead a century in the spontaneity and individuality of his figures—one is wearing what is believed to be the first portrayal of spectacles in art (ring the bell; open Mon–Fri 9–12 and 3:30–7).

Around Treviso

Just up the Sile from Treviso, **Canizzano** has some of the area's most ancient working water-wheels. For centuries Treviso ground Venice's wheat; in 1764 the Sile had 133 water-wheels, mostly owned by Venetian aristocrats or convents, who transported the flour down the river to the lagoon in big barges. Another couple of kilometres further on, in the parish church of **Santa Cristina di Quinto**, there's a beautiful altarpiece of the *Madonna and saints* by Lorenzo Lotto. Like Giovanni Bellini, Lotto places the figures in a classical alcove, the columns of which are continued by the ornate frame—not so much to fool the eye as to draw it into the central mystery. Quinto is also the site of the **Parco del Sile**, with its watermill and landscapes of water and reeds (open only Sat 2–sunset and Sun 9–sunset).

    Istrana, a couple of kilometres northwest of Quinto, is the site of a charming Rococo villa by Giorgio Massari, the 18th-century **Villa Lattes**; inside there's a collection of music boxes (open Tues and Fri 9–12, Sat and Sun 9–12 and 3–6; adm).

WHERE TO STAY (tel prefix 0422)
In Treviso there are a couple of pleasant, moderately priced hotels worth a mention. For convenience, there's the modern ******Continental** near the station at Via Roma 16, tel

57 216, offering doubles with bath for L125–165 000. For a bit of charm and air conditioning, not too much further from the station, try **Le Beccherie**, in the heart of the city on Piazza Ancilotto 11, tel 540 871 (L64 000 with breakfast). Cheapest of all is *Alla Colomba**, Via Ortazzo 25, tel 542 284 (L25 000 without bath).

If you're driving, however, you can stay just north of town in Paderno di Ponzano at a lovely villa, *****Relais El Toulà**, Via Postumia 63, tel 969 191. With only 10 elegant and luxurious double rooms you're assured lots of special touches and supreme tranquillity; El Toulà is one of Italy's poshest hotels. The extensive grounds include a swimming-pool; tennis courts are nearby, and there's a charming bar and excellent restaurant. Prices are also luxury: bed and breakfast L260–450 000; closed in Aug.

EATING OUT

More people eat than stay in Treviso, and the city's fine restaurants are a tempting reason to follow the crowd. Besides cherries, Treviso produces the Veneto's finest red *radicchio* (chicory); a typical dish is *sopa coada*—a baked pigeon casserole. For an aperitif, try a glass of Trevisian Prosecco.

The restaurant of the above hotel, **Le Beccherie** (tel 540 871), is one of Treviso's bastions of local atmosphere and cooking—a great place to try *pasta e fagioli* with red *radicchio*; complete meals L35 000; closed Thurs eve, Fri and July. The city's most acclaimed restaurant, **El Toulà da Alfredo** (Via Collalto 26, tel 540 275), disdains tradition for a lovely, elegant Belle Epoque decor and an imaginative menu that includes in addition to Veneto specialities (try their *sopa coada*) French and Viennese dishes. Closed Mon and the middle of Aug; call ahead (L65 000).

In a beautiful medieval building, **Al Bersagliere** (Via Barberia 21, tel 541 988) has more *sopa coada* and Venetian specialities such as squid in its own ink, risotto, and liver Venetian-style. Delicious antipasti too; around L45 000; closed Sun and Aug. A fair bargain and a boon to homesick Americans, **Toni del Spin**, Via Inferiore 7, tel 543 829, offers at the end of a Veneto meal (*bigoli*, risotto, *risi e bisi*, or in the winter, roast suckling pig) American apple pie! Closed Sun and in Aug; L20–25 000. Another inexpensive choice, **All'Oca Bianca**, Vicolo della Torre 7, tel 541 850, has decent home cooking for around L15 000; closed Wed.

North of Treviso:
Oderzo, Conegliano, and Vittorio Veneto

North and west of Treviso is the Marca Trevigiana, the medieval territory ruled by the lords of the city and, in the 14th century, one of the first *terra firma* properties annexed by Venice. Part of it—Ásolo, Masèr, Possagno, and Castelfranco—may be found under 'North of Padua'. What remains—the towns of Oderzo, Conegliano, and Vittorio Veneto are synonymous with Prosecco, the seductive fizzy white wine that constantly tempts citizens of the Veneto from their appointed tasks for a little nip 'in the shade' (*nell'ombretta*).

The second temptation is red chicory, or *radicchio*, which the local literature describes as an 'edible flower, produced by a long series of farms with primary ambitions, and prepared under the most strange and unexpected cooking ways'. To find it at its most edible, if not 'strange', come in December.

GETTING AROUND

Buses run every hour or so from Treviso to Oderzo. Trains from Padua, Venice, and Conegliano run only once or twice a day north to Belluno, via Conegliano and Vittorio Veneto; another, longer but more scenic route goes by way of Montebelluna and Feltre. The Dolomiti-Bus Company has daily routes directly into the mountains (Agordo, Arabba, Falcade, Colle S. Lucia) from Venice if you want to go direct; in the summer it's advisable to reserve a ticket at the ATP office in Piazzale Roma (tel 522 2099).

TOURIST INFORMATION

Oderzo: Palazzo Porcia, Piazza Castello 1, tel (0422) 717 627
Conegliano: Viale Carducci 32, tel (0438) 21 230
Vittorio Veneto: Piazza del Popolo 18, tel (0438) 57 243
Alpago: Piazza 11 Gennaio 1945, in Tambre, tel (0437) 49 277

Oderzo

No one has ever heard of Oderzo, 27 km northeast of Treviso, but in its Roman heyday, when it was called *Opitergium*, its renown spread as far as Egypt, where it was recorded in the first century BC. Pompey destroyed it, Julius Caesar rebuilt it and made it an important communications centre for the region, reason enough for passing barbarians to smash it. It avoided history for most of the succeeding centuries, and today it's *Opitergium*'s remains that are the town's biggest attraction, especially the hunt mosaics in the **Museo Civico**, Via Garibaldi (Tues–Sat 2:30–5:30, Sun 10–12 and 3–6); the **Pinacoteca**, nearby at Via Garibaldi 80, has a large collection of engravings by Alberto Martini, a homegrown surrealist (May–Sept Mon–Fri 3–7; Oct–April 2:30–6:30).

Besides Romans and surrealists, Oderzo is known for its red red full-bodied wines; French ex-pats like Merlot and Cabernet, and *Raboso delle grave del Piave* all of which you can discover along the 68-km *Strada del Vino Rosso* winding from Oderzo to Conegliano. Non-vinous detours on the way include **Portobuffolè**, a small town north of Oderzo with the uncanny eerie emptiness of a De Chirico painting; its walls are intact, as is the curious late Renaissance **Casa di Gaia da Camino**, sometimes used for exhibitions. Otherwise, a pair of little churches may tempt you off the road: **Ormelle's Chiesetta dei Cavalieri Templari**, one of a very few Templar foundations to survive in Italy, and the church of **San Giorgio** in **San Polo di Piave**, with late Gothic frescoes, including a Last Supper with a seafood menu.

Conegliano

The old castled town of **Conegliano**, north of Treviso on N. 13, is the capital of Prosecco, home of Italy's first wine school, founded in 1876, and the birthplace of Giambattista Cima (1460–1518)—'the sweet shepherd among Venetian painters', as Mary McCarthy called him, the son of a seller of hides, who used his native countryside as a background in many of his works. If you haven't seen the originals, reproductions are displayed at his birthplace, the **Casa di Cima** (Via Cima 24, behind the cathedral; open Sat and Sun 4–6, Dec–Feb 3–5; adm). An original and beautiful Cima, *Madonna with Child, Saints, and Angels* (1493) forms the altarpiece of the 14th-century **Duomo**, its façade frescoed by Ludovico Pozzoserrato. He and some of his more inept 16th-century fellows also frescoed the inside of the adjacent **Scuola di Santa Maria dei Battuti** (the hall of a confraternity of flagellants); open 9–12 except Wed.

The Duomo is on Conegliano's finest street, **Via Venti Settembre**, lined with old palaces. The **Castle** on the hill, though founded in the 10th century, has mostly been reconstructed to house the **Museo Civico** (9–12 and 3:30–7, winter 9–12 and 2–5:30, closed Mon; adm), with its permanent exhibition on a local obsession—grapes—this time in art instead of in the bottle. The views over the rolling Prosecco countryside make the walk up worthwhile; to see and taste it at its best on ground level, take the 42-kilometre **Strada del vino bianco**—the white-wine road—between Conegliano and **Valdobbiàdene** to the west. On the way, be sure to visit the parish church of **San Pietro di Feletto**, founded around the year 1000 and frescoed in the 15th century by an unknown itinerant painter. His 'Poor Man's Bible' is a jewel of popular religious art; his *Nativity*, especially, is more moving than many from more famous brushes.

Vittorio Veneto

The Venetian Pre-Alps bore a heavy share of battles in both World Wars, and the hills around Asiago, Monte Grappa and the Piave, are often crowned with British, Italian or French war cemeteries. **Vittorio Veneto**, north of Conegliano, saw Italy's final battle in the First World War (October 1918) and has a street named after it in every city in Italy. The Vittorio in its name, however, comes not from the victory but from Italy's first king, Vittorio Emanuele II; in 1866, to celebrate the birth of Italy, two rival towns were united—**Cèneda** down below, and the upper, walled town of **Serravalle**.

Cèneda, which has developed into the commercial half of Vittorio, is mostly to be visited for its 16th-century **Loggia** attributed to Sansovino and now home of the **Museo della Battaglia**, devoted to the long, final engagement (open 10–2 and 4–6:30, from Oct–April 10–12 and 2–5, closed Mon, same ticket for S. Lorenzo and museum in Serravalle). Also worth seeking out is the church of **Santa Maria del Meschio**, for a lovely *Annunziazione* by Andrea Previtali (early 16th-century), where the Virgin has a view of a delightful early spring landscape through her window.

Serravalle, which the tourist office tries to promote as a 'little Florence of the north' has retained most of its austere Renaissance character, its old palaces, squares, ancient tower and gates. Like Cèneda, it has a museum in its shield-encrusted **Loggia Serravallese** (1460s), this sheltering local odds and ends and a lovely terracotta *Madonna and Child* by Sansovino, belonging to the **Museo del Cenedese** (open 10–12 and 4:30–6:30, Oct–April 10–12 and 3–5, closed Tues). The same ticket (see above) will get you in to see the fine mid-15th-century fresco cycle in **San Lorenzo dei Battuti** (another flagellants' church) by the south gate (open 3:30–4:30, closed Tues; arrange visits through the Museo del Cenedese).

On the far side of Piazza M. Flaminio, the 18th-century **Duomo** has an 1545 altarpiece by Titian of the *Madonna and saints* but little else to recommend it. Serravalle's other attractions require more effort to see, especially if you're relying on your pedal extremities. There's the **Pieve di Sant'Andrea di Bigonzo**, towards Cèneda, with 15th-century frescoes on the life of St Andrew, by local painters Antonello da Serravalle and Frigimelica. Even better is the 1336 *Tomb of Rizzardo da Camino* in the church of **Santa Giustina**, near the ruins of Serravalle's castle.

Bosco del Cansiglio and the Alpago

Vittorio is the base for visiting the enchanting **Bosco del Cansiglio**, a forest of beech and red pine interspersed with flowery meadows on a lofty karstic plateau. Known as the Republic of Venice's *Bosco da reme*, the 'wood of oars', it was administered by a special *consilium*, who saw that the trees were planted to grow straight and suitable for galley duty. The penalty for cutting one down was death. **Fregona**, linked by bus with Vittorio Veneto, is a small town noted for its production of a heady dessert wine called Vin Santo and a good base for walks in the woods, and the **Grotte del Calieròn**, a series of caves driven through the karst by a torrent. Mt Cansiglio itself offers the closest downhill skiing to Venice.

The slopes may also be reached from the beautiful **Alpago** valley on the northern side. The Alpago, the Veneto's 'balcony of flowers' has a picture postcard lake, **Lago di Santa Croce**, where the boating, fishing, and watersports have yet to become trendy and expensive. The lake is the focal point for the Alpago's little villages, celebrated for their kitchens more than anything, and **Valdenogher**, site of the pretty 15th-century Palazzo d'Alessandria, with mullioned windows and a portico. Art historians have identified the lovely natural amphitheatre of the **Val Belluna**, leading north from the Alpago into the Dolomites, as the background in Titian's *Sacred and Profane Love* (in the Borghese Gallery, Rome).

WHERE TO STAY AND EATING OUT

San Polo di Piave is worth a stop not only for its church but its superb restaurant, **Gambrinus**, Via Gambrinus 22, tel (0422) 855 043, in a beautiful setting—a garden full of birds and soft lights, and unusual dishes like a fruit risotto, guinea fowl with radicchio, eel from the Sile, or rabbit with basil (L40–50 000, closed Mon and Jan).

Conegliano (tel prefix 0438) is a popular day-trip or stopover and as such has a number of excellent restaurants, one of which is in the central and handsome *****Canon d'Oro**, Via XX Settembre 129, tel 34 246 (L49 000 without bath, L72–82 000 with); in the restaurant try homecooked dishes like *bollito misto* and *vitello tonnato* (veal in tuna sauce) and wash it down with the good house wine (closed Sat; L30 000). Conegliano's most celebrated restaurant, **Tre Panoce**, Via Vecchia Trevigiana, tel 60 071, is located just outside town in an old farmhouse crowning a hill of vineyards, with outdoor dining available in the summer. The food matches the lovely surroundings, prepared with fresh ingredients from the country; the menu changes daily, but game specialities and mushroom dishes appear frequently (closed Mon and all of Aug; L45 000). Another excellent choice, unfortunately closed during the same period, **Al Salisà**, Via XX Settembre 2, tel (0438) 24 288, is more consciously elegant and features succulent snails (*lumache*) and game specialities in season, especially venison. Good local wine list, frequent lunch specials; around L35 000; closed Tues eve, Wed, and Aug.

In Vittorio Veneto (tel prefix 0438), *****Hotel Terme**, Via delle Terme 4, tel 554 345, has good, comfortable rooms and an excellent kitchen, serving specialities with *radicchio* and garden-fresh vegetables for L35 000 (closed Mon); rooms with bath, L95 000.

In the Alpago there are some 6000 rooms to rent in private homes and one of the top restaurants in Venetia, **Dolada**, located in Plois, overlooking the surroundings and Lake Santa Croce, at Via Dolada 9, tel (0437) 479 141; closed Mon, except in July and Aug. Wood panelling, candlelight and romance accompany homemade pasta, the celebrated *zuppa dolada*, superb fish, duck and lamb dishes and an exceptional wine list, all for around L50 000. In Puos d'Alpago, **San Lorenzo**, Via IV Novembre 57, tel 43 52, is another exceptional restaurant in the land of good food; snails (a local speciality) and stuffed breast of veal are among the antipasti. Pasta with wild asparagus is a delicious choice in spring for primo, followed by fish from the Lago di Santa Croce, and there's lots of other choices as well (L30 000, closed Wed and June).

Belluno and Feltre

TOURIST INFORMATION
Belluno: Piazza Martiri 27, tel (0437) 28 746; also Via Rodolfo Psaro 21, tel (0437) 940 083; refuge info from the CAI at Via Ricci 1.
Feltre: Largo Castaldi 7, tel (0439) 32 032.

Belluno

The Veneto's northernmost provincial capital, Belluno is as notable for its artistic or historic monuments as for its magnificent setting at the junction of the Piave and Ardo rivers, with the first peaks of the Dolomites as a backdrop. It also a transportation hub for the mountains, and a good place to pick up information on hikes and ski resorts in the eastern Dolomites.

The most important building in Belluno is the **Duomo**, a serene 16th-century work by Venice's Tullio Lombardo, but never completed and several times rebuilt after earthquakes. The 18th-century campanile was designed by Filippo Juvarra (court architect to the House of Savoy) and from its top the stunning views of the town and mountains are enough to make a trip to Belluno worthwhile. Piazza del Duomo is shared by the 15th-century **Palazzo dei Rettori**, the ornate residence of Belluno's Venetian governors, and the **Torre Civica**, a relic of the town's medieval castle. Around the corner, in Via Duomo, the **Museo Civico** (10–12 and 3–6, Sun 10–12, closed Mon) is a treat for fans of that extroverted Baroque virtuoso Sebastiano Ricci and his nephew and collaborator Marco, natives of Belluno. Another native represented in the museum, sculptor Andrea Brustolon (1662–1732) was a leading figure of his day, whose gifted technical skills made him as popular as the fact that he never attempted to do anything original.

Via Duomo gives onto little **Piazza del Mercato** with its porticoes and fountain dating from 1410, one of the most charming corners of the old town. The main street Via Mezzaterra leads south from here to the 14th-century **Porta Ruga**, with a postcard view of the Piave gorge and the mountains. Just off Via Mezzaterra, the church of **San Pietro** has a painted high altarpiece by Sebastiano Ricci and carved ones in the chapel by Brustolon.

If you don't have the time or stamina for a major foray into the mountains, take the bus to **Nevegal**, 11 km south of Belluno. Nevegal has a little ski resort and a chairlift to the

179

Rifugio Brigata Alpina Cadore (1600 m), with a pretty alpine garden. From here it's an easy three-hour walk up to the **Col Visentin**, site of another refuge that commands a unique panorama: north across the sea of Dolomite peaks and south to the Venetian lagoon.

Feltre

West from Belluno the road skirts the Piave and the southern flank of the Dolomites on its way to Feltre, one of the prettiest and least visited 'art towns' in the Veneto, a Renaissance time capsule in a breathtaking setting. Its loyalty to Venice during the War of the Cambrai earned it a thorough sacking and razing by the troops of Emperor Maximilian in 1510; but this same loyalty was also rewarded immediately afterwards when Venice footed the bill to have it rebuilt. Its centre has changed little since, especially the houses along the main **Via Mezzaterra**; many of their façades frescoed by Lorenzo Luzzo (1467–1512), whose pallor lent him his punk nickname, *Il Morto da Feltre*, the 'Dead Man of Feltre'.

The jewel strung on Via Mezzaterra is **Piazza Maggiore**, one of those sublime stage pieces of urban design that Italians do better than anyone. The centre has the mandatory winged lion on a column (though on closer inspection it looks more like a vampire bat) and statues of two famous sons, Vittorino da Feltre, a leading light in Renaissance education, whose school in Mantua was a paragon of liberal classical education, and Panfilo Castaldi, the first to use moveable type in Italy. Around the piazza is the surviving keep of the medieval castle, the 1599 church of **San Rocco** (with a fountain between the steps by Tullio Lombardo), and the 16th-century **Palazzo dei Rettori** (Municipio), decked out with a Palladian portico. Inside there's a bijou wooden and painted **Teatro Comunale** (1730) which saw the production of Goldoni's first plays. It owes much of its current appearance to an early 1800s rebuilding, and a recent restoration (open mornings on request).

From the Piazza, Via Luzzo leads down to the 15th-century eastern gate, the **Porta Imperiale** and the Palazzo Villabuono (no. 23), now the **Museo Civico** (open 10–1, weekends also from 4–6, closed Mon; adm). The museum has a collection of local Etruscan and Roman artefacts, including an altar to *Anna perenna* (the year, associated with the all-important dole); among its paintings are works by 'The Dead Man' (especially his Giorgionesque *Madonna with saints*), and canvases by Gentile Bellini, and Cima da Conegliano). The *Transfiguration*, Il Morto da Feltre's most acclaimed work, is nearby in the sacristy of the church **Ognissanti** on Borgo Ruga, beyond the gate by the museum.

Back towards the centre, on Via del Paradiso 8, the **Museo Rizzarda** (open June–Sept 10–1 and 4–7, closed Mon; adm) stars a collection of beautiful works in wrought iron, much of it from the forge of the local master Carlo Rizzarda (1883–1931) along with 19th and 20th-century paintings. Feltre keeps its **Duomo** in Via Castaldi, at the foot of the stairs down to the station. Unlike the buildings in the old centre, it has gone through some serious changes, but has retained a rare treasure: a 6th-century cross from Byzantium, with fifty-two scenes from the New Testament.

From Feltre it's an easy, 5 km-walk southeast to the Romanesque **Sanctuary of Santi Vittore e Corona** (1100) on Monte Miesna. Its frescoes go back to the 13th century, and the views go as far as the southern plains. Another excursion from Feltre—to the northwest is a spine of scoured peaks called the **Vette Feltrine**, with a not terribly difficult trail leading from the hamlet of Aune up to the **Rifugio G. Dal Paz** (1993 m). At the foot of the Vette, 3 km from Feltre is **Pedavena**, home of the Heineken-Dreher brewery, next to a beer garden and restaurant, and a park and mini-zoo for the small fry. It also has Belluno's finest country house, the17th-century **Villa Pasole**.

WHERE TO STAY AND EATING OUT (tel prefix 0437)
Belluno caters mostly for ski bunnies, but don't be deterred. ***Hotel Astor**, Piazza dei Martiri 26-E, tel 24 921, offers good value and comfortable, central rooms for L65 000, all with bath. *Da Mares**, Via F. Pellegrini 6, tel 34 012, has adequate rooms, none with bath, for L30–40 000. The best place to eat is the hardest to find, located behind a plain door in the heart of town—**Al Sasso**, Via Consiglio 12, tel 27 701. The cooking is simple—homemade pasta and gnocchi, rabbit and kid, all served in a traditional setting (closed Mon and last two weeks of July; L20 000). **Al Borgo**, Via Ancoretta 8, tel 24 006, has good home cooking—*pasta e fagioli*, polenta with mushrooms; L30 000, closed Mon eve and Tues.

In Feltre, the finest hotel is in a garden near the station: **Viale del Piave**, tel 2003, with every creature comfort and rooms from L75–105 000; a bit further up, closer to the centre, is the less costly ***Cavallino**, Via Garibaldi 8, tel 81 547, where a simple room with bath will set you back L40–45 000. Or stay and dine higher up, in the mountains at Croce d'Aune: the alpine ***Croce d'Aune**, tel 98 921 has doubles for L22–32 000 without bath, or L50 000 with.

Part V

THE DOLOMITES, TRENTINO and ALTO ADIGE/SÜD TIROL

Tre Cime di Lavaredo

The Dolomites

There are mountains and there are the Dolomites. Born as massive corals in the primordial ocean, and heaved up from the seabed 60 million years ago, tempests and blizzards over the aeons have whittled away the malleable calcite that laces the Dolomites to form an extraordinary landscape. Otherworldly and majestic peaks claw and scratch at the sky between the valleys of the Adige and the Piave rivers, a petrified tempest of jagged needles, pinnacles and sheer cliffs.

These most romantic of mountains were named after a wandering French mineralogist with a fantastic name, Dieudonné Sylvain Guy Tancrède de Gratet de Dolomieu, who in 1789 was the first to describe their mineral content. They have since adorned countless jigsaw puzzles and attracted thousands of nature-lovers, hikers, sportsmen, mountain-climbers and skiers, who can slide down the slippery slopes even in the summer on the glaciers of **Marmolada** (3341 m), the highest peak in the range. In the summer the snow fields convert to bouquets of wild flowers, streaked with brilliant blue gentians, yellow alpine poppies, buttercups, edelweiss, and pink rhododendron. The air and light in autumn are so sharp and fine they can break your heart.

Culturally, especially in the bilingual Alto Adige/Süd Tirol, the Dolomites are more than half Austrian. In isolated mountain valleys people speak German and little Italian, while others still speak Ladin (Romansch), a language that owes its origins to the days when the Emperor Tiberius sent Roman soldiers to crush the Celts in the mountain valleys of Switzerland and the Tyrol. Some of the soldiers stayed behind in the valleys, and their descendants became known as the Ladini, or Latins. The cuisine in the Dolomites profits from both Italy and Austria, which makes the region a great place to eat apple strudel and pasta al dente, though not a good place to make yourself understood if you only speak English.

Prices skyrocket in the Dolomites during their high season (Christmas holidays, end of January to Easter, mid-July to mid-Sept). To avoid high prices and colour-coordinated coachloads of Austro-Italian swingers and Gucci-equipped alpinists, try to go in June or October, when the alpine refuges are open but not packed to the gills, or go after the New Year holidays for skiing, when everyone else has to go back to work and the resorts offer big discounts.

Highlights of the Dolomites

There are so many lovely walks and drives in the Dolomites it seems a bit presumptuous to put one above another, though the stupendous **Great Dolomites Road** between Bolzano and Cortina justly deserves its fame. Other sensational **drives** are around the Pale di San Martino; through the passes of the Sella Group; along the western slopes of the Brenta Dolomites from Pinzolo to Folgarida; and around Cortina, to Misurina, Auronzo, the Val di Sesto and down the Val di Landro.

It's also difficult to pinpoint the most memorable **walks**. It's never too far to a cable car or chair lift that can whisk you half-way up a mountain to begin your rambles. Among the best, requiring no special equipment, are two easy but ravishing paths in Panevéggio Natural Park; a beautiful walk above Misurina around Tre Cime di Lavaredo; above Santa Cristina to Sassolungo; around Madonna di Campiglio and Molveno in the Brenta Group; around Colle Santa Lucia; and above Merano, among countless others. If you've had some mountain experience, one of the most famous hikes begins in the Val di Fassa, to the bizarre Torri del Vaiolet on Catinaccio (or Rosengarten); another awesome experience is to hike the Via Bocchette above Madonna di Campiglio. The High Trails of Dolomites (see below) were laid out to take in the best scenery and are accessible from many points. The Pale di San Martino, the Brenta, Cristallo, Tofane, Marmolada, and Sella Groups offer challenges to skilled climbers. Every tourist office has trail maps for their districts and can advise on the degree of difficulty.

The prettiest **lakes**, though again among hundreds it seems unfair to mention only a few, are sapphire Misurina, Carezza, and Alleghe, and the strikingly-hued Tovel and Braies. The prettiest **valleys**: the Val di Non with its orchards, the emerald Val di Sole, the grand Val di Fassa, the sunny Val Gardena, the rural Tyrolean Pusteria, and the picturesque Val di Sesto, the wild Valle di Ega, the enchanting Val di Genova, and the ravishing Val Zoldana.

Man-made sights pale before the handiwork of angels, but the **cities** of Trento, Bressanone, Vipiteno, Pieve di Cadore, Rovereto, Bolzano and Merano are all worth visits; as are the ancient **towns** of Cencenighe, Cavalese, Borgo Valsugana, Pergine, and Malles.

183

The mountains are also endowed with a fine collection of medieval **castles**—Castel Tirolo above Merano; Castello di Sabbionara at Avio; Castel di Pietra at Fiera di Primiero; Castello Toblino; Castel Telvana at Borgo Valsugana; Castello Wolkenstein at Ponte Gardena; Sluderno castle; as well as several around Cles, Appiano, and Naturno. Quite a few now house hotels or restaurants. The **ecclesiastical highlights** include the ancient abbey Novacella near Bressanone; the curious hermitage of San Romedio at Cles; the frescoes at San Rocco at Tesero, San Vigilio at Pinzolo, and at Malles' parish church and Benedictine abbey.

For **skiing** and other **winter sports**, Cortina d'Ampezzo has the best facilities (and highest prices), with San Martino di Castrozza, Madonna di Campiglio, Auronzo, Canazei, Selva di Cadore, Sappada, Solda, and San Candido coming in close behind.

GETTING AROUND
Even the heirs of the Romans can make the trains go only so far in the mountains. The line north from Venice, Treviso, and Conegliano (see preceding section) passes through Pieve di Cadore before petering out in Calalzo, 70 km from Cortina d'Ampezzo ($2\frac{1}{2}$ hours from Venice). The western Dolomites in the Trentino/Alto Adige are linked by the main line between Verona and Munich/Innsbruck, which passes by way of Trento ($1\frac{1}{2}$ hours), Bolzano ($2\frac{1}{2}$ hours) to the Brenner Pass (4 hours), with branches to Merano and Malles/Venosta to the west and to Brunico and San Candido/Innichen to the east on the line to Vienna. By bus: The Dolomites are exceptionally well served by two major bus companies—*Dolomiti Bus* in the east and *SAD Buses* in the west. Pick up their schedules at the main bus stations or tourist offices; many departures coincide with trains from the south. Besides their normal runs, the bus companies add special scenic tours in July and August from the major centres.

Hiking
One is almost tempted to lapse into Italian hyperbole about hiking in the Dolomites—but suffice it to say it's as close as some of us will ever get to heaven. There are routes for everyone, from couch potatoes to rock-grappling Indiana Joneses, and seven High Trails of the Eastern Dolomites specially designed for those 'vagabonds of the path' who fall in between the two extremes. The trails range from 120–180 km in length, and are designed to take the average walker two weeks—though it doesn't hurt to plan a few days on top of that for rests and detours. The High Trails have the virtue of keeping you on top of mountains and plateaux for nearly their entire length. While they do not require any special climbing skill (trails with a death-defying *via ferrata* ('iron ladder') or other obstacles almost always have detours for the less intrepid), they do demand a stout pair of hiking boots with good rubber soles and protection against sudden storms, even in the middle of summer. Strategically-placed alpine refuges provide shelter, but if you come in early June or October before the refuges open you'll need to carry camping gear. The refuges are open from 20 June to 20 September; in July and August it's wise to book a bed or camp bed in advance to avoid disappointment.

The High Trails are:
No 1: From Lake Braies to Belluno, the most popular route.
No 2: 'Trail of the Legends', from Bressanone to Feltre.
No 3: 'Trail of the Chamois', from Villabassa to Longarone.

No 4: The Grohmann route, from San Candido to Pieve di Cadore.
No 5: The Titian route, from Sesto Pusteria to Pieve di Cadore.
No 6: 'Trail of the Silences', from the sources of the Piave to Vittorio Veneto.
No 7: Belluno Pre-Alps to the Alpago (a region covered in the preceding section).

There are two good sets of maps that include the above trails and others as well, and point out the location of the alpine refuges: *Carta dei Sentieri e Rifugi*, Edit. Tabacco Udine or *Maps Kompass-Wanderkarten*, Edit. Fleishmann-Starnberg. Both are scale 1:50,000, and are readily available at news-stands in the region. There is also an extensive literature and guides covering the paths if you can read Italian or German; alternatively, the tourist office in Belluno offers free booklets on each trail in English that contain everything you need to know before you go, including the telephone numbers of the refuges. They also give you a good idea of the level of difficulty of each trail, so read them thoroughly before setting out.

Alpine refuges (*rifugi alpini*) vary. Many are owned by the Italian Alpine club, while others are privately owned, primarily by ski resorts. Some are along trails, while others may be reached via cable car. All offer bed and board. Prices vary mainly by altitude: the higher up and more difficult of access, the more expensive. Camp beds range from L5–15 000, beds from L12–20 000; complete meals around L12 000.

Besides these, there are the *baita* (wooden hut) and *casera* (stone hut) and bivouacs (beds but no food) along some trails: these generally have no custodians but offer shelter.

Skiing

The Dolomites are like a candy shop for winter sports junkies. As the sunny side of the Alps, they enjoy good clear weather and when it snows, it falls delightfully dry and powdery. There are slopes of all levels of difficulty, country trails, toboggan and bobsled runs, ice rinks and speed-skating courses; if all the ski runs were laid end to end they would stretch from the Brenner Pass to Reggio Calabria. There are bonuses as well: ski schools in July, and indoor, heated pools in the middle of winter. The only problem comes in trying to choose which out of scores of places to aim for.

Write in advance to the tourist information offices: to Belluno for their *Dolomiti Neve* pamphlets, to Trento for *Snowy Planet* or Bolzano for *Ski Panorama: South Tyrol*, all of which have suggestions that may narrow down the field. An easier option is to book a week's *Settimana Bianca* package (room and board at a hotel, ski-pass and instruction) from CIT or other travel offices all over Italy. This is especially good value outside the peak season. If you have your own transport and want to try as many resorts as possible, the *Superski Dolomiti* pass gives you unlimited access to most of the slopes for periods of one, two, or three weeks—the longer the period, the more economical the pass. Nearly all resorts hire out equipment and offer ski instruction; some have winter caravan camping.

The Eastern Dolomites: the Cadore

Much of the district north of Belluno along the upper Piave, known as the Cadore, was incorporated into Italy only after the First World War. Its glitzy, gorgeous, somewhat

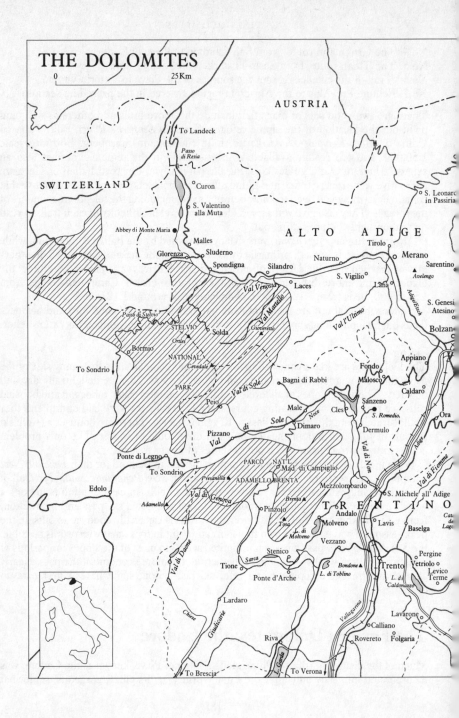

THE DOLOMITES

0   25Km

AUSTRIA

To Landeck

Passo di Resia

SWITZERLAND

Curon

S. Valentino alla Muta

S. Leonar in Passiria

ALTO ADIGE

Tirolo

Merano

Sarentino

Avelengo

Abbey di Monte Maria

Malles

Glorenza

Sluderno

Spondigna

Silandro

Naturno

S. Vigilio

Lana

S. Genesi Atesino

Val Venosta

Laces

Val l'Ultimo

Bolzan

Passo di Stelvio

STELVIO

Val Martello

Solda

Giovereno

Appiano

Orlies

Bormjo

NATIONAL

Cevedale

Fondo

Malosco

Caldaro

PARK

Val di Sole

Bagni di Rabbi

Sanzeno

To Sondrio

Peio

Male

Noce

Cles

S. Romedio.

Ora

di

Sole

Dimaro

Dermulo

Val di Nom

Pizzano

Val

Ponte di Legno

PARCO NAT'L

Mad. di Campiglio

To Sondrio

Val di Fiemme

Presanélla

ADAMELLO BRENTA

Mezzolombardo

S. Michele all' Adige

Edolo

Val di Genova

Brenta

Pinzolo

TRENTINO

Cat Lago

Adamello

Tosa

Molveno

Andalo

Lavis

Baselga

L. di Molveno

Vezzano

Pergine

Vetriolo

Val di Daone

Stenico

Bondone

Trento

Levico Terme

Sarca

L. di Toblino

L. di Caldonazzo

Tione

Ponte d'Arche

Chiese

Giudicarie

Lardaro

Lavarone

Vallagarina

Calliano

Folgaria

Riva

Rovereto

To Brescia

L. Garda

To Verona

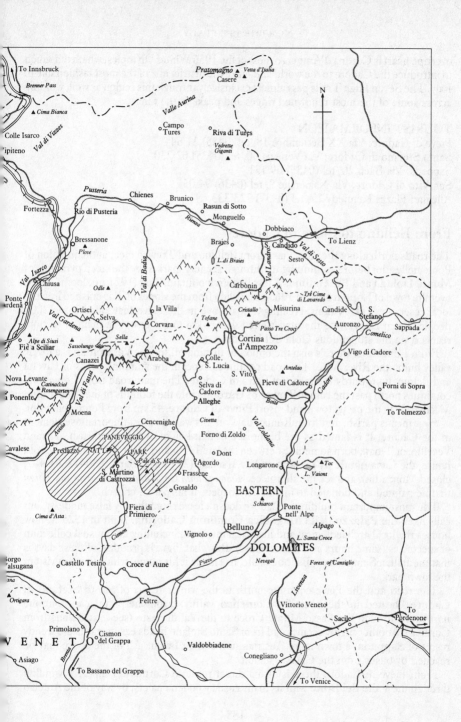

overripe heart is Cortina d'Ampezzo, host of the 1956 Winter Olympics, which did much to introduce the Cadore to the world and make the district one of the most fashionable in Italy. The Seven High Trails pass almost exclusively through this region as well, winding across some of the most renowned ridges and peaks in the range.

TOURIST INFORMATION
Pieve di Cadore: Via XX Settembre 18, tel (0435) 31 644
Santo Stefano di Cadore: Via Venezia 40, tel (0435) 62 230
Sappada: Via Bach 20, tel (0435) 69 131
San Vito di Cadore: Via Nazionale 9, tel (0436) 94 05
Alleghe: Piazza Kennedy 17, tel (0437) 723 333

From Belluno to Pieve di Cadore

The roads north along the river Piave from Belluno and Treviso meet at the junction of Ponte nelle Alpi before continuing up through scenery marked by the steep pyramids of **Monte Dolada** and **Piz Gallina**. A less benign mountain, **Toc** (1921 m), looms ahead over the town of **Longarone**. In 1963 a landslide from the slopes of Toc crashed into the local reservoir, Lake Vaiont, creating a tidal wave in the Piave that killed some 2000 people. From Longarone the now-ruined dam, 6 km to the east, is a main attraction, reached via the stupendous **Gola del Vaiont**.

From Longarone there's also the option of turning off for the **Val Zoldana**, a lovely valley lining the River Maè. The road continues beneath the stunning peaks of Civetta and Pelmo, up towards the resort of Selva di Cadore. The main road from Longarone continues north past the ruined **Tower of Gardona** into the foothills of the Antelao and Marmarole to the pretty town and resort **Pieve di Cadore**, 45 km from Ponte nelle Alpi.

Pieve means parish, and from Roman days on this was the most important settlement in the Cadore. It is famed as the birthplace of that knight of the paintbrush, Tiziano Vecellio, or Titian, born sometime between the late 1470s and 1490. You can visit his old house, the **Casa natale di Tiziano** on Via Arsenale (23 June–7 Sept, 9:30–12:30, 4–7, closed Mon; adm), and see the altarpiece *Madonna with Child and SS. Andrew and Titian* that he painted and donated to one of the chapels of his parish church.

The most important building in Cadore doesn't leave room for any false modesty, but calls itself the **Palazzo della Magnifica Comunità Cadorina**. Built in 1525, it now houses the local archaeological and historical museum, including an unusual collection of spectacles (same hours as Titian's house). But what Pieve is proudest of these days is that the Italian Santa Claus, Babbo Natale, has made it his home, which you can visit in the town park.

The road and the Piave continue north to the winter resort of **Santo Stefano di Cadore**, located in the beautiful **Comélico valley**. From here you can continue northwest through the Passo Monte Croce to the Val di Sesto (see 'Excursions from Cortina'). Another highly scenic road from Santo Stefano heads east towards the trendy resort of **Sappada**, a town more Austrian in feel than Italian. All of the above may be reached by buses from the Calalzo station.

From Pieve di Cadore there is also a direct route to Cortina d'Ampezzo, winding through the **Valle del Boite** with its many rustic wooden chalets, by way of the Antelao massif, nicknamed the 'King of Cadore', and **Monte Pelmo,** one of the most unusual and striking peaks in the Dolomites. The road passes by way of two summer/winter resorts, **Borca di Cadore** and the more important **San Vito di Cadore,** an excellent base for ascending Pelmo and nearby peaks.

WHERE TO STAY AND EATING OUT
As in the case of most Dolomite resorts, guests tend (or are usually obliged) to dine in their hotels on half- or full-pension terms.

Near Pieve di Cadore in the hamlet of Tai, the ****Canada,** Via Manzago 15, tel (0435) 31 741, is one of the most charming hotels in the Cadore, with a lovely garden in a beautiful setting; open all year, L45 000 without bath, L55–75 000 with. One reason for Sappada's popularity is its abundance of reasonably priced accommodation. A couple of good choices are ****Corona Ferrea,** at Borgata Kratter, Via Kratten 17, tel (0435) 69 103, open 20 June–20 Sept and 20 Dec to 15 April; comfortable rooms, all with bath for L55–80 000. The small ****Sierra Hof,** Via Soravia 54, tel 69 110, is near the centre of the village; all rooms have bath and cost from L45–65 000; closed May, Oct and Nov. In San Vito di Cadore, there are a number of comfortable hotels: ******Marcora,** Via Roma 28, tel (0436) 9101, a moderately sized choice with a pool in a fine setting, open 20 June–10 Sept and 20 Dec to 10 April; L120– 170 000. Another pleasant choice in San Vito, ****Il Cardo,** in Via Belvedere, tel (0436) 94 59, is open all year and has rooms, all with bath, for L50–60 000.

Cortina d'Ampezzo

GETTING AROUND
Cortina's bus station is just off Via Marconi and is served by SAD and Dolomiti buses; for information call 2741. Services are greatly augmented June–Sept, when buses serve virtually every paved road in the region. The nearest train station is Dobbiaco/ Toblach, 35 km north (on the Bolzano line), with timely bus connections to Cortina.

TOURIST INFORMATION
Piazzetta S. Francesco 8, tel (0436) 3231, near the central Piazza Venezia. This is the place to go to find a room (besides the hotels, there are thousands in private houses), good maps of surrounding trails and to learn about excursions. The local alpine guide organization is next door and open in July and August (tel 4740).

The Sporting Life
Cortina's the sort of place where David Niven and Audrey Hepburn would hang out in a café wearing sunglasses, but it enjoys the best location in the Dolomites: a lofty (1224 m), sunny, cross-shaped meadow at the junction of the Boite and Bigontina valleys, in the centre of a ring of extraordinary mountains—Pelmo 'the Throne of God'; Civetta, the great mount 'owl'; hair-raising Cristallo, the 'crystal' mountain, shaped like a funnel; Sorapis, licked by stony flames; and the Cinque Torri, the 'five towers'. Cortina claims that the world's first ski contest was organized here in 1903, but it was the 1956 Olympics which endowed Cortina with superb winter sports facilities; here you can ski-jump, speed-skate, fly down bobsled and luge runs, and do figures of eight in the ice stadium,

not to mention the thousand and one downhill and cross-country ski runs in the vicinity. In the summer, Cortina, which has a number of 'Green Week' discount packages similar to the winter 'White Weeks', is an excellent base for hikers and alpinists and excursions of all kinds into the mountains, while in town there's a riding school, tennis, and summer/winter swimming-pools, and activities like the Ice Disco Dance in the Olympic Ice Stadium.

Devoted heart and soul to the merry, sporting life, Cortina is almost as well known for its night-time activities, especially in winter, when the *après ski* fraternity fills its clubs and discotheques and trips the light fantastic until the wee hours of dawn. The few historic buildings Cortina had burned down in 1976, but it doesn't give a damn—this is no town for the diligent scholar. But whatever worldly pleasure and delight this snowy fleshpot offers, it comes at a price, rating right up with Capri, Portofino, and Venice herself on the bottom line of the tab; those on a budget survive by camping and dining à la supermarket.

Cortina has more than its share of trendy shops and a museum of contemporary art you can take in if it rains—the **Museo Ciasa de Ra Regoles**, Via Parco Angolo on the Corso Italia, with works by De Pisis, Morandi, De Chirico and more (open Dec–Easter and July to mid-Sept from 4–7:30, sometimes in the morning; adm). Two cable cars from Cortina wait to whisk you up to the mountains, both at the end of town bus lines: in the north, near the Olympic stadium, to **Tofana di Mezzo** (3244 m; L21 000 round-trip) with its privately run alpine refuges, and in the west, to **Tondi di Faloria** (2343 m; L18 000). All-day ski passes for Faloria and Cristallo are available at the office on Via de Zeto 8 in Cortina.

If you prefer to glide off the beaten track, make your way to the **Creste Bianche**, on the north face of Cristallo, or the **Bus di Tofana**, near the Dibona refuge, and **Vallorita**, a 1300 m sugary white drop. There's also a cross-country course for hardy souls, stretching all the way to Dobbiaco in the Pusteria.

WHERE TO STAY (tel prefix 0436)

Expect to run up against the full-board requirement nearly everywhere in Cortina in its high season—mortifying to the pocketbook though not to the flesh; the local cuisine is as *haute* as the price.

If you're putting on the dog in Cortina, the *******Miramonti Majestic** is the place to do it (Via Pezziè 103, tel 4201, open July–Sept, and Dec–March). Warm, traditional, and rustic, it has pretty wooden balconies affording magnificent views. The well-designed rooms have most imaginable creature comforts; there's an indoor pool, tennis courts, exercise facilities, and sauna; doubles without bath range from L100–200 000, with bath L130–360 000. A close second in the glamour category, CIGA's *******Cristallo Palace**, Via R. Menardi 42, tel 4281, offers almost as many sports facilities, including tennis courts and swimming-pool, good food and lovely large rooms with truly dolomitic views; open July–Sept and Dec–March. All doubles have bath (L200–400 000). If you'd rather be in the centre of the action, ******De La Poste**, Piazza Roma 14, tel 4271, is a large alpine chalet with classy rooms and balconies, and a terrace and cosy bar that see much of Cortina's busy social life, especially in the evening (closed 20 Oct–20 Dec; doubles from L110–360 000).

In the moderate range, another alpine chalet, the *****Hotel Corona**, Via Val di Sotto 10, tel 3251 (10 minutes from the centre) is memorable for a modern art collection even more extensive than the one in the museum; it's also more convenient for the ski lift. (Open June–Sept and Dec–March; L55–100 000 without bath.) *****Impero**, Via C. Battisti 66, tel 4246, has no such pretensions, and no restaurant but adequate rooms open all year (all with bath; L65–90 000). The charmer in this price category, the 800-year old farmhouse, now a family-run inn, the ****Menardi**, Via Majon 110, tel 2400, is furnished with antiques and bedecked with fresh flowers. (Open 20 June–20 Sept, and 20 Dec–10 April; rooms with bath L64–120 000.) Among the bargains (by Cortina standards), you can't beat ***Cavallino**, Corso Italia 142, tel 2614; open all year; sparkling doubles are L38–55 000 without bath.

EATING OUT

Both of Cortina's best and most fashionable restaurants are outside the city and most easily reached by car. **Il Meloncino**, at Gillardon 17, tel 861 043, is in the suburban district of Gillardon en route to Falzarego. With great views over Cortina, this small, intimate restaurant offers a delicious menu to complement its romantic setting; the risotto with myrtleberries is a real treat. Reservations a must; you may have to settle for lunch as dinner dates are sometimes booked up a month in advance (closed Tues, June and Nov; L40–50 000). The more elegant **El Toulà**, 123 Via Ronco (tel 3339), is closer to Cortina, near Pocol. Located in a refurbished wooden farmhouse, the restaurant specializes in perfect grilled meats, roast lamb, and desserts with a Tyrolean touch. Extensive wine list; open only from Dec–March and 15 July–15 Sept, closed Mon; L80 000). **Al Camin**, Via Alverà 99, tel 862 010, is a cosy restaurant with lots of wood and a big fireplace, serving the tasty local editions of polenta and goulash and more for around L30 000.

Excursions From Cortina

TOURIST INFORMATION
Auronzo: Via Roma 10, tel (0435) 93 59
Dobbiaco: Via Roma, tel (0474) 72 132
Agordo: Piazza Libertà 33, tel (0437) 62 105
Falcade: Piazza Municipio 1, tel (0437) 59 242
Frassenè: tel (0437) 67 035

As a major crossroads, Cortina offers numerous forays into the surrounding mountains. The classic Dolomites excursion is to take the Great Dolomites Road between Cortina and Bolzano, but as most people approach from the west, you'll find it described under the Bolzano section, p. 210.

A popular and beautiful short trip from Cortina is on the N. 48 over the lofty **Tre Croci pass** to **Lake Misurina**, one of the loveliest of Dolomite lakes, shimmering below the jagged peaks of Sorapis and the remarkable triple-spired **Tre Cime di Lavaredo**, 15 km northeast of Cortina. The colours of Misurina are so brilliant they would look touched-up on a postcard; as a resort it makes a fine alternative to Cortina, especially if ice-skating is your sport. From Misurina it's a magnificent 7-km drive up to the **Rifugio Auronzo**, located just beneath the Tre Cime di Lavaredo. From the refuge it's an easy walk to the 1916 **Bersaglieri Memorial**, honouring Italy's famous sharpshooters. More fine views await from **Monte Piana**, a lofty meadow 6 km north of Misurina.

Circular routes from Misurina to Cortina

There are two possible circular routes from Misurina back to Cortina that make rewarding, full-day excursions. Both begin to the east via **Auronzo**, past a peak known as the **Corno del Doge** for its resemblance to the Venetian Doge's bonnet. Auronzo, surrounded by fragrant spruce forests, on the shores of an artificial lake, is another resort town, with a cable car and chair lifts up **Monte Agudo**.

From Auronzo you can circle south around Pieve di Cadore and the Valle di Boite (161 km altogether; see 'Pieve to Cortina', above) or take the longer route around to the north (224 km) through the **Comélico** and the beautiful **Val di Sesto**, noted for its traditional wooden houses. The route passes into the Alto Adige region through **San Candido/Innichen**, a pretty summer/winter resort on the river Drava; it has a Benedictine monastery and a lovely Romanesque collegiate church, the 13th-century **SS. Candidus e Corbinian**. The turn back to Cortina (N. 51) is at **Dobbiaco/Toblach**, one of the original Dolomite resorts, in a magnificent setting, with good skiing, a nearby lake, and a railway station. The large **castle** in the old part of town was built for Venice's arch-enemy, the Emperor Maximilian, in 1500.

Dobbiaco to Cortina

The road passes the wooded Lago di Dobbiaco and enters into the dramatic **Val di Landro**, with the Cristallo group looming ahead over the town of **Carbonin/Schluderbach**. The road south of here is known as the 'Alemagna' for it was long the main route south from Germany: it passes by way of **Ospitale**, one of many towns in the region named after the hostels that once sheltered pilgrims on their way to Rome, and a pair of little lakes, the Black and the White, before the lonely ruins of the **Castel Sant'Umberto**. The road then circles around castle-crowned Podestagno, before descending into the Ampezzo with the Le Tofane group storming up to the right.

Cortina to Colle Santa Lucia and Agordo

There are two routes to this region south of Cortina: the main one traces the Great Dolomites Road through the Falzarego Pass, while the lesser-known but equally pretty route takes the Giau Pass through to **Selva di Cadore**, at the head of Val Zoldana and the road to Longarone. **Colle Santa Lucia** near here is a photographer's paradise with its old agricultural hamlets and famous view of the Dolomites as a backdrop (31 km from Cortina).

From here the road passes **Caprile** and the lovely **Lago di Alleghe**, under the massive peaks of Civetta. At the fine old village of Cencenighe there's the option of turning off for Falcade and San Martino di Castrozza (see East of Trento). **Agordo** (45 km) is an attractive town and resort in the Val Cordevole, along one of the principal branches of the Piave. The Passo Duran above Agordo leads to the Valle di Zoldo and the village of **Dont** (21 km)—there are splendid views of Civetta and Pelmo, and, if you're interested, you can buy samples of local woodcarving.

WHERE TO STAY AND EATING OUT

On Lake Misurina there are a couple of good choices: ***Lavaredo**, Via Monte Piana, tel (0436) 39 127, has tennis courts and a good restaurant, and is open all year (L50–75 000 with bath, L45 000 without), while the **Dolomiti des Alpes**, Via Monte

Piana 26, tel (0436) 39 031, just above the lake, has a sauna-solarium (closed Oct to mid-Dec; all rooms with bath, L43–65 000). In nearby Auronzo there are far more choices: at **Juventus, Via Padova 26, tel (0435) 92 21, you can be right on Lake Auronzo's beach; comfortable rooms from L50–55 000 without bath, L60–68 000 with. Also close to the beach, the *Vienna, Via Verona 2, tel (0435) 93 94, has rooms for L25–40 000 without bath, and L40–50 000 with. A good restaurant in Auronzo, **Dal Cavaliere** on Via Cimagogna, tel (0435) 98 34, serves delicious suckling pig and risotto with herbs or mushrooms in a traditional wood-panelled decor (L35 000, closed Wed).

In Dobbiaco/Toblach, the ***Cristallo-Walch, Viale Roma 11, tel (0474) 72 138, is a fine resort hotel in a beautiful setting, with an indoor pool and sauna (L65–100 000; closed May and Oct–Nov). For real mountain splendour, however, stay at the ***Alpengasthof Ratsberg, on top of Monte Rota (cable car), Monterota 10, Radsberg, tel (0474) 72 213, with a lovely park, indoor pool and views for L35–45 000.

In Selva di Cadore, a fine, economical place to stay and eat is the **Giglio Rosso, at Pescul, tel (0437) 720 310, where all rooms have baths (L38–45 000) and the restaurant does a fine bilberry risotto and turkey in beer for only L20 000 (open Dec–March and June–Sept). In Caprile, (near Alleghe) the 120-year-old ***Alla Posta, Piazza Dogliani 19, tel (0437) 721 171, is the most prestigious hotel, with TVs in each of its comfortable rooms; fairly good restaurant (L65–90 000).

The Western Dolomites: Trentino

The autonomous province of Trentino contains some of the finest scenery of the western Dolomites, especially in the Val di Fassa on the western slopes of Marmolada and in the isolated, but hauntingly majestic Brenta Group to the west of the Adige; it also includes the north shore of Lake Garda (under which section it is described). Unlike the Alto Adige/Süd Tyrol further north, Trentino is mostly Italian in language and heritage, sprinkled with a Ladin minority in the valleys. Many of the 200 alpine refuges in Trentino are operated by the *Società degli Alpinisti Tridentini* (SAT), which is a good source for mountain information. Contact the Society in Trento: Via Manci 57, tel (0461) 21 522. Trento itself is one of Northern Italy's finest little cities, worth a visit even if mountains aren't your cup of tea.

GETTING AROUND
Trento is on the main FS line between Verona and Brenner; another line links the city with Bassano, passing through the Valsugana. A private rail line goes from Trento up to Cles, the *Ferrovia Trento-Malè*. Otherwise buses are the main form of public transport; service, especially out of season in the western reaches, is skeletal, though if you look wholesome enough hitch-hiking is fairly easy. In addition to the main Dolomite bus lines, *Atesina Trento* provides links to the southern half of the region as well as connecting Trento to Riva del Garda, Feltre, Belluno, and Bassano.

TOURIST INFORMATION
Rovereto: Via Dante 63, tel (0464) 430 363.
Folgaria: Via Roma 62, tel (0464) 71 133.

From Verona to Trento: the Val Largarina

Following the Adige up from Verona, passing through the Valpolicella region and the Monti Lessini, the road enters Trentino near **Avio**, dominated by the proud 14th-century **Castello di Sabbionara**. Its guardhouse preserves a wonderful fresco cycle of battling knights, the *Parata dei Combattenti*, while in the keep the frescoes portray scenes of courtly love. The castle was the first property of the Italian version of the National Trust, the Fondo per l'Ambiente Italiano, and is open 9–1, 9–sunset in the summer, closed Mon; adm.

Further up the road and the river Adige, past a sea of vineyards, **Rovereto** is the second city of Trentino, built around an imposing Venetian castle; from 1416–87 the city formed the northern extent of the Serenissima, before the Trentini, with the aid of the Tyroleans, pushed the Venetians back to Verona. This area was also hotly contested in the First World War, and the castle contains an evocative **War Museum** devoted primarily to that conflict (open 9–12 and 2–6). After the War, cannons from each of the nineteen belligerents were melted down to make the largest bell in Italy, the **Campana dei Caduti**, located in the southern quarter of Rovereto; it is rung in memory of the fallen every day at sundown. Rovereto was the home town of the great archaeologist Paolo Orsi, who willed his private collection of statues, busts and vases from Magna Graecia to the city, displayed in the **Musei Civici** near the centre of town. The Italian Futurist Fortunato Depero (1892–1960) worked for many years in Rovereto, and left the city a collection of his vivid, poster-like works, now in the **Museo Depero**.

To the west of Rovereto are two small summer/winter resorts on a lofty plateau (1000 m) below Monte Cornetto: **Folgaria**, in a neighbourhood of mouldering Austrian fortifications left over from World War I, and the larger **Lavarone**, near the lake of the same name, where Sigmund Freud sojourned three summers. In the tiny village of **Luserna**, near Lavarone, the inhabitants speak Cimbro, a dialect of High German.

Across the Adige from Rovereto, **Isera** is the centre for the production of Marzemino wine, one of Trentino's finest reds. To the north, visible from the road to Trento, the ruined but still imposing **Castle of Beseno** towers over the small town of Calliano, visible from the highway.

WHERE TO STAY AND EATING OUT   (tel prefix 0464)
In Rovereto, the *****Rovereto**, Corso Rosmini 82/d, tel 435 222, is a fine central hotel for an overnight stay, with comfortable air-conditioned rooms, all with bath for L110 000. Bargains are few—***Villa Cristina**, Via Abetone 48, tel 421 482, where rooms are 40 000 without bath, and 50 000 with. The place to eat is **Al Borgo**, Via Garibaldi 13, tel 436 300, a surprisingly sophisticated little restaurant in the heart of town, featuring delicious dishes like ham and spinach in puff pastry, risotto with lemon, or turbot with artichokes, all accompanied by piano music in the evening (L45–55 000, closd Mon). In Lavarone Freud stayed at the *****Hotel du Lac**, in Frazione Chiesa, tel 73 112; an indoor swimming-pool and tennis courts, in addition to its pretty setting on the lake, make it a fine place to forget your favourite neurosis (L65 000 with bath, L49 000 without).

Trento

In the 16th century Emperor Charles V, haughty ruler of most of Europe, found his Germanic possessions in the throes of the Reformation and his Catholic domains rigidly bracing themselves for an hysterical reaction. A staunch Catholic himself, Charles sought to heal the growing rift in his realm by calling a council of the Church to look into some urgently needed counter-reforms. The pope finally agreed in 1536, but another nine years passed while the two quibbled about venue—Charles wanted it on Imperial turf, while the pope insisted on an Italian city. Trento, an Italian city ruled by a powerful bishop prince, but part of the Holy Roman Empire, was found to be the perfect compromise. The Council of Trent (1545–63), one of the major events of the Counter-Reformation, was too late to bring the Protestant strays back into the fold, though it played an important role in defining the role of the bishops as pastors, in educating parish priests—and in putting an end to the Renaissance, by establishing the Church's totalitarian control over the arts.

Influential in bringing the Council to Trento was the city's greatest ruler, Bernardo Clesio, Bishop of Trento, Count of Tyrol, president of the secret council of the Spanish King Ferdinand, and later Supreme Chancellor to Ferdinand's grandson, Charles V. A great patron of the arts, he personally brought at least the tail end of the Renaissance to the city.

The Council put Trent on the map, but Trento has much more to offer than memories of the Counter-Reformation. Lying at the foot of Monte Bondone, between the banks of the Adige and the Fersina, it is refreshingly unpretentious and charming; many of its gently winding streets are embellished with colourful al fresco frescoes, and the former palace of its bishop has a cycle of medieval frescoes that alone is worth the trip.

GETTING AROUND
The bus and FS railway station are next to each other by the Piazza Dante. FS information, tel 34 545; bus information tel 984 700. The Trento-Malè station, with trains up the Val di Non to Cles, is up the street on Via G. Segantini.

TOURIST INFORMATION
No province in Italy has such an efficient and enthusiastic tourist board. The regional tourist office is at Corso 3 Novembre 132, tel (0461) 980 000.

The city office is on Via Alfieri 4, across the Piazza Dante from the station, tel (0461) 983 880, and there's an information office at Piazza Duomo, tel 981 289.

To the Duomo
Trento's points of interest are easily seen on foot. The statues of the great poet and other celebrated Italians in the **Piazza Dante**, amid the public gardens in front of the station, were erected in 1896 by Trento's irredentist societies in defiance of their Austrian rulers. Next to the station itself, the attractive 12th-century collegiate church of **San Lorenzo** stands in a sunken lawn.

From San Lorenzo, Via Andrea Pozzo and Via D. Orfane lead to the gracious pink **Santa Maria Maggiore**, a simple and elegant Renaissance temple with ornate portals and a beautiful organ gallery from 1534. Beyond this, streets open into the **Piazza**

195

Duomo, Trento's loveliest square, lorded over by an 18th-century **fountain of Neptune** with his trident, recalling the city's Roman name, *Tridentum*. The 16th-century **Palazzo Cazuffi**, with exterior frescoes stands on one side, facing the **Duomo**, an austere marble temple designed in the 13th century and completed in 1515. Although it took three hundred years to build, the style is all plain Romanesque, its extrovert columns on the east side its only flourish. But it sounds good—the campanile has one of the prettiest bells in Italy. In its stately interior, the Council of Trent held its three major sessions, and its decrees were given divine blessing before the huge crucifix still to be seen in a right-hand chapel. The baldacchino over the altar is a replica of the one in St Peter's. Excavations in 1977 unearthed a 6th-century basilica under the cathedral, built to house the relics of Trento's patron, San Vigilio.

Next to the cathedral, the Palazzo Pretorio, crowned with swallowtail battlements and the tall, medieval **Torre Civica**, houses the excellent **Museo Diocesano Tridentino** (open 9–12 and 2–6, closed Wed; adm), containing items from the Duomo Treasure and churches throughout Trentino. There are paintings of the Council of Trent; also a local 16th-century portrayal of a *Mass of St Gregory*, its nonchalant congregation including a large band of pious skeletons; three pretty 12th-century ivory caskets made by the Saracens; an unusual 12th-century enamelled reliquary case and four charming 15th-century wooden altarpieces from the church of San Zeno in the Val di Non, portraying three local martyrs in scenes observed by a man in a beaver hat. The museum's greatest treasure, however, waits in the last room: a cycle of six early 15th-century Flemish tapestries by Peter Van Aelst, masterpieces of woven portraiture and detail, purchased and brought to Trento by Bernardo Clesio.

From Piazza Duomo, be sure to stroll down Via Belenzani, lined with fine Renaissance palaces. The best, **Palazzo Geremia**, was one of the first built in Trento, and is embellished with 16th-century frescoes of the Wheel of Fortune and the local citizens receiving the Emperor Maximilian.

Castello di Buonconsiglio

From Via Belenzani, Via Roma/Via Gian Antonio Manci leads to the residence of Trento's mighty bishop-princes, the Castello di Buonconsiglio. Because of its importance on the main highway between Germany and Italy, the German Emperors in the Middle Ages sought to keep the city under control by granting Trento's bishops a regal temporal status that they possessed until Napoleon. The castle actually consists of two buildings—the 13th-century Castelvecchio and the 1530 Magno Palazzo, built by bishop Clesio. The castle houses the provincial museum of art (open 9–12 and 2–5, closed Mon).

Of the castle's richly frescoed rooms, the most memorable one has mythological figures on the ceiling, touched up to conform to Counter-Reformation modesty levels—some of the gods are decked out in turn-of-the-century swimsuits, while the goddesses look like Tarzan's Jane. The great mirrors in the Sala degli Specchi were added in the 18th century to replace the Flemish tapestries now in the cathedral museum. The best art of the castle is reserved for last: the ravishing, colourful **Frescoes of the Months** in the Torre dell'Aquila, painted by an anonymous artist around the year 1400. While nobles sport and flirt in the foreground, peasants perform their month-by-month labour in the background, tending their flocks, making cheese, planting and harvesting their fields, and making wine. In one scene is the oldest-known depiction of Trento, dominated by the castle itself; in another, a gracious noble family engages in one of the first recorded snowball fights, in front of the castle at Stenico (see below).

On a more solemn note, the Castello di Buonconsiglio was the site of the imprisonment and trial in 1916 of the Italian patriot Cesare Battisti and his two companions, executed by the Austrians for high treason. Their cells, the courtroom where they were tried, and the ditch where they were shot may be seen; Battisti's prominent memorial, a marble circle of columns, stands on the hill of Doss Trento west of town.

Around Trento: Monte Bondone

The slopes of Trento's mountain neighbour, Monte Bondone, are easily reached by cable car, departing from the Ponte di San Lorenzo in Trento (behind the bus station) and climbing as far as **Sardagna** (from 7 am–6:30 pm). From Sardagna there are fine views over the city, and at least three buses a day that continue up to **Vaneze** and **Vason**, Monte Bondone's ski resorts; from Vason another cable car ascends to one of Bondone's three summits (2098 m). Further along the road towards Riva, **Viotte** is the site of a nature reserve, an alpine refuge, and near the latter, a **Botanical Garden**, founded in 1938 on the banks of two artificial lakes, and planted with over two thousand species of high altitude flora from around the world (open May–Oct).

ACTIVITIES
Trento hosts a lively festival in honour of its patron saint Vigilio every year from 20–26 June. One of the main events is the *Palio dell'Oca*, in which teams from each of the city's neighbourhoods don 17th-century costumes and race down the Adige on rafts, trying to slip a ring over the neck of a papier-mâché goose suspended over the river. On the last day, the *Ciusi-Gobj Masquerade* commemorates a day back in the Middle Ages when Trento hired a group of workers from Feltre to reinforce the walls. Food supplies being low at the time, Trento's bishop realized that the city could not afford to feed the workers and sent them back home—but they returned in the night to raid its stores. Such a memorable battle ensued that it is re-enacted in costume on 26 June in the Piazza Duomo—the Ciusi are from Feltre, and they have five chances to break the ranks of Trento's Gobj to make off with the prize: a hot pot of bubbling polenta. Be sure to ask the tourist office for a copy of the monthly *Viva Trento* for a complete listing of current events.

WHERE TO STAY   (tel prefix 0461)
Trento isn't as well endowed with lodgings as the mountain resorts in its province, and one may wonder where all the bishops attending the Council of Trent put up off and on for nearly twenty years. Some are said to have slept at the predecessor of the ****Albergo Accademia, near Santa Maria Maggiore at Vicolo Colico 4/6, tel 981 011; two other buildings have since been added to form the modern hotel. The panelled rooms are comfortable and air-conditioned, and you can pick up German language programmes on the TVs in every room (L110 000). The ***Alessandro Vittoria, Via Romagnosi 14–16, tel 980 089, is located near the centre, on the far side of the Piazza Dante, and is quiet and snug, and the only hotel in Trento to have a statue of Queen Victoria, although one doubts if she would approve of the decorative scheme

or frigo-bars and TVs in the rooms (L125 000). *Al Cavallino Bianco, a block from the cathedral on Via Cavour 29, tel 31 542, is the pick of the economical choices, if only for its lobby, which resembles a backyard, and the cheap Chinese restaurant downstairs. Rooms are L56 000 with bath, L45 000 without.

If you have a car, one of the nicest places to stay is the ***Villa Madruzzo, 3 km east of Trento in Cognola, tel 986 220. Located in a leafy park, in a charming 19th-century villa, the rooms are modern and comfortable; L105 000, all with bath.

EATING OUT

Trentino cuisine is basically alpine: popular dishes include *canderli*, a kind of gnocchi made with salami and parsley; *patao*, a minestrone of yellow flour and sauerkraut, and *osei scampadi*, veal birds cooked with sage. Trentino produces some 23 DOC wines, and is especially notable for its whites and increasingly, for its sparkling wines—for a red, try Marzemino or Cabernet Sauvignon; for a white, try the superb Riesling Renano, fruity Chardonnay, Pinot Bianco or Pinot Grigio.

Trento's most celebrated restaurant, the Chiesa, Via S. Marco 64, tel 985 577, is located in an elegant 17th-century palazzo near the Castello di Buonconsiglio. It is famous for its 'Apple Party Menu' in which Trentino's delicious apples make an appearance in every dish; other choices include smoked trout and a tempting cheese strudel, or even a 1500s menu based on the preferred dishes of Bernardo Clesio, accompanied by an extensive wine list and scrumptious desserts. Closed Sun eve, Mon, and mid–Aug to mid–Sept; be sure to reserve (L40–45 000). The restaurant in the Accademia hotel (see above) is one of Trento's finest (tel 981 580), with a menu that changes monthly but often features local ingredients like crayfish and trout; it has a fine choice of regional wines (L30–35 000, closed Mon.)

The popular Ristorante-Pizzeria Forst, located in the middle of Trento in the 16th-century palace on Oss Mazzurana 38, tel 235 590, is the place to drink beer and Trentino's wines, eat a pizza *tirolese* (with mushrooms and speck) for L6000 or a full menu in the dining room upstairs for L20 000. The Taverna-Enoteca Al Tino, Via S. Trinità 10, tel 984 109 (on the other side of the Duomo, near Piazza Vittoria), has good, L14 000 full meals, or pizza in a jolly atmosphere of wine casks.

East of Trento

TOURIST INFORMATION

Levico Terme: Via Vittorio Emanuele 3, tel (0461) 706 101
San Martino di Castrozza: Via Passo Rolle 165, tel (0439) 68 101
Fiera di Primiero: Via Fiume 10, tel (0439) 62 407

The Valsugana

The Valsugana follows the course of the Brenta, and is mainly visited for its two lakes, Caldonazzo and Levico. Pergine, a few kilometres before the Lago di Caldonazzo, is the most interesting town in the valley, with its ruined castle and medieval streets. San Cristoforo below is the main resort on the lake. From Vetriolo Terme you can hike up to the summit of Panarotta for splendid views of Caldonazzo, the adjacent lake Levico, and its resort of Levico Terme. Both lakes are excellent for sailing and wind-surfing.

Further down-river, the old town of **Borgo Valsugana** lies under the well-preserved 14th-century **Castel Telvana**, a ghostly eminence when illuminated at night. There are pretty views from the Val di Sella above Borgo; from nearby **Castello Tesino** a winding road leads to San Martino (75 km).

Pale di San Martino

The stunning, pinnacle-crowned Pale di San Martino (3191 m) is the principal mountain group of the southern Dolomites, and **San Martino di Castrozza**, dramatically lying at its foot is the biggest winter resort south of Cortina d'Ampezzo (complete with helicopters up to some of the more difficult runs—skating, and a bobsled run), as well as a superb base for summer climbing and walking excursions. If the Beautiful People at Cortina make your flesh crawl, it's a possible alternative, though, like Cortina, the village is mostly phony alpine schmaltz (the Austrians demolished the medieval town in World War I, leaving only the ancient church).

Among the most popular excursions from San Martino (be sure to pick up the map with its itineraries at the tourist office) is the ascent by cable car and chair lift to the summit of **Rosetta**. On the whole, however, the Pale is a mountain group reserved for experienced climbers. If you're not among them, there are less demanding walks up Monte Cavallazza, facing the Pale (3 hours); or closer at hand, to the Col Fosco or more ambitiously, to Panevéggio.

Panevéggio National Park

Much of the breathtaking region around San Martino lies in the precincts of the **National Park Panevéggio-Pale di San Martino**, a wilderness of venerable woods, emerald meadows, rushing streams, wildflowers, and wildlife, one of the truly unspoiled corners in Italy. Access to the park is from the visitors' centre (from San Martino, it's just a few kilometres beyond the **Passo di Rolle**), in the village of **Panevéggio**, where there's a little natural history museum. There are two splendid paths that take in awesome vistas, including not only the Pale di San Martino, but the distinctive peaks of Marmolada, Pelmo, and Civetta. The forests here are not only beautiful, but in past centuries provided Venice with the timber for its fleet and Stradivarius and his colleagues from Cremona with the resonant wood for their fiddles. Within the park there are only a few places to camp, and a firm rule that no one is allowed to stay for more than 24 hours.

The Pale di San Martino is encircled by a grandly scenic road. The northern part of the route towards Agordo passes through the villages of **Canale d'Agordo** and **Falcade**, the latter a ski resort (see the 'Eastern Dolomites'). The southern route, also via Agordo, passes first through **Frassenè**, a summer resort, then climbs through the forests of Gosaldo to the **Passo di Cereda** and the resort **Fiera di Primiero**, which like Cortina stands at the crossing of two valleys, the Cismon and Canali. There's skiing in the winter here, and in the summer a popular outing is the hour's walk to the sinister ruins of the **Castel di Pietra**, precariously balancing on a jagged rock—according to legend, it was built by Attila the Hun. Two traditional alpine villages in the area are **Mezzano** and **Tonadico**.

WHERE TO STAY AND EATING OUT
Levico Terme: Standing out among the many hotels here is the ***Bellavista, tel
(0461) 706 474, with a thermal pool and pleasant air-conditioned rooms for L65–
85 000, all with private bath. The most highly recommended restaurant in town is the
small but good **La Stua**, Via C. Battisti 62, tel (0461) 707 028, serving Trentino
specialities with a woodland touch, according to season—truffles in the autumn, berries
in the summer (L25–30 000).

In San Martino most of the hotels are just to the south in Siror, like the ****Excelsior
Hotel Cimone, tel (0439) 68 262, with very cosy rooms for L90–125 000, and the
***San Martino**, tel (0439) 68 011, with an indoor pool, tennis courts, and sauna
(L50–55 000 without bath, L65–80 000 with). The **Suisse, tel (0439) 68 087 is a
simple but comfortable bed and breakfast for L35–43 000 without bath and L42–50 000
with.

Val di Fiemme and Val di Fassa

The Val di Fassa is the region to the north of Panevéggio, and takes in the magnificent
scenery dominated by the western slopes of the mighty Marmolada group.

TOURIST INFORMATION
Cavalese: Via Fratelli Bronzetti 4, tel (0462) 30 298
Predazzo: Via SS. Filippo e Giacomo, tel (0462) 51 237
Canazei/Alba: Via Costa, tel (0462) 62 466

Cavalese and the Val di Fiemme

If you're approaching from San Martino, you can join the main route north at Predazzo;
alternatively, from Trento, the road follows the river Avisio past a region of rocks eroded
into spiky 'pyramids' near **Segonzano**, then enters the **Val di Fiemme** near its chief
town **Cavalese**. For many years, thanks to the bishops of Trento, the Val di Fiemme was
virtually independent, ruled by its own *Regolani* who held their outdoor parliament in the
park of the Pieve (parish church); you can still see their circle of stone benches, the
Banco de la Reson. The 'Magnifica Comunità' of Cavalese still has considerable say in
local affairs, running the Val di Fiemme from the grand **Palazzo della Comunità**, the
former bishops' palace, its façade painted with fine frescoes. Local rule had its disadvantages for some. In nearby **Doss delle Strìe**, eleven witches were burnt alive in 1505.
A cable car from Cavalese ascends to **Mt Cermis** (2229 m).

The lake-spangled mountains between Cermis and the Val Sugana, the **Catena dei
Lagorài**, are for the most part accessible only on foot, making them one of the least
developed areas in the Dolomites. **Tesero**, just east of Cavalese, is a charming
traditional village; its old church of San Rocco is frescoed with the 'Sunday Christ',
surrounded by the tools forbidden on the Sabbath; at Panchià up the road there's a pretty
covered bridge spanning the Avisio. Both have good downhill ski runs.

Val di Fassa

Beyond Predazzo, the road enters the Val di Fassa, where the seven *comuni* preserve
their Ladin dialects. The main base for exploring the magnificent peaks in the area—

Marmolada, Sassolungo, and Sella—is the town of **Canazei**, all of its buildings dating from 1912, when a fire destroyed the town. Here you can pick up literature on the numerous trails, cable cars, and alpine refuges in the area; C. Artoni's *200 Itinerari in Val di Fassa* is a good bet for serious exploration. In nearby **Campitello** the parish church has another curious 15th-century fresco on the subject of Sabbath-breaking, apparently a major problem among local workaholics.

Vigo di Fassa is a centre of Ladin culture in the valley, where you can see *tabià*—the traditional log cabins of the Ladini, and learn more about their culture at the **Museo Ladino di Fassa**, spread out among several *tabià* at San Giovanni di Vigo di Fassa. From San Giovanni it's a 20-minute walk to the Gothic church of **Santa Giuliana a Vigo**, with fine quattrocento frescoes and a carved and gilded triptych by Giorgio Arzt of Bolzano (1517). From Vigo a cable car crawls up the Catinaccio group to the west, where you can walk up to a peculiar sheer triple pinnacle, the **Torri del Vaiolet**. **Moena**, another modern community, is the largest town in the valley and an important winter sports centre.

WHERE TO STAY AND EATING OUT
In Cavalese, one of the nicest hotels has the funniest name, the *****Trunka Lunka**, tel (0462) 30 233; it has only 21 rooms, all with bath and TV, a sauna and solarium (L75–85 000). Another hotel in Cavalese, *****San Valier**, tel (0462) 31 285, has an indoor pool, sauna, and pretty setting (L70–100 000). Up on the top of Mt Cermis, *****Sporting**, tel 31 650, has a pool and sauna as well as magnificent views; all 46 rooms have bath for only L40 000. In Canazei, there are hotels in all price ranges: the *****Bellevue**, tel (0462) 61 104, has great mountain views and pleasant rooms, all with bath; outside of July and Aug, prices drop considerably (L65–95 000). *****Il Caminetto**, tel (0462) 61 230, is another good choice, like the Bellevue open all year; L65–95 000. ****Oswald**, tel (0462) 61 125, has comfortable, air-conditioned rooms, all with bath, L45–50 000.

West of Trento: the Brenta Dolomites

TOURIST INFORMATION
Andalo: Piazza Paganella, tel (0461) 585 836
Fai della Paganella: tel (0461) 583 130
Tione di Trento: Via D. Chiesa 3, tel (0465) 23 090
Molveno: Piazza Marconi 1, tel (0461) 586 924
Pinzolo: tel (0465) 51 007

Around Monte Paganella

The Brenta Group, though a bit distant from the other Dolomites, is as marvellous and strange, a challenge for experienced alpinists, though there are a number of less demanding walks for non-alpinists as well. Even if you don't have time to plunge into the heart of the Brenta Dolomites, it's easy to visit the eastern flank of the mountains from Trento, first heading north via **San Michele all'Adige** and **Mezzocorona**, the land of the 'prince of Trentino wines', Teròldego, as well as spumante. From the crossroads at

Mezzolombardo, the scenic road climbs to three well-equipped summer/winter resorts, served by four buses a day from the city: **Fai della Paganella, Andalo** (both with cable cars to the summit of Monte Paganella—2125 m) and **Molveno**, located near a pretty lake and a base for hiking. From Molveno the road continues south to Ponte Arche, where it meets the roads south to Riva del Garda; on the way, in a swamp near the village of Fiavé, archaeologists have discovered some of the oldest houses in Italy. Or at least their foundations—hundreds of wooden piles as much as 5000 years old, planted in the lagoons by a culture very like the famous lake dwellers of Switzerland. East of Ponte Arche is pretty **Lake Toblino** with its castle; to the southwest lies the Giudicarie.

The Giudicarie

The Valley of Giudicarie runs from Molveno down to the Lago d'Idro, near Brescia. Along the way it passes San Lorenzo in Banale, where a track north up the **Val d'Ambiez** provides a quick route for hikers to approach the highest peaks of the Brenta group. Further on, the lovely castle at **Stenico** retains some faded but good Renaissance frescoes (guided tours, daily except Mon 9–12 and 2–5:30; Jan–March, 9–12 and 2–5; adm). From Stenico, the road along the north bank of the river leads to the narrow Val d'Algone, with a waterfall near Airone, and another track into the mountains.

Trentino's most ruggedly stark scenery lies to the south, along the upper reaches of the River Chiese in the **Val di Daone** (N. 237) up to the artificial lakes of Malga Boazzo and Malga Bissina. These lie at the foot of lofty Monte Fumo (3418 m) in the Adamello group. The other principal river running through the Giudicarie is the Sarca, which feeds Lake Garda. North of **Tione**, the valley capital, the main road follows the Sarca up to **Pinzolo**, an attractive town where the exterior of the parish church of **San Vigilio** (in the cemetery, at the northern end of town) was frescoed by the itinerant Lombard artist Simone Baschenis in 1539, portraying a vividly eerie medieval-style *Dance of Death*. Placid, business-like skeletons conduct princes, popes, soldiers, and everyone else to their end, with a couplet of elegant poetry for each. More of Baschenis' precise, luminous work can be see inside the church.

Pinzolo is a good base for exploring the glacier-clad Brenta and Adamello mountains, with their scores of lakes, as well as the lovely **Val di Genova**, part of the **Parco Naturale Adamello-Brenta**, one of the last Alpine refuges of the brown bear. The mouth of the Val di Genova is graced by the lofty **Cascate di Nardìs**, a woodland waterfall flowing from the glacier on **Presanella** (3254 m)—in Pinzolo you can find a guide to make the ascent. Before the waterfall, the chapel of **Santo Stefano** at Carisolo has more frescoes by Simone Baschenis. To the east a chair lift (the world's fastest, they claim) rises to the lower slopes of **Cima Tosa**, the highest peak of the Brenta Dolomites.

WHERE TO STAY AND EATING OUT

In San Michele all'Adige, you can dine well at **Da Silvio**, Via Brennero 2, tel (0461) 650 324. Ultra-modern in decor, serving imaginative dishes, Silvio's delicious speciality is called the Altamira, a selection of mixed meats grilled at your table, with your choice of sauces; two menus from 25–45 000, closed Mon. In Molveno, the most comfortable hotel is the ***Belvedere**, tel (0461) 586 933, with fine rooms, all with bath, overlooking the lake, as well as an indoor pool and solarium (L80–110 000). An older hotel, the

***Molveno**, tel (0461) 586 934, offers tennis and an outdoor pool among its amenities (rooms without bath L58–85 000, with bath L72–105 000). Overlooking Lake Toblino 12 km west of Trento, the charming *Castel Toblino**, tel (0461) 44 036, has four rooms to let. The castle and the setting are romantic, even if the rooms are simple, and the restaurant serves good Trentino cuisine. Closed Tues from Nov–Feb, rooms without bath L50 000, meals around L30 000.

In Pinzolo, the ***Centro Pineta**, tel (0465) 52 758, is a pleasant, medium-sized hotel, warm in the winter and cool in the summer and pine-scented all year round (L75–100 000, all rooms with bath). In the centre, there is the friendly and well-run ***Corona**, tel 51 030 (all rooms with bath, L72–90 000).

There are plenty of good restaurants in and around Pinzolo: at Le Pozze 8, the little **Prima o Poi**, tel (0465) 57 175 serves such delicacies as a pâté made with trout, homemade pasta and gnocchi, and mushroom dishes for L35–40 000 (closed on Wed and in June). At Fisto, near Spiazzo (south of Pinzolo), **La Pila** is in a restored old bakery; it specializes in the traditional *cucina povera* delights of the area: polenta with sausage, hare and pheasant, and red potato *gnocchi*—made with beetroot (about L25 000). In Giustino, also south of Pinzolo, the family-run **Ristorante Mildas** has some impressive seafood (rare for this region), game dishes, roast kid, a good selection of Trentino wines (try *Marzerino*, a rich red made in a very small area in these mountains), and a talking blackbird to greet you at the door (L30 000 and up).

Brenta Dolomites: the Northern Valleys

TOURIST INFORMATION
Madonna di Campiglio: Via Pradalago 4, tel (0465) 42 000
Malè: Viale Marconi 7, tel (0463) 91 280
Fondo: Piazza S. Giovanni 14, tel (0463) 80 133

Madonna di Campiglio

From Pinzolo the road zigzags up to the most important resort in the Brenta Dolomites, Madonna di Campiglio, with extensive winter sports facilities including a ski-jump, 31 lifts, speed-skating, a regular skating rink, and an indoor pool; in the summer it offers experienced climbers the chance to try their mettle on ice and a wild, rocky terrain; for inexperienced walkers it has the most scenic trails in the group. Even if you only have enough spunk to get into a chair lift and a funicular you can enjoy the marvellous views of the Dolomites from the **Passo del Grostè**, some 2260 m above Campiglio to the east, or from **Pradalago** (cable car) to the west. Each side has its attractions; the rugged coral shafts of the highest peaks on the east, and a score of small lakes along an easy path to the west.

Get the tourist office's trail map to do Campiglio's classic walk, through the beautiful Val di Brenta and Valsinella just to the south. A more difficult path, the fabulous **Via Bocchette**, takes in the region's most bizarre naked pinnacles and fantastic cliffs, but should only be attempted with proper training and equipment if you don't want to become another statistic.

North of Campiglio the road passes through Passo Campo di Carlo Magno, so named from the legend that Charlemagne stopped here on his way to Rome to receive the Emperor's crown. **Folgarida**, beyond the pass, is another well-endowed winter resort.

Val di Sole

Occupying the upper reaches of the Noce river, Italy's 'Sun Valley' is a cosy region of soft green meadows and villages, with a backdrop of lofty peaks of Monte Cevedale. The scenic roads up the **Val di Peio** and **Val di Rabbi** lead into the **Parco Nazionale dello Stelvio** but don't go very far: the main entrance from the east is through Spondigna in Alto-Adige (see p. 214); pick up information at the visitor centre in **Bagni di Rabbi**.

Many of the Val di Sole villages have exceptional frescoes on their churches: **Pellizzano**, with a charming *Annunciation* over the door, and **Peio**, with one of the biggest and most endearing St Christophers in Italy (it's good luck to see him before starting a journey, so they paint him extra large). Beyond the turn-off for Peio, the main route N. 42 passes **Ossana**, with a strong castle, continuing along the glacier-coated flank of Presanella, before leaving Trentino at the **Passo del Tonale**, one of the highest and most scenic passes in the Dolomites.

Malè, the capital of the Val di Sole, is the site of an ethnographical museum, the **Museo della Civiltà Solandra**, with handicrafts and agricultural and domestic implements. Although the old Trento-Malè railway no longer goes all the way to Malè, buses coincide with trains at Cles station. Malè is an important woodworking centre and has good skiing in the winter.

Val di Non

The wooded Val di Non, the enchanting valley along the lower course of the River Noce, produces some of Italy's finest apples, especially Golden Delicious and a variety unique in Europe called 'Renetta del Canada', which look more like potatoes than apples but make a pretty fair pie. The valley is especially lovely in the spring, when its apple blossoms, emerald meadows, and snow-clad mountains glow with colour.

Cles, the main town of the Val di Non (linked by train to Trento), stands on the large artificial lake of Santa Giustina. It is the home town of Trento's great bishop Bernardo Clesio, who was born in the **Castello Cles**, the best of a score of castles in the valley. Cles has several Renaissance buildings, but the most attractive and unusual is across the lake, just east of Sanzeno, the **Santuario di San Romedio**.

This popular pilgrimage shrine, set on a tall crag above a delightful mountain stream, marks the cave where the 10th-century hermit Romedio lived with his pet bear, as a kind of alpine St Jerome. Over the centuries the shrine expanded, spilling down the rock in a strange stack of chapels, courtyards, and stairs in several styles—the end result lies somewhere between a doll's house and a monastery. Up on top, besides some indifferent frescoes, there is a portal with barbaric-looking reliefs from the original 11th-century shrine. Leading to it, the steps and corridors are lined with homemade ex-votos— including a disarming small painting that records in graphic detail how Romedio saved an entire family from being crushed under a tram. At the bottom, there is a fine Renaissance courtyard, a bar, and one of the ghastliest souvenir shops ever. Part of the charm of visiting San Romedio is in the surrounding countryside, following the back roads to hidden villages like **Coredo** or **Cavareno**.

South of Cles, a 15-km road leads to another breathtaking alpine lake, **Lago di Tovel**, deep in the folds of the Brenta Dolomites. Unique among mountain lakes, Tovel once was famous for its ruby redness at certain periods, courtesy of a rare alga, *Glendodinium sanguineum* on its surface. A few years back, the algae suddenly disappeared—no one knows why—and Tovel now must be content with a brilliant, though typical, sapphire blue. If you liked Simone Baschenis' Dance of Death at Pinzolo, you can see more of his work, in a somewhat lighter vein, in the parish church at **Tuenno**, on the road to Lake Tovel.

From Lake Santa Giustina you can head east to Bolzano, through the **Passo Mendola**, or continue down the Val di Non past its orchards and old castles, most notably at **Taio** and **Vigo**, while **Sfruz**, a small town above the valley, is a fine cross-country skiing centre and base for walks. The road continues south to Trento via San Michele all'Adige.

WHERE TO STAY AND EATING OUT

Madonna di Campiglio is the one resort in the Brenta Dolomites with lodgings and facilities to please the most demanding customers, and prices tend to be accordingly high. You can shoot long drives in the Alps at the course of the ******Golf Hotel**, up at the Passo Carlo Magno, tel (0465) 410 035. A former summer residence of the Habsburgs, the hotel is open in winter for skiers as well; excellent rooms for L155–185 000. In Campiglio itself the ******Relais Club des Alpes**, tel (0465) 40 000, is large and well furnished, with a large indoor pool; each of the airy rooms has air conditioning and televisions, L185–210 000. Good value in Campiglio, *****Palù**, tel (0465) 41 280, is a small, older hotel with comfortable air-conditioned rooms, all with TVs and private baths for L85–100 000. Campiglio also has many self-catering flats; contact the local Associazione Albergatori, tel (0465) 42 660.

Near Madonna, on the road to Dimaro, tel (0465) 41 231, **Genzianella** is the place to try Trentino specialities the way they're meant to be from the gnocchi to the polenta, down to the bread and butter; L30 000, closed May and June. Near the entrance of the Val di Peio, at Comasine, you can dine well in a charming, 15th-century mill, **Il Mulino**, tel (0463) 74 244. The spacious interior has been attractively converted into a multi-level dining room, where such mountain specialities as goat with wild apples, trout, and venison are excellently prepared. Closed Tues and Oct; L30 000.

Cles has a fine resort hotel in its *****Punto Verde**, tel (0463) 21 275, open all year with tennis, indoor pool, and sauna, all rooms with private bath, L70–85 000. There are two little hotels by Lake Tovel, open summers only. ***Albergo Lago Rosso**, tel (0463) 41 242, is a shade quieter; rooms without bath L43 000.

Alto Adige/Süd Tirol

Everything has two names on the sunny side of the Alps, in the bilingual province of Bolzano/Bozen, otherwise known as the Alto Adige/Süd Tirol. And yet ethnically the inhabitants are neither German nor Italian, but Ladin, a people who spent most of their history ruled by the bishops of Brixen (Bressanone) and the Counts of Tyrol, based near

Merano. After the abdication of the 'Ugly Duchess', Margaret of Tyrol in 1363, the whole region passed at least nominally to the Habsburgs. German influence was thus stronger here than in Trentino, and when Napoleon put the Süd Tirol under Austrian control it had no objection—unlike Trentino which chafed and yearned to join Venetia.

After World War I Italy gained Trentino, and in the 1920s absorbed the lands up to the Brenner Pass as the natural frontier. Mussolini, a rather nasty cultural imperialist, immediately invented Italian names for all the towns and tried to stick the Italian language down the inhabitants' throats until Hitler told him to lay off. It was not a good beginning, and if the Trentini, led by Cesare Battisti, defied the Austrians, the people of Süd Tirol, with their majority pro-Austrian party (the PPST) tend to be among the most disaffected Italians; if it weren't for the Italian vote from the southern half of the autonomous region of Trentino-Alto Adige, separatism would be a serious problem. Occasionally the more vicious malcontents show their resentment by sabotaging the train tracks and other unpleasant little tricks. The central Italian government, for its part, has done much to mollify the region, giving it a great deal of autonomy and enough economic perks to make it one of the country's wealthiest provinces.

Its position as one of the great historical crossroads between north and south, its brilliant Alpine scenery, its winter sport traditions (Bolzano traditionally produces Italy's finest skiers), and renowned climatic spa at Merano made the Süd Tirol a tourist destination long before other parts of the Dolomites. The region has a special mountain information telephone number: (0471) 993 809, and a snow and winter traffic number: (0471) 993 812 so you can ring ahead to find out what you're getting into.

Alto Adige/Süd Tirol also produces some of Italy's best wine, especially white, and lots of it—there are some forty vines for every inhabitant. Most reliable bottlers are Herrnhofer, Bellendorf, Kehlburg, von Elzenbaum and Hofstatter; good whites to try are light and smooth Riesling Renano, dry and snappy Gewürztraminer, Weissburgunder (Pinot Bianco), Welschriesling (known elsewhere at Riesling Italico), Sylvaner (dry and delicate perfume), and Muller-Thurgau (light and fruity).

Bolzano/Bozen

The lively, cultured capital of Alto Adige, Bolzano is an excellent base for visiting the mountains. Located on the banks of the Isarco (Eisack) and the Talvera (Talfer), which just downstream merge to form the Adige, with mountains rising on either side, Bolzano was an important market town in the Middle Ages, a tradition it remembers in its busy food market today. With its high, narrow, gabled houses and arcaded streets it looks the part of a piece of Austria that got away. In the summer, however, you may want to base yourself somewhere higher in the mountains; the high humidity turns Bolzano into a sauna.

GETTING AROUND
Trains for Trento, Bressanone, Vipiteno, and Innsbruck; Merano and Malles; and for Brunico, Dobbiaco, and Lienz depart from the station a block from the central Piazza Walther. The bus station is across the street on Via Garibaldi, tel 971 259. From here you can pick up a bus to Cortina and to nearly every town in the Alto Adige.

TOURIST INFORMATION
The office for the city of Bolzano is at Piazza Walther 8, tel (0471) 975 656 (be sure to ask for its monthly calendar of events). For the region Alto Adige/Süd Tirol and mountains: Piazza Parrochia 11/12, tel 993 840. Guided mountaineering and group day-trips are available with the Club Alpino Italiano, Piazza Erbe 45, tel 21 172 (or if German's your forte, the Alpenverein Südtirol, Via dei Bottai 25, tel 78 729). There are a number of tourist offices in the centre of town that can help book you into resorts and economical *Settimana Bianca* or *Settimana Verde* (ski week and summer week) packages.

Piazza Walther
Bolzano's cultural fusion manifests itself unexpectedly in the town's pretty parlour, the **Piazza Waltherpatz**. In the centre there's a statue of Germany's greatest minnesinger, Walther von der Vogelweide, and at his feet slouch travellers from around the world munching on Big Macs from America's biggest chain, located just behind the great troubadour. In front of Walther stands Bolzano's Gothic **Duomo** with its colourful roof and pretty tower. The art, however, is a block behind the cathedral, in the former **Dominican cloister** (now the Music Conservatory) where the chapel of San Giovanni contains fine 14th-century frescoes by an admirer of Giotto.

From here Via Goethe/Goethestrasse leads up to the jovial **Piazza Erbe**, Bolzano's commercial hub, where a fountain of Neptune watches over the daily fruit and vegetable market. To the right begins the city's main street, the moody **Via Portici/Laubengastrasse**, lined with shops under its Tyrolean arcades, while at the back of the Piazza Erbe lies the church of the **Francescani** with its pretty Gothic cloister, fresco fragments, and a beautiful 1500 altarpiece by woodcarver Hans Klocker. Near here as well, on Via Museo/Museostrasse, is Bolzano's **Museo Civico** (open 9–12 and 2:30–5:30, Sun 10–1, closed Mon), with a small archaeological section, Gothic and Baroque art and wood carvings, and folk items. It stands near the bridge over the Talvera; to the right, off in its own field, is the **Castel Mareccio**, with its five stout towers and 13th-century core, now used as a conference centre and no longer open to the public.

For a fine view of the castle and craggy mountains beyond Bolzano, cross the Talvera and stroll up its riverside park, the **Lungotalvera Bolzano**; bearing straight from the bridge, however, Corso Libertà/Freiheitstrasse leads to **Gries**, a suburb with two important churches—the imposing, Baroque **Abbey Church of the Benedettini** in the main piazza and the old **parish church of Gries**, with a beautifully carved 15th-century wooden altar by Michael Pacher (open 10–12 and 2–3).

Walks around Bolzano
There are two fine walks you can take with views over Bolzano. Beyond the Gries parish church, at the end of Via Knoller/Knollerstrasse begins the **Passeggiata del Guncina**, at least 1.5 km in length, with an inn at the top for refreshments. A bit longer but more dramatic, the **Passeggiata Sant'Osvaldo** begins near the train station at Via Renico/Rentscherstrasse and descends by the head of the Lungotalvera promenade. A bit further up the river, the 1237 **Castel Roncolo**/Schloss Runkelstein guards the passage on its impregnable rock, though it will admit visitors to admire its fascinating 14th-century frescoes of chivalric knights (guided tours daily exc Sun, Mon 10–5 pm; closed Dec–Feb).

There are three cable cars from Bolzano, but the most rewarding is that from Via Renon/Rittnerstrasse next to the station, climbing 1221 m up the slopes of Mt Renon/ Rittner to **Soprabolzano/Oberbozen**. The views of the Dolomites are splendid, but for a truly strange sight, continue from here on the rack railway up to **Collalbo/ Klopbenstein**, and from there follow the path to the **Longomoso Pyramids**—rocks eroded to form a dense forest of needles and bizarre stone drapery. More fine views of the Dolomites can be had from the San Genesio/Jenesien cable car, departing from Via Sarentino (across the Talvera and before the Castel Roncolo).

WHERE TO STAY (tel prefix 0471)

Bolzano is well equipped with hotels. The most lavish and sophisticated, the CIGA chain's ******Park Hotel Laurin**, Via Laurin 4, tel 980 500, is a lovely hotel built at the turn of the century in Viennese Jugendstil, located in a fine old park and rose garden near the centre of Bolzano. It has a heated swimming-pool, and the lounge and public area are furnished with fine antiques clustered around the black marble fireplaces. The excellent rooms are large and very comfortable, L125–180 000. In the Piazza Walther, the long-established ******Grifone-Greif**, tel 977 056, may be in the very heart and soul of Bolzano, with a café giving on to the busy square, but at the back there's a fine swimming-pool in a garden. Rooms are very pleasant, though not all have private bath. Downstairs is one of Bolzano's best restaurants, with outdoor dining in good weather (L90–100 000 without bath, L155 000 with; meals around L40 000).

For peace and quiet, the little 11-room *****Eberle**, Passeggiata Sant'Osvaldo 1, tel 26 125, also offers guests a pool, tennis, sauna and gym in addition to cosy rooms (L55–70 000). A charming choice in the centre, just behind the Piazza Walther, ****Herzog**, Piazza del Grano/Kornplatz 2, tel 26 267, is an inn in the old style, furnished with hand-painted wooden furniture; TVs in every room as well (L48 000 without bath, L54–70 000 with). If it's hot in Bolzano, take the Colle cable car (Italy's oldest) from the opposite bank of the Eisack (from the train station) up to the refreshing breezes of Colle/Kohlern, where there aretwo small but very pleasant hotels—****Kohlern**, Colle 11, tel 971 428, with 14 rooms, all with bath for L30–38 000, or the ***Klaus**, Colle 14, tel 971 294, an old farmhouse with 10 rooms, no baths; L28 000.

EATING OUT

Like the language, the cuisine of Alto Adige/Süd Tirol is a bit more than half German— you can even get speck (smoked prosciutto) on pizza. Entries that frequently pop up on the menu include Wienerschnitzel, sauerkraut dishes, goulash, knödel (breadcrumb dumplings in a variety of styles), *Terlaner* (wine soup) with apple, cheese, and poppy-seed strudels, Sacher torte, and rich mousse for dessert.

The restaurant in the Hotel Laurin (see above), the **Belle Epoque**, not only has an elegant, turn-of-the-century decor, but also delicious, reasonably priced antipasti, fish dishes and great desserts (varied menus, like the L21 000 business menu, or L30– 50 000 à la carte). Contemporary elegance and very good Italian food may be had at **Da Abramo** in Piazza Gries 16, tel 280 141; specialities include seafood in the antipasti, first and second courses; divine risotto (L30–50 000, closed Sun, and part of June and July). There's a restaurant in the Castel Mareccio, the **Maretsch**, tel 979 439, serving traditional Süd Tirol dishes, either inside or in the courtyard of the castle (closed Sun and half of Aug; L35 000). At Via Grappolo/Weintraubeng 2 (tel 970 247), the **Rathaus Keller**, next to the Baroque Municipio/Rathaus is a locally popular joint with a Tyrolean atmosphere, with meals for L20–25 000.

East of Bolzano: the Dolomites

Bolzano lies just to the west of the Süd Tirol's most spectacular Dolomite scenery. Scores of Alpine refuges, chair lifts and cable cars, and fast buses from Bolzano to towns and funicular stations in the valleys make access easy. Bolzano's tourist office has information on trails and refuges; for more detailed information, buy a copy of *I Rifugi Dell'Alto Adigio* by Willy Dondio.

TOURIST INFORMATION
Ortisei/St Ulrich: Via Rezia 1, tel (0471) 76 328
Santa Cristina: Via Chemun 25, tel (0471) 73 046
Selva di Valgardena/Wolkenstein: tel (0471) 75 122
Corvara/Kurfa: Palazzo Comunale, tel (0471) 836 176
Nova Levante/Welschnofen: Via Carezza 5, tel (0471) 613 126

Val Gardena/Grodnerta

The most accessible and certainly one of the most beautiful excursions from Bolzano is to the take the Brenner road north to the Ladin-speaking Val Gardena, lying between the Alpe di Siusi/Seiser Alm and jagged Odle/Geislergruppe. The dominant feature of the **Alpe di Siusi** is a magnificent plateau, noted for its skiing in winter and seemingly endless meadows of flowers in the late spring; there are numerous lifts up from the Val Gardena, or a road up from the resort town of **Siusi** on the Brenner road north of Bolzano. A classic, not strenuous hike from Siusi is the 4-hour trek up **Monte Puez**, rewarded with remarkable views and an optional stay at one of the *grandes dames* of 19th-century alpine refuges, **Rifugio Bolzano di Monte Puez**.

The road enters the Val Gardena at **Ponte Gardena/Waidbruck**, under the medieval **Trostburg Castle**, open for tours May–Oct, 10–4; closed Mon. The first and largest town of the valley, **Ortisei/St Ulrich**, has specialized in wood carving for centuries, especially in figures for churches (a good sampling may be seen in the local church), and is the site of a wood-carving school. Ortisei, and the next two villages in the valley, **Santa Cristina** and **Selva di Val Gardena/Wolkenstein** are also well-equipped resorts, with cable cars ascending the Alpe di Siusi. Selva, dominated by the forbidding wall of the Sella group that blocks the head of the valley, is the favourite summer resort of Italy's former President Pertini. Santa Cristina has a cable car up into the Odle group and up to the foot of the most distinctive peak in the region, the spiralling, dream-like **Sassolungo/Langkofel** (3180 m).

From the crossroads in Selva you have a choice of two spectacular routes, either over the **Passo di Sella** to Canazei in Trentino, where you can pick up the Great Dolomites Road (see below), or over the grand **Passo di Gardena** down into the **Val Badia**, another beautiful valley that has retained its Ladin culture. **Corvara** and **La Villa/Stern** are the main resorts in the valley. The north road through the valley leads to San Lorenzo, near Brunico, while the south road descends to Arabba.

Catinaccio/Rosengarten

The other main group easily accessible from Bolzano, Catinaccio/Rosengarten, is among the most celebrated of all the Dolomites. Its name first appears in a 13th-century Tyrolean epic poem, describing how King Lauren of the Dwarfs was made prisoner and dragged away from his mountain realm. Furiously Lauren put a curse on the roses that had betrayed him, that no one would ever see them again, neither by night nor by day. But he neglected to mention the dawn or the twilight, when the enchanted roses redden the stony face of Rosengarten.

From Bolzano, the road to Rosengarten begins at Cardana/ Kardaun, just east of town, and passes through the breathtaking narrow gorge of the **Val d'Ega/Eggental**. As the road nears the valley's main settlement and winter and summer resort, **Nova Levante/Welschnofen**, the craggy peaks of the **Latemar** group loom up to the right, while the massive wall of Rosengarten rises to the left. You can reach the slopes of Rosengarten from Nova Levante or the Passo Costalunga/Karer, near gorgeous Lake Carezza, up the road from Nova Levante. For an even more spectacular approach, continue along the road, which becomes increasingly magical, to **Pozza di Fassa** on the east slopes of Rosengarten (see 'Trentino').

The Great Dolomites Road: Bolzano to Cortina d'Ampezzo

The road just described from Bolzano through the Val d'Ega to Rosengarten and Pozza, is the first leg of the fabled 110-km Strada delle Dolomiti, or the Great Dolomites Road. Buses from Bolzano or Cortina make the journey in summer three times a day, and you should take one—for who could bear to keep their eyes on these mountain roads and miss some of Europe's greatest scenery?

After Pozza the road continues up the Fassa Valley of Trentino to the resort of Canazei, the best base for the ascent of the Dolomites' mightiest peaks, **Marmolada**. The road from Canazei climbs in zigzags, past the peculiar tower of **Sassolungo** and Sella glowering on the left, on its way to the **Passo Pordoi**, with fabulous views of Sella and Marmolada.

From the pass the road writhes down towards **Arabba**, a ski resort, and **Pieve di Livinallongo**, below the odd-shaped **Col di Lana**, its summit blown off by an Italian mine in World War I. The road climbs again, past the haunting, eroding **Castello d'Andraz** (just after the settlement of Andraz) to the **Sasso di Stria** (Witch's Rock) and the tunnel at **Passo di Falzarego**.

From here the road begins the descent to Cortina, with views of the strange **Cinque Torri** (Five Towers) and nearly vertical slopes of the Tofane, before reaching the top of the Boite valley, with views over Cortina (see p. 189).

WHERE TO STAY AND EATING OUT   (tel prefix 0471)
The Val Gardena is well equipped with excellent hostelries. In Ortisei, the ******Aquila-Adler**, Via Rezia 7, tel 76 203, is the most glamorous hotel, open mid-Dec to mid-March and mid-May–Oct. Located in a large garden, with an indoor pool and tennis courts, some rooms lack private baths, but all are very cosy (L76–150 000 without, L100–185 000 with).

In Santa Cristina, ******Sporthotel**, at Sacun 17, tel 76 780, has lovely mountain views, an indoor pool and sauna, and tennis, all in a quiet park (open Easter–Oct); all 32 rooms have bath, L85–100 000. Several hotels are just outside Santa Cristina at Monte Pana, open only for the summer and winter seasons: a pleasant one, *****Cendevaves**, Via Monte Pana 17, tel 76 562 has an indoor pool and good views (L55–65 000).

In Selva, the small but very comfortable ******Alpenroyal**, Via La Pozza 90, tel 75 178, is one of the few in town open all year, with plenty of facilities to keep its guests fit and happy—indoor pool, whirlpool baths, sauna, solarium, and fitness room. All rooms have private baths and TVs; L55–95 000. A good economical choice, ****Freina**, Via Centro 403, tel 75 110, is convenient to the slopes; each of its 12 rooms has a bath, and even though at least half-pension is required, it's a pleasure because the food is excellent—stop here if you're just passing through (L65 000 half-pension per person, L75 000 full-pension, meals L15–20 000 on the menu, a bit more à la carte).

In Nova Levante the ******Posta Cavallino Bianco/Weisses Rössel**, Strada Carezza 30, tel 613 113, is a fine resort hotel, its name recalling the former postal relay station but its facilities—indoor and outdoor pools, tennis, and much more—are contemporary and very comfortable. Open mid-Dec to mid-April and mid-June to mid-Sept, rooms are L87–100 000. Good value in Nova Levante, open all year, is the *****Stella-Stern**, Strada Carezza 51, tel 613 125, with nice rooms, all with bath, an indoor pool and fitness room; L50–60 000.

North Towards the Brenner Pass

TOURIST INFORMATION
Bressanone/Brixen: Viale della Stazione 9, tel (0472) 22 401
Brunico/Bruneck: Via Europa 22, tel (0474) 85 722
Vipiteno/Sterzing: Piazza Città 3, tel (0472) 65 325

Val Isarco

North of Bolzano and Ponte Gardena lies the Val Isarco/Eisacktal, the main route to the Brenner Pass. On the way to Bressanone, the ancient town of **Chiusa/Klausen** lies under its 17th-century monastery and is a base for visits to the quiet Val di Funès.

Bressanone/Brixen was the capital of the region for a millennium, ruled by bishops continually at odds with the Counts of Tyrol. Now a popular resort under Monte Plose, the city is one of the most charming in the Alto Adige with its medieval buildings and arcaded streets, but its ancient **Duomo** was metamorphosed into a dull Baroque church in the 18th century. Fortunately the remodellers neglected the Romanesque cloister with its fine 14th-century frescoes. Even earlier frescoes decorate the cathedral's 11th-century **Baptistry**. The cathedral treasure and a fine collection of *presepi* (carved Christmas cribs) may be seen in the Museo Diocesano in the **Hofburg**; this former bishop's palace has an exquisite arcaded, three-storey courtyard (open 10–12 and 2–5, closed Sun).

Besides excursions on Mount Plose, Bressanone is a good base for visiting **Schloss Velthurns**, built for the local bishop in the 16th century in the hills to the southwest, open for guided tours at 10, 11, 2:30 and 3:30; closed Mon and Dec–Feb. Another short excursion from Bressanone is to the fortified **Convento di Novacella/Neustift**, some 3 km north of town, at the head of the Pusteria (tours at 11, 2, 3 and 4; closed Sun; adm). Begun for the Augustine Order in 1142, the Convent is a fascinating study in the evolution of architecture, with its 12th-century tower, its fine Baroque church, its beautiful frescoed 14th-century cloister, its strange, round 12th–16th century Chapel of San Michele. Visits also include a small art gallery and the library with a collection of medieval manuscripts.

The Pusteria

The Pusteria/Pustertal is the wide and pleasant valley running along the river Rienza, east to Dobbiaco/Toblach. Dotted with typical Tyrolean villages and castles, many of its attractive little churches contain works by the valley's master 15th-century woodcarver Michael Pacher, most notably in the 13th-century parish church of **San Lorenzo di Sebato**. Prominent near here is the **Castel Badia convent** (Sonnenburg), now a hotel.

The capital of the Pusteria, **Brunico/Bruneck** is a pleasant town and transportation hub of the region. From here you can head north into the heavily wooded **Val di Tures**, where **Campo Tures/Sand in Taufers** is the main centre, clustered under its medieval baronial castle, **Burg Taufers**. Glacier alpinists come for the **Vedrette Giganti**, reached from Riva di Tures (with a pretty waterfall), while extremists may carry on north of Campo up the Valle Aurina to **Casere/Kasern** and 2 km beyond to the tiny hamlet of **Pratomagno**, the northernmost village in Italy.

East of Brunico, **Monguelfo/Welsberg** is a resort under a 12th-century castle; from here a road turns south into the Val di Braies/Prags. The **Lago di Braies**, fast in the Dolomites' embrace, is celebrated for its intense green colour. East of Monguelfo the road continues to Dobbiaco/Toblach (see 'Excursions from Cortina').

The Upper Val Isarco to Brenner

Vipiteno, the main town between Bressanone and the pass, formerly belonged to the great banking empire of the Fuggers. The attraction it held for them was its mines, which flourished in the Renaissance but have been abandoned since the 18th century. But in the 15th and 16th centuries they were quite lucrative, judging by the splendid houses they built for themselves, complete with battlements. The end of the main corso is framed by the tall **Torre di Città**; in the Piazza Città the **Museo Multscher** is devoted to a handful of rather elegant works of the 15th-century painter Hans Multscher (open 9–11 and 3–5, closed Sun). To house pilgrims on their way to Rome, the Knights Templar built a **hospital** on the edge of Vipiteno in 1241, though most of what you see today dates from the 16th century. Excursions into the mountains around Vipiteno include the scenic **Val di Ridanna** with skiing to the west, the tranquil **Val di Vizze** to the east, and through the **Val Passiria** and the **Passo Giovo** towards Merano.

Colle Isarco/Gossensass is another summer/winter resort, with skiing and hiking on Cima Bianca and in the Val di Fléres. Beyond this lies the **Brenner Pass** (1375 m), the lowest of Alpine passes and the route of countless invaders from the north; during World War II it was heavily bombed. From here it is 125 km to Innsbruck.

WHERE TO STAY AND EATING OUT   (tel prefix 0472)
Bressanone is perhaps better known for a hotel for than any of its sights, a venerable inn that recalls a day back in the year 1500 when the king of Portugal sent an Indian elephant

to Emperor Maximilian as a gift for his zoological park. The elephant, on his way to his new home, spent a week in Bressanone's best hostelry. The locals were so impressed that they had his portrait done by the door of the inn for all to see, and there it remains to this day, on the front of the ****Elefant, Via Rio Bianco 4, tel 22 288. Of the old Renaissance inn, only the fresco remains, but inside the ceilings and walls retain antique panelling, and there are beautiful tile stoves. Many of the lovely rooms are furnished with antiques, though no one remembers which one the elephant slept in. There's a swimming-pool and pleasure garden, as well as a dairy and vegetable garden that provides many of the fresh ingredients for the Tyrolean and international dishes served in the Elefant's fine restaurant; everything, however, closes down between Nov and Feb (rooms, all with bath, L140–150 000, meals L40–50 000). A more reasonable choice ***Chiavi d'Oro, Via Torre Bianca 10, tel 22 379, where rooms are L30–33 000 without bath, and L35–42 000 with.

Bressanone has a pair of good reasonably-priced restaurants. The finch, or **Fink**, Portici Minori 4, tel 23 883 is decked out in the traditional woodsy style, and offers a variety of cold meats, saddle of venison, *polenta nera* (made from buckwheat), and other local dishes, topped off with a large selection of cheeses (L20–25 000, closed Wed eve, Thurs, and last two weeks of June). **Bel Riposo**, Via Vigenti 2, tel 22 548, offers wholesome, rib-sticking cooking: *zuppa della Val d'Isarco* (with cheese and garlic), *gnocchetti* (dumplings in broth) and venison (L20 000).

In Vipiteno, **Hotel Krone**, Via Città Vecchia 31, tel 765 210 is the place to sleep and eat for the total mitteleuropean experience, geraniums, gardens and Biedermeier rooms; refined Tyrolean cuisine, including a separate and utterly lavish dessert menu, and an Italian touch—a separate olive oil menu (L30 000).

The Upper Adige

TOURIST INFORMATION
Merano/Meran: Corso Libertà 45, tel (0473) 35 223
Naturno/Naturns: tel (0473) 87 287

Merano

Just 25 km up the Adige from Bozen, **Merano** (Meran in German) has something no other Tyrolean town can claim—radioactive waters. Since the 1830s it has been a favoured spa; there are also plenty of opportunities for skiing, in the big recreation area called Meran 2000, on the slopes above the town. It is an attractive place, full of flowers, grapes, and wine with a stern 15th-century Gothic **Cathedral** and a fine medieval centre, set around the arcaded Via dei Portici.

From the Torre delle Polvere/Pulvertürm, between the Cathedral and the river, the **Passeggiata Tappeiner/Tappeinerweg** leads up into the mountains, with memorable views, a favourite promenade of the Meraner. As a strategic spot in the alpine passes, this area bristles with castles; **Castel Tirolo/Schloss Tirol**, north of town in Tiroler Dorf, is one of the best, headquarters of the independent Counts of Tyrol before the Habsburgs snatched up the province in 1363. It has some frescoes of saints and Romanesque carvings in the chapel (daily exc Mon, 9:30–12, 2–5 pm; adm; closed in winter). Nearby **Brunnenberg** was the last home of Ezra Pound, the American poet who talked trash on the radio for Mussolini—after the war he was locked up in a Washington mental hospital, and finally allowed to return to Italy to die (it now houses an agricultural museum, open daily exc Tues, 9:30–11:30; adm; closed Dec–Easter).

Schloss Schenna, north of Merano,has an impressive collection of arms and armour (daily exc Sun, guided tours 10–12, 2–5 pm; adm; closed Dec–Feb). It stands at the foot of a valley called the **Passeiertal**, well known to all Austrians as the home of their national hero, Andreas Hofer, a country innkeeper who led the local resistance against Napoleon. The valley continues north to St Leonhard in Passeier, from which you can get across the mountains to Vipiteno/Sterzing.

East of Merano, the valley of the Val Venosta, or Vinschgau, follows the Adige west to the Austrian border. To the south, it skirts the peaks of **Ortler**, one of the tallest patches of Alps. At **Naturno/Naturns**, the little church of San Prokulus has some fragments of frescoes that may be as old as the 8th century. Six miles further, **Castelbello/Kastelbell** hangs over the valley; a narrow but very scenic road digresses north up another valley, the Schnalstal, passing a little lake called the Stausee. **Latsch**, on the Adige, has cableways up in this direction, the only year-round skiing area in the region.

Two genuine treats await anyone who makes it as far up the valley as Sluderno/Schluderns, the next town up the Adige: **Churburg** castle, with gloriously painted loggias and a fine collection of armour; and the **Marienburg monastery**, a 17th-century Benedictine house, gleaming white with a crown of towers and gables. It makes a grand sight in its woodland setting, and there are more good 12th-century frescoes in the chapel crypt (still a working monastery, but you may visit daily exc Sat afternoon and Sun; 10:45–3 pm; in summer tours at 10, 11, 3 and 4:30).

From here the main road, route 38, crawls up to the Stelvio pass by an endless series of twists and bends. The Adige, however, turns north towards Austria, passing first the romantically ruined castle of **Lichtenberg** and a pretty lake called the **Reschensee**. It's an artificial lake, with the church tower from a submerged village still sticking up above its calm surface. **St Valentino** and **Resia/Reschen** are the last small ski resorts before the border; there are trails where you can do a little cross-country run through three nations (Switzerland is close by too), without any Customs men making nuisances of themselves.

If you don't go right up the valley but leave the Adige at **Spondigna/Spondinig** and continue along the N. 38, you'll enter **Stelvio National Park**, the largest in Italy, founded in 1935 and encompassing the grand alpine massif of Ortles-Cevedale. A tenth of the park's 134,620 hectares is ice—and among its one hundred glaciers, it has one of Europe's largest, the 2000-hectare *Ghiacciaio dei Forni*. The peaks offer many exciting climbs, on **Gran Zebrù** (3850 m), **Ortles** (3905 m) and **Cevedale** (3778 m); the park encompasses over fifty lakes and Europe's second-highest pass, the **Passo di Stelvio**, through which you can continue to Bormio and into Lombardy between the months of June and October; or ski, even in August.

Stelvio is administered by the provinces of Sondrio, Trentino, and Bolzano, all of which have visitors' centres that can tell you where to find the 1500 km of marked trails, the best flowers, alpine refuges, or where to watch for chamois, the not very shy marmots, eagles, and other wildlife, including the ibex, reintroduced in 1968. Unfortunately, the insatiable Italian hunter shot the last bear in these mountains in 1908. Hunting is now illegal in the Lombard section of the park, but continues in Trentino and Alto Adige, causing no end of controversy each autumn between the anti-hunting and hunting factions.

WHERE TO STAY AND EATING OUT (tel prefix 0473)

In Merano you can sleep like a lord in one of several renovated castles set in greenery: ******Schloss Rendegg**, tel 34 364 (L180–250 000 with breakfast) or *****Schloss Labers**, tel 34 484, a castle villa (L110–155 000 with breakfast). Franz Kafka, however, preferred the luxurious ******Hotel Palace**, Via Cavour 4, tel set in beautifully maintained grounds with a pool; L220–380 000 with breakfast; it has a good restaurant in its **Tiffany Grill**, tel 34 734, a rarefied pub-style restaurant serving unusual dishes like breast of pheasant in bilberries, or salmon and sole in lemon sauce for L45–55 000, closed Tues.

Gourmets visiting Merano reserve a room months in advance at the *****Villa Mozart**, Via S. Marco 26, tel 30 630, to feast in its refined Austrian-Succession dining room—open for hotel guests only. Owned by Andreas Hellrigl, who also runs the famous Palio restaurant in New York, there is only a fixed menu for around L80 000 (closed Nov-Mar). If you can't get a room at the Mozart, you can try Hellrigl's other Merano restaurant, **Andrea**, Via G. Galilei 44, tel 37 400, specializing in local dishes (*zuppa al vino Terlano*, rack of lamb in rosemary, etc). Two menus available: the works for L80 000, or a smaller version at L60 000, both minus wine; closed Mon and mid-Jan–mid-Mar. An excellent, and less economically ruinous meal of soup, trout or venison, and a superb dessert may be had at **Terlaner Weinstube**, Via Portici 231, tel 35 571 for L25–30 000; closed Mon and mid-Jan–mid–Feb.

Part VI

FRIULI–VENEZIA GIULIA

Relief depicting craftsmen at the Archaeology Museum, Aquileia

For most English or American visitors, this region east of Venice is *terra incognita* with a jumbly name that sometimes turns up on the wine list in Italian restaurants. Trieste, at the far end of Italy, evokes cloudy images of pre- and post-War intrigue, a kind of *Third Man* on the Mediterranean. In between Trieste and Venice the imagination fails.

One problem is that the region is burdened with a history as messy as its name. In Roman days Aquileia was the most important city and seat of the patriarchate. Its ecclesiastical and temporal authority was gradually usurped by Cividale del Friuli, the Lombard capital in the Dark Ages, and then in the Middle Ages by Udine, before all was snatched away by the Venetians in the 14th century. Trieste was sometimes under the doge's thumb, sometimes Venice's bitter rival under the Counts of Gorizia or the Austrians. Napoleon threw the region in with the 'Kingdom of Illyria', a piece of real estate subsequently picked up by the Austro-Hungarian Empire. Italy inherited it in 1918, along with all of Istria down to Fiume (modern Rijeka). A major dispute broke out over the territory following World War II. The Allies forced Tito to leave Trieste, occupying it themselves as a neutral free port until 1954, when it was readmitted into Italy, leaving the rest of Istria to Yugoslavia. A disastrous earthquake in 1976 shook the core of Friuli, killing a thousand people, levelling entire towns, and causing widespread structural damage that has taken more than a decade to repair. Now rebuilt with modern apartments and bungalows, the central Friulian plain bears an uncanny resemblance to the American Midwest.

Weary of being marginal, Friuli-Venezia Giulia is now grasping for an identity of its own, but it's like trying to put together pieces from several different jigsaw puzzles. The population in the east speaks Slovenian, while the north has a sizeable German minority.

In Trieste there are large Jewish, Greek, and Serb minorities, and in the middle, around Udine, a Friulian ethnic majority, like the Ladini in the South Tyrol, speak a language similar to the Swiss Rhaeto-Romansch. In 1963 the central government threw up its hands in despair and gave the region autonomy.

Wine

The Friuli region produces some of Italy's finest wines, with no fewer than seven of its own D.O.C. regions. Visiting wine lovers should pick up a copy of *The Golden Land* from the tourist office for a complete description of the various vintages and producers whose cellars are open to visitors. The best known region is Collio (around Cormons), famous for its white wines, especially Pinot Bianco and Riesling. The Colli Orientali, a much larger region, also does good whites and a brisk red, Refosco. Rochi di Cialla and Giovanni Dri are just two of the best-known labels. The other D.O.C. regions— Aquileia, Isonzo, Carso, Latisana, and Grave del Friuli produce good reds: names to look for are Schiopettino, Carso Terreno, and Riva Rossa.

Friuli-Venezia Giulia Itineraries

The two greatest monuments in the region are the cathedral of Aquileia, with its fabulous 4th-century mosaics, and the Tempietto Longobardo in Cividale del Friuli, a unique relic of the Dark Ages. There are four good beaches between Venice and Trieste: Caorle and Bibione (both in the Veneto) and Lignano-Sabbiadoro and Grado. The Carnic (Corniche) and West Julian Alps offer less expensive and less crowded resort alternatives to the Dolomites.

You could see the highlights of the region in four days by car, starting from Venice and ending up in the Cadore region of the Dolomites, with the first day in ancient Aquileia and nearby Grado, an attractive beach resort with a medieval core (114 km from Venice). The next day: Trieste (52 km), including the Archduke's palace at Miramare and the Grotta del Gigante in Trieste's unusual *Carso* hinterland. Third day: the 8th-century wonders of Cividale del Friuli and Udine, an art city (105 km). Day 4: Codroipo, site of the villa of the last doge, and from there into the mountains, either via the interesting small town of Spilimbergo to the resort area of Piancavallo, ending up in the Eastern Dolomites at Longarone (85 km from Udine); or north, following the scenic valley of the Tagliamento to Pieve di Cadore (200 km).

By public transport you can follow the same itinerary, except on the last day from Udine options are a train west through Codroipo and Pordenone to Conegliano, one of the crossroads of the Veneto, from where you can return to Venice or head north to Pieve di Cadore; alternatively, take the train north to Carnia from Udine, and bus from there to Sappada.

From Venice to Trieste: the Coast

GETTING AROUND

Trains from Venice run roughly every two hours (to Trieste 2¹/₂–3¹/₂ hours); buses depart less frequently from Piazzale Roma, though Caorle and Bibione are easiest reached by direct bus from Venice. Otherwise, take the train to S. Donà di Piave and the local bus from there. For Bibione or Lignano-Sabbiadoro, train to Latisana and bus in 30 mins to the coast.

TOURIST INFORMATION
Caorle: Piazza Papa Giovanni 1, tel (0421) 81 085
Lignano-Sabbiadoro: Via Latisana 42, tel (0431) 71 821

Old Roman Towns and Beaches
The N.14 from Venice passes first Marco Polo airport and then **Altino**, the modern name of the Roman city of Altinum. Once renowned for its wealth and villas, Attila the Hun put it to the sack—only the first of many hardships that led its inhabitants to found a new city on the island of Torcello in the Venetian lagoon. What Attila and the Lombards didn't wreck was removed to Torcello, so that all that remains in the **Museum** (9–6 closed Mon) are mosaics and a few odds and ends.

The route continues over the Piave near **San Donà di Piave**; it was near here that Ernest Hemingway, a member of the Red Cross, was wounded in 1918, an experience that became the germ of *A Farewell to Arms*. From San Donà a detour to **Caorle** (the Roman port Caprulae) is tempting, not only for its attractive old fishermen's town on an isthmus, its beaches, and its pretty lagoon beloved of wildfowl, but for the splendid gilded Venetian *pala* on the altar of the **Cathedral** built in 1075. The **Valle Grande** along the inner lagoon preserves a relic of the primordial pine grove that once scented the shore from Grado to Ravenna. **Bibione** on the far side of the lagoon is another pleasant resort.

Caorle was the port of ancient Concordia Sagittaria, and besides the usual Italian seaside amenities, it has two unusual landmarks: the cylindrical brick, conical-roofed **campanile** of the cathedral, built in 1100 and a rare example of the style outside Ravenna, and the 'lighthouse church' of the Madonna dell'Angelo, isolated on a point. **Portogruaro**, the ancient Concordia Sagittaria, is a seductive old town laid out under the delicately worked but very tilted campanile of its cathedral, worth a visit for its frescoes. Portogruaro preserves its ancient gates and winding arcaded streets. Finds excavated in town and the townlet of Concordia (2 km) are displayed in the **museum** (9–12, 3–6, winter and holidays 9–1, closed Mon).

Lignano-Sabbiadoro

From **Latisana** you can follow the crowds south to the Laguna di Marano and the fastest-growing resort area on the Adriatic, **Lignano-Sabbiadoro**. With a lovely 9-km sandy beach and scores of new hotels, apartments, bungalows and camp sites, Lignano-Sabbiadoro and its two adjacent resorts of **Lignano-Pianeta** (the prettiest section, under the pinewoods) and smart **Lignano Riviera** offer fun in the sun and Vienna sausages just like Mutter makes: a veritable Austrian riviera.

Palmanova

In the Renaissance, despite all Alberti's theories on town planning, only a handful of entirely new towns were ever constructed; none of them has survived more completely than **Palmanova**. Built in 1593 by the Venetians as a bulwark against the Austrians and Turks, it is a fine example of 16th-century 'ideal' radial military planning, with a geometrical *tour de force*: the star formed by its walls has nine points, while the large, somewhat eerie, piazza in the heart of town is a perfect hexagon that originally contained the arsenal servicing the nine bastions. Even though most of the walls and moat are now overgrown, their stone softly moulded into serpentine hills and gullies, they are still defended by young conscripts. At the **Museo Storico** (10–12, 4–7; holidays, morning only; closed Mon), ask about the torchlight tour of the recently discovered walkways within the walls. From Palmanova there are frequent buses to Aquileia, Grado, and Udine.

WHERE TO STAY AND EATING OUT

In the beach resorts, count on high-season prices from mid-June to the end of August. Seafood is naturally the speciality on the table, and the further east you go, the more likely you are to find it prepared Dalmatian-style in olive oil—wash it all down with the good white wine of Collio.

In Caorle: The best hotel is the seaside *****Airone**, Via Pola 1, tel (0421) 81 570, open 20 May–20 Sept, with a pool as well as a private beach and great rooms for L70–85 000, all with bath. For dinner, try **Duilio**, Via Strada Nuova 19, tel (0421) 81 087, celebrated for its succulent seafood in the antipasti, in the pasta, and as the main course. A charming setting, a huge wine list, and reasonably priced menus (L25–35 000) are added attractions; ordering à la carte expect to pay around L45 000 (closed Mon and in Jan).

Lignano-Sabbiadoro: The majority of hotels are in the proper Lignano-Sabbiadoro area, which is also a good place to look for bungalows. Nothing really stands out—all have been built in the last twenty-five years, but a couple of reasonable possibilities with beaches are ****Miramare**, Via Aquileia 49, tel (0431) 71 260, with parking and a garden as well as a beach (open May–Sept, doubles L42–55 000 with bath), or the not very different ***Pensione Astro**, Viale Miramare 48, tel (0431) 71 309, open 15 May–22 Sept; rooms from L30 000 without bath to L55 000 with. Eating out is a pleasure at **Al Cason**, Viale Tagliamento 3, tel (0431) 427 201, open Easter–Oct, housed in an old thatched fishing cottage. Good seafood dishes, and an exquisite Adriatic fry among other choices; L35 000.

In shady Lignano-Pianeta you can lodge first class at the ******Greif**, Via Arco del Grecale 25, tel (0431) 422 261, a large resort hotel with a pool and garden, parking and private beach; open 19 May–15 Sept; L105–170 000. The *****Medusa Splendid**, Raggio dello Scirocco 33, tel (0431) 422 211, is more intimate, and also has a pool, very good rooms, and a garden for L60–75 000. Inexpensive and open all year, ***La Pigna**, Via dei Cantieri 2, tel (0431) 428 463, has rooms for L35 000 without bath, L45 000 with.

Lignano Riviera: The fashionable place to stay is the ******Eurotel**, Calle Mendelssohn 13, tel (0431) 428 992, enjoying perhaps the most beautiful setting in the area with lovely rooms, heated pool and more (open May–Sept; L55–100 000). For dinner at the small, family-run and very convivial **Bidin**, Corso Europa 1, tel (0431) 71 988, reservations are a must. Simple, honest and delicious cooking for L30–45 000; closed Wed.

Aquileia and Grado

If Palmanova is unique in its plan, Aquileia is unique in that it's the only major Roman city in the north to die on the vine, so to speak. While most of the other Roman metropolises are still notable towns or cities, Aquileia has dwindled to 3000 inhabitants who no longer receive emperors, but tend the vineyards and the tourists who flock to see the most important archaeological site in Northern Italy. Grado, the nicest resort on the coast, has its own palaeo-Christian treasures and its own Venetian-style lagoon.

GETTING AROUND
To reach Aquileia and Grado, take the train from Venice or Trieste to Cervignano and bus from there; there are also direct buses from Udine. Between Grado and Trieste, the airport Ronchi dei Legionari has flights from London and other Italian airports.

TOURIST INFORMATION
Aquileia: Piazza Capitolo, tel (0431) 91 087 (April–Nov only)
Grado: Viale Dante 68, tel (0431) 80 035

Aquileia

Founded as a Roman colony in 181 BC, Aquileia ('Eagle') earned its name from the eagles that flew over the town while plans were being laid for Augustus' German campaign. It was a good augury. Augustus himself was in and out, and received Herod the Great here. The famous Patriarchate of Aquileia was founded in 313, but after the sack of the city by Attila (452) and the Lombards (568), the patriarch moved to a safer home in Grado, the ancient foreport of Aquileia. When Aquileia wanted it back in the 7th century, Grado refused to surrender the title, and for four hundred years rival patriarchs sat in Grado and in Cividale dei Friuli, the Lombard capital. When they were reconciled in 1019, Aquileia's great basilica was rebuilt, but it was the old city's last hurrah. Aquileia's port on the Natissa silted up, malaria chased out the remaining citizens, and the patriarchate moved on to Udine and became a mere archbishopric.

The Basilica
Aquileia's magnificent **Basilica** with its lofty campanile is a landmark on the Friulian plain for miles around (open 8:30–12 and 3–7). The basilica was founded in 313 by the first Patriarch, Theodore, and when it was rebuilt in 1023 Theodore's floor was merely covered up. Rediscovered and uncovered in this century, the pavement is a vast, ancient carpet of vivid and often whimsical mosaics where portraits, animals and geometric patterns happily mingle with Christian and pagan scenes. Original 1031 frescoes survive in the apse, where you can see Patriarch Poppo dedicating the basilica he clutches in his hands, accompanied by Emperor Conrad II and Gisela of Swabia. Bas-reliefs in the northeast chapel portraying Christ with St Thomas of Canterbury, carved only a few years after his martyrdom, show just how fast news of church politics travelled in the 1170s. Another treasure is the 11th-century San Sepolcro, a tabernacle built in the form of the Holy Sepulchre in Jerusalem.

Next to the San Sepolcro is the entrance to the **Cripta degli Scavi** (9–2, holidays 9–1, closed Mon; same ticket for museum), containing more great mosaics from 313, sandwiched in between those of the Romans and the 8th century. Another crypt, the **Cripta degli Affreschi**, is adorned with colourful 12th-century Byzantine-style frescoes.

The Museo Archeologico
This museum, housed in an old palace across the main road from the basilica (same

hours as crypt; ring if gate is closed) contains an excellent collection from Roman Aquileia, including a fine set of highly individualistic Republican portrait busts; unlike the Greeks who idealized themselves in marble (or perhaps were just better-looking), the Romans insisted that all their warts, cauliflower ears, and crumpled Roman noses be preserved for posterity. Among the bas-reliefs there's a smith with his tools, amber and gold ornaments, and a thousand and one household items that breathe life into ancient Aquileia. The ancient Aquileians could be lighthearted: there are flies of gold and a wee, bronze figurine of a springing cat.

The Excavations
A circular walk, beginning on the Via Sacra behind the basilica, takes in most of Aquileia's excavations; an unfortunate proximity to Venice, that quarrying magpie, has shorn them of most of their grandeur. The Via Sacra first passes by the recently unearthed **Roman houses and palaeo-Christian oratories** (with some beautiful mosaics intact), then continues up through the considerable ruins of the ancient **harbour**. Continue straight and bear right after the crossroads with the modern road Via Gemina to the **Palaeo-Christian Museum** (same hours as archaeology museum), with reliefs and sarcophagi and a walkway over the undulating mossy mosaics. Return by way of the Via Gemina to the Via Giulia Augusta and turn left (the main Palmanova-Grado road). On the right of this you can see the old Roman road, on the left, the **Forum** with its re-erected columns. Just off a fork to the right, the **Grand Mausoleum** (1st century AD) was brought here from the distant suburbs. The meagre ruins of the amphitheatre, the baths (terme), and another tomb, the **Sepolcreto**, are on Via XXIV Maggio and Via Acidino, north of the village's central Piazza Garibaldi.

Grado
Aquileia had an inner port and an outer port, or *Grado*, on the island that still bears its ancient name. Modern Grado lies over the causeway 11 km to the south, the queen of its own little lagoon and archipelago. Even the narrow alleys of its picturesque old town, the **Castrum Gradense**, are called *calli* as in Venice. With a long beach and a thermal spa that specializes in baking its visitors in hot sand baths, Grado is a popular resort.

In the 6th century the Patriarch of Nova Aquileia, as he called himself, was installed in the **Duomo** (Basilica of Santa Eufemia), a simple solid temple preserving a fine 6th-century mosaic floor, though the scriptural adages and geometrical patterns that cover it seem austere after the garden on the floor of Aquileia's basilica. A fine silver Venetian-style *pala* glows on the altar. An alley of early sarcophagi separates Santa Eufemia from another, smaller basilica, **Santa Maria delle Grazie** and the octagonal, 6th-century **Baptistry**, both with mosaic floors.

From Grado there are daily excursions in the summer into the lagoon, where several of the islets have traditional thatched fishermen's cottages, or *casoni*. If you're lucky you'll see herons in the mystery-laden fens of the lagoon. There are also frequent sea connections to Trieste and the Istrian coast in the summer (see 'Trieste'), and to the quaint fishing village of **Porto Buso**.

WHERE TO STAY AND EATING OUT   (tel prefix 0431)
Aquileia: **La Colombara**, Via S. Zilli 34, tel 91 513, a bit out of the centre, serves up the finest cuisine in the ruined city, specializing in seafood prepared in a number of excellent

and unusual ways; good wines from the Collio (L38 000; closed Mon and 2 weeks in Jan). The old *Aquila Nera, Piazza Garibaldi 5, tel 91 045, offers adequate rooms and home cooking in Aquileia's quiet main square (open all year; L36 000 without bath, L42 000 with).

Grado: Again, tons of choices—a couple that stand out are the ****Antica Villa Bernt, Via Colombo 5, tel 82 516, a refurbished old villa with only 22 lovely rooms, all with bath, air conditioning, and TV for L120–145 000, open May–Sept; and the ****Savoy, Via Carducci 33, tel 81 171, in the centre of Grado, with its thermal pool, garden, parking, and very comfortable rooms (L60–100 000). To avoid the full-pension tyranny, try the pleasant **Villa Lucilla in the pine woods, three blocks from the beach at Viale del Capricorno 3, tel 80 814, open May–Sept (garden, parking and you can bring Fido; all rooms with bath L35–42 000).

The most celebrated restaurant in Grado, the Antica Trattoria da Nico, Via Marina 10 in the old town, tel 80 470, is run by the jolly Nico who meets Grado's sizeable fishing fleet at dawn to select the pick of the catch, which he expertly prepares and serves up in a proper marine decor. Menu adapted to the catch—around L45–55 000, closed Thurs and Jan. Colussi, Via Roma 1 (a block from the bus station), tel 80 110, offers the most traditional Friuli and Veneto cuisine in Grado—try the baked *rombo* (turbot) with white wine; closed Mon; around L30 000.

Trieste

Once the main seaport of the Austro-Hungarian Empire, two world wars have made Trieste the woebegone widow of the Adriatic, a grandiose neoclassical city shorn of its *raison d'être*; its tourist slogan these days may just as well be 'Gateway to Yugoslavia'. But even if you're just passing through it's worth a stop, not perhaps for its bombastic architecture, but for its unique atmosphere, spiced with its Hungarian-Slovenian heritage and a nostalgia that coats the city like the dust on Miss Havisham's wedding cake in *Great Expectations*.

But Trieste, if a bit of a museum, is a lively, bright, neon-lit one, who in the summer puts a rose in her hair and becomes a pert seaside flirt. With Venice, she carries the advantage of being a natural link between central Europe and the Mediterranean, and as Europe grows closer together there is some hope that at least a bit of the old trade and excitement will return. Meanwhile Trieste isn't napping; with help from the Italian government, she holds her own as a 'Science City' with a number of brand-new research centres, including three UN-funded agencies intended to apply modern physics to problems of the third world.

You may remember Trieste best for her fine natural port and karst hills, or for the throngs of Yugoslavs in black leather jackets who come, lured by the bright lights and smart goods, to drop big dinars in Trieste's shops, or perhaps for the extraordinary kitsch quality of her monuments. In Venice one of the games visitors play is counting the stone lions, but in Trieste it's huge, stony breasts—it has more of them than any city in the world.

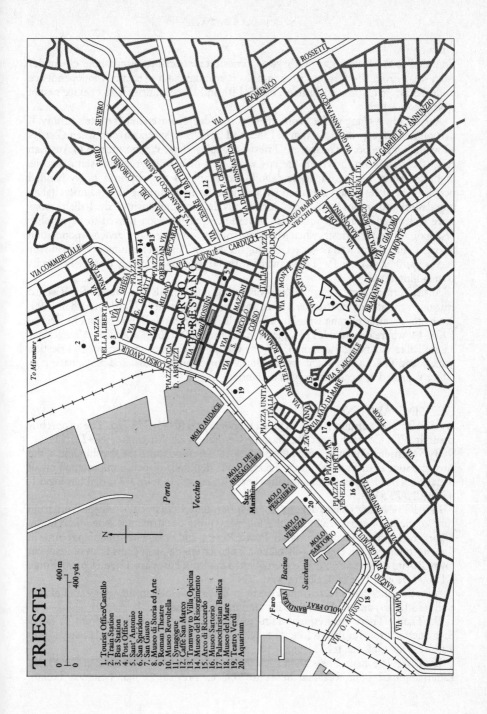

TRIESTE

0
0

400 m
400 yds

Z

1. Tourist Office/Castello
2. Train Station
3. Bus Station
4. Post Office
5. Sant Antonio
6. San Spiridone
7. San Giusto
8. Museo di Storia ed Arte
9. Roman Theatre
10. Museo Revoltella
11. Synagogue
12. Caffè San Marco
13. Tramway to Villa Opicina
14. Museo del Risorgimento
15. Arco di Riccardo
16. Museo Sartorio
17. Palaeochristian Basilica
18. Museo del Mare
19. Teatro Verdi
20. Aquarium

History

Founded as the Celtic port of Tergeste, Trieste first became an important city under Augustus. From the 9th to 13th centuries it maintained a precarious independence under its arrogant, princely bishops; by the 14th and 15th centuries it was Venice's chief rival in the Adriatic.

Austria, always longing for a convenient port, is deeply woven into Trieste's history. It first offered the city its protection in 1382, and in 1719 its special favour, when Charles VI made it a free port. These were Trieste's happiest days. When returned to Austrian rule after Napoleon, however, the city was bereft of both its free-port status and its medieval heart, as the Viennese rebuilt the centre of the city in a heavy-handed neoclassical style. They governed in a similar fashion, turning the majority Italian population into ardent Irredentists, turbulently desiring union with Italy. Italian troops were welcomed in 1918, but Italian government all too soon proved to be another disappointment for Trieste, when Mussolini tried to force the heterogeneous population into an Italian cultural strait-jacket, larding the city with Fascist monuments. World War II was another disaster for Trieste when it found itself permanently divorced from its Istrian hinterland.

At the turn of the century Trieste was full of intellectuals and literati. Sir Richard Burton, translator of the *Arabian Nights*, was consul here from 1870 to his death in 1890. James Joyce, after eloping with Nora Barnacle, taught in the Berlitz school in Trieste 1905–14, where he wrote his only play and *A Portrait of the Artist as a Young Man*. Rainer Maria Rilke was nearby at Duino. But the Grand Cafés, once the symbol of Triestine society and filled with fervent cross-cultural conversation, ideas, and plots, have now either vanished or deal primarily in memories.

GETTING AROUND

By Air: Trieste's airport is at Ronchi dei Legionari, tel (0481) 773 225. The airport bus is run by Flli. Cosulich, near the Stazione Centrale, Viale Miramare, tel 422 711.

By Steamer: The mammoth offices of Lloyd Triestino (once the flagship line of the Austro-Hungarian Empire) on the Piazza Unità dell'Italia dispense information on all departures from Trieste, and most anywhere else as well. Inquire at Via dell'Orologio 1, tel (040) 778 5428.

Lloyd Triestino's *Dionea* departs from the Bersaglieri Wharf daily (except Wed) from June to Sept for Istria, calling at the following ports on a rotating schedule: Grado, Koper, Izola, Piran, Umag, Novigrad, Porec, Rovinj, and Pula. The same ship returns in the afternoon, so you could easily make a Yugoslavian day-trip (Pula is an old Roman town, Rovinj a big resort, Porec a pretty Venetian town). Fares are: Grado L6500, Porec L13 000, Rovinj L15 000, all one-way.

Adriatic Lines has a ferry from Trieste to Zadar (9 hours) in the winter and also to Split (23 hours) and Dubrovnik (32 hours) in the summer.

By Train: There are frequent trains to Venice, Gorizia, and Udine from Trieste's Stazione Centrale on Piazza Libertà 8, tel 418 207. Trains for Yugoslavia depart from Trieste-Villa Opicina, tel 211 682.

By Bus: The main bus station is in front of the Stazione Centrale, in the Piazza Libertà, tel 62 030. Regional buses to Venice, Treviso, Padua; Belluno, Trento,

S. Candido and Sappada in the Dolomites; Milan, Mantova, and Genoa. Buses to Yugoslavia, Istria, Rijeka, Zara, Dubrovnik, and Zagreb.

TOURIST INFORMATION
Trieste: Piazza della Cattedrale 3, tel (040) 750 002; Stazione Centrale, tel 420 182.
Sistiana: Via Sistiana 56/b, tel (040) 299 166
Muggia: Corso Puccini 6, tel (040) 295 972

Piazza dell'Unità d'Italia
From the train or bus station, the Corso Cavour leads directly into the **Borgo Teresiano**, the commercial centre laid out in an orderly grid by MariaTheresa's tidy planners and planted with neoclassical architecture. The street passes over the **Canale Grande**, an inlet with mooring for small craft. At its head stands the classical temple church of **Sant'Antonio**, and near it, the blue-domed Serbian Orthodox **Santo Spiridone**, an exotic orchid in a regimented garden.

Trieste's whale of a heart, the vast **Piazza dell'Unità d'Italia**, is one of Italy's largest squares. Facing the harbour, it is framed by the hefty **Palazzo del Comune**, topped by two Moors who ring the bell in the clock tower; on one side the **Palazzo di Governo** glows in its bright skin of neoclassical mosaics, on the other broods the huge palace of Lloyd Triestino. Flowers brighten the piazza in the summer, while in winter, plants that look appropriately like cabbages hold pride of place in the planters unless they are cowering beneath the mighty *bora*, a northeast wind that whips over the Carso. The centrepiece of all this, a mind-boggling pile of rocks and statuary, purported to represent the *Four Continents* (1750) may send you staggering off for a drink at the piazza's **Caffè degli Specchi**, in business since 1839 and once famous for the meetings of Italian Irredentists held within.

Up the Capitoline Hill
Catch bus 24 from the station or Piazza dell'Unità to ascend the Capitoline Hill, the nucleus of Roman and medieval Trieste. In the 5th century the Triestini raised the first of two basilicas here to their patron San Giusto, a martyr drowned during the persecution of Diocletian. An adjacent basilica, built in the 11th century, was linked to the first in the 14th century, lending the **Cathedral of San Giusto** its curious plan. The doorway, under a splendid Gothic rose window, is framed by the fragments of a Roman sarcophagus: six funerary busts gaze solemnly ahead like a corporate board of directors, while embedded in the adjacent, squat campanile there's a frieze that looks like a fashion plate for Roman armour. The interior (closed 12–3) has some fine mosaics, especially the 13th-century *Christ with SS. Giusto and Servulus*, as well as good 12th-century frescoes. Buried on the right is Don Carlos of Spain, the Great Pretender of Spain's 19th-century Carlist Wars. He died as an exile in Trieste in 1855, but there are still a few Carlists in Spain, occasionally causing trouble in the name of his heirs.

Next to San Giusto are the fragments of the Roman forum and a 1st-century basilica, of which two columns have been re-erected. The excellent view over Trieste is marred by a 1933 Monument to The Fallen, admirably extolling the principal fascist virtues of strength and vulgarity. The 15th-century **Castello** was begun by the Venetians and finished by the Austrians, and offers more views and a small **Museo Civico** (9–1, closed Mon), with a collection of armour and weapons.

Just down the lane from the cathedral is the **Museo di Storia ed Arte** and the **Orto Lapidario** (both 9–1, closed Mon; adm). The first houses some intriguing finds from ancient Tergeste and a famous 5th-century deer-head silver *rhyton*, or drinking vessel, from ancient Tarentum. The Orto Lapidario contains Roman altars, steles, a red granite Egyptian sarcophagus and the neoclassical tomb of the great antiquarian J. J. Winckel-mann (d. 1768), murdered in Trieste when he attempted to seduce a Tuscan cook.

On the way down to the centre, stop at the well-preserved 1st-century **Roman theatre** on the Via Teatro Romano.

Other Sites Around Trieste

The **Museo Revoltella**, in Piazza Venezia (from Piazza Unità, continue along the harbour past the Stazione Marittimo; entrance on Via Diaz 27; open 9–1, closed Mon), was founded by one of the financiers of the Suez Canal, a big boon to Trieste's port. It has a gallery of 19th-century art that evokes the city's golden days, as well as modern works by Picasso, Morandi, Braque, Kokoschka, De Pisis, and more.

On the other side of town (off Via Carducci, between Piazza Oberdan and the Capitoline Hill), Via Cesare Battisti 18 is the address of Trieste's best surviving Belle Epoque coffee house, the **Caffè San Marco**, physically unchanged since it opened in 1914, its name and the Venetian scenes painted on the walls betraying the owner's pro-Italian sentiments. According to the Triestini, the masked carnival figures in the oval over the bar portray Vittorio Emanuele and Mussolini. You won't find a classier joint to shoot a round of billiards or sit at a marble table to chug down one of the local micro-cappuccinos. A block over lies Via S. Francesco and the most beautiful **Synagogue** in Italy, built in 1910 on ancient Syriac models.

Habsburgs and Karst: Excursions from Trieste

You can't go too far without running into Yugoslavia. For a short jaunt, take the old Opicina **Tranvia** (tramway) from Piazza Oberdan up to Poggioreale for the fine panorama from the belvedere **Vedetta d'Opicina**.

Another popular excursion is to **Miramare**, some 7 km up the coast (bus 60 from Piazza Oberdan to Barcola, change to line 36 for Miramare; in summer, boat excursions from Riva Mandracchio). On the way, watch for the **Faro della Vittoria**, a powerful lighthouse and 1927 war memorial to sailors, crowned by a heavy-sinewed, big-busted Valkyrie in a majorette's costume.

Miramare

Perched on its own little promontory overlooking the sea, the castle of Miramare hides a dark history behind its charming 19th-century façade. Built by the Habsburg Archduke Maximilian and his Belgian wife Carlotta, visitors are greeted by a stone sphinx with a cryptic smile that seems to ask the world—why did Maximilian leave this pleasure palace and like a *dummkopf* let Napoleon III's financiers con him into becoming Mexico's puppet emperor in 1864, and why did he linger around there to face the firing squad three years later? Was he an idealist, as his apologists claim, or too much of a Habsburg to know any better?

Carlotta, after desperately trying to rally European support for her husband, went mad after his execution and survived him by fifty years in Belgium, while Miramare rapidly acquired the ominous reputation for putting a curse on anyone who slept within its walls; most unfortunately another Habsburg—the Archduke Ferdinand—lodged here on his way to assassination in Sarajevo, the incident that sparked off World War I. When the Americans occupied it in 1946, their commander insisted on sleeping out in the park in a tent. You can hear the whole sad story at the *son et lumière* show 'Miramare's Imperial Dream' (in English on Tues at 9 or 9:30 pm in July and Aug. The castle itself is open 9–1, also June and July 3–6; adm). Miramare's charming park was designed by Maximilian, who made a better botanist than emperor; it's free and open daily until sunset.

The Carso

Most of Trieste's slender province is within the Carso, which derives its name from its karst topography. Karst is pliable limestone, easily eroded by the rain into remarkable shapes—here pale cliffs that form Italy's most dramatic Adriatic coastline north of the Gargano peninsula; inland the karst has been buffeted into petrified waves of rock dotted with *dolinas* (swallow holes), while underground, aeons of dripping water have formed vast caverns, subterranean lakes and rivers inhabited by blind amphibians. Vines grow wherever they can be made to fit, and elsewhere the landscape is dominated by sumac, which autumn ignites into a hundred shades of scarlet.

Beyond Miramare and the industrial shipbuilding town of Monfalcone lies the fishing village of **Duino**, with its two castles; the ruined **Castello Vecchio** and the 15th-century **Castello Nuovo**, perched on a promontory over the sea. Castello Nuovo has long been owned by the Princes von Thurn und Taxis, one of whom played host to Rainer Maria Rilke here from 1910–14, when the poet composed his famous *Duino Elegies*. The castle is now a Rilke study centre, and there's a scenic 'Rilke walk' along the promontory. Nearby **Sistiana** is a pretty resort with a yacht harbour in its own little bay.

Born in a karstic abyss in Yugoslavia, the **Timavo river** continues underground for 30 km before reappearing near the winsome Romanesque church and inland village of **San Giovanni di Duino**. Also inland are the caves, the most famous of which, the **Grotta del Gigante** in Opicina, is the largest and easiest to visit (bus 45 every half-hour from the Piazza Oberdan). So vast it could swallow the entire basilica of St Peter, the Grotto is embellished with well-lit stalactites and stalagmites. A **Museum of Speleology** has displays on cave geology and exhibits of palaeolithic and neolithic remains discovered on the site (open winter 10–12 and 2–6:30, summer 9–12 and 2–7, closed Mon; adm). The cave is not far from **Sgonico** (bus 46 from Piazza Oberdan), site of a karstic botanical garden, while bus 40, also from Oberdan, offers an excursion through some fine scenery to the perilous karstic cliffs in the **Val Rojanda**, site of an alpine school. The famous white Lippizaner horses are raised and receive their first dance lessons just over the Yugoslav border in Lipica. Other buses (and in the summer, boats) head south to **Muggia**, an attractive old Venetian fishing port and Italy's last bit of Istria.

ACTIVITIES
Carnival is celebrated with a Venetian flair in Muggia. From November to March, there's opera season at Teatro Comunale Verdi in Trieste. Summer boat tours of the

Triestine Riviera depart from Trieste's Riva del Mandracchio. Frequent spectacles are performed at the castle on summer evenings; occasional classical plays are put on at the Teatro Romano, and in the first week of July, Trieste holds a Science Fiction film festival. Nearest beaches are at Riviera di Barcola, Sistiana and Grignano.

WHERE TO STAY   (tel prefix 040)

On Trieste's finest square, the Piazza Unità d'Italia, stands the city's finest hotel, the ****Duchi d'Aosta, tel 62 08l, in a neo-Renaissance palace erected in 1873. Now owned by the CIGA chain, it basks in a dignified Belle Epoque ambience; upstairs the luxurious rooms are fitted with all modern comforts. Harry's Grill, the hotel's restaurant, serves excellent international specialities (rooms L125–200 000, meals L70 000). Another fine neoclassical building, the **Hotel Al Teatro, Via Capo di Piazza G. Bartoli 1 (near Piazza Unità), tel 64 123 is, as its name suggests, near the opera. The hotel served as British headquarters after World War II and is a bit of a nostalgic trip back to the Trieste of yore (L46–55 000 without bath, L68–75 000 with). There are many less expensive choices in the centre (look around the Via Roma, Via Diaz, or Via XXX Octobre), but it's more fun to take the Tranvia up to Opicina and lodge at the little *Diana, near the station at Via Nazionale 11, tel 211 176, with bathless doubles for only L25 000, or the classier **Daneu, Via Nazionale 194, tel 214 214; doubles L38–43 000 without bath, L42–48 000 with. Both have restaurants.

There are also a large number of seaside choices in Duino and Sistiana. Among them, the ***Duino Park, Via Duino 60/c, tel 208 184, has a pool and a private beach, and a TV in every room (L65–95 000). The **Sistiana, Via Sistiana 19, in Sistiana, tel 299 235, offers pleasant doubles for L33 000 without bath, L38 000 with; bar and restaurant on premises.

EATING OUT

Trieste is a good place to eat dumplings instead of pasta—the Slovenian and Hungarian influences are strong in the kitchen. A famous first course is *jota*, a kind of minestrone with beans, potatoes, and sauerkraut, or you could try *kaiserknödel* (bread dumplings with grated cheese, ham, and parsley). For seconds, there's a wide variety of fish like *sardoni* (big sardines), fried or marinated, and both tasty and inexpensive. Goulash, roast pork, and *stinco* (veal knuckle) are also popular. The middle-European influence, however, is especially noticeable in the desserts: the lovely strudels, the *gnocchi di susine* (plums), or *zavate*, a warm cream pastry.

The ideal place to partake of this *cucina Triestina* is at Suban, Via Comici 2, in the suburb of San Giovanni, tel 54 368 (ring to book and take a taxi; closed Mon and most of Aug). Founded out in the country in 1863, urban growth has since absorbed this wonderful old inn, though it manages to maintain much of its old feel and its fine views over Trieste. Suban offers a famous *jota*, *sevapcici* (Slovenian grilled meat fritters), sinful desserts, and good wines, all for L38–50 000; closed Mon, Tues, and most of Aug. The elegant seafront Nastro Azzurro, Riva N. Saura 12, tel 305 789, is near the fish market and specializes in its wares; the seafood antipasti and fritto di mare are mouth-watering (L35–60 000, depending on what fish you choose). Nearby, the Trattoria Alla Cantine Sociale, Riva N. Sauro 18, tel 300 689, is a more popular-based seafood restaurant, with good *triglia* (red mullet); L25 000.

The trendiest and smartest restaurant in Trieste is also by the sea, the **Elefante Bianco**, Riva 3 Novembre, tel 60 889, with Italian nouvelle cuisine served up in an atmosphere of greenery, wrought iron, and wood—try the *panzerotti* stuffed with pesto or shrimps with orange (L45 000; closed Sun). Up in the castle, **La Bottega del Vino** (tel 733 235, closed Tues) features heavy timbers and a medieval cellar ambience, though in the summer you dine out with views over the city. One section is devoted to wine-tasting. The menu is limited but offers scrumptious crêpes for L32 000; closed Tues and Jan. **Bella Trieste**, Via Pane Bianco 96 (in the Serrola quarter: take bus 29 from Piazza Goldoni, get off at Via dei Soncini and turn right), tel 815 262, is a little cathedral of good home cooking. Order the *gnocchi alla crema* and the *cospicuo* (a variety platter of meats); L25 000.

Eastern Friuli: Gorizia, Udine and Cividale

GETTING AROUND
Gorizia and Cormons are linked by rail from Trieste, Pordenone and Venice. Gorizia, Cormons and Udine are on the line from Trieste. Gorizia's station is at Piazzale Martiri della Libertà, tel 22 013; coaches are at Via IX Agosto 11, tel 84 566.

TOURIST INFORMATION
Gorizia: Corso Verdi 100/E, tel (0481) 83 870
Gradisca d'Isonzo: Via M Ciotti, Palazzo Torriani, tel (0481) 99 217
At either office, you can pick up brochures on the wine road in Collio, with a list of cellars and trattorias on the way.

Gorizia

Capital of one of Italy's smallest provinces, the frontier city of Gorizia (Gorica in Slovenian) was for centuries ruled by a powerful dynasty of counts, who were always ready to stir up trouble against Venice, with the winking approval of the Kings of Hungary. When the last Count died in 1500 without an heir, Gorizia was inherited by Emperor Maximilian and the Habsburgs. The Austrians later provided the wide boulevards and gardens that made Gorizia an 'Austrian Nice' (minus the seashore) and their fierce defence of the area in World War I, especially around Monte San Michele and Redipuglia, resulted in bitter battles that left over 300,000 Austrian, Hungarian, and Italian dead. But while Gorizia saw much less fighting in World War II, its troubles began with some confused post-war diplomacy that made it a kind of Berlin, cut in two between Italy and Yugoslavia in such a thoughtless manner that the city almost died. Things were improved in 1979, when residents on either side of the barbed wire fence were granted a 16-km zone around the city to transact their affairs freely, making it a congenial East-West prototype for the opening of the Berlin Wall; it is the site of an annual Eastern European trade fair and a number of Friulian, Slovenian, and Italian cultural exchanges.

Crowning Gorizia, **Borgo Castello** is a little village within the city, built inside the 1509 Venetian fortress that also incorporates the 12th-century **Castle** of the Counts of Gorizia; it has good views over Gorizia and 17th-century furniture inside (open

9–12 and 2–5, closed Mon). The Borgo contains solemn medieval houses, the 1386 church of **Santo Spirito**, and the **Formentini House**, now the museum of history, art, and handicrafts (same hours as castle). The **Duomo**, tinkered with repeatedly since the 14th century, contains a treasure bestowed by Maria Theresa.

All the area around Gorizia is called the **Collio**, the most important wine region in Friuli. West of Gorizia, in the many-towered town of **Gradisca d'Isonzo**, you can taste any or all Friulian wines at the **Enoteca Regionale Serenissima**, open 10–1 and 4–11, closed Wed. **Cormons** near Gradisca is the only town in Italy to put up a statue to Emperor Maximilian; it is also the main producer of Collio wine, where you can visit the **Cantina Produttori Vini del Collio**, tel (0481) 60 579; besides its *Vino della Pace*, made from vines from all over the world, which the cantina sends out annually to the world's heads of state, it has an outdoor sculpture garden.

WHERE TO STAY AND EATING OUT   (tel prefix 0481)
As a border town, Gorizia sees much coming and going. The nicest place to stay is the ***Palace**, Corso Italia 63, tel 82 166, with large modern rooms, TV, air conditioning, etc for L45–82 000. ***Motel Nanut**, Via Trieste 116, tel 20 595, has a pool and tennis and fine rooms for L70 -75 000 with bath. The Nanut can also claim a good if simple restaurant, with a delicious home-cooked menu of gnocchi, goulash, and vino di Collio for L15–20 000; closed Sat eve, Sun and mid-July–mid-Aug. For something smaller and simpler, *Sandro**, Via Santa Chiara 18, tel 83 223 has doubles with bath for L45 000.

Up in Gorizia's Borgo Castello, you can sup in medieval splendour at the **Lanterna d'Oro al Castello**, Via Monache 12, tel 535 565, featuring Friuli specialities like *prosciutto di San Daniele*, and well-prepared dishes of venison, kid and boar; closed Mon (L35 000). Another choice, **Transalpina**, Via Caprin 30, tel 32 984, features the same good prosciutto, homemade pasta, *gnocchi piquante*, and fish for seconds, and a rich tiramisù for dessert; L30 000.

In Cormons, ***Felcaro**, Via S. Giovanni 45, tel 60 214, is an 18th-century villa on the slopes of Monte Quarin, surrounded by vines and gardens; amenities include tennis courts, sauna, pool, and an excellent restaurant (rooms, L38–42 000 without bath, L52–65 000 with; meals L30 000). Cormons has several fine restaurants. **Al Giardinetto**, Via Matteotti 54, tel 60 257, is in the centre of town in a charming setting, with an Hungarian-flavoured menu: gnocchi with plums, goulash, rack of pork, Sachertorte and poppy seed cakes . . . (L35 000; closed Mon eve, Tues, and July). Outside the centre, on a hilltop in Subida, **Al Cacciatore della Subida**, tel 60 531 (closed Tues and Wed), enjoys a charming country setting, complemented by charming local cuisine; the cold breast of pheasant in mushroom cream is a popular summer dish; eat it outside under the pergola. Excellent Collio wines (L35–45 000; closed Tues, Wed, and 2 weeks in Feb).

Udine and Cividale

Legend states that Udine's *castello* sits on a mound erected by Hun warriors, who carried the soil to the site in their helmets so that their commander Attila could watch the burning of Aquileia. The story is apocryphal, but Udine went on to take Aquileia's position as Friuli's capital after the 13th century and become seat of Aquileia's patriarch from 1238 to 1751. Udine's chief rivals were Cividale and Venice, and after a nine-year resistance Udine surrendered to the latter in 1420. In World War II it was the last city in Italy to be liberated (May 1945).

GETTING AROUND
Udine is linked by train with Venice, Pordenone, and Trieste; Cividale is most easily visited by bus or train from Udine (20 minutes). If you're travelling by air, Udine has buses to Ronchi dei Legionari airport; the terminal is at Via Savorgnana 18, tel 292 923. Udine's railway station is on Viale Europa Unità, tel 503 656; the bus station is across and a bit up the street, tel 506 941. Car hire firms are near the station on Viale Europa Unità: Hertz at no. 127, tel 503 403; Avis at no. 33, tel 501 149; Maggiore at no. 26, tel 290 956.

TOURIST INFORMATION
Udine: Via dei Missionari 2/1 or Via Piave 27, tel (0432) 295 972
Cividale del Friuli: Largo Boiani 4, tel (0432) 731 398

Udine

Udine, the capital of Friuli, is an attractive city of old streets interwoven with little canals; not surprisingly, it's also the centre of Friulian nationalism, where you're likely to hear people in the street conversing in the mysterious Friulian tongue. Unless you've been smitten by the works of Giambattista Tiepolo, none of Udine's attractions are exceptional, but the whole is admirable and off the major tourist trails.

Piazza della Libertà
The heart of Udine, the Piazza della Libertà, has been called 'the most beautiful Venetian square on terra firma'. Its most striking building, the candy-striped **Loggia del Lionello**, was built by a goldsmith in 1448 and faithfully reconstructed after a fire in 1876; a second loggia, the **Loggia di San Giovanni** (1533), supports a clock tower and a bell rung by two Venetian-inspired 'Moors'. There is the usual Venetian column topped by a lion of St Mark, accompanied by a statue of Justice with Bette Davis eyes; below this is a rather unhappy monument to the unhappy Peace Treaty of Campo Formio, in which Napoleon gave this part of Italy to Austria.

Palladio's rugged **Arco Bollari** (1556) is the gateway to the hill of the **Castello**, former seat of the Patriarch and the Venetian governor. In 1487 the latter built the sweeping portico that still shields visitors from inclement weather but could do nothing against the 1976 earthquake, a jolt that severely damaged all the buildings on the hill. Its civic and art museums should reopen in 1990. Among the paintings are works by Tiepolo, Pordenone, Pellegrino di San Daniele, and Carpaccio; in the modern gallery are works by the brothers Afro, Mirko, and Dino Basaldella, natives of Udine. There are fine views of the Alps from the walls. Across the way, **S. Maria di Castello** was the first church in Udine. Though restored many times since, it preserves a mix of rather faded frescoes from the 13–16th centuries.

Down in the City

The oft-altered **Duomo**, a couple of blocks from the Piazza Libertà, has a charming 14th-century lunette over the door with comical figures so weathered they look like gingerbread—any religious symbolism in them would be entirely accidental. The interior is a dignified Baroque symphony of grey and gold, framing a handful of works by Tiepolo. In the heavy-set campanile there's a small **Cathedral Museum** (Tues, Thurs, and Sat 9–12, though at the time of writing closed, tel 506 830 to see if it's reopened), adorned with excellent 1349 frescoes of the *Funeral of St Nicholas* by Vitale da Bologna and a beautiful 1343 *sarcophagus of the Blessed Bertrando di S. Genesio*, one of the greatest works of medieval Friuli. The **Oratorio della Purità**, added to the cathedral in 1757, is a Tiepolo shrine, with its partly frescoed, partly painted *Assumption* on the ceiling, the altarpiece of the Immaculate Conception, and the chiaroscuro frescoes on the walls by Tiepolo's son Giandomenico; ask the sacristan to open it for you.

The church of **San Francesco**, near the Duomo (down Via Calzolai) is an austere 14th-century church on Piazza Venerio; from here turn left on Via Savorgnana for the more ornate **San Giacomo**, with its clock tower and lifesize figures gazing over the arcaded **Piazza Matteotti**, one of Udine's finest squares and the site of its market for centuries; piazza decorations include a fountain by Giovanni da Udine, a votive column of 1487 dedicated to the Virgin Mary, and a lovely carved wellhead from the same period, tucked beside the church. An unusual feature of San Giacomo is the outdoor altar on the balcony over the door, once used to celebrate mass on market days.

Three museums have recently re-opened just to the west of Piazza Matteotti; all have the same hours: 9:30–12:30 and 3–6, Sun 9:30–12:30, closed Mon. At Via Zanon 24, in the Torre di Santa Maria, the **Museo della Città** documents the 1000 years of Udine's existence, its guilds, confraternities, and the Friulian language. The **Museo Friulano delle Arti e Tradizione Populari**, Via Viola 3, is dedicated to aspects of Friulian life—rooms from a traditional house, rural artefacts, costumes, etc. And at Via Giardini 22 (the next street north), there's a **Museo del Risorgimento e della Resistenza**.

From Piazza Matteotti, Via Sarpi leads around to join the Riva Bartolini with Palladio's **Palazzo Antonini** (now the Banca d'Italia). The Tiepolo trail, however, continues in the other direction: from the Piazza Libertà, take Via Manin through a gate to the Piazza Patriarcato (near the tourist office) and the **Palazzo Arcivescovile**, built in two stages, in the 16th and 18th centuries, and frescoed with fine Old Testament scenes by Giambattista Tiepolo (open Mon–Fri 8–12). More recent art (Severini, Carrà, De Chirico, Morandi, De Kooning, Segal, Lichtenstein, Dufy, etc.) is on display in the new **Teatro/Galleria d'Arte Moderno**, located on the northern fringes of the old town at Viale P. Diacono 22 (take Riva Bartolini to Via Palladio and straight along Vias Mazzini, Mantica and A. L. Moro—or hop on bus 2, or 2b which is circular from the station; open 9:30–12 and 3–6, closed Mon and Sun afternoons).

Cividale del Friuli

Only a hop and a skip from Udine in the valley of the Natisone, Cividale del Friuli is a grand old town, founded in 50 BC by Julius Caesar as *Forum Iulii*, a name that was adopted for the entire Friuli region. The Lombards invaded in 568 and made Cividale the capital of their first duchy. The city grew so important that the Patriarch of Aquileia moved here in 737, initiating a magnificent 8th century, documented by Paulus Diaconus, the contemporary Lombard historian. Born in Cividale, Diaconus is one of the chief sources scholars have for the Dark Ages. Cividale's patriarchal state endured from 1077–1366, when Udine took control. Though many of the town's monuments were damaged in the 1976 earthquake, all have since been repaired.

South Bank

From the Cividale Città station, the Corso leads to the main piazza, with the 13th–15th century **Palazzo Comunale**, a statue of Julius Caesar, and the **Duomo**, begun in 1453 and given its plain but attractive Renaissance façade by Pietro Lombardo. It contains unique treasures: the 12th-century silver altarpiece, the *Pala di Pelegrino II*, with its 25 saints and two archangels; a fine gilded equestrian monument (1617) and the Renaissance sarcophagus of Patriarch Nicolo Donato. In the **Treasury** you can see the sword of Patriarch Marquardo, with which he entered Cividale in 1366 after his investiture by the Emperor himself. In commemoration it is dusted off for use in the first Sunday Mass of the New Year, the *Messa di Spadone*, celebrated with a plethora of pomp and pageantry. Also in the precincts of the Duomo is the **Museo Cristiano** (both treasury and museum open 9:30–12 and 3–5:30; Sun 11:30–12, 3:30–5:30), which contains two masterpieces from the 8th century: the octagonal *Baptistry of Callisto* and the *Altar of Ratchis*, dating back to 749, a period when there was still considerable confusion about the way hands and arms are attached to the human form. Yet compare this charming primitive work with the six virgins in the Tempietto (see below).

The **Museo Archeologico Nazionale** has recently been transferred to the Palazzo Pretorio, designed by Palladio, across from the the Duomo (daily exc Mon, 9–1:30, Sun 9–12:30; adm). The collection is celebrated for the glories of its early medieval section; some of the most intriguing items came from the sarcophagus of the 6th-century Lombard Duke Gisulphus—a fibula, cross, and ring all beautifully wrought of gold. There are ancient weapons and ivory chessmen from a knight's tomb, the early 9th-century *Pax del Duca Orso* is adorned with an ivory crucifix in a golden frame, studded with jewels; there is a 1400 embroidered altar cover, a 10th-century ivory casket, the delightful *Psalter of Egbert of Tièves* (990), owned by St Elizabeth of Hungary, an 8th-century copy of Paulus Diaconus' *History of the Lombards*, and much more.

Corso Ponte d'Aquileia descends to the Natisone and the 1442 **Ponte del Diavolo**. In the Middle Ages, it was a common folk belief that bridges were magical, and many stories grew up telling how they were erected overnight by the Devil himself. In Cividale's case, Satan hung around in the morning to snatch the first soul that ventured across as his payment. But the wily Cividalesi outsmarted him by sending over a cat.

The Tempietto Longobardo

The Tempietto Longobardo (Santa Maria in Valle) lies on the banks of the Natisone in Piazzetta San Biagio. It is the greatest work of the 8th century in Italy, despite the fact that it had to be restored in the 13th century after an earthquake shattered three-quarters of its ornamentation and all of its mosaics. The stucco reliefs that remain,

Virgin Saints in the Tempietto Longobardo, Cividale del Friuli

however, are ravishing, uncanny and perhaps even miraculous: there are six gently smiling white virgin saints, standing at either side of a beautiful and intricately carved window, all positioned over an even more intricately carved arch with a vine motif—a love letter from the Dark Ages to posterity. Artistically, Europe wasn't to see the likes of the Tempietto Longobardo again for 400 years.

Besides the stuccoes there is a finely carved and inlaid wooden choir of 1371 and some excellent frescoes of the same period, replacing the lost mosaics; the *Adoration of the Magi* is lovely (open daily 9–12, 3–6; Sun 9–1; closed Mon afternoons; the custodian lives in Via Monastero Maggiore).

On the same north bank of the Natisone, there's the mysterious **Ipogeo Celtico** under the house at Via Monastero 21 (8–1, 3:30–5:40; closed Mon afternoons and Sun; ask at the neighbouring bar for the key). This peculiar man-made cave is believed to have served as a funeral chamber in the 3rd century BC, though no one's sure, because there's nothing to compare it with. Later the Romans and Lombards used it as a prison, where unfortunates would have had to look at the three monstrous, carved heads that peer out of the walls seemingly from the dawn of time itself.

WHERE TO STAY AND EATING OUT   (tel prefix 0432)
In Udine, the ******Astoria Hotel Italia**, Piazza XX Settembre 24, tel 505 091, is the *grande dame* of the city's hotels, conveniently located in the heart of town, its very comfortable rooms cost L120–145 000; it also has one of Udine's finest restaurants, specializing in meat and fish dishes in the Veneto style (L35 000). Near the station, the ****Vienna**, Viale Europa Unità 47, tel 294 446, is nothing special, but quite adequate for an overnight stay; rooms L42 000 without bath, L50 000 with. The ***Piccolo Friuli**, Via Magrini 9, tel 290 817 (near Piazza Matteotti—Via Zanon to Via Murati), has rooms a couple of stars ahead of its official rating, with baths in every room (L38–47 000). The ***Trieste**, a couple of blocks from the station on Via R. Battistig 11, tel 504 171, offers plain, functional doubles for L35 000 without bath.

There are several well-known restaurants in Udine. One, **All'Antica Maddalena**, Via Pellicerie 4, tel 25 111, in the centre of town, consists of two small but lovely Renaissance and Baroque dining rooms, where good Veneto cuisine is served, with an emphasis on seafood, truffles in season, and steaks with various sauces prepared at your table (L35–40 000; closed Sun and Mon lunch). **Alla Buona Vite**, Via Treppo 10 (near Piazza Patriarcato),tel 21 053, is Venetian in its ownership and menu. Good seafood antipasti and seafood risotto, liver alla veneziano, bigoli, and that good lagoon cuisine in a refined setting (L40 000; closed Mon and Aug). The oldest of them all, **Alla Vedova**, Via Tavagnacco 8, tel 470 291, is quite a way from the historic centre, off the road to Tarvisio; but what better way to spend an evening than at a table near the great hearth (or outdoors in the summer), dining on wild duck with risotto? The house's red Refrosco is famous (L30–35 000; closed Sun eve, Mon, and Aug). **Da Arturo**, near Piazza 1 Maggio and Basilica della Grazie on Via Pracchiuso 75, is a good neighbourhood trattoria that will fill you on local Friulian specialities for L15–20 000.

For an exceptional meal, you'll have to drive or catch a bus up to the village of Tricesimo and its gourmet haven, **Da Boschetti**, Piazza Mazzini 9, tel 851 230, where the highly innovative chef bases his dishes entirely on the availability of fresh ingredients and old Friulian traditions—try *pappardelle* with porcini mushrooms, or scallops with French beans in almond oil, or steamed salmon with vegetables and exquisite desserts. There's a *menu degustazione* for L48 000, à la carte you'll pay about L60 000; closed Mon and part of Aug.

Cividale del Friuli's hotel ****Al Castello** in Via del Castello 18, in the suburb of Fortino, tel 733 242, is not in a castle but a former fortified Jesuit Seminary. It offers Cividale's most atmospheric rooms for L52–60 000, as well as a good restaurant (L30 000). Less expensive, the **Locanda Pomo d'Oro**, Piazza S. Giovanni 19, tel 731 489, has doubles without bath for L32 000 and a good little restaurant besides. If you're making a day trip, stop in at **Alla Frasca**, Via di Rubesi 10, tel 731 270 (closed Mon), with a charming Renaissance atmosphere and tasty Friulian dishes, specializing in the kind of mushrooms and truffles that make Italians melt, served with polenta (L30 000; closed Mon and Feb). In Cividale, try the local cake: *Gubana*, filled with a spiral of nuts—a recipe so precious that like wine it's DOC.

The Carnia and central Friuli

Sadly, this region, and its once-lovely old towns of Gemona and Venzone, were the epicentre of the great '76 earthquake and few of their monuments survive, though they are now traversed by a bright new autostrada, one of Italy's most recent engineering marvels. The mountain valleys, especially in the eastern Julian Alps, are Slovenian-speaking, and if the peaks lack the imposing grandeur of their Dolomite neighbours, they also lack their crowds and lofty prices in their summer and winter resorts.

TOURIST INFORMATION
Tarvisio: Via Roma 10, tel (0428) 2135
Forni di Sopra: Via Cadore 1, tel (0433) 88 024
Arta Terme: Via Roma 22/24, tel (0433) 92 002
Pordenone: Piazza della Motta 13, tel (0434) 21 912

The Carnia

The mountains around the pass at **Tarvisio** 'a Window on Europe' (near the Austrian and Yugoslav borders) are stern, but cradle an up-and-coming winter and summer resort, **Sella Nevea**, near two pretty lakes at the national park in **Fusine**. One of the prettiest excursions in the area is up to **Lago del Predil** under Monte Magante on the Yugoslav frontier. The old frontier town between Italy and Austria was until 1918 **Pontebba**, 16 km west of Tarvisio; in its church **Santa Maria Maggiore**, there's a beautiful carved wooden altarpiece called the *Flügelaltar* (altar of wings) from 1516.

Tolmezzo is the main town of the Carnia and the transportation hub of the mountains, with buses to most of the villages. To the west of Tolmezzo the scenery grows increasingly delightful. Resorts have sprung up at **Arta Terme**, with its mineral springs, **Ravascletto** and **Villa Santina**. The district around **Paularo** is especially rich in *casolari*, the unusual wooden multi-storeyed chalets resembling walk-up barns. **Forni di Sopra** has a fine 15th-century triptych in the Romanesque church of San Floriano, and good skiing, as does **Forni di Sotto**, a village rebuilt after the Nazis burnt it to the ground in reprisal for partisan activities. **Sauris** has a beautiful lake with ski slopes on the surrounding mountains. From **Comeglians** begins the lovely scenic road up to **Sappada** in the Cadore (see p. 188).

Udine to Pordenone

West from Udine you can take a detour through the Friulian heartland to **San Daniele del Friuli**, famous for its sweet cured hams and the fine frescoes by Pellegrino da San Daniele in the church of **Sant' Antonio**. **Spilimbergo**, on the west bank of the Tagliamento, is the site of the 'painted castle' with lovely exterior frescoes, a Gothic cathedral with paintings by Pordenone, and a Mosaic school, founded in 1922 and open for tours. Another town in the district, **Maniago**, produced swords and daggers for the Republic of Venice, and now manufactures cutlery, axes, nailclippers and more, all on display in the *comunale* cutlery shop.

On the main Udine-Pordenone road, **Codroipo** is the site of the enormous **Villa Manin** (1738), residence of Venice's last doge, Lodovico Manin. When he was elected, his chief rival declared: 'A Friulian as Doge! The Republic is dead.' The prediction was correct, but the villa, with its air-headed frescoes and elegant park, recalls better days. Napoleon was one of its guests, if not a welcome one (interior open 9:30–12:30 and 2–5, closed Mon; adm).

Pordenone

Pordenone is a working city and provincial capital that gave its name to the Renaissance artist G. A. Sacchiense, whose works may be seen in the **Museo Civico** in the pretty 15th-century Palazzo Richiere (9:30–12:30 and 3–6:30, closed Mon) and in the **Duomo** (where his odd masterpiece, the *Madonna della Misericordia*, hangs). The cathedral has a beautiful campanile in Romanesque brickwork. The bizarre **Palazzo Comunale**, focal point of Pordenone's arcaded Corso, has a Venetian clock tower topped by two bell-ringing Moors, superimposed on a graceful 13th-century building. The city has a number of shady green parks along the river Noncello.

South of Pordenone, the wee hamlet of **Sesto al Reghena** is the site of the fortified **Abbey of Santa Maria in Sylvis**, founded by the Lombards in the 8th century. It possesses some fine early bas-reliefs, a 13th-century *Annunciation*, and unique frescoes; look especially for the *Albero della Vita*, depicting Christ crucified on a voluptuous pomegranate tree.

Sacile to the west is a pleasant town on the willowy banks of the Livenza, which has, ever since 1351, held a bird festival (the 'Dei Osei') on the last Sunday in August. Thousands of songbirds are assembled in the main piazza, and prizes are awarded to the birds and the person who can do the best imitation of their songs. To the north, the mountain basin of **Piancavallo** (1300 m) is the most important winter resort in Friuli, under the towering slopes of Monte Cavallo. From **Montereale** a 50-km road threads through a steep mountain gorge to Longarone in the Eastern Dolomites.

WHERE TO STAY AND EATING OUT

If chance finds you sleepy in Tarvisio, one of the prettiest places to stay is in the nearby hamlet Fusine, at the little *****Edelweiss**, tel (0428) 61 050 (bathless rooms L40 000). In Forni di Sopra, there's a more plush ******Edelweiss**, Via Nazionale 11, tel (0433) 88 017, with a good restaurant (rooms L60 000, meals L30 000, closed Oct and Nov).

In a 15th-century tower in Spilimbergo, **La Torre Orientale**, Via de Mezzo 2, tel (0427) 2998 is an intimate, elegant little restaurant, with a menu ranging from the famous prosciutto di San Daniele, gnocchetti with ricotta, sweet and sour duck (*all'agro*); excellent wine list (L35 000 or more, closed Tues, Sun eve, and most of Aug).

Visitors to the Villa Manin can stay for lunch or dinner in one of the wings of the palace at **Del Doge**, tel (0432) 906 591—dishes range from the international to typical Friulian: the homemade pasta is delicious, especially the spaghetti 'del Doge' with black olives and basil; good fresh trout, too (L40 000, closed Mon).

In Pordenone, the most rewarding activity is to be had at the table, at **Noncello**, Via Marconi 34, tel (0434) 523 014; in its handsome dining room of wood and flowers, try some of the seafood antipasti, homemade pasta dishes, and immaculately prepared fresh fish (L35–40 000, closed Sun and Aug; reserve). For quick meals, pizza, or an in-expensive sit-down dinner, try Pordenone's **Alla Tavola Calda**, Piazza Risorgimento, tel (0434) 255 058 (L15 000 for a meal, closed Tues). One of Friuli's best restaurants is 9 km north of Pordenone in San Quirino: **La Primula**, Via S. Rocco 35, tel (0434) 91 005, famous in the area since 1875. The decor is rustic, with large fireplaces and wrought iron, but the cuisine is delicate and refined and imaginative—green crêpes filled with ricotta and porcini mushrooms, a honey and cinnamon risotto, a salad of frog and beans (honestly, it tastes better than it sounds). The unadventurous will find equally good traditional dishes and an amazing wine cellar (L40–50 000, closed Sun eve, Tues, and most of July).

Part VII

EMILIA–ROMAGNA

Torrechiara, Parma

Between the sparkling wines of Lombardy, the elegant Soave of the Veneto and the full-bodied Chianti of Tuscany, Emilia-Romagna seems at first a glass of warm beer. It is mostly flat, on the southern plain of the Po, hot and humid in the summer, cold and fog-bound in the winter. Most tourists see it only from the train window when chugging between Venice and Florence.

But for anyone interested in cracking the surface of this glossiest and most complex of nations, Emilia-Romagna is an essential region to know. For this is Middle Italy, agricultural, wealthy, progressive, a barometer of Italian highs and lows—the birthplace of the country's socialist movement but also of Mussolini and Fascism. In Emilia-Romagna hard-working cities like Modena, Parma, and Bologna share space with Rimini, Italy's vast, madcap international resort, with Ravenna, the artistic jewel of the region with its stupendous Byzantine mosaics, and with traditional Apennine villages. Emilia-Romagna is the cradle of Italy's greatest and most innovative film directors— Fellini, Bertolucci, Pasolini, and Antonioni; of musical giants like Verdi, Toscanini, Pavarotti, Tebaldi, and Bergonzi; of diverse talents like Marconi, Savonarola, Ariosto, and Ferrari.

As a united region, Emilia-Romagna is a child of the Risorgimento. Emilia, the land west of Bologna, was named after a Roman road, the long, straight Via Aemilia, built by M. Aemilius Lepidus between Piacenza and Rimini. Nearly all of Emilia's large cities grew up along it at intervals, like beads on a string. Romagna, the land to the east of Bologna, recalls the period from the 5th century to 751 when this was 'Rome', when Ravenna was the last enclave of the Roman Empire in the west, ruled by the Exarchs of the Eastern Roman Empire of Byzantium. By the Middle Ages most of these cities had

238

gone their own way, controlled by dynasties of dukes and *signori*—the Farnese, Este, Malatesta, Bentivoglio, and da Polenta families—who claimed at least nominal allegiance to the pope, and held the front line between the Papal States and the not always friendly Venetians and Milanese.

In Emilia-Romagna you'll find, besides the unique art of the Byzantines and Goths in Ravenna, some of Italy's finest Romanesque churches (Parma and Modena), two of its crookedest towers (Bologna), some of its most beautiful Renaissance art (Parma, Bologna, and Ferrara) and the early Renaissance's most unusual building, the Malatesta Temple in Rimini. The province of Parma has some of Italy's finest castles and a host of spas, most famously at Salsomaggiore. You can ski, hike, ride, or hang-glide in the Apennines, observe the wildfowl in the Po Delta, sunbathe in style on the Adriatic, go duty-free shopping in San Marino, visit Italy's ceramics capital at Faenza, or attend a grand opera in Parma, Reggio, Bologna, or Modena. You'll find the best food in Italy in Emilia-Romagna; this is the home of Parmesan cheese and Parma ham, tortellini, lasagne, spaghetti bolognese, and a hundred different kinds of sausages, balsamic vinegar and eels. It is also the home of Lambrusco, which foams like a beer when it's first poured, only to reveal a sparkling, elegant, and full-bodied wine below.

Itineraries

The region's art and architectural highlights are easily seen in eight days or so:

From west to east: a half-day in **Piacenza** (the Piazza dei Cavalli, Duomo, Palazzo Farnese); from there, bus to **Busseto** with its Verdian memories (half-day). **Parma** (bus or train from Busseto) requires an entire day or more to take in its magnificent cathedral and Baptistry, its museums in the Farnese palace, and its frescoes by Correggio. Leave half a day for **Modena's** cathedral and museum, and at least two and a half days for **Bologna**, perhaps Italy's most underestimated art city. **Faenza's** great ceramics museum and shops deserve a half-day, easily shared with **Rimini's** Malatesta temple, a short walk from the station. Give **Ravenna's** marvellous churches and monuments a very full day, or even two, and **Ferrara's** cathedral, Este castle, and fine Renaissance palaces a day as well.

But it would be a shame to race through the monuments of the flatlands without taking a breather in the country. From Piacenza you can visit the attractive Roman ruins at **Velleia**, or ancient **Bobbio**, with its monastery founded in the Dark Ages by an Irish monk, or the fine medieval village of **Castell'Arquato**. In Parma it's worthwhile hiring a car to visit its fine castles, especially **Torrechiara** and **Soragna**, or the Farnese's 'little Versailles', in **Colorno**. There are several interesting old towns north of Reggio Emilia like **Novellara, Guastalla**, and **Luzzara**, home of Italy's museum of naif painting.

From Modena you can take a lovely detour into the northern Apennines, not to be sniffed at for mountain scenery; the resort of **Sestola** is an excellent base for excursions around Monte Cimone, the tallest peak in the Northern Apennines. In the spring **Vignola**, also south of Modena, is a wonderland of cherry blossoms. Southern Forlì province, especially around **Portico di Romagna, Santa Sofia**, and **Campigna**, is also good for mountain excursions. The wetlands and forests of the **Po Delta** and the great medieval **abbey of Pomposa** are worth a visit from Ferrara, which also has a string of seven beach resorts, which are quieter and more Italian than **Rimini, Riccione**, and

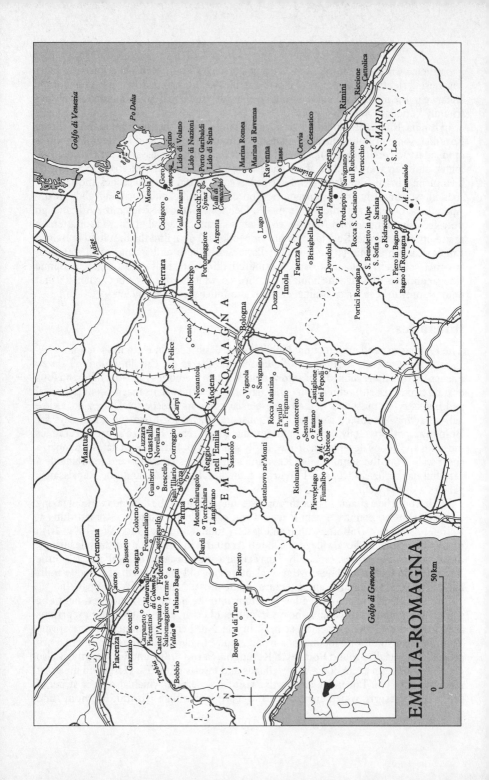

Cattolica further south. All are an easy excursion bus hop from the pygmy mountain **Republic of San Marino.**

Piacenza

Competing with the more famous and obvious charms of nearby Parma and Cremona, Piacenza is the unassuming wallflower of Renaissance art cities. Nevertheless, it can boast of two of the most gallant horses in Italy, a Botticelli, and an amazing liver.

A Roman colony of 218 BC that grew up where the Via Aemilia met the Po, Piacenza was an important *comune* in the 12th and 13th centuries and a member of the Lombard League in 1314. It spent much of the subsequent centuries under the Farnese thumb, as part of the Duchy of Parma. In 1848, after a plebiscite, Piacenza became the first city to unite with Piedmont in the new nation of Italy, earning itself the nickname 'Primogenita'.

GETTING AROUND
The station, on Piazzale Marconi, is about a 10-minute walk from the centre: frequent connections to Milan (1½ hours), Parma (1 hour), and Cremona. The bus station is in the Piazza Castello, near the Palazzo Farnese, with buses to Cremona, Bobbio (10 a day, 1 hour 20 mins), Grazzano Visconti, Alseno and Salsomaggiore, Castell'Arquato (1 hour), Busseto, and Fidenza. Buses to the excavations in Velleia (1 hour 40 mins) are infrequent—if you go, make sure you aren't stranded.

TOURIST INFORMATION
Piazzetta dei Mercanti 10 (flanking Piazza Cavalli) tel (0523) 29 324

Piazza dei Cavalli
Piacenza's excellent Piazza dei Cavalli (to get there from the station, cut across the park to Via G. Alberoni and Via Roma, then turn left on Via Carducci) takes its name from its two bronze horses with flowing manes, the **Cavalli**, masterpieces of the early Baroque cast in the 1620s by Francesco Mochi. Riding them are two members of the Farnese clan: Alessandro, the 'Prince of Parma', who served as Philip II of Spain's governor in the Low Countries during the Counter-Reformation (not a position from which to win a popularity contest, despite the fine statue), and his son Ranuccio. The piazza also contains the Gothic **Palazzo del Comune** (1280), with its swallowtail crenellations and rose window, and the 13th-century church of **San Francesco**, noted for its Gothic interior.

The Lombard-Romanesque **Duomo** (1122–1233), rising up at the end of the main street, Via XX Settembre, is an imposing pile; viewed from the side and apse it's a picturesque confusion of columns, caryatids, and galleries in the shadow of the mighty campanile and octagonal lantern. The interior is transitional (from Romanesque to Gothic) and includes some good 15th-century frescoes. From here Via Chiapponi leads to **Sant'Antonio**, Piacenza's most ancient church, with an 11th-century octagonal lantern believed to be the first built in Italy and a fine Gothic porch called the 'Paradiso'. Just southwest, on Via San Siro and Via Santa Franca and across from a picturesque derelict Art Nouveau theatre, the **Ricci Oddi Gallery** has a well-arranged collection that offers an excellent idea of what Italian artists were up to between the years 1800 and 1930 (open 10–12, also 3–5; winter 2–4; adm).

Palazzo Farnese

From the Piazza dei Cavalli, Corso Cavour leads to the pachydermic, unfinished Palazzo Farnese, local headquarters of the ducal family, begun in 1558. Recently restored, the palace now houses the collections of the **Museo Civico**: Botticelli's lovely *Tondo* is the highlight of the paintings, and in the archaeological section you can see the most famous bronze of the Etruscan civilization: the *Fegato di Piacenza*, a model of a sheep (or some say human) liver, designed for the apprentice augur, diagrammed and inscribed with the names of the Etruscan deities. The Etruscans used the liver as a microcosm for the sky, divided into sections ruled over by various gods, and looked for blemishes to see which gods had anything to communicate. Other sections of the museum contain medieval arms, and a collection of 18th- and 19th-century coaches.

Northwest of Palazzo Farnese, beyond Piazza Casali, **San Sisto** with its courtyard is a fine Renaissance church of 1511, designed by Alessio Tramello; within is the tomb of Duchess Margaret of Parma (d. 1586), ruler of the Netherlands from 1559–1567. Even better is Tramello's **Madonna di Campagna** (1530) located at the west end of Piacenza, on Via Campagna, and prettily frescoed by Pordenone.

If you're in Piacenza on a Sunday afternoon between 3 and 6, head southwest (2 km) to **San Lazzaro Alberoni**; this is the only time that the Collegio Alberoni will let visitors in to see its fine collection of Flemish tapestries; among its 16th–18th- century Flemish and Italian paintings, look for Antonello da Messina's *Christ at the Column*—an unusual composition with the Renaissance's most sorrowful Christ.

Environs of Piacenza

The rarely visited hills and mountains south of Piacenza offer several possibilities for excursions or road stops. The main Genoa road, along the Trebbia valley, passes through **Bobbio** (46 km), the site of the monastery found by St Colombanus in 612. Columbanus was one of several scholarly Irish monks who came to illiterate Italy as missionaries in the Dark Ages, and his monastery dominated the neighbourhood for centuries. Traces of Columbanus' church survive in the **Basilica**, rebuilt in the 15th century, as was the saint's tomb. The **Museo di San Colombano** contains a famous 4th-century ivory bucket with reliefs, Romanesque statuary, and painting; in the town of Bobbio, clustered around the monastery and castle, there are many fine old stone houses.

Emilia's best-preserved Roman town is prettily situated on a hillside, 33 km south of Piacenzo. **Velleia** was never very large, but it retains an interesting forum, temple, amphitheatre and mysterious large stones carved to resemble bathtub plugs. Most of the items excavated are now in Parma, though bits and pieces remain in the antiquarium on the site (open daily 9 until sunset). If you're driving you can cut over the hills from here to Lugagnano and **Castell'Arquato**, a lovely walled hill town built around an asymmetrical **Palazzo Pretorio** (1293) and a Romanesque church of the same period—a picturesque ensemble Piacenza likes to put on its brochures. Just as picturesque, closer to Piacenza, but not as authentic, **Grazzano Visconti** was recently rebuilt in the medieval style. The result is charming, and the village is a good place to purchase ornamental wrought iron.

WHERE TO STAY   (tel prefix 0529)
Piacenza's most prestigious hotel, the ****Grande Albergo Roma, Via Cittadella 14, tel 23 201, is just off the Piazza dei Cavalli; it offers old-fashioned service, comfortable air-conditioned rooms, and a garage for L64–75 000 without bath, L95–115 000 with. The ***Nazionale, also conveniently near the piazza at Via Genova 33–35, tel 754 000, has pleasant rooms, frigo-bars, and a garage for L55–70 000 with.

Near the station there are a couple of plain, simple choices—*Daturi, Piazzale Marconi 41, tel 20 823, offers bathless rooms for L30 000, L34 000 with bath. The *Rangoni, Piazzale Marconi, tel 21 778, offers much the same for the same price.

EATING OUT
Piacenza can claim an exceptional gourmet restaurant, the delightful Antica Osteria del Teatro, near Sant' Antonio's on Via Verdi 16, tel 23 777, where local recipes merge delectably with French nouvelle cuisine under the chef's magic touch. Expect delicious surprises, but not on Sun eve, Mon, or Aug (L55–80 000). The nearby Ginetto, Piazza San Antonio 8, tel 35 785, is the Osteria's main rival for honours at the table, its tantalizing menu also featuring a French touch or two—vol-au-vent and quiche compete with crêpes filled with artichokes and cheese, or with spinach and ricotta, and a celebrated strawberry torte (L45 000, closed Sun and Aug). If dining in the vicinity of Italy's biggest nuclear plant won't spoil your appetite, you can eat very well at Valentino, Via Roma 29/b, tel 811 233, in Caorso (16 km from Piacenza, towards Cremona), a restaurant that has carefully revived many old local and Lombard recipes like *zuppa di zucca* (pumpkin soup with almonds), but also risotto with wild asparagus, artichokes in pastry, duck with cherries, and a superb *vino della casa* (L45 000, closed Mon).

From Piacenza to Parma

Around the Via Aemilia between Piacenza and Parma there are enough sights to occupy an entire day. Just east of Piacenza, Alseno is famous for its Abbey of Chiaravalle della Colomba (4 km north of town) with a Romanesque church and beautiful brick cloister. More elaborate Romanesque awaits at Fidenza, the Roman *Fidentia Iulia*, known for centuries as the Borgo San Donnino until Mussolini resurrected its old, more imperial-sounding name. Fidenza's interest is concentrated in its 13th-century Duomo, its porch adorned with statues by the followers of the great Antelami, the master of Parma's Baptistry.

South of Fidenza, Salsomaggiore with its 109 hotels is the largest and best known of a cluster of saline water spas specializing in arthritic and rheumatic cures. The Italian royal family favoured it in the Belle Epoque, and many of Italy's operatic celebrities still find the waters a tonic for weary throats. Its main baths, the Terme Berzieri, are concentrated in an intriguing half-baked Liberty spa. Better, stop in at the Palazzo dei Congressi on Viale Romagnosi. Once this was the city's grandest hotel, built in Salsomaggiore's pre-World War I golden era and owned by Cesar Ritz; past clientele included the likes of Caruso, Toscanini and Queen Margherita. Its lobby is still one of the grandest in Italy, a Liberty-arabesque fantasy with exquisitely colourful frescoes by Italy's Art Nouveau master Galileo Chini. Another important spa nearby is Tabiano Bagni with sulphur springs.

Busseto

Lying some 15 km north of Fidenza on the Cremona road, Busseto is an attractive walled town, neatly rectangular with an arcaded main street and a discreet Renaissance castle. Italians know it best as the musically inclined village that gave the world Giuseppe Verdi. To Italians, Verdi is more than just another great composer; he was the genius who expressed the national spirit of the Risorgimento in music: Italy's answer to Richard Wagner.

Opera buffs can have a field day and take in the complete 'Swan of Busseto' tour, beginning at **Roncole**, 9 km southeast of Busseto, where the composer was born in 1813, son of a grocer and tavern-keeper (daily exc Mon and the month of January; summer 10–12 and 2–7, winter 10–12:30, 2–5; adm expensive, but the ticket includes the sights listed below as well). While in Roncole, you may also visit the parish church where little Giuseppe was baptized and played the organ.

In Busseto proper a statue of Verdi relaxes in an armchair near the medieval castle, or **Rocca**, built by the Pallavicino lord Oberto, who became the subject of Verdi's first and seldom heard opera, *Oberto*. In the Rocca the **Teatro Verdi**, modelled on La Scala, was built in the composer's honour in 1845; Verdi frequently attended performances here. The Rocca's Palazzo Pallavicino is now the **Museo Civico**, packed full of Verdian memorabilia (theatre, castle, and museum open same hours as above). The ticket, however, does not include the **Villa Verdi**, or Villa Sant'Agata, built with the proceeds from *Rigoletto* in Sant'Agata di Villanova, 3 km north of Busseto. Privately owned, guided tours are offered of the house and replica of the room in a Milanese hotel where Verdi died in 1901 (April–Oct; daily exc Mon, 9–12, 3–7; adm).

The Castles of Parma

The province of Parma is known for its beautiful castles, some of which lie between Busseto and Parma. The **Palace of Soragna** was begun in the 8th century as a castle and converted into a stocky brick palace ten centuries later by its current owners, the Princes of Meli Lupi. It contains good period furnishings and frescoes by Parmigianino, Gentile da Fabriano, and others (open 1 March–30 Nov 9–12 and 3–7; adm). In **Fontanellato** the fairytale **Castello di Sanvitale** is much more castle-like, surrounded by a proper moat that's still in use and adorned inside with frescoes; the rich, sensuous Diana and Acteon in the boudoir are by Parmigianino (open all year round 9:30–12:30 and 3–6, closed Mon; adm). Another imposing fortress, **Castel Guelfo**, once belonged to the Ghibelline Pallavicino family of Busseto but was renamed as an insult by its Guelph captors in 1407 (no adm).

In **Colorno**, just north of Parma, one of the Farnese dukes, Ranuccio II ('Little Froggy') converted an old castle into a 'miniature Versailles' in 1660. It has beautiful gardens and an orangery—and tunnels; the later Bourbon rulers must have been a bit nervous, for they created escape hatches for themselves leading all over the countryside, one supposedly running all the way to Parma (open weekdays, 11–12).

WHERE TO STAY AND EATING OUT   (tel prefix 0524)
Most of the accommodation and food in the area between Piacenza and Parma is concentrated in Salsomaggiore, beginning with the *******Grand Hotel & Milano**, Via

Dante 1, tel 572 241, the plush place in town to take the waters, with lovely air-conditioned rooms, heated pool in a pretty garden, open April–Oct (L140–175 000). The ***Valentini, Viale Porro 10, tel 78 251, is another old favourite, with its own spa, swimming-pool, parking, all in a quiet park setting (L55–65 000 without bath, L68–80 000 with; open 23 March–16 Nov). In the same pleasant neighbourhood, **Villa Moderna, Viale Porro 9, tel 71 270, has good rooms and parking facilities, all rooms with bath L38 000. Al Tartufo, Viale Marconi 30, tel 573 696, is a large restaurant that has become the classic place to eat in Salsomaggiore; besides *tartufi* (truffles) starring in many of the dishes, you can try the chef's famous grilled mushrooms. Good wine list; L50 000. Also in Salsomaggiore, on the flowery banks of a lakelet filled with trout and carp, is the peaceful Alle Querce da Giorgio, Via Parma 85, tel 572 484. The patron will suggest a menu, and it will probably include porcini mushrooms, truffles and homemade pasta among other good things (L40 000, closed Jan, Feb, and Mon except in Sept and Oct).

The finest place to stay in Busseto is, naturally, named after one of Verdi's operas and is owned by the family of a tenor who often performs in them, Carlo Bergonzi: ***I Due Foscari, Piazza Carlo Rossi 15, tel 92 337, is small, very comfortable and will probably have no vacancies unless you reserve in advance; air conditioning is not the least of its charms; all rooms have bath, L62 000. Here, too, you can find one of Busseto's best restaurants, featuring solid, traditional Parmigianino cooking for around L40 000 (closed Mon and Aug). Verdi-ites in Roncole can lunch (or on Saturday, dine) at one of the region's best-known and yet simplest restaurants, Guareschi, Via Processione 160, tel 92 495, where many of the ingredients of its specialities are made, or grown, on the family farm, including the Lambrusco, the salamis and prosciutto, the pasta, the vegetables, all well prepared and delicious (closed Fri and all of July, L35–45 000).

Near Fontanellato, in the village of Sanguinaro, ***Tre Pozzi, Via Casalbarbato 129/b, tel (0521) 825 347, is a fine medium-sized hotel in a rural setting (all rooms with bath, L75 000). The hotel restaurant (tel 825 119) is a fine one that likes to sprinkle its dishes with truffles and *funghi* of all kinds; L40 000, closed 20 July–10 Aug.

Parma

The French daily *Le Monde* rated Parma as the best Italian city to live in, for its prosperity and quality of life. Even the air in Parma is lighter and less muggy in the summer than that in other cities along the Po. One of Italy's great art cities and the second city in Emilia-Romagna after Bologna, Parma's many admirers can cite her splendid churches and elegant lanes, her works of art and antiquities, the lyrical strains of grand opera that waft from her Teatro Regio—a house that honed the talents of young Arturo Toscanini—and the glories of its famous cheese and ham at table as reasons not only to visit, but to return again and again.

Parma is the place to see the masterpieces of Benedetto Antelami (1177–1233), the great sculptor from Provence whose Baptistry here introduced the Italians to the idea of a building as a unified work of art in its architecture and scuptural programme. Parma's distinctive school of painting began relatively late, with the arrival of Antonio Allegri Correggio (1494–1534), whose highly personal and self-taught techniques of *sfumato*

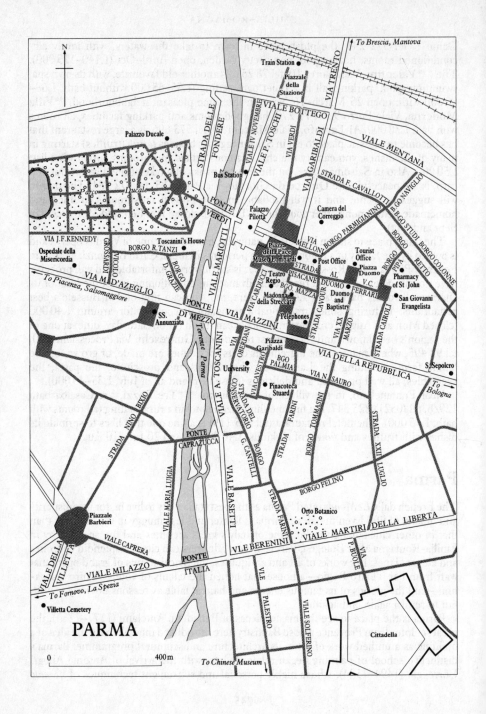

PARMA

0 ———————— 400m

To Brescia, Mantova
Train Station
Piazzale della Stazione
VIA TRENTO
VIALE BOTTEGO
VIALE MENTANA
Palazzo Ducale
STRADA DELLE FONDERE
VIA IV NOVEMBRE
VIALE P. TOSCHI
VIA VERDI
VIA GARIBALDI
Bus Station
Parco Ducale
PONTE VERDI
STRADA F. CAVALLOTTI
B.GO NAVIGLIO
Palazzo Pilotta
Camera del Correggio
B.GO STUDI BORGO COLONNE
VIA J.F. KENNEDY
Toscanini's House
GROSSARDI
BORGO R. TANZI
VICOLO D. GRAZIE
VIA MELLONI
BORGO PARMIGIANINO
BORGO PIPA
BORGO RETTO
Ospedale della Misericordia
To Piacenza, Salsomaggiore
VIA M. D'AZEGLIO
D. BORGO
VIALE MARIOTTI
Piazza della Pace
Museo Lombardi
Post Office
Tourist Office
Piazza Duomo
Pharmacy of St John
San Giovanni Evangelista
STRADA AL PISACANE
Teatro Regio
VIA CARDUCCI
BGO MAZZALI
V.C. FERRARI
Madonna della Streccata
STRADA CAVOUR
Duomo and Baptistry
VIA XX MARZO
STRADA CAIROLI
PONTE DI MEZZO
VIA MAZZINI
Telephones
SS. Annunziata
Torrente Parma
VIA A. TOSCANINI
VIA OBERDAN
Piazza Garibaldi
BGO PALMIA
VIA DELLA REPUBBLICA
S. Sepolcro
To Bologna
University
VIA CAVESTRO
STRADA DEL CONSERVATORIO
Pinacoteca Stuard
VIA N. SAURO
STRADA FARINI
STRADA TOMMASINI
STRADA XXII LUGLIO
PONTE CAPRAZUCCA
STRADA NINO BIXIO
BORGO G. CANTELLI
BORGO FELINO
VIALE MARIA LUIGIA
VIALE BASETTI
STRADA FARINI
Orto Botanico
VIALE MARTIRI DELLA LIBERTA
Piazzale Barbieri
VIALE CAPRERA
VLE BERENINI
VIA P. BUOLE
VIALE DELLA VILLETTA
PONTE ITALIA
VIALE MILAZZO
VLE PALESTRO
VIALE SOLFERINO
Cittadella
To Fornovo, La Spezia
Villetta Cemetery
To Chinese Museum

and sensuous subtlety deeply influenced his many followers, most notably Francesco Mazzola, better known as Parmigianino.

History

Parma is a fine example of how Italians have learned to adapt and even prosper in the face of continual political uncertainty. After starting out as a small Roman way-station on the Via Aemilia, the fledgeling medieval town of Parma found itself insecurely poised on the edge of the 'spheres of influence', of pope and emperor, a conflict echoed internally by the factions of the da Correggio and the Rossi families. Throughout the Middle Ages and Renaissance Parma changed hands among the Visconti, della Scala, Este, Sforza and other local strongmen before its incorporation in the Papal States in 1521. Even this endured only until 1545, when Pope Paul III required a tax farm for his natural son, Pier Luigi Farnese, and created the Duchy of Parma and Piacenza to fill the bill.

Pier Luigi's own ambitions led shortly to his assassination by a Spanish-led conspiracy, but all in all, the duchy gave Parma a measure of stability, remaining in the family until 1748, when, upon the extinction of the Farnese line, it passed into the hands of the Bourbons of France. At first the enlightened French attempted a programme of reform; checked by the nobility and rural discontent, the Bourbons soon learned to collect their rents and not make waves. Their rule continued until 1815. This year marked the arrival of Parma's best-loved ruler, Napoleon's nymphomaniac widow, Marie Louise, who received the duchy from the Congress of Vienna. In 1859 the city was incorporated into the Kingdom of Italy.

GETTING AROUND

Parma is easy to reach by rail, positioned on the main line from Turin and Milan to Bologna, Florence and Rome. The station is on the north edge of the centre, on Via Altissimo, at the end of Strada Garibaldi; bus No. 1 can take you into the centre. The bus station is on Viale P. Toschi, between the railway station and the Palazzo della Pilotta, with good service to all points in the province.

TOURIST INFORMATION
Piazza del Duomo 5, tel (0521) 234 735

Palazzo della Pilotta

Arriving by train or bus in Parma, one of the first buildings you notice is also, unfortunately, the most pathetic: the ungainly, bomb-mutilated **Palazzo della Pilotta**, built for the Farnese, and named after *pelote*, a ball game once played in its courtyard. The palace's appearance is not improved by having the municipal car park in its shadow. Yet looks are deceiving, for within this patched-up shell are Parma's greatest treasures. A grand staircase leads to the first-floor **Museo Archeologico Nazionale** (open 9–2, 9–1 holidays; closed Mon; adm), founded in 1760 and containing finds from the excavations at Roman Velleia. The single most important exhibit is the **Tabula Alimentaria**, a large bronze tablet that records the contributions of private citizens to the dole in Trajan's time, as well as many fine bronzes, Etruscan and Greek ceramics, and the statuary from the collections of ducal antiquarians.

On the second floor the **Galleria Nazionale** (separate adm; expensive; open 9–8 pm) was founded even earlier, in 1752. To reach the gallery you pass first through the wooden **Teatro Farnese**, built in 1620 and modelled on Palladio's Teatro Olimpico in Vicenza, though being Farnese, this one had to be considerably larger; it also had moveable stage scenes, unlike the permanent set in Vicenza. In 1945 a bomb tore most of the theatre into splinters and sawdust, but it has since been carefully reconstructed.

The gallery's paintings are dramatically arranged in chronological order along platforms and catwalks on four levels. Most of the works are from Emilia-Romagna and Tuscany. The Early Renaissance collection features works by the Tuscans Gaddi, Spinello Aretino, Giovanni di Paolo and Fra Angelico and the Emilians Simone dei Crocifissi and Loschi (whose charming *St Jerome* holds a toddler lion paternally by the paw). Further along there's a lovely portrait sketch by Leonardo, *La Scapigliata*, four fine works by the Venetian Cima da Conegliano, and a portrait by Sebastiano del Piombo of the handsome young Medici pope, *Clement VII*. Some of Correggio's most celebrated works are here, the tender *Madonna di San Girolamo* and the *Madonna della Scodella* among others, as well as Parmigianino's *Marriage of St Catherine* and the flirtatious *Turkish Slave*, and works by Garofalo. Among the non-Italians are works by Peter Brueghel the Younger, Van Dyck, and Holbein's famous portrait of the sharp-featured Erasmus.

Also in the Palazzo, opposite the gallery, is the **Palatine Library**, with a vast collection of incunabula, codices, manuscripts, and a number of editions published by the city's famous printer Bodoni, who gave his name to the popular type he invented (9–12; free).

Piazza della Pace
Behind the palazzo and over the bridge lies the extensive **Parco Ducale** with its shady cafés and duck pond, while in front is the **Piazza della Pace**, with its statue of a rugged World War II partisan. Just off the Via Melloni is the **Camera del Correggio** (daily exc Mon; 9–1; adm) in the ex-convent of San Paolo. In 1519 its worldly abbess, Giovanna Piacenza, hired Correggio to fresco her refectory with sensuous mythological scenes; Correggio portrayed the abbess herself as the goddess Diana over the fireplace. The decorative scheme in the vault is unique: sixteen vignettes of putti, set over sixteen mythological emblems. Some of these can be decoded: Pan, the punishment of Hera, the three Graces; others cannot. Attempts have been made, though not necessarily convincing ones, to claim the whole as a vast Hermetic allegory. Certainly it is one of the most provocative works of the High Renaissance, embodying a symbolic language that may be lost to us for ever. The second room contains fine 1514 frescoes and grotesques by Araldi.

Also near the Piazza della Pace on Strada Garibaldi 15, the **Glauco Lombardi Museum** is devoted to the life and times of the former Empress of France and Duchess of Parma, the much-loved Marie Louise (Oct–Apr, 9:30–12:30 and 3–5, Sun 9:30–12:30; summer 9:30–12:30, 4–6 pm; Sun, 9:30–1, closed Mon and in July). A block up is the celebrated **Teatro Regio**, built by Marie Louise in 1829. The Regio is one of Italy's operatic holy-of-holies, and undoubtedly the best place to hear local favourite Verdi. Its audiences have a reputation for being the most contentious and demanding in the nation;

intimidated tenors and sopranos from all over the world submit each year either to avalanches of flowers or catcalls from the famous upper balconies, the *loggioni*. Toscanini got his start here playing in the orchestra, which has since been renamed in his honour.

Piazza Duomo

Strada Pisacane connects the Piazza della Pace to the Piazza Duomo, the heart of medieval Parma and the site of its remarkable cathedral and baptistry. The exterior of the **Duomo** is ambitious, angular Romanesque, embellished with rows of shallow loggias; three tiers of them cross the façade, creating an illusion of depth around the central arched window, and the pattern continues in the rich decoration of the sides, apses, and dome. The best part of the façade is the latest, the projecting central portal of 1281, with 13th-century reliefs of the Labours of the Months. The fine interior (7:30–12 and 3–7) contains two masterpieces: a bas-relief of the *Deposition* by Benedetto Antelami, an outstanding late 12th-century sculptor influenced by the art of southern France, and one of the true precursors of the Renaissance; and in the dome, Correggio's *Assumption* (1520), a work of art celebrated since the days of Vasari for its almost three-dimensional portrayal of clouds, angels and saints.

The octagonal **Baptistry** is a huge jewel of Italian Romanesque, constructed of pale rose-coloured marble from Verona and surrounded by four levels of restrained loggias that echo those of the Duomo. Along with those of Florence and Pisa, it is the biggest and most impressive in Italy. It was designed in 1196 by Antelami, who carved the remarkable ribbon frieze of animals and allegories that encircles the lower part of the exterior. Like Correggio's ceiling in San Paolo, this is a possible case of lost allegories. Among the 79 figures are symbols of the four Evangelists (lion, ox, eagle and man), set at the cardinal points; most of the figures—animals, archers, griffins, sea serpents, winged cats—are repeated somewhere on the frieze, in mirror images.

Antelami is also responsible for the doorways dedicated to the Virgin Mary and the Last Judgement, and the statues in the niches. Inside are the master's famous reliefs of the Twelve Months, and also spring and winter. The lovely 13th-century frescoes, freshly restored, are by an unknown but masterly hand—be sure to bring enough lire coins to light them up (9–12, 3–6:30; adm expensive).

Save some lire, however, for **San Giovanni Evangelista**, the church just behind the cathedral (open 7–12 and 3:30–7:30). Under its Baroque skin it shelters one of the masterpieces of the High Renaissance, Correggio's *Vision of St John* fresco in the dome. Unfortunately when the church was remodelled in 1587 all of Correggio's other ceiling decorations were lost, though a fresco of St John writing down his vision survives over the door north of the altar. Other frescoes here are by Parmigianino. Near the church you can visit the ancient **Pharmacy of St John** on Borgo Pipa, open 9–1:30, which has been dispensing drugs since 1298 and contains old jars, pots, 16th-century decoration and medieval pharmaceutical instruments.

Piazza Garibaldi

In company with the rest of the old gents of Parma, Garibaldi and Correggio, or at least their statues, spend their day in the modern centre of Parma, the **Piazza Garibaldi**. Here, too, stands the yellow **Palazzo del Governatore** (17th century) with its intricate sundial. Behind the palazzo, the church of **Madonna della Steccata** was built in 1539 on Bramante's original design for St Peter's. Its sumptuously ornamented interior contains excellent 16th-century frescoes in its chapels by Parmigianino and his contemporaries.

Paganini, Toscanini, and Stendhal

There are three musical and literary pilgrimages one can make in Parma. The first is to the tomb of the embalmed wizard of catgut and bow, Paganini, who lies decked out in virtuoso splendour in **Villetta Cemetery** (a 15-minute walk from the centre of Parma, open 8–12 and 2–5, till 7 in the summer). The **Birthplace of Arturo Toscanini** (1867–1957) is at Via Rudolfo Tanzi 13, between the Ponte di Mezzo and the Parco Ducale; it contains memorabilia and every record he ever made (daily, 10–1; ring in advance, 285 449).

Stendhal *aficionados* will be glad to know that there really is a **Charterhouse of Parma** (the Certosa), though these days it's much more tranquil. Located 4 km east of town (bus No 10), it was founded in 1281 but totally rebuilt in the 17th century, and now serves as a school. The cloister is closed for restoration, but you may visit the church's frescoed interior from 9–12 and 3–6, winter 2–4.

Four Castles

Further afield, there are Parma's famous castles (see 'The Castles of Parma', above for those to the north of the city). In the foothills south of the city towers **Torrechiara** (on the bus route from Parma to Langhirano) a castle made of brick and fantasy, entirely unchanged since the 15th century. Defended by four mighty towers, its outer wall encloses a small village; inside there is an elegant court and good frescoes by an artist named Bembo, who exceeded himself in the beautiful 'Golden Room' (open 9:30–1; closed Mon; adm; ring in advance, 855 255).

Bardi castle, another showpiece of the 1400s, perches atop its own hill southwest of Parma; it retains its beautiful beamed ceilings and 16th-century frescoes. According to legend the castle is named after the last of Hannibal's elephants, who wandered here to die in the Punic Wars; records of a castle on this site go back to the 800s (to visit the interior, ring first, tel (0525) 71 321). Off the main road to Reggio Emilia lies **Montechiarugolo**. Built in 1406 and architecturally resembling Torrechiara it contains fine 15th- and 16th-century paintings (Sat and Sun, 2–4, 2–6 in summer, tel 659 343). At **Compiano**, further up in the mountains, there is a half-ruined castle with something surprisingly rare in Italy—ghosts.

In the Middle Ages, the road through Parma over the Apennines was part of the *Via Romea*, the pilgrims' route to Rome and the ports for the Holy Land. The pilgrims—Italy's original tourist trade—contributed much to the prosperity of the area. The villages along the way all have simple, lovely Romanesque churches. **Vicofertile**, **Bardone** and **Berceto** all have interesting and well-preserved sculptural details, but the best of all is at **Talignano**, where over the portal is a unique scene of St Michael weighing out the souls of men at the Last Judgement. If you're travelling in this direction today, by car, you'll pass into Tuscany via a most remarkable super highway, a bit of braggadocio Italian engineering that alternates tunnels and long bridges for over 15 miles, hardly ever touching the ground.

ACTIVITIES

The opera season at the Teatro Regio runs from November to April, with many concerts during the rest of the year; there are also occasional performances at the Teatro Farnese. At the end of August there's a conductors' competition, and in October one for lyric singers. For plant tours of Parma's prime products, prosciutto and Parmesan cheese, call their cooperatives: the Prosciutto Consorzio, tel 208 187; the Parmigiano Consorzio, tel 23 253.

In Parma there are a number of antique shops along Via N. Saura and vicinity; young designer boutiques cluster around Borgo Angelo Mazza. Books in English may be found upstairs at Feltrinelli's, Strada della Repubblica 2, near Piazza Garibaldi.

WHERE TO STAY   (tel prefix 0521)

Parma's fairgrounds are bustling in May and September, months when you may well find no room at the inn if you haven't reserved a couple of months in advance.

The very modern ******Palace Hotel Maria Luigia**, Viale Mentana 140 (near the station), tel 281 031, offers very good and very quiet air-conditioned rooms. The rooms are stylish and most have their own TV, but there's not a lot of atmosphere (L160 000). Its main rival, the ******Park Hotel Stendhal**, near the heart of town at Via Bodoni 3, tel 208 057, offers the same amenities in a less modern setting, also L150 000. The *****Torino**, near the centre at Borgo A. Mazza 7, tel 281 046, offers in addition to its convenient location, a garage, plush rooms, and breakfast—only L70 000.

The **Croce di Malta**, Borgo Palmia 8, tel 35 643, a block from Piazza Garibaldi, is pleasant, quiet and small, L45 000 without bath in the high season. The ***Centrale**, Via N. Sauro 5, tel 25 086, is also just off Via Farini and the best budget choice, with old-fashioned rooms, bright posters,and friendly owners (L25 000, without bath). Parma also has a new youth hostel, **Ostello Cittadella**, housed in the Farnese's 17th-century pentagonal fortress south of the centre (Via P. Boule, tel 581 546, bus No 9 or 10 from the station); IYHF card required, L10 000 per person per night. Near the station, ***Brozzi**, Via Trento 11, tel 771 157, has simple but good rooms (L28 000 without bath) and an excellent restaurant serving Parma's specialities (L25 000). Another choice, ***Lazzaro**, is at Via XX Marzo 14, tel 208 944, where a double with bath is a mere L32 000.

EATING OUT

The pig is like the music of Verdi; nothing in it of waste.
supposed old Parma saying

It wouldn't do to mull over the meaning of this cryptic epigram for too long, but isn't it just like the Parmigiani to connect metaphorically their two ruling passions: music and food. Whatever they do with the rest of the pig, the best of it goes into the celebrated, world-beating Parma Ham. Any genuine Italian *prosciutto* junkie can distinguish hams from one region from those of another, and there is a consensus that the pigs from the mournful prairies of Emilia make the smoothest and best.

Parma is one of Emilia-Romagna's gastronomic capitals, famous for its hearty pasta dishes, topped naturally with parmesan (properly *parmigiano*) cheese, as well as for *stracotto* (roast beef), *carpaccio* (raw beef), refined recipes for horsemeat and for its various methods of serving artichokes (*carciofi*)—in fritters, pasta dishes, and in crêpes.

An ideal place to dip into Parma's specialities is **Parizzi**, Via Repubblica 71, tel 285 952, a large, cheerful restaurant with delicious antipasti of prosciutto di Parma and salami, followed by crêpes alla parmigiana, or asparagus in pastry, or *cappelletti*, Parma's favourite shape of pasta, followed by *scaloppe Parizzi*, with fontina and ham, and great desserts. Definitely reserve, closed Sun eve, Mon and 20 July–20 Aug (L40–60 000). **La Greppia**, Strada Garibaldi 39, tel 33 686, is another old favourite, housed in a former stable, with a delicious selection of *pasta di verdure* (made with spinach or tomatoes) and other original vegetable dishes, and good second courses, including veal in a sauce of hazelnuts, all prepared before your eyes in the glass kitchen (L45–75 000), closed Thurs and Fri.

The **Vecchio Molinetto**, Via Milazzo 39, near the Villetta cemetery, tel 52 672, is an unpretentious place offering good honest local cuisine—great risotto baked with veal and *involtini alla Molinetto*, L28 000. More traditional, moderately priced Parma cuisine is served at the **Trattoria dei Corrieri**, Via Conservatorio 1, tel 234 426, located in the centre of town in an old postal relay station. Typical salami and ham antipasti, pasta with parmesan cheese and a filling and tasty *bollito misto* (boiled meats) L25–30 000.

Outside town, in Sacca di Colorno, **Stendhal-Da Bruno**, Via Sacca, tel 815 493, is the perfect complement to a visit to the Farnese palace, inhabited in Stendhal's time by Marie Louise. Fish is the speciality here—eels and small fry from the rivers, and denizens of the deep brought in daily from Chioggia. Great homemade charcuterie, desserts, wine all served in a serene setting for around L43 000.

Reggio Emilia

A bright, prosperous agricultural city, Reggio nell'Emilia, now usually called just Reggio Emilia, is the Roman *Regium Lepidi*; it lines either side of the Via Emilia, modern name of the Roman Via Aemilia, which also divides the old part of the city from the new streets to the north. From 1409 to 1796 Reggio was ruled by the Este family of Ferrara, during which time its most famous son, Lodovico Ariosto (1474–1533), author of *Orlando Furioso* was born. Nowadays it is noted for its numerous dance schools, its balsamic vinegar and its version of parmesan cheese, Parmigiano–Reggiano, which tastes exactly the same as Parma's to any sane person.

TOURIST INFORMATION
Piazza C. Prampolini 5, tel (0522) 451 152

The **Piazza Prampolini**, just south of the Via Aemilia, is the civic and ecclesiastical heart of Reggio, with its peculiar **Duomo** topped by a single octagonal tower. Most of its original Romanesque features were remodelled in the 16th century, though on the façade the fine statues of Adam and Eve remain, and in the tower niche, a copper Madonna flanked by the cathedral donors. On the same piazza, the **Palazzo Comunale** (begun in 1414 and often remodelled) was where the Tricolore was proclaimed the Italian national flag during the second congress of Napoleon's Cispadane Republic. Beyond the city market behind the cathedral, 16th-century **San Prospero** is noted for its fine choir, with frescoes and inlaid stalls.

North of the Via Emilia

In the centre of Reggio's new broad streets is the vast Piazza Cavour and the renowned 19th-century **Teatro Municipale**, crowned by a surplus of musing statuary; high-quality operas, concerts, and plays are performed here from December to March. The **Musei Civici**, near a powerful monument to the Martyrs of the Resistance, have various collections—Natural History, archaeology in the **Museo Chierici** (with the buxom Neolithic 'Chiozza Venus'), the Museum of the Risorgimento and Resistance, and the Museo Numismatico (9–1, closed Mon).

In Reggio's public garden at the back of the theatre, there's an imposing funerary monument of a Roman family (50 BC) discovered in Boretto. Nearby is the very eclectic **Galleria Parmeggiani**; if nothing else, note the 16th-century Moorish-style doorway brought over from Valencia. Many of the works of art inside are Spanish as well, including an El Greco.

Three km east of Reggio, in San Maurizio, there is a 16th century villa, **Il Mauriziano**. Home of Ariosto's family, some of the rooms have been restored to look as they were when the poet came to visit from his new home in Ferrara.

Between Reggio and the Po

Some 15 km from Reggio, **Correggio** is a pretty town with old arcaded streets, the birthplace of the painter Antonio Allegri, better known as Correggio. His home on Borgo Vecchio was reconstructed in 1755. The **Palazzo dei Principi**, begun in 1506, contains the town's Civic Museum, with a Christ by Mantegna and some lovely cinquecento Flemish tapestries (open 9–1, closed Mon). The Renaissance church of **San Quirino** is attributed to the Farnese family's favourite architect, Vignola—a local boy whose best works are all in Rome. In **Novellara** the 14th-century Gonzaga dukes built a fine castle, the **Rocca**; this now serves both as the town hall and museum, housing medieval and Renaissance frescoes and a unique collection of chemists' jars.

Gualtieri, the Lombard *Castrum Walterii*, has a Spanish-style *plaza mayor*, the arcaded **Piazza Bentivoglio** and the 16th-century brickwork **Palazzo Bentivoglio** with frescoes; those in the *Sala dei Giganti* are especially good. Another old Lombard town, **Guastalla** (Wartstal) was a capital of the Gonzaga and conserves many 16th-century memories, including a statue of Ferrante Gonzaga the Condottiere, as well as the **Basilica del Pieve,** a fine Romanesque church begun in the 10th century, and the 1671 Teatro Ruggeri. Further down the Po, on the outskirts of **Luzzara**, the former convent of Agostiano has been converted into the bright and charming **Museo Comunale dei Pittori Naif,** with a permanent collection of *naif* (self-taught, 'naive') art, many of the works by leading Italian *naif,* Antonio Ligabue. There are also frequent temporary exhibits, and a New Year's competition and show that lasts throughout January. The museum was founded by Cesare Zavattini, one of Italy's great neo-realist directors and a collaborator of Vittorio Da Sica.

Brescello, the old Roman town of Brixellum, is adorned wih a statue by Sansovino of Ercole II d'Este in the guise of his namesake Hercules. The town is famous in Italian popular culture as the hometown of Guareschi's *Don Camillo*, the conservative post-War priest eternally, fraternally at war with the Communist mayor Peppone—a series of films was made from these stories in the fifties.

South of Reggio, **Canossa** will ring a bell with anyone who ever studied medieval history. It was the original family seat of the powerful feudal family of da Canossa, longtime Counts of Tuscany, whose last member was the mighty and charismatic Countess Matilda. In 1077, after Emperor Henry IV deposed Pope Gregory VII and the pope in turn excommunicated the emperor, Matilda, a partisan of the Guelphs, was instrumental in bringing Henry to Canossa on his knees in the snow to apologize to Gregory. It was a turning-point in European history; for the next two centuries, popes would hold the upper hand over the kings and barons of Europe. Today Canossa is scenic and tranquil, with a ruined castle as a dim reminder of the days of Countess Matilda, though every now and then the Italians like to stage an historical pageant by the castle.

WHERE TO STAY   (tel prefix 0522)
Reggio's top hotel, the ******Grand Hotel Astoria**, Viale L. Nobili 2, tel 35 245, offers fine views over the municipal gardens. It has its own garage, comfortable, air-conditioned rooms, and great service (L85–155 000). The historic *****Scudo d'Italia**, Via Vescovado 5, tel 34 345, has lodged most of Reggio's visiting actors and opera singers in its slightly old-fashioned but very pleasant rooms; it has one of Reggio's best restaurants downstairs (rooms, all with bath, L78 000, meals L30 000). The ****Posta Dipendenza**, on Via San Giuseppe 7, tel 40 046, is conveniently located in the town centre (but don't confuse it with the more costly Hotel Posta). Its 15 doubles, all with bath and TV, go for L75 000. If you're not travelling on an expense account, try ***Sirena**, Viale Ramazzini 2, tel 39 718, with a garage and pleasant rooms; L29 000 without bath, L40 000 with, or ***Stella**, Via Blasmatorti 5, tel 32 280, for the same prices.

In the north, Guastalla has the most in the way of accommodation. *****Old River**, Viale Po 2–4, tel 824 676, offers excellent air-conditioned rooms (this can be crucial in August) in a pleasant green setting, garage, all rooms with bath L78 000. The humbler, smaller, but adequate ***Pacian**, Via Trieste 3, tel 824 195, has rooms for L28 000 without bath, L41 000 with.

EATING OUT
Like Parma, Reggio is a major producer of parmesan cheese (its proper name is Parmigiano-Reggiano); like Modena it distils *aceto balsamico*, or balsamic vinegar, as valuable as frankincense in the Middle Ages. The best place to delve into its delights is the friendly **Osteria Campana**, Via Simonazzi 14b, tel 39 673; among its regional dishes, is Emilia's favourite *tortellini di zucca*, (filled with pumpkin); ask about their daily specials (L35 000, closed Mon, Tues eve and Aug).

For a gourmet *nuova cucina* experience, head 16 km west towards the village of Sant'Ilario d'Enza and the large, bright, and jovial **L'Istrione**, on Via Brunetto Ferrari 34, tel 672 201, where the prize-winning owner and chef produces little miracles; the *foie gras all'aceto balsamico* is a genuine treat. Closed Tues and in Aug, L45 000.

Modena

Modena puts on a class act—'Mink City' they call it, the city with Italy's highest per capita income, a city with 'a psychological need for racing cars' according to Mr Enzo Ferrari, who made his famous flame-red chariots here until his death in 1989. Modena has an Italian monopoly on such beasts—the Maserati plant is just outside town. Sleek and speedy, but also lyric, Modena was the cradle of Luciano Pavarotti; its scenographic streets take on an air of mystery and romance when enveloped in the winter mists rising from the Po.

Known in Roman days as Mutina, Modena first came to note in the 11th–12th centuries under Countess Matilda (see above, Canossa), a powerful ally of the pope. When it became an independent *comune*, however, Modena's Ghibelline party was to dominate in response to the Guelph politics of the city's chief rival, Bologna. In 1288 the city came under control of the Este dukes of Ferrara, and the Este Duchy of Modena endured until 1796.

GETTING AROUND
There are frequent rail connections with Bologna (30 min), Parma (45 min) and Milan (2½ hours); also to Mantua (1 hour). The station is on Piazza Dante, a 10-minute walk from the centre (or take bus No 1 or 2); for train information, tel 218 226.

The coach station is at Viale Monte Kosica and Via Fabrinana, tel 225 469. There are frequent connections to Bologna, Ferrara, and provincial towns in the Apennines.

TOURIST INFORMATION
Corso Canalgrande 3, tel (059) 225 585, also Via Scudari 30, tel (059) 222 482

Duomo di San Geminiano
The Via Emilia is Modena's main thoroughfare, and it is in the centre of this city that the old Roman highway picks up one of its loveliest gems, the **Piazza Grande**, address of Modena's celebrated Romanesque **Duomo di San Geminiano**. Begun with funds and support from Countess Matilda in 1099, the cathedral was designed by a master-builder named Lanfranco and completed in the 13th century; a thorough cleaning in 1985 has restored it to its original ivory appearance.

Curiously, the main features of the cathedral are 12th-century Ghibelline Lombard, and scholars believe Lanfranco designed it thus at the bidding of Modena's burghers as a show of independence, both from Matilda and the powerful Abbey of Nonantola (see below). Complementing the Duomo's fine proportions are the magnificent carvings by the 12th-century sculptor Wiligelmo over the three main entrances. Little is known about Wiligelmo, but he is one of the very earliest medieval sculptors to leave his name, and his work was undoubtedly a strong influence on later sculptors across central Italy. His friezes on either side of the main Lion Portal are believed to illustrate scenes from the medieval mystery play on the Book of Genesis, the *Jeu d'Adam*. Wiligelmo's South Portal depicts the life of Modena's 4th-century patron, St Geminiano, and he is also responsible for the delicate floral decorations on the door facing the piazza, where you can also make out the weights and measures carved into the façade during the days when the daily market was held in the square.

Wiligelmo's anonymous contemporary, the 'Master of the Metopes', executed the eight fascinating reliefs of mythological creatures and allegorical subjects on top of the buttresses—monsters relegated to the ends of the cathedral just as they are relegated to the ends of the earth. Those on the cathedral are copies; the originals, which deserve a much better look, are in the adjacent **Museo Lapidario** on Via Lanfranco

(8:30–7:30 pm, Sun 9:30–1; inquire in the Sacristry). Yet another sculptor is responsible for the 12th-century carving of King Arthur in the lunette over the Porta della Pescheria.

Later work in the 12th century, including the rose window, was done by the Campionese masters, a school of master builders and sculptors from around Lake Lugano in Lombardy; they added the final touches to Lanfranco's charming interior, with its rhythm of arches supported by slender columns and ponderous piers. The altar is split in the Lombard style, the choir raised above the crypt. This is supported by lion pillars and adorned with remarkable tinted bas-reliefs of the Passion by the Campionese masters. The mighty, if slightly askew campanile, called the **Ghirlandina**, was also completed by the Campionese masters; at 276 ft, it is the tallest church tower in Italy after those of Cremona and Venice. It houses a famous trophy: an ancient wooden bucket stolen during a raid on Bologna in 1325, when the two cities were at war. It is the subject of a 17th-century mock-heroic epic, *La Secchia Rapita*. The Bolognese make periodic attempts to steal it back; according to rumour, they have it now, and what you see is only a replica. At the base of the campanile is a photo memorial to Modena's martyred partisans. You can climb to the top of the tower for the bird's-eye view of the city (Mon–Sat 9–12:30 and 3:30–7; key available from the porters in the Municipio across the piazza).

Palazzo dei Musei

The other main sight in Modena is the Palazzo dei Musei (with your back to the cathedral, turn left on the Via Emilia), housing the **Biblioteca Estense** (10–1, closed Sun). Among its famous collection of illuminated manuscripts is one of the most fabulous anywhere, the *Bible of Borso d'Este*, made for the Duke of Modena, a gorgeously coloured 1200-page marvel, illustrated in the 15th century by the Emilians Taddeo Crivelli and Franco Rossi. Due to re-open soon, the **Museo Civico di Storia e Arte Medioevale** has a collection of art from the Duomo, ceramics, fabrics and everyday items.

Upstairs, the **Galleria Estense** (9–2, holidays 9–1, closed Mon) is a well-arranged collection founded by Francesco I d'Este, whose excellent bust by Gian Lorenzo Bernini greets visitors at the entrance. His taste wasn't quite as good as that of some other dukes, but here's your chance to see a Tomaso da Modena outside of Treviso, as well as some good early Emilian works, a good Flemish collection, Venetian Renaissance artists (Palma Vecchio's *Portrait of a Lady*; also paintings by Tintoretto, Cima da Conegliano, and Veronese), bronzes by Il Riccio of Padua, the beautiful *Madonna Campori* of Correggio, Velazquez's *Portrait of Francesco I d'Este*, and an early altar by El Greco.

On the way back to the Piazza Grande, stop by to see the *Deposition* by Guido Mazzoni (1476) in **San Giovanni Battista**. From Piazza Grande Via C. Battista leads to the huge Baroque **Palazzo Ducale**, now the National Military Academy and off limits unless you happen to stumble into Modena on the Sunday nearest 4 November. Between this behemoth and the station the main landmark is the interesting neo-Romanesque **Tempio Monumentale**, erected in 1923.

Nine kilometres east of Modena lies the **Abbey of Nonantola**, founded in 652 by the Lombard abbot Anselmo, rebuilt in the 12th century and suffering various Baroque vicissitudes since. The portal, however, retains its beautiful carving by the workshop of Wiligelmo. The church is dedicated to Pope St Sylvester, buried in the choir, while the crypt contains 64 columns with carved capitals and the tomb of another holy pope, St Adrian III.

ACTIVITIES
Modena sponsors an Antiques Fair on the 4th Saturday and Sunday of every month in the Piazza Grande (except in July and December). Sept–May is the concert, ballet, and opera season at the Teatro Comunale, while from late October to May plays are performed at the Teatro Storico.

WHERE TO STAY (tel prefix 059)
The palatial ******Canalgrande**, Corso Canalgrande 6, tel 217 160, has richly decorated public rooms, with frescoes on the ceiling and chandeliers, and plush, air-conditioned bedrooms with modern comforts. Ancient trees grace the hotel's pretty garden (L85–165 000). The *****Hotel Estense**, Via Berengario 11, tel 242 057, is a few minutes' walk east of Piazza Grande, offering unpretentious but comfortable rooms with the option of air conditioning; guarded parking for your car; L30–55 000 without bath, L42–75 000 with. Even more centrally located at Via Farini 44, tel 223 618, *****Roma** has rooms in a 17th-century Este property, fitted out with a garage (L55–80 000, all rooms with bath). The ****Albergo Centrale**, near the cathedral on Via Rismondo 57, tel 243 248, has freshly renovated rooms; L26–40000 without bath, L30–54 000 with. An economical choice, ***Sole**, Via Malatesta 45, tel 214 245, is also near the Duomo, with seven basic but nice rooms without bath, L33 000.

EATING OUT
Modena's kitchen has a long and notable tradition. In the heart of Emilia's pig country, it prides itself on its varieties of salumeria and its prosciutto; minced pork fills its tortellini and its famous main course, *zampone*, pig's trotter, which is boiled and sliced. Modena's balsamic vinegar is distilled from Trebbiana grapes; after a few years of being diligently poured from one barrel to another it achieves a delicate taste, between sweet and sour. The plump cherries of Vignola are among the best in Italy. Modena is also the best place to taste true, natural Lambrusco, which must be drunk young (a year or so old) to be perfectly lively and sparkling; the test is to see if the foam vanishes instantly when poured into a glass. There are three main kinds: the grand *Lambrusco di Sorbana*, the mighty *Lambrusco di Santa Croce*, and the amiable *Lambrusco di Castelvetro*.

The cathedral of Modenese cuisine is a restaurant almost as famous as the real cathedral, **Fini**, Piazzetta San Francesco, tel 214 250. Founded in 1912, Fini has an almost endless menu of hearty regional pasta (lasagne and tortellini prepared in a variety of ways, the *pasticcio di tortellini* is exceptional), meat dishes such as the famous *zampone* and *bollito misto*, and appetizers (hams and sausages and salami), all deliciously prepared; closed Mon, Tues and 27 July– 25 Aug, L50–60 000. Two newcomers on the Modena restaurant scene are rapidly gaining a reputation as well: the very elegant **Borso d'Este**, Piazza Roma 5, tel 214 114, with a light, experimental menu of such dishes as shrimp and artichoke salad, risotto with Venetian radicchio and marrow flowers, duck in balsamic vinegar. Equally imaginative desserts, and French and Italian wines; closed Sat lunch, Sun and Aug (L50–70 000). The other newcomer **Vinicio**, Via Cantelli 3, tel 217 810, does an excellent job of adapting the rather heavy local cooking to modern tastes—try tortelli with ricotta and spinach. Good salads and vegetables, and meat courses prepared with balsamic vinegar; excellent wine list (L45 000). **Zelmira**, Via S. Giacomo 27, tel 222 351, is a fine, old-fashioned restaurant serving good old-fashioned Modenese cooking for L28–33 000.

The Modenese Apennines

At Modena you have your chance to break away from the flatlands of the Po by taking a detour south into the Apennines. Near the border with Tuscany the mountains achieve majestic proportions and are usually covered with snow—and skiers. Otherwise, you won't find a prettier place for a walk or a picnic in all of Emilia-Romagna.

GETTING AROUND
From Modena's coach station there are five buses a day to Fiumalbo, to Fanano-Sestola four a day, to Vignola every hour.

TOURIST INFORMATION
Sestola: Via Passerini 18, tel (0536) 82 324. For a ski report, (0536) 223 222.

Cherries, Pinnacles, and Bathroom tiles
The hills just south of Modena have perfect updraughts for hang-gliding and sail planes, especially around **Pavullo** and **Montecreto**, In April the emerald green foothill region around **Vignola** and **Savignano** is covered with the lacy blossoms of Vignola's famous cherry trees. The third week of April is given over to a cherry blossom festival; June, however, is the time for cherry gluttony—and Vignola produces the best in the land. From here you can continue further south to **Guiglia** and the peculiar erosion pinnacles of Rocca Malatina, located in the **Parco Naturale dei Sassi**. There is a fine 11th-century country church just south of Guiglia, at **Pieve Trebbio**, with lovely primitive capitals inside.

To the southwest of Modena, **Sassuolo** is the centre of Italy's flourishing ceramic tile industry, which has been booming since the country's famous designers have discovered that people spend money on decorating their bathrooms and kitchens as well as their persons. It also produces *Nocino*, a liqueur flavoured by green walnuts that must be picked on St John's Day.

The most striking scenery is to be had around **Sestola**, a winter and summer resort near the highest peak of the Northern Apennines, **Monte Cimone** (2165 m). From Sestola you can visit a pretty glacial lake, the **Lago della Ninfa** and the **Giardino Esperia**, planted by the local Alpine club in 1950 at the Passo del Lupo. The garden is interesting as the Passo del Lupo is a botanical frontier, and contains both Alpine and Apennine flowers, trees, and herbs. To the east, near Montefiorino, there are more fascinatingly strange early medieval carvings in the church of **Rubbiano**. Montefiorino was a stronghold of the Resistance in World War II and declared a free republic for two months in 1944; there is a small museum of the Resistance in the village.

Another excursion from Sestola is to **Pian Cavallaro** and from there to the summit of Monte Cimone for a unique view—on a clear day you can see both the Tyrrhenian and Adriatic seas, and all the way north to the Julian Alps and Mont Blanc. You can also make the ascent from the old village of **Fiumalbo**, just below the Passo Abetone that separates Emilia from Tuscany. Two other mountain lakes are just south of Fiumalbo: **Lago Santo** and **Lago Bacio**, connected by an easy footpath. Not as pretty but more unusual is the small **Lago Pratignano**, in the meadows south of Fanano. In the spring its banks are strewn with unusual wild flowers and carnivorous plants—bring your waders.

WHERE TO STAY

In Sestola, ******San Marco**, Via Delle Rose 2, tel (0536) 62 330, is a delightful hotel in a Renaissance villa, surrounded by a lovely garden and tennis courts in the midst of a pine grove; open June–Sept and 20 Dec–March, L75–105 000. Near San Marco, *****Tirolo**, Via delle Rose 19, tel (0536) 62 523, is also endowed with tennis courts and very comfortable rooms (end of June–Sept, Christmas–March, L40–50 000). Pleasant, small, and open all year, ****Sport Hotel**, Via delle Ville 116, tel (0536) 62 502, has rooms for L28–35 000 without bath and 35–42 000 with. Sestola's best restaurant is **Il Faggio**, Via Libertà 68, tel (0536) 62 211, where the dishes are all based on fresh, locally available ingredients—try the venison or boar (L35 000).

In Fiumalbo, there are numerous small hotels, especially at Dogana Nuova near the ski resort, and a youth hostel, **Cimone** up at Il Chioso, 10 km north of Abetone, tel (0536) 73 137, open all year; L10 000 a person a night.

BOLOGNA

'You must write all the beautiful things of Italy,' said the Venetian on the train, but the man from Bologna vehemently shook his finger. 'No, no,' he insisted. 'You must write the truth!' And it is precisely that, a fervent insistence on the plain truth as opposed to the typical Italian delight in appearance and *bella figura* that sets Bologna apart. A homespun realism and attention to the detail of the visible, material world are the main character- istics of the Bolognese school of art (art scholars may recall Petrarch's comment that while only an educated man is amazed by a Giotto, anyone can understand a Bolognese picture). The city's handsome, harmonic, and well-preserved centre disdains imported marble or ornate stucco, preferring honest red brick. Bologna's municipal government, long in the hands of the Italian Communist Party, is considered the least corrupt and most efficient of any large city in the whole country. In the 11th century it was the desire for truth and law that led to the founding of the University of Bologna, whose first scholars occupied themselves with the task of interpreting the law codes of Justinian in settling disputes over investitures between pope and emperor. And it is Bolognese sincerity and honest ingredients in the kitchen that has made *la cucina bolognese*, by common consent, the best in all Italy.

'La Dotta', 'La Grassa', and 'La Rossa' (The Learned, The Fat, and The Red) are Bologna's sobriquets. It may be full of socialist virtue but the city is very wealthy and cosy, with a quality of life often compared to Sweden's. The casual observer could well come away with the impression that the reddest thing about Bologna is its telephone booths and its suburban street names—Via Stalingrado, Via Yuri Gagarin, and Viale Lenin. But Bologna is hardly a stolid place—its bars and cafés and squares are brimming with youth and life, and there is a full calendar of concerts from New Wave to jazz to Renaissance madrigals, as well as avant-garde ballet, theatre, and art exhibitions. But visitor beware: in July and August Bologna is as exciting as the luncheon meat that bears its name.

History

Born as the prosperous Etruscan outpost of Felsina, and renamed Bononia by the Gauls, Bologna grew up at the junction of the Via Emilia and the main road over the Apennines from Florence. Dominated by Ravenna for centuries, Bologna broke away in the 11th century and became an independent *comune* in the 12th and 13th centuries, a golden age when it was one of the principal cities of the Lombard League and a prominent Guelph community. As such it warred with Ghibelline Modena, and defeated that city in the Battle of Fossalta in 1249, capturing Enzo, King of Sardinia and natural son of Emperor Frederick II, whom Bologna kept as a reluctant guest in a nice little castle until his death in 1272.

Bologna became an unwilling part of the Papal States in 1278, though for the next few centuries power was held by various regimes: Milanese Viscontis and rebel Viscontis, papal legates, and most famously the Bentivoglio family (1401–1506), whose name translates quaintly as 'Wish-you-well' and who heralded the flowering of local culture despite a sensational family saga of assassination, high-living and questionable legitimacy—the paternity of Annibale, father of the great art patron Giovanni II, was decided by a throw of the dice. Like their allies and protectors the Medici of Florence, the Bentivoglio never aspired to the status of princes, preferring to hold various offices as 'first citizens', while keeping all effective power in their hands. Giovanni II ruled for 43 years, until ousted by Pope Julius II, after which Bologna was ruled directly by a papal legate.

Bologna witnessed one of the turning-points in Italian history when Charles V insisted on being crowned emperor in its basilica of San Petronio instead of in Rome, which his imperial troops had mercilessly sacked two years previously. Charles felt that going to Rome would seem like an act of contrition, and such was the low standing of papal authority that when he told Pope Clement VII that he did not need to seek crowns, but that crowns sought after him, the pope could only agree. Charles's coronation, on 24 February 1530, both as Emperor and King of Italy, was celebrated with tremendous pomp (marred only when the weight of his imperial suite caused the collapse of a temporary wooden bridge from the Palazzo di Podestà to San Petronio, resulting in a score of casualties). Although no one knew it at the time, Charles would be the last emperor ever to be crowned by a pope, ending a 700-year tradition that began with Charlemagne; at the same time it marked the beginning of three centuries of foreign domination in Italy and the first symptoms of death for the Renaissance. Luigi Barzini notes that from then on the Italians put away their bright clothes and began to wear black in the Spanish style, as if they were in mourning—just as they would don black shirts under Mussolini.

In the 19th century Bologna was the birthplace of Guglielmo Marconi, who carried out his first experiments on the radio at the Villa Grifoni, and of Ottorino Respighi the composer (1819–1930), whose music was popularized abroad by his fellow Emilian, Toscanini. But it was also at this time that Bologna took the lead in the Italian socialist movement—as well as enduring the brunt of the fascist reaction of the twenties. And though it was on the Gothic Line from 1943–45 and the scene of fervid partisan activity—one of the very few big cities to free itself before the Allied troops arrived—Bologna emerged from the War relatively unscathed. The city's historic centre is considered one of the best-preserved and maintained in Italy, much to the credit of the city administration's policy of 'active preservation'—old houses in the centre are gutted and renovated for municipal public housing, maintaining the character and diversity of the old quarters.

Nor is this the first time that Bologna has found a creative solution to its housing needs. One of the first things you notice in Bologna is how every street is lined with arcades, or *portici*. The original ones date from the 12th century when the *comune*, faced with a housing shortage caused by 10,000 university students, ordered rooms to be built over the streets on to existing buildings. Over time the Bolognese became attached to them and the shelter they provided from the weather; now it claims 35 km of *portici*, more than any other city in the world.

GETTING AROUND

By Air: Bologna's airport G. Marconi is to the northwest in the Borgo Panigale, tel 311 578; city bus No 91 links it to the Station. Bologna has flight connections with London, Rome, Pisa, Sardinia and Sicily.

By Train: Bologna is one of the prime nodes of the FS rail network, with frequent and fast connections to Venice, Florence, Milan, Ravenna, and Rimini, and just about anywhere else. For information tel 246 490. Because of the tragic ultra-Right bombing here in August 1980 that killed 85 people, Bologna is the one station in Italy certain to inspect your bags minutely if you leave them at the *Consigna*. The station itself is a 10–15-minute walk from the centre; bus 21 or 22 will get you there quicker.

By Bus: The bus station is near the FS at Piazza XX Settembre, tel 248 374, with buses every hour for Ferrara, Imola, Modena, and Ravenna. City bus information may be had at 1/1 Piazza Re Enzo near Piazza Maggiore, tel 247 005. Bus 3 goes to the Fiera and Modern Art museum, bus 22 to the Porta Saragossa.

By Car: Bologna is easy to get to, just off the A1 between Milan and Florence; A13 connects the city to Venice, A14 to Ravenna and Rimini. It's not so easy, however, to negotiate through, with a typical Italian imbroglio of pedestrian and one-way streets without any place to park. Most of the sights, however, are within easy walking distance of each other.

TOURIST INFORMATION

Piazza Maggiore 6, tel (051) 239 660; Via G. Marconi 45, tel 236 602; also at the station, tel 246 541.

Piazza Maggiore

The centre stage of Bolognese public life is the Piazza Maggiore and its antechamber, the **Piazza Nettuno**. The latter is graced with the virile and vaguely outrageous **Fountain of Neptune**, 'who has abandoned the fishes to make friends with the

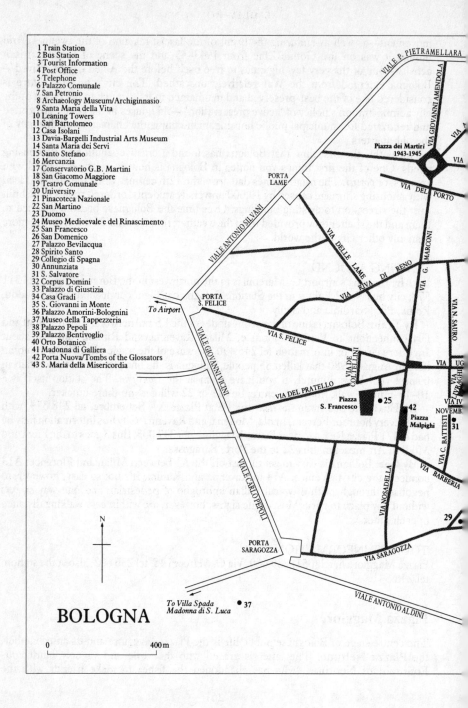

1 Train Station
2 Bus Station
3 Tourist Information
4 Post Office
5 Telephone
6 Palazzo Comunale
7 San Petronio
8 Archaeology Museum/Archiginnasio
9 Santa Maria della Vita
10 Leaning Towers
11 San Bartolomeo
12 Casa Isolani
13 Davia-Bargelli Industrial Arts Museum
14 Santa Maria dei Servi
15 Santo Stefano
16 Mercanzia
17 Conservatorio G.B. Martini
18 San Giacomo Maggiore
19 Teatro Comunale
20 University
21 Pinacoteca Nazionale
22 San Martino
23 Duomo
24 Museo Medioevale e del Rinascimento
25 San Francesco
26 San Domenico
27 Palazzo Bevilacqua
28 Spirito Santo
29 Collegio di Spagna
30 Annunziata
31 S. Salvatore
32 Corpus Domini
33 Palazzo di Giustizia
34 Casa Gradi
35 S. Giovanni in Monte
36 Palazzo Amorini-Bolognini
37 Museo della Tappezzeria
38 Palazzo Pepoli
39 Palazzo Bentivoglio
40 Orto Botanico
41 Madonna di Galliera
42 Porta Nuova/Tombs of the Glossators
43 S. Maria della Misericordia

VIALE P. PIETRAMELLARA

VIA GIOVANNI AMENDOLA

Piazza dei Martiri
1943-1945

VIA DEL PORTO

PORTA
LAME

VIALE ANTONIO SILVANI

VIA DELLE LAME

VIA RIVA DI RENO

VIA G. MARCONI

VIA N. SAURO

PORTA
S. FELICE

To Airport

VIALE GIOVANNI VICINI

VIA S. FELICE

VIA DE
COLTELLINI

VIA UG

VIA IV
NOVEMB.

31

VIA DEL PRATELLO

Piazza
S. Francesco

• 25

42

Piazza
Malpighi

VIA C. BATTISTI

VIALE CARLO PEPOLI

VIA NOSADELLA

VIA BARBERIA

29 •

N

PORTA
SARAGOZZA

VIA SARAGOZZA

BOLOGNA

To Villa Spada
Madonna di S. Luca   • 37

VIALE ANTONIO ALDINI

0 _____ 400 m

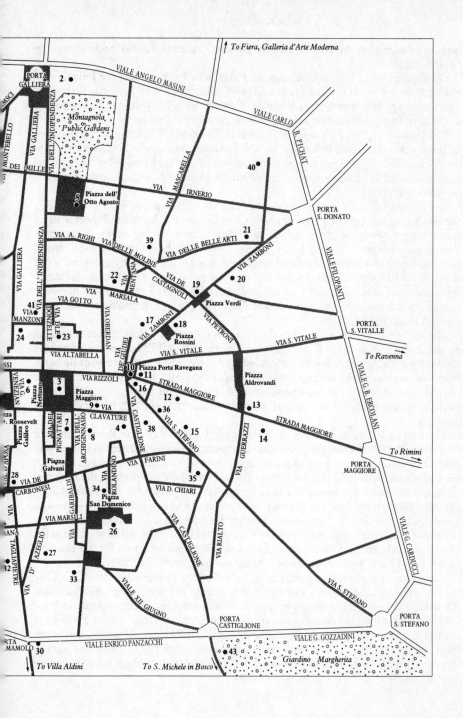

pigeons', designed in the 16th century by Tomaso Laureti of Palermo and executed by Giambologna.

Occupying part of both squares are the **Palazzo di Re Enzo** and the **Palazzo del Podestà**, begun about the same time and remodelled in 1484 by Aristotile Fieravanti, who went on to design part of the Kremlin. The corners of the **Voltone** (the big portico in front) contain 16th-century statues of Bologna's four patron saints.

The **Basilica di San Petronio**, by Antonio da Vicenza (1390), is the largest structure on the square, yet had the Bolognese had their own way, this temple to their patron saint would have been far grander, and even larger than St Peter's in Rome— but the Cardinal Legate ordered them to spend their money on the university's Archiginnasio instead of on municipal prestige.

San Petronio's façade was never finished. The white and red marble stripes, recalling the city's heraldic emblem, only made it up to the door. The **central portal** has a remarkable doorway, with bas-reliefs of biblical scenes by one of the finest early Renaissance sculptors, Iacopo della Quercia of Siena. He began them in 1425, just as Lorenzo Ghiberti was finishing the more famous doors of the Baptistry in Florence (for which job della Quercia had been one of the unsuccessful contestants). Like Ghiberti's, these doors are landmarks in the visual revolution of the early Renaissance. They seem strangely modern—especially the panel of Adam and Eve, which would not look out of place in Rockefeller Center.

Missing from the front of San Petronio, however, is Michelangelo's colossal bronze statue of Pope Julius II, commissioned by that pope in 1506, after he regained the city for the Papal States. Julius also commissioned a large castle in the centre of Bologna. Both were torn to bits by the population as soon as the Pope's luck changed; and to rub salt into his wounded pride, the bronze was sold as scrap to his arch-enemy, Alfonso I of Ferrara, who melted it down to cast an enormous cannon—which he fondly called 'Julius'.

The lofty, spacious interior saw the crowning of Charles V as Holy Roman Emperor and, according to tradition, the conversion of a visiting monk named Martin Luther who became so nauseated by papal pomp and pageantry that he decided to go ahead and start the Reformation. In 1655 the astronomer Cassini traced the meridian on the floor and designed the huge astronomical clock, which tells the time with the shaft of light admitted through an oculus in the roof. Two of the chapels are noteworthy—one with 15th-century frescoes of Heaven and a rather alarming Hell, and another containing Lorenzo Costa's *Madonna and Saints*, both to the left as you enter. In the museum at the end of the aisle are models of some of the grand schemes proposed for the church's façade (10–12 and 4–6, closed Tues, Thurs, and Sat afternoons).

The crenellated **Palazzo Comunale**, to the right, incorporates the 1287 Casa Accurso (the arcaded section), and the 1425 annexe by the fierce-sounding Fieravante Fieravanti, father of Aristotile. Over the main door presides a bronze statue of Pope Gregory XIII, a native of Bologna and the reformer of the calendar. Under a canopy to the left is a beautiful terracotta Madonna by Nicolò dell'Arca, a Renaissance sculptor from Apulia who left his best work in Bologna. Inside, reached by Bramante's grand staircase (1505), the municipal art collection, contains an important collection of Bolognese art (open 9–2, 9–12:30 Sun, closed Tues).

Via dell'Archiginnasio

Bologna's excellent **Museo Civico Archeologico** is just to the left of San Petronio, on Via dell'Archiginnasio 2 (open 9–2, Sun and holidays 9–12:30, closed Mon; adm). In its dim and dusty wooden cases is crammed one of Italy's best collections of antiquities: beautifully wrought items from the Iron Age Villanova culture, native Italics who were eventually conquered by the Etruscans; and works from Bologna's beginnings as the Etruscan colony of *Felsina*. Felsina may have been a frontier town but it is richly represented here with tomb art, proto-chesspieces shaped like gravestones and the embossed bronze *Situla* (urn) *di Certosa*, similar to works found in Tuscany. The Etruscans traded through their port of Spina (near Comacchio) with the Greeks, whose lovely Attic vases are one of the highlights of the museum. There are a few items from Gallic Bononia, Roman artefacts (a lovely copy of Phidias' bust of Athena Lemnia), and an excellent Egyptian collection.

Further down the street is the **Archiginnasio** (open Mon–Sat 9–1:45), its walls covered with the escutcheons and memorials of famous university scholars. After 1800 this became the municipal library, but if you ask the porter, he'll admit you to the old anatomical theatre, shattered by a bomb in the War and painstakingly rebuilt in 1950. The monument in the piazza in front of the Archiginnasio commemorates Luigi Galvani, the 18th-century Bolognese discoverer of electrical currents in animals who gave his life and name ('galvanize') to physics.

Just off the Piazza Maggiore on Via Clavature, the church of **Santa Maria della Vita** is worth a visit for the terracotta *Lament Over the Dead Christ* by Nicolò dell'Arca, a work harrowing in its grief and terror, a 15th-century version of Edvard Munch's *Scream*.

Two Leaning Towers

In the passage under Via Rizzoli (the main street flanking the Piazza Maggiore) you can see the remains of the old Roman Via Aemilia which followed the same route. To the left the end of Via Rizzoli is framed by the beautiful **Piazza Porta Ravegnana** and a pair of towers that might have wandered off the set of *The Cabinet of Dr Caligari*. After the initial shock wears off, however, fondness invariably sets in for this odd couple, the Laurel and Hardy of architecture. The taller one only manages to look respectable because the other is so hilarious.

According to legend, the towers were built in 1119 as a competition between two powerful families. The winner, the svelte 97 m **Torre degli Asinelli** is only 1 m shorter than the campanile of St Mark's in Venice, and certainly the highest in Bologna, which once had 180 such skyscrapers. It tilts about 1 metre out of true, though the 500 steps that lead to the top are more likely to make your head spin than the tilt. The view over Bologna is worth the trouble, however (open daily 7–7; adm). Its side-kick, the **Torre Garisenda**, sways tipsily to the south, 3.2 m out of true; the Garisenda contingent failed to prepare a solid foundation, and when they saw their tower pitching precariously, gave up. In 1360 it became such a threat to public safety that its top was lopped off, leaving only a squat, 48 m stump; inscribed in its base you can read what Dante wrote about it in the *Inferno*.

From the towers, five streets fan out to gates in the eastern walls of the old city. One of these, the palace-lined **Strada Maggiore**, follows the route of the Via Aemilia, passing first in front of **San Bartolomeo**, notable for its two works by Bolognese masters: Albani's *Annunciation* in a chapel on the south aisle and Guido Reni's *Madonna*. In the 19th century Italians considered the 'Divine Guido' as their greatest artist; since then he has taken a precipitous and admittedly deserved fall from fashion. At No 13 Strada Maggiore, the **Casa Isolani** is one of the best-preserved 13th-century houses left in Bologna; at No 44 the 18th-century **Palazzo dei Giganti** (or Davia) contains the **Museum of Industrial Art** and the **Galleria Davia-Bargellini**, housing Vitale da Bologna's famous *Madonna with Teeth*, perhaps the most characteristic work of the Bolognese school (open 9–2, Sun 9–12:30, closed Mon). At this point the *portici* of the street intermingle with those of the arcades of the city's Gothic jewel, **Santa Maria dei Servi**, which contains among its works of art a rare *Madonna* by Cimabue (in the apse) which you'll need to illuminate to see.

Santo Stefano

Via Santo Stefano, another of the streets radiating from the two towers, may be reached from Santa Maria dei Servi on Via Guerrazzi (where, at No 13, the 14-year old Mozart was elected to the Academia Filarmonica). A few blocks up is Bologna's most charming church, or rather quartet of churches, with a cloister and two chapels thrown in, now all known as **Santo Stefano**. Three of the churches of this unique and harmonious Romanesque ensemble face the Piazza Santo Stefano—the **Crocifisso**, with an altar on its façade, begun in the 11th century and containing an ancient crypt below its raised choir. To the left is the entrance to **San Sepolcro**, a curious, polygonal temple containing the equally curious tomb of Bologna's patron San Petronio, supposedly designed after Jerusalem's Holy Sepulchre and adorned with bas-reliefs. The church of **SS. Vitale e Agricola**, to the left of this, is Bologna's oldest, built in the 5th century, with bits and pieces of old Roman buildings and alabaster windows. The **Cortile di Pilato** beyond this contains an 8th-century Lombard bathtub that has somehow gained the sinister reputation as the basin where Pontius Pilate washed his hands. From here you can enter the fourth church, the 13th-century **Trinità**, and the lovely 11th-century **Cloister**, and the **Museum**, with works by Simone de' Crocifissi and others (all open 9–12 and 3–6).

The lovely Gothic **Palazzo della Mercanzia** (1384) is further up Via Santo Stefano; it has an ornate loggia by the architect of San Petronio, Antonio di Vincenzo.

Via Zamboni

Again from the leaning towers, Via Zamboni leads directly to Piazza Rossini. Rossini (composer of the *Barber of Seville* and *William Tell*), studied from 1806–10 at the **Conservatorio G.B. Martini** on the piazza and spent much of his life in a nearby palazzo. The Conservatory houses a museum and gallery with original scores by Mozart, Monteverdi and Rossini, and oddly, paintings by Thomas Gainsborough (open weekdays 9–1). Also on the square, **San Giacomo Maggiore**, begun in 1267 and enlarged since, was the parish church of the Bentivoglio, who adorned it with art. Giovanni II hired the Ferrarese Lorenzo Costa to paint the frescoes in the **Cappella Bentivoglio** of the *Triumph of Death*, the *Apocalypse*, and *Madonna Enthroned* in the midst of

Giovanni II and his family. The Bentivoglio seem pleasant enough, though the mobs of Bologna hardly found them so; when the Bentivoglio were deposed they tore their palace apart brick by brick. The fresco itself was commissioned in thanksgiving for Giovanni's escape from hired assassins. The fine altarpiece in the chapel is by Francesco Francia, a native of Bologna, while the high-mounted tomb opposite, of Anton Galeazzo Bentivoglio (1435) is by della Quercia. Be sure to ask the sacristan to let you into the **Oratory of Santa Cecilia**, frescoed by Costa and Francia.

The **Teatro Comunale**, further up Via Zamboni in Piazza Verdi, was built in 1763 over the ruins of the Bentivoglio Palace by Antonio Bibiena. The Bibiena clan of theatre and stage designers were in demand all over Europe in the 17th and 18th centuries, and did much to popularize the typical Baroque tiers of boxes, which the Teatro Comunale preserves behinds its 1933 façade.

The University
Beyond this is the **University**, which was moved in 1803 from the too-central Archiginnasio (where the students could cause trouble) into Pellegrino Tibaldi's Mannerist **Palazzo Poggi**, topped by the eclectic observation tower, or *speculum*, and adorned with Tibaldi's frescoes of Ulysses. Famed for medicine, astronomical studies (Copernicus studied here), and the sciences, Bologna was best known for its studies of jurisprudence, ever since its founding by the Glossatori (who 'glossed' or annotated Justinian's codes); the university maintained its reputation as one of the best schools in Europe until the Counter-Reformation, when the papal repression wiped out free thought in Italy. One its students, Vacarius, founded the law school at Oxford in 1144.

There are a number of small museums connected to the university, including a museum of the university itself on Via Zamboni 33. The **Botanical Garden**, open weekday mornings, is at Via Irnerio 42, or, for a sobering picture of what Fido looks like under the skin, the **Anatomy Museum of Domestic Animals**, at Via Belmeloro 12 (on request, weekdays 9–1); the **Museum of Human Anatomy**, Via Irnerio 48, is open Mon–Fri 10–12, while on Saturdays from 10–1 you can pore through the **Museum of Astronomy**, Via Zamboni 33.

Pinacoteca Nazionale
Across from the university, at Via Belle Arti 56, Bologna's most important artworks are housed in the Pinacoteca Nazionale (open 9–2, Sun 9–1, closed Mon; adm). Represented here are 14th-century Bolognese artists, of which Vitale da Bologna emerges as the star with his intense *St George and the Dragon* and other detached frescoes; also some by visiting artists like Giotto, the Vivarini brothers and Cima da Conegliano of Venice, and a fine collection of works from the Ferrara school (Costa, Cossa, and Ercole de' Roberti's *St Michael Archangel* and a fragment of a tearful *Magdalene*). Later Bolognese paintings are by Francesco Francia, Aspertini, Marco Zoppo, and Tibaldi. Raphael's *S. Cecilia in Estasi* was moved here from a local church; near it are pictures by Perugino, Giulio Romano, and Parmigianino. Beyond these are fine works of Bologna's 16th–18th century eclectic revival—the Carracci brothers, Guido Reni, and Guercino.

Via Belle Arti, heading back towards the centre, passes several fine old palaces and ends at the intersection with Via Mentana. Turn left here for **San Martino**, which was remodelled in the 15th century; Paolo Uccello painted a fresco at that time, lost until

1981 when a delightful fragment was discovered. Other masterpieceshere are by Francia and Costa.

North and West of Piazza Maggiore

The Via dell'Indipendenza is the main thoroughfare linking the Piazza Maggiore to the station. In its northern reaches is the attractive **Montagnola Public Garden** and the bustling **Piazza Otto Agosto**, site of a busy popular market on Fridays and Saturdays. The 10th-century **Duomo di San Pietro**, on Via dell'Indipendenza near Piazza Nettuno was remodelled in the Baroque style, and like Venice's old cathedral, was the local symbol of the Vatican's authority as opposed to that of the municipality, embodied in the basilica of the city's patron saint. And as such, it received little affection and is not very interesting, unless you are a devotee of St Anne, whose skull is the chief treasure, a gift of Henry VI of England. The Romanesque campanile is a survivor of the original structure, and it's worth while strolling down Via Altabella and its adjacent lanes for a view of medieval Bologna, with its ancient towers.

Opposite the cathedral, Via Manzoni leads to the Palazzi Fava, site of the **Museo Civico Medioevale e del Rinascimento**, with an interesting collection of armour, ceramics, Majolica plates, the carved tombs of medieval scholars, ivory works, glass, a 13th-century English cope, and more (open 9–2, Sun 9–12:30, closed Tues; adm).

Via Ugo Bassi, the westerly section of the Via Aemilia, leads to the narrow and lively **Piazza Malpighi**, with one of Bologna's old city gates, the 13th-century **Tombs of the Glossatori**, and the lovely Gothic **San Francesco**, with its fine old towers and beautiful 14th-century marble altar screen sculpted by Pier Paolo dalle Masegne. At Via Barberia 13, just south of Piazza Malpighi, you can learn about the art of weaving rugs and tapestries at the **Museo Storico Didattico della Tappezzeria** (open weekdays 9:30–12, and pm Thurs and Sat from 3:30–7). Back towards the centre, Via C. Battisti runs south of Via Ugo Bassi to the 17th-century **San Salvatore**, with a striking

San Francesco Church

Mannerist *Marriage of St Catherine* (1534) by Girolamo da Carpi, a work generally acclaimed as his masterpiece, and a polyptych by Vitale da Bologna.

South of Piazza Maggiore

From the Archiginnasio, continue south down Via Garibaldi to **San Domenico**, built in 1251 to house the relics of St Dominic, founder of the Order of Preaching Friars. Dominic built a convent on this site and died here in 1221, and though the exterior and interior of his church have been frequently remodelled, it's well worth a visit for his tomb, the *Arca di San Domenico*, to which many hands contributed, including those of Nicolò Pisano and his school, who executed the beautiful reliefs of the saint's life; Nicolò dell'Arca, who received his name from this work, added the cover of the sarcophagus and the fine statues on top, while a 20-year-old Michelangelo sculpted SS. Petronius and Proculus and an angel. Among the other works, look for a bust of St Dominic by Nicolò dell'Arca and the beautiful wooden inlaid choir stalls.

From San Domenico, Via Marsili leads to Via D'Azeglio, with the **Palazzo Bevilacqua**, a 15th-century Tuscan-style palace where the Council of Trent took refuge from a plague in Trent in 1547. Just north of here, at Via Val D'Aposa 6, is the lovely brick and terracotta façade of **Spirito Santo**. Via Marsili, now Via Urbana, continues to the **Collegio di Spagna**, the Spanish college founded in 1365 by Cardinal Albornoz for Spanish students. In the Middle Ages Bologna had many such colleges, but this one (an official piece of Spanish territory at the time) is the only one to survive. Cervantes studied here, as did St Ignatius.

From here Via Saragozza wends down to the **Porta Saragozza**, from where begins the portico to beat all porticoes—winding 4 km up the hill to the **Sanctuary of the Madonna di San Luca**. The church was built to house an icon attributed to St Luke, and the 666-arch portico was added between 1674 and 1793; the views from the sanctuary over Bologna are famous (if you're not up to walking, there's a bus from the Porta Saragozza). Other famous viewpoints in the hills south of Bologna are from **San Michele in Bosco**, a hospital in a former Olivetan convent (bus 28) and from the **Villa Aldini** (bus 12), built on the site where Napoleon admired the panorama of the city skyline. From the villa you can walk down towards the Porta Mamola and the fine 15th-century church of the **Annunziata**.

To the northeast of Bologna, in the Zona Fieristica, the **Galleria d'Arte Moderna** is at Piazza della Costituzione 3, with an especially strong collection by Giorgio Morandi (open 10am–8pm, closed Tues).

ACTIVITIES

During the school term, you have only to seek out the student bars around the university and the posters in their windows to find out about concerts, films, exhibitions, and dances; alternatively, check out the listings in Bologna's oddly named local paper, *Il Resto del Carlino*, which does not mean 'the remains of little Charles' as many foreigners suspect, but the change from an old coin called a Carlino; when you bought a cigar, instead of change you could have a newspaper. In June especially, but also in July and August, dance and music are performed in the Piazza Maggiore. The drama season at the Teatro Duse runs from November to May, while operas are performed at the Teatro

Comunale for a brief season in the winter. Every April Bologna hosts the International Childrens' Book Fair; otherwise look in at Feltrinelli, Via dei Giudei 6/c for books in English. Bologna is also the only city in Italy to have a municipally run gay organization, the Cassero di Porta on Via Saragozza, tel 433 395, which sponsors films and discussions during the week and discos on the weekends.

Bologna is a good city for nightowls: try **Osteria dell'Orsa**, by the University at Via Mentana 1/F, tel (051) 270 744, which has dinners (around L25 000), wine, and live Italian jazz on Wednesday and Friday nights—when you should reserve (open until 2 am). **Mabuse**, also by the University at Via delle Moline 2/F, tel (051) 228 971, is a 'multimedia' bar, specializing in the visual arts, poetry, and sporadic concerts. Quaffers of German beer can wash away any lingering *weltschmerz* at **Del Cantinone**, Via del Pratello 56/a, tel (051) 523 524 (open till 2 am; dinners available for L18 000); this area, around Via del Pratello and Piazza Malpighi, is one of the liveliest after dark; **Margot**, Via del Pratello, tel (051) 267 498 has wine and inexpensive meals in the L15 000 range until 4 am; **Master Club**, Via del Pratello 13, tel (051) 267 400 has regular jazz concerts.

WHERE TO STAY (tel prefix 051)

The ***** **Royal Hotel Carlton**, Via Montebello 8, tel 249 361, is an ultra-modern palace in the centre of Bologna, with six floors of deluxe, flamboyant designer rooms. The lobby and bar are striking, and there's a spacious underground garage. All rooms are carpeted, air-conditioned, and furnished with colour televisions and frigo-bar; L300 000. Most of Bologna's other smart hotels are on the outskirts of the city. For a swimming-pool, baby-sitting service, and air conditioning, check in at the ******Crest**, Piazza della Costituzione in the Fair district, tel 372 172, with very nice rooms for L95–190 000. ******Grand Hotel Elite**, to the west outside Porta S. Felice at Via Aurelio Saffi 36, tel 437 417, is an elegant and very comfortable hotel, air-conditioned with TVs and frigo-bars in the rooms. It is the proud possessor of one of Bologna's best restaurants, the Cordon Bleu (see below); rooms L95–180 000.

A minute from the Piazza Maggiore, on Via D'Azeglio 9, the ***Hotel Roma**, tel 274 400, is a fine choice in medieval Bologna, offering large, if slightly eccentric, air-conditioned rooms with good beds; another charming feature is its roof garden bar, L85–95 000. ***Nettuno**, Via Galliera 65, tel 247 508, is only a few blocks from the station; friendly management, 1950s-era rooms, L78–90 000. **Orologio**, in the heart of town at Via IV Novembre 10, tel 231 253, has cosy rooms for L35–72 000 with bath, or L26–52 000 without.

There are no bargains in Bologna, but rooms are cheaper at *Farini**, a couple of blocks from the Piazza Maggiore on Via Farini 13, tel 271 969, an older hotel run by a charming older man; large old-fashioned rooms for L30–48 000 with bath, L28–40 000 without. Brighter but a bit further from the centre, *Pensione Ferraresi**, Via Livraghi 1 (off Via Ugo Bassi), tel 221 802, with very pleasant rooms upstairs for L40–48 000.

EATING OUT (See also ACTIVITIES, above)

In Italy's gastronomic capital, eating out is a pleasure, whether you plump for a meal at a star restaurant or head for one of the city's traditional late night inns, or *osterie*. Locally they call it *cucina petroniana*, and it gave Italy its tagliatelle, tortellini (filled with cheese) and lasagne, which the Bolognese like to tint green with spinach. *Alla bolognese* means with a meat and tomato sauce that only Bologna really knows how to prepare. The city is known for Italy's best pâtés, its mixed platters of salami, its veal dishes, and, of late, for its innovations in the kitchen. Colli Bolognesi wines are produced in the hills just to the south of the city, and for an authentic Bolognese repast, order a fruity amber-coloured Albana, white Trebbiano, or dry Sauvignon to accompany your antipasti; a Bianco dei Colli with your tagliatelle, or a heartier Barbera bolognese for pasta dishes from the oven; with veal dishes, a Merlot dei Colli; with red meat, the robust Cabernet dei Colli; if you order seafood, a Riesling or energetic Pignoletto from the Colli, the latter of which is also good with cheese.

One of Bologna's most innovative and unusual restaurants is the **Cordon Bleu** in the Hotel Elite (see above); innovative in that the chef's speciality is the revival of recipes from the Renaissance; it appears that the old doges and popes, the Farnese, Este, Sforza, and Medici tribes were into Nouvelle Cuisine—many dishes feature exciting combinations of meat or fish with fruit, served with unusual wines from all over Italy. There are two *menu degustazione* offerings—the *piccolo* (with wine) and the *grande* (without) both around L80 000; closed Sun and 25 July–25 Aug. Bologna's most celebrated restaurant, **Pappagallo**, in the pretty Piazza della Mercanzia 30, tel 232 807, has an enchanting dining room formerly frequented by such notables as Alfred Hitchcock and Albert Einstein. The new management and chef have yet to receive the unreserved approval of the Bolognese, but it's worth a visit for its local specialities and great wines and atmosphere (L55–70 000; closed Mon and Aug).

South of San Francesco, a new restaurant, **Silverio**, Via Nosadella 37/1, tel 330 604, is the talk of the town, its pale green and grey dining rooms furnished with beautiful antiques and serving gourmet delights—old-fashioned *cappellettone* and delicious second courses, desserts, and wines, all for L35–50 000. Closed Mon. **Il Tartufo**, Via del Porto 34, tel 521 057, features both traditional Emilian dishes and delightful new creations like rabbit with black truffles or lamb in vinegar (L40–50 000).

Le Tre Fecce, located in the medieval Casa Isolani on Strada Maggiore 19, tel 231 200, is another delightful place to dine in 'Fat city'; complementing the beautiful Gothic decor are dishes like tagliatelle with asparagus tips and breast of pheasant with white grapes, rich desserts and fine Trebbiano wine (L50 000; closed Sun eve, Mon and mid-June–mid-July). Near the cathedral, **Notai**, Via dei Pignattari 1, tel 228 694 is a Bolognese classic, with a piano bar upstairs and an elegant Victorian dining room down, with delicious and unusual filled pasta dishes and unorthodox but succulent variations on local favourites that change every month, and Bologna's best wine list (L60 000 for a marvellous *menu degustazione*). Another favourite, **Franco Rossi**, Via Goito 3, has a very pleasant and friendly ambience, and specialities based on Bolognese traditions—tagliatelle and good risotto, duck with green peppercorns or devilled scampi (L45–65 000, closed Sun in summer, Tues in winter).

There are even good bargains to be had at the Bolognese table: **Da Bertino**, Via Lame 55, tel 522 230, offers properly prepared and very tasty Bolognese cuisine without fancy frills; closed Sun; full meals with wine L20–30 000. **Boni**, an old-timer on Via Saragozza 88, tel 585 060, closed Sat, will make you happy with tortelli in cream, roast meats, and omelettes with balsamic vinegar for around L20 000. For a bit more you can dine at one of the city's best, **Trattoria Sale e Pepe**, Via de' Coltelli 9, tel 228 532, with innovative specialities cooked to a T with a Neapolitan touch, great desserts and wine for L25 000.

One of the liveliest places in town is the **Hostaria Alla Botte**, Via Sant'Isala 30, tel 333 678—try their *tortellaccio dalla Botte* for primo (L25 000, closed Tues); or join the students at **Osteria del Matusél**, by the University at Via Bertoloni 2/2, tel 231 718, where you can fill up on onion soup or potato gnocchi, couscous or curry, and a glass of house wine for L15 000 (open till 12:45, closed Sun).

Bologna is also your chance to try something out of the ordinary: vegetarian at **Clorofilla**, Strada Maggiore 64, tel 235 343 (L11 000, closed Sun); Italian natural foods at the **Centro Naturista**, Via Albari 6, tel 278 860 (L10 000, closed Sun); Macrobiotic at **Oggi si vola**, Via Urbana 7, tel 585 308 (L12 000, closed Sun); Argentine at **Marsala**, Via Marsala 17/19, tel 273 881 (L20 000, closed Sun). There are two good Chinese restaurants on Via S. Vitale: **Pechino**, no. 15, tel 232 504 (L20 000) and **Tonshen**, no. 71, tel 267 543 (L15 000); French at the **Torre Eiffel**, Via Rolandino 1/2, tel 230 938 (L24 000, closed Mon), or American at **McDonald's**, Via Indipendenza 2.

East of Bologna

Between Bologna and the Adriatic are a hotchpotch of attractions—Italy's most important trotting course and the Imola motorway, the Rubicon and the fine medieval town of Brisighella, Faenza, Italy's most famous ceramics town, and Forlì, decorated by Mussolini.

GETTING AROUND

Between Bologna and Rimini trains are fast, frequent, and occasionally furious (in August). Driving, you will have a choice between Autostrada A14 or nerveracking Route 9. For trips into the Apennines you'll have to rely on buses from Forlì. For Brisighella there are trains from Faenza; Bagno di Romagna and other towns near the Tuscan frontier can be reached by bus from Forlì.

Imola

Between Bologna and Rimini there are a number of possible excursions. Nearest to Bologna, **Imola** is locally as well known for its restaurant, a pilgrimage shrine for grand gourmets, as it is internationally for motor racing. As in Roman days the Via Aemilia divides the town in two; an old convent at Via Emilia 80 has a small **Pinacoteca**, with local works (open only first and third Sun of each month 10–12). In the 18th-century cathedral you can pay your respects at the tomb of Imola's patron saint Cassian, a schoolteacher whose martyrdom was particularly unpleasant: he was stabbed with the pens of his students. **Imola Castle** to the south of the Via Aemilia was defended by Caterina Sforza, widow of the last Lord of Imola, until its capture by Cesare Borgia in 1500. In the nearby village of **Dozza**, the castle houses the **Enoteca Regionale Emilia-Romagna**, where you can sample the region's wines from 10–12 and 4–7.

Faenza

'Faience ware' was born in the 16th century in Faenza, with the invention of a new style of majolica: a piece was given a solid white glaze, then rapidly, almost impressionistically, decorated with two tones of yellow and blue. It caused a sensation, in such demand throughout Europe that Faenza became a household word.

Today Faenza has regained much of its 16th-century renown as a ceramics centre. There are 500 students enrolled in its Istituto d'Arte per la Ceramica and experimental laboratory, as well as some 60 artists from around the world who run workshops in town. For a state-of-the-art tour, be sure to visit the workshops of Carlo Zauli, on Via della Croce 6; Ivo Sassi, Via S. Filippo Neri 3; Goffredo Gaeta, Via Ceonia; as well as old-timers Angelo Biancini, on Via San Nevolone and Domenico Matteucci on Piazza II Giugno 8. Among several buildings and palaces adorned with majolica, the most splendid is the Liberty-style **Palazzo Matteucci** in Corso Mazzini. Pick up a town plan at the **Consorzio Ceramisti Faenza**, Voltone Molinella 2, near Piazza del Popolo, tel (0546) 22 308.

The **Museo Internazionale delle Ceramiche**, in the centre of town on Viale Baccarini, was founded in 1908 and repaired after its bombing in the War (open 9:30–2:30 and 3:30–5:30, Sun 9:30–1, closed Mon; adm). It houses a magnificent collection of ceramics from all over Italy; pieces from Faenza adorned with giraffe-necked Renaissance ladies were typical nuptial gifts. There are fine Liberty-style pieces by Domenico Baccarini and Francesco Nonni, and downstairs an excellent collection of ceramic art by Picasso, Matisse, Chagall, and Rouault. Faenza's unfinished Renaissance **Duomo** in the central Piazza della Libertà, has some good period sculpture inside; the **Museum**, on Via Severoli (open 9:30–12:30, 2:30–4:30, closed weekend afternoons), contains a good collection of paintings of Romagna artists, sculpture by Alfonso Lombardi and works formerly attributed to Donatello.

Brisighella

Some 12 km south of Faenza on the Florence road, Brisighella is a charming village and thermal spa in the Lamone Valley. The sharp cliffs overhead are crowned by splendid towers of the 12th-century **Rocca** and the **Torre dell'Orologio**, the latter originally a respectable guard tower with a clock slapped on front in the 18th century. Brisighella produced much of the clay fired in Faenza's kilns—next to the village you can see the walls left in the hills by the old quarries. So precious was this cargo borne by the village's mule caravans that a protected, elevated passageway, the **Via degli Asini**, was built through the centre of town, which, in case of attack, could be sealed up at either end. In the Rocca you can visit the **Museo del Lavoro Contadino**, with a collection devoted to the region's peasant culture and work (open 10–12 and 3:30–7:30, closed Mon; weekends only in the winter). On the edge of town there's an ancient Romanesque church, the **Pieve del Tho**. Several ceramics workshops still operate in Brisighella; from the end of June to the first week of July the city hosts an elaborate Medieval Festival, with music, games, feasts, plays, and more.

WHERE TO STAY AND EATING OUT

To Imola's **Ristorante San Domenico** on Via G. Sacchi 1 come gastronomic pilgrims from around the world. Consistently rated in the top five in the country, this holy temple of Italian culinary traditions offers a constantly changing menu of the day, sublimely prepared with the lightest and most delicate of touches. The dining room is as beautiful as the desserts, and the wine list is exquisite enough to shatter a plastic credit card. If you stay away from the champagne, dinner at San Domenico's should run around L100 000; call (0542) 29 000 for reservations, except on Mon and 25 July–27 Aug. Breathing on its sacred heels is a much newer establishment, **Naldi**, Via Santerno 13, tel (0542) 29 581, offering tempting and innovative variations on Emilia-Romagna recipes—pâtés with black truffles, tortellini in walnut cream, stuffed chicken breasts in a charming setting for L45 000.

Italy's best Russian restaurant is located nearby at Toscanella di Dozza: **Katiuscia**, Via Emilia 103/a, tel (0542) 672 349, where you can get mellow on glasnost over bortsch, chicken Kiev, vodka, and much more (L40 000, closed Mon).

In central Faenza, the ***Albergo Vittoria**, Corso Garibaldi 23, tel (0546) 21 508, is an attractive hotel with 19th-century furnishings and a dining room with a fine frescoed ceiling. Rooms without bath L55 000, with L70 000. **Cavallino**, Via Emilia Levante 32, tel (0546) 30 226, is a pleasant choice just outside the centre, with a garage; rooms with bath L50 000. **Torricelli**, Piazza C. Battisti 8, tel (0546) 22 287, is closer to the centre: L35 000 without bath and L42 000 with. **Amici Miei**, Corso Mazzini 54, tel (0546) 661 600, is the most elegant place to eat in Faenza, with its charming antique furnishings, local specialities and a good wine list; L35–40 000.

Brisighella has among its numerous restaurants two exceptional choices: **Gigiolè**, Piazza Carducci 5, tel (0546) 81 209, whose chef has done detailed research into Romagna's medieval traditions at table—ravioli stuffed with rabbit and mint, veal with wild fennel, mulberry pudding, and more (L45 000; closed Mon and 15 Feb–14 Mar, and 2 weeks in July). The second, **La Grotta Osteria con Uso di Cucina**, Via Metelli 1, tel (0546) 81 829, offers three daily menus—the bargain, the regional, and the *degustazione*, the latter highly imaginative. Rated one of the best restaurants in Emilia-Romagna, the prices are amazing—you can dine well for L15–25 000, depending on which menu you select; closed Tues and 15–31 Jan and 1–15 June.

Mussolini's Birthplace, the Blood of Jove, and Trotters

TOURIST INFORMATION
Forlì: Corso della Repubblica 23, tel (0543) 25 532.
Bagno di Romagna: Via Lungosavio 14, tel (0543) 911 026.

Forlì

Forum Livii on the Via Aemilia was elided over the years into Forlì, a city split between an attractive old town and the architectural legacy of Mussolini, who was born in nearby Predappio. The centrepiece of old Forlì is the striking 12th-century **Basilica di San Mercuriale**, with a good campanile, a 13th-century lunette of the Magi by the school of Antelami, and an interesting interior. The **Duomo**, on Corso Garibaldi, has a temple façade; note the painting inside of 15th-century firemen. On Corso della Repubblica, the good **Museo Archeologico e Pinacoteca Saffi** (open 9–2, Sun 10–1, closed Sat), contains works by local artist Marco Palmezzano, Fra Angelico, and others, as well as Flemish tapestries, ethnographic exhibits, and ceramics. The nearby **Santa Maria dei Servi** merits a stop for the finely sculpted tomb of Luffo Numai (1502); further south Forlì's castle, the picturesque 15th-century **Rocca di Ravaldino**, was another possession of Caterina Sforza and the birthplace of her son Giovanni de' Medici (better known as 'Giovanni delle Bande Nere', a famous *condottiere* and father of Cosimo I, first Duke of Tuscany). It now serves as a prison.

Into the Apennines

South of Forlì there are three principal routes into Tuscany, each passing through pretty mountain scenery. Some of the best is in the Montone Valley, the main route to Florence. On the way there is the planned Renaissance townlet of **Terra del Sole**, begun in 1564 in the form of a perfect rectangle, not far from the small spa of **Castrocaro Terme**. Ruined medieval castles haunt the next towns, **Dovadola** and **Rocca San Casciano**. Dante's beloved Beatrice spent several summers in the old medieval town of **Portico di Romagna**; the Portinari house where she lodged can still be seen in the main street. Near the Tuscan frontier, the 9th-century abbey of **San Benedetto in Alpe** sheltered Dante after his unsuccessful bid to return to Florence from exile (described in the *Inferno*, Canto XVI, 94–105). In San Benedetto you can hire horses to explore the region's valleys, especially the lovely **Valle dell'Acquacheta** with its bucolic, stepped waterfall. The rapid Brusia river is popular with canoeists and kayakers.

The narrow alternative road (Ter. 9) passes through the Sangiovese ('Blood of Jove') wine country around **Predappio**, where Mussolini was born, the son of an anarchistic blacksmith, and where his remains were buried in the local cemetery in 1957, near those of his common-law wife, Rachele. Mussolini made his hometown the seat of the local *comune* and embellished it with public buildings, leaving the old *comune*, **Predappio Alta**, alone under its overgrown castle. In Predappio Alta, the **Cà de Sanvès** is the place to taste the local ruby reds, open 10–12 and 3 to midnight, closed Tues.

From Forlimpopoli on the Via Emilia, the road heads south for **Bertinoro**, an old town famous for its wine and hospitality. And such were the squabbles over guests in old Bertinoro that a column was erected in front of the 14th-century **Palazzo Comunale** and hung with rings, one belonging to each family. To whichever ring a stranger tethered his horse decided which family would be his host. Nearby **Polenta** has a fine 9th-century Byzantine-Romanesque temple. The main SS310 continues into the scenic Upper Bidente valley, where the **Ridracoli dam** and Romagna Aqueduct have recently been completed in the midst of a heavily forested region (open weekends only). There are ski facilities in the valley at Monte Campigna near the old Tuscan town of **Santa Sofia**. Further south, near **Balze**, there's more skiing at Monte Fumaiolo, on whose slopes the river Tiber (Tevere) begins its 418 km journey to Rome. **San Piero in Bagno** and **Bagno di Romagna**, with thermal and mud baths, are popular summer resorts here.

Cesena

Cesena, site of the European Trotting Championships in August, was in the 14th–15th centuries one of the jewels of the Malatesta clan. Their castle still dominates the town, while a 1452 basilica built for Domenico Malatesta Novello is the main sight, housing the **Biblioteca Malatestiana** (open 8–1 and Mon 4–8) with a priceless collection of manuscripts. Between Cesena and Rimini, at **Savignano** the road crosses a poor excuse for a stream that most authorities accept as the shadowy Rubicon, which divided what was then Gaul from Roman Italy, and which Julius Caesar crossed with his army, breaking the law but hoping there would be no one to oppose his entry into Rome. Today it separates respectable Emilia-Romagna from the international bikini beach boogaroo at Rimini.

WHERE TO STAY AND EATING OUT

In Forlì the best place to stay and eat is the ******Principe**, just outside the centre at Viale Bologna 153, tel(0543) 34 630, air-conditioned, comfortable modern rooms for L95–120 000; the restaurant, open for dinner only, serves good land- and seafood like salmon tarragon; around L35 000, closed Fri and Aug. For a treat local gourmets travel 8 km to Forlimpopoli to dine at **Al Maneggio**, in Selbagnone, tel (0543) 74 20 42, located in a villa next to a delightful garden; the kitchen's specialities are based on an elegant simplicity; superb risotto, *gamberone*, desserts, and wines (L45–50 000). In Bagno di Romagna, ******Hotel Tosco-Romagnolo**, Piazza Dante 2, tel (0543) 911 014, open Easter–Nov is a charming place to stay, relax, and dine in one of Italy's most enchanting restaurants, **Paolo Teverini** where the food is based on Romagna-Tuscan country traditions—delicious pâtés, crêpes, rack of lamb, and wines, from L40 000; rooms L90–130 000. If your pockets tend to be more flushed than flush, Bagno di Romagna's ***Giovanna**, Via Manin 35, tel (0543) 911 057 will put you up in one of its 7 rooms with a bath for a mere L23–26 000.

Ferrara

There's been a certain mystique attached to Ferrara ever since Jacob Burckhardt called it 'the first modern city in Europe' in his classic *Civilization of the Italian Renaissance*. Whether or not Burckhardt was right can be debated endlessly; what is certain, however, is that the famous 'additions' laid out in the Renaissance to the medieval city were far too ambitious. Ferrara, even in the most brilliant days of the Court of Este, never had more than 30,000 citizens—not enough to fill up the long, straight, rational streets laid out in the 9-km circuit of the walls.

But what was a failure in the Renaissance is a happy success today; if Italian art cities can be said to come and go in fashion, Ferrara is definitely in, popularized by a well-received international campaign to save its uniquely well-preserved walls. Protected within these bastions is a charming Medieval-Renaissance city. Thanks to the rather tyrannical Este, it was one of the brightest stars of Renaissance culture, with its own fine school of art, led by the great Cosmè Tura, Ercole de' Roberti, Lorenza Costa, and Francesco del Cossa. Poets supported by the Este produced three of the Renaissance's greatest *ottava rima* epic poems—Boiardo's *Orlando Innamorato* (1483), Ariosto's better known continuation of the same story, *Orlando Furioso* (1532), and Tasso's *Gerusalemme Liberata* (1581), all of which praise the ducal family.

FERRARA

0 ———— 400 m
0 ———— 400 yds

VIA PORTA CATENA

VIALE ORLANDO FURIOSO

VIALE XXV APRILE

BELVEDERE

VIA BAGARO

VIA PAVONE

ERCOLE I D'ESTE

VIA BORSO

● 26

VIA GUARINI

Parco Massari

● 27

Cimiterio Israelitico

VIALE PO

● 2

● 3

CORSO PORTA PO

● 24

● 29

● 25

VIA ARIOSTO

● 23

VIA CAVOUR

VIA ARMARI

● 28

CORSO PORTA MARE

PIAZZA ARIOSTEA

VIA BORGO DEI LEONI

VIA PALESTRO

VIA MONTEBELLO

VIA CASSOLI

VIALE

CORSO VITTORIO VENETO

Stadio

CORSO B. ROSSETTI

PIAZZA PIAVE

PIAZZA XXIV MAGGIO

IV NOVEMBRE

CORSO ISONZO

VIA ARPAGRANDE

VIA PIANGIPANE

RAMPARIS PAOLO

PIAZZA SACRATI GARIBALDI

PIAZZA CASTELLO

1
5
8
21
6

PIAZZA CATTEDRALE

VIA CORSO

VIA GIOVECCA

VIA MORTARA S. ROCCO

RAMTARI

VIA CALDIROLO

VIA IPPOLITO D'ESTE

Po di Volano

CORSO PORTA RENO

PIAZZA TRENTO E TRIESTE

VIA SCIENZE

VIA SAVONAROLA

10
11
13

● 20
● 19
12

VIA BASSI

15
16

14

VIA SCANDIANA

VIA GHISILIERI

VIA BORGOVADO

VIA MAYR

VIA D'ESTE

VIA POMPOSA

VIA BOLOGNA

VIALE

VIA XX SETTEMBRE

VIALE BALUARDI

18

VIA PORTA D'AMORE

17

VIALE ALFONSO

VIALE VOLANO

● 22

VIA COLOMBAROLA

1. Tourist Office/ Telephones
2. Train Station
3. Bus Station
4. Post Office
5. Castello Estense
6. Palazzo Comunale
7. Duomo
8. Teatro Comunale
9. San Francesco
10. Casa Romei

11. Savanarola's House
12. Corpus Domini
13. Palazzina di Marfisa d' Este
14. Palazzo Schifanoia
15. Oratorio dell' Annunziata
16. Santa Maria in Vado
17. Palazzo di Ludovico il Moro
(Archaeology Museum)
18. Sant' Antonio in Polesine
19. Ariosto's Family House

20. Palazzo Paradiso
21. Palazzo Roverella
22. San Giorgio
23. Palazzo del Diamante
24. Ariosto's House
25. San Benedetto
26. Certosa/S. Cristoforo
27. Civic Museum of Modern Art
28. Chiesa del Gesù
29. San Maurello

N

History

Ferrara grew up on a formerly navigable branch of the Po, and until the 17th century based its economy on river tolls, the salt pans of Comacchio, and the rich agricultural land of the Delta. Always ruled by a powerful local family, it was the rise of the Este in 1250 that made Ferrara a great Guelph city, an outpost of papal power in the north. The Este family produced some of the most interesting characters of the Renaissance; there was Nicolò II (1361–88), the friend of Petrarch; Alberto (1388–93) who founded the university of Ferrara; Nicolò III (1393–1441), reputedly the father of hundreds of children on both banks of the Po, and the villain who perpetrated one of the tragic love stories of his day. He had his young wife Parisina and natural son Ugo executed for their love. The other sons of Nicolò III, Leonello, Borso and Ercole I (1471–1505), met happier fates and were responsible for the city's great cultural flowering. Ercole I had the first addition to the city (known as the Herculean Addition) designed by his architect Biagio Rossetti. His offspring, Isabella (wife of Francesco Gonzaga), Beatrice (married to Lodovico Sforza, *Il Moro*), and Cardinal Ippolito were among the cultured and influential people of their day. His heir Alfonso I (1505–34) married the beautiful and unjustly maligned Lucrezia Borgia, who ran a brilliant and fashionable court, patronizing Ariosto and Titian, while her husband spent his days casting huge cannons. Their son, Ercole II (1534–59) married Renée (or Renata) daughter of Louis XII of France and a Calvinist, who welcomed Rabelais to Ferrara and sheltered John Calvin himself in Ferrara under an assumed name; eventually relations with Rome became so touchy that she had to be sent away.

The last Este Duke, Alfonso II (1559–97), patron of the unstable and unruly Tasso, was considered the best-educated and most courtly ruler of his day—at the expense of his overtaxed and discontented people. When he died without an heir, Ferrara was glad to see the last of the family and was ruled thereafter by a papal legate (though a branch of the Este family continued to rule as dukes of Modena and Reggio until the time of Napoleon). Without the largesse of the dukes, Ferrara became an artistic backwater; in the early 1700s even the great Duomo suffered a remodelling at the hands of Baroque vandals. During World War I, however, the 'Metaphysical School' of painting (De Chirico, Carrà, De Pisis, Morandi, etc) had its origins in the city. Inspired by the great frescoes in the Palazzo Schifanoia, the Metaphysicists sought in their art to distil and perceive the ambiguity of reality.

GETTING AROUND

Ferrara's railway station is a 15-minute walk west of the centre (or take city bus 1 or 9). Rail connections are frequent to Bologna, Venice, and Ravenna; for information, tel 770 340. The bus station is near the corner of the Rampari di San Paolo and the Corso Isonzo, tel 25 815; a fine network of lines goes to the coast, to Bologna, Modena, Ravenna, and Rovigo.

Because it is flat and a large number of streets are closed to traffic, bicycles have become the favourite method of transport. The city may be running a bicycle rental scheme; inquire at the tourist office. If not, try the Deposito da Felisatti, at Via Palestro 27.

TOURIST INFORMATION
Piazzetta Municipale 19, tel (0532) 48 280.

The Castle and the Cathedral
A grim symbol of Este power looms over the exact centre of Ferrara, the imposing **Castello Estense** (open 9–1 and 2:30–6, Sat and Sun 9 am–8 pm; adm expensive). Designed to look like a Victorian factory building, it would have succeeded except for the broad moat and drawbridges. It was begun in 1385 by Nicolò II after a local revolt, though later Este transformed it into their chief residence, its crenellations replaced by white marble balustrades, its great halls adorned with art. A few decorated rooms survive: the *Salone* and *Saletta dei Giochi* (the games room, belonging to the children) and the fine *Sala dell'Aurora* (the dukes' bedroom) and *Camerina dei Bacchanali* are the most interesting. The tour includes Renée's Calvinist chapel, the dungeon where Ugo and Parisina languished before their beheading, and the prison where Giulio and Ferrante, brothers of Alfonso I, spent their lives after attempting a conspiracy. Even the life of a cultured duke wasn't all peaches and cream.

The Corso dei Martiri leads first to the **Palazzo del Comune**, built in 1243 and adorned with statues of Nicolò III and Borso; in the Piazza della Repubblica stands a statue of Savonarola, a native of Ferrara. Beyond this the pretty rose-coloured **Duomo**, begun in 1135 by Wiligelmo, was finished a century later. Its glory is a marble portico, carved with a magnificent 13th-century scene of the *Last Judgement* by an unknown sculptor; Maestro Nicolò executed the bas-reliefs of St George in the lunette over the door. The lovely candy-striped campanile is from the 15th century; the arcade on the north side retains its original twisted columns. The interior was remodelled in the 17th century and contains much good art, although the best is in the **Cathedral Museum** (10–12 and 3–5, 4–6 in summer; closed Sun), featuring the lovely marble *Madonna of the Pomegranate* by Iacopo della Quercia, a master early Renaissance sculptor from Siena, and a set of famous organ shutters painted by Cosmè Tura, with an *Annunciation* and a *St George*, and a relief of the months that once adorned the cathedral exterior. The picturesque market portico flanking the cathedral in the Piazza Trento e Trieste was erected in 1473.

Renaissance Palaces
From behind the cathedral Via Voltapaletto, Via Savonarola will take you in a few minutes to the **Casa Romei** (8:30–12:30 and 3–6:30, closed Mon; adm), a fine example of a typical Renaissance palace, built for a banker who married an Este in 1445. Besides its charming frescoes, fireplaces and elegant courtyards, there are some expressive detached frescoes moved here from Sant'Andrea and other deconsecrated churches. Further down, behind the church of San Girolamo is the **Corpus Domini** (9:30–11:30 and 3:30–5, closed weekends), containing the austere tombs of Alfonso I, Alfonso II and Lucrezia Borgia.

A block up Via Ugo Bassi, in a garden at Corso della Giovecca 170, the late Renaissance **Palazzina di Marfisa d'Este** once formed part of a much larger complex of buildings, now unfortunately lost. Marfisa, a friend of Tasso, was beautiful and

279

eccentric, and the subject of several ghost stories; it seems that she enjoyed riding through the city at midnight in a wolf-drawn carriage. The interior of her little palace, with its unusual *grotteschi* frescoes on the ceiling, has been admirably restored and fitted with period furnishings (adm).

Palazzo Schifanoia
Ferrara's most famous palace, the **Palazzo Schifanoia** (1385), stands a few blocks east at Via Scandiana 23 (Via Ugo Bassi to Via Madama). Schifanoia translates as 'disgust with boredom', and it would be difficult to stay bored in the delightful **Salone dei Mesi**, a secular masterpiece painted for Borso d'Este by Cosmè Tura, Ercole de' Roberti and Francesco del Cossa. The scenes of mythological and allegorical subjects peopled by charming 15th-century aristocrats are believed to have been inspired by Petrarch's *Triumphs*—in each month a different god is seen to 'triumph', most famously Venus in the month of April, with a rare scene of a Renaissance kiss. The palace has other rooms with beautiful ceilings, housing an eclectic collection of medieval (note the alabaster Passion of Christ from Nottingham), ancient, and Egyptian art, open daily 7am–7pm; adm.

Palazzo di Lodovico Il Moro
Turn right at the walls at the end of the street and continue to Via XX Settembre. At No 124 stands the elegant **Palazzo di Lodovico il Moro** designed by Rossetti and erroneously named after Beatrice d'Este's Milanese husband, though it never belonged to him. It has frescoes on the ground floor by Raphael's pupil, Garofalo, and upstairs the excellent **Museo Archeologico Nazionale**, recently restored, with its collection of finds from some 4000 tombs in the Greek-Etruscan necropolis of Spina (near Comacchio), including excellent 5th–4th-century BC Attic vases, a splendid gold diadem, a tripod from Vulci, and two pirogues (canoes) carved from tree-trunks in a later Roman period. Spina was the Etruscan port on the Adriatic; until the Gauls chased the Etruscans out of Emilia-Romagna in the 4th century BC the town knew a long period of prosperity.

Just outside the walls (through the Porta Romana) **San Giorgio** was Ferrara's cathedral until the 12th century, worth a look for the sumptuous 1475 **Tomb of Lorenzo Roverella**, Pope Julius II's physician. Within the walls, near the museum and just off Via Beatrice d'Este, the convent of **Sant' Antonio in Polesine** has some fine frescoes, mostly from the 14th century, and inlaid choir stalls (open 9–11:30 and 3–5, closed Sun).

On the way back to the centre, on the Via delle Scienze in the heart of medieval Ferrara, the 13th-century **Palazzo Paradiso**, was the former seat of the university. Today it holds a library devoted to Ariosto, with the complete manuscript of *Orlando Furioso* and Ariosto's tomb.

The Herculean Addition
North of the castle are the streets laid out by Biagio Rossetti for Ercole I, the Herculean Addition, which more than doubled the size of 15th-century Ferrara. Not long after the fall of the Este dynasty, travellers noted that many of the streets here were abandoned

and overgrown; even today they feel somewhat melancholy and quiet. Rossetti's show-piece **Palazzo dei Diamanti**, in the very centre of the Addition, takes its name from the 8500 pointed diamond-shaped stones that stud the façade—diamonds being not only the best friends but also the emblem of the Este. It houses the **Pinacoteca Nazionale** (9–2, Sun 9–1, closed Mon; adm) with works mainly of the Ferrara school—Turà, Cossa, Costa, Roberti, the sweet Raphaelesque Garofalo (a favourite of the 18th century), and Dossi, as well as detached frescoes from old churches and palaces. There's also a Carpaccio, *Death of the Virgin*, and 19th- and 20th-century art on the ground floor in a separate museum, the **Gallerie Civiche d'Arte Moderna** (open 9–1, 3:30–7; 3–6 in winter; adm).

The Diamond Palace lies at the junction of two main streets; down one, the Corso Porto di Po, Via Ariosto leads to the **Casa di Ariosto** (8–12 and 3–6, closed holidays) which the poet built for himself, 'small', he described it modestly, 'but suited to me'.

To the east of the Diamond Palace, on the Corso Porta Mare 9, the **Palazzo Massari** (open Apr–Sept 9–1 and 4–7; winter 9:30–1 and 3–6:30; adm but free first Sun and Mon of each month), houses the **Civic Museum of Modern Art** and the **Documentary Museum of the Metaphysicists**, with slides and reproductions of major metaphysical works, covering the origins of the movement in Ferrara. The nearby **Palazzina dei Cavalieri di Malta**, Corso Porta Mare 7, seat of the Knights of Malta 1826–34, contains a collection of 19th-century and 'Liberty' art (same hours).

The Via Borso from the Massari Palace leads to the **Certosa**, founded by Borso d'Este in 1452, now the city cemetery; its church of **San Cristoforo** is embellished with a huge luck-giving St Christopher. The **Cimitero Israelitico**, along the walls of Via Porta Mare, was founded in the 17th century, when Ferrara had a considerable Jewish population, many of whom were refugees from Spain; strewn with wild flowers, it is one of the prettiest spots in the city.

The Walls

Ferrara's well-preserved 9-km circuit of red brick walls are easiest seen by bicycle. Dating mainly from the 15th and 16th centuries, the best stretch is between the Porta Mare and the northern ex-Porta degli Angeli, built by Rossetti. Plans are in hand to extend a pedestrian and bicycle-only 'Green Addition' from the walls to the banks of the Po.

Around Ferrara

Most of the region around Ferrara is flat and somewhat dreary. **Argenta**, on the river Reno to the southeast of Ferrara, is mainly visited for its restaurant (see below). Its attractive quattrocento church of **San Domenico** now houses a small art gallery, with works by Garofalo and others. **Cento**, under its 14th-century castle (on the main road to Modena), was the birthplace of the Baroque painter Guercino (1591–1666) and the ancestors of Disraeli; a representative collection of the former's paintings is in the **Pinacoteca Civica** on Via Matteotti 10.

WHERE TO STAY

(tel prefix 0532)

The ****Ripagrande, Via Ripagrande 23, tel 34 733, housed in the Renaissance Beccari-Freguglia palace in the medieval quarter of town, offers the most memorable lodgings in Ferrara. The ground floor retains its Renaissance decor, heavy-beamed ceiling, and a fine restaurant as well. The 40 rooms upstairs are very modern, all equipped with kitchenettes and sitting rooms, air conditioning, and colour TV. Pleasant courtyards at the back; parking; and bicycle rentals available to guests (L110–160 000). Another top hotel, the ****Astra, Viale Cavour 55, tel 26 234, on the main street to the station, is a sturdy, long established, and well-furnished hotel, with air conditioning, frigo-bars, and a good restaurant (L90–160 000). ***Europa, Corso Giovecca 49, tel 33 460, is a fine old hotel in a 17th-century palace, with parking and breakfast only; doubles without bath L48–52 000, with L68 000. Right on the same square as the castle, the **Annunziata, Piazza Repubblica 5, tel 34 855, has pleasant rooms and showers in the hall for L33–36 000. The *Nazionale, Corso Porta Reno 32, tel 35 210, is also in the heart of town, near the cathedral; fine rooms, all doubles have private bath (L40 000). Another choice by the station is Stazione, Piazzale Castellina 1, tel 56 565 (L40 000 with bath, L30 000 without).

EATING OUT

Ferrara's most famous dish (and the favourite of Lucrezia Borgia) is *salama da sugo*—a kind of salami that is cured for a year, then gently boiled and eaten with a spoon. The bakers of Ferrara are famous for their X-shaped bread *ciupèta*; little caps of pasta, *capelletti*, often filled with pumpkin, are another local speciality. When Renée of France came to Ferrara she brought her own vines, the origins of the local viniculture and the delicious *Vino di Bosco*. The Aldobrando, Porta Mare 45, tel 752 648, bases its menu solidly on Ferrara's cuisine, especially *salama da sugo*; closed Sun, L35 000. One trendy place in town, the Ristorantino, Vicolo Mozzo Agucchie 15, tel 761 517, also serves local specialities, with especially good capelletti and imaginative second courses served in a large and attractive dining room (L30–35 000). For fish, Le Chat qui Rit, Via Carlo Mayr 21, tel 761 347, serves up the best in town, shipped directly every day from Chioggia and delicately prepared, accompanied by an excellent wine list (L50 000; closed Tues and 20 July–1 Sept). Italia, Largo di Castello 32, tel 35 775, offers dishes like *salama da sugo* and capelletti, fish, and grilled lamb for L25–35 000.

Ferrara also has a unique place to drink: Al Brindisi, Via degli Adelardi 11 near the cathedral, tel 37 015. It occupies the same address as the ancient Taverna da Chiucchiolino, opened in 1435, and although the furnishings are much newer, the atmosphere is often just as jovial as it was in the 15th century. For coffee and delicious pastries, try the Caffè Europa, at Via della Giovecca 51.

In Argenta, the restaurant the Italians rave about is called Trigabolo, Piazza Garibaldi 4/5, tel (0532) 804 121, another gourmet enclave in an unlikely spot. In its elegant dining room you can feast on delicious first courses like ravioli stuffed with artichokes with basil sauce, cannoli with turbot in clam sauce, ravioli with guinea fowl, *zuppa di pesce*, and more, according to season, while for seconds there are delicacies like goose liver with pears or veal with lettuce cream and almonds. Great wine list and rich desserts; *menu degustazione* L75 000. Closed Tues and the first three weeks of July.

The Coast: from the Po to Ravenna

Buses from Ferrara radiate to the flatlands of the coast. For most people the main attractions along this coast are the Po Delta and magnificent Romanesque abbey of Pomposa, though there are plenty of Italian family lidos in the vicinity if you're tempted to join the summer ice cream, pizza, and parasol brigades.

TOURIST INFORMATION
Lido degli Estensi, Viale Carducci 31, tel (0533) 87 464.
Pomposa: Via Lungomare (summer only) (0533) 88 228.
Lido di Volano: Via Imperiale 11 (summer only) tel (0533) 85 115.
Porto Garibaldi: Viale dei Mille (summer only), tel (0533) 87 580

Bosco della Mésola and the Po Delta

Alfonso II d'Este was the first to start draining the marshes south of the Po Delta. Much of what doesn't support rice paddies these days has been included in the **Parco del Delta del Po**, one of Italy's most important wetlands and a birdwatcher's paradise (see p. 131 Rovigo). Part of the primordial coastal pine forest survives intact in the **Bosco della Mésola**, now a nature reserve; visitors are admitted on Sundays and holidays only from 8 am to sunset. Not far to the east, this varied and ever-changing coastline offers something completely different—a marooned 100-acre patch of dunes, once part of the coast. It's called the 'Moraro', near Italba. Excursion boats plying the small, narrow canals between the reeds explore the mouth of the Po di Goro and the Valle di Gorino, departing from the picturesque fishing hamlets of Gorino, Goro, or Mésola; for information, contact Vincenzino and Luigi Schiavi, Via Vicolo del Faro 1, Gorino, tel (0533) 99 815; or the Hotel Uspa, Piazza Libertà 9, Gorino, tel (0533) 99 817.

Abbey of Pomposa
The main road SS309 follows the old Roman coastal road, the Via Romea. Just over the Po di Goro, it passes through **Mésola** town, with an old hunting lodge, the 'Delizia Estenese' of Alfonso I d'Este, then continues down to the haunting and serene **Abbey of Pomposa**, an 8th-century Benedictine foundation, formerly on its own islet; in its atmosphere of total tranquillity the monk Guido d'Arezzo invented the modern musical scale in the early 11th century. Uninhabited since the 17th century, the abbey is dwarfed by its great **campanile**, adorned with a unique series of mullioned windows which progress tier by tier from a narrow slit on the bottom to a grand *quadrifore* (four arches) on top. The **Church** (7th–11th centuries) has a lovely Byzantine atrium and an interior embellished with colourful 14th-century frescoes, many by the charming Vitale da Bologna; other good frescoes by his school are in the monks' Chapter House. The abbot governed the surrounding territory from the beautifully austere 11th-century **Palazzo della Ragione**. A **Museum** contains items relating to the monastery. The complex is open daily 8–12 and 2–5.

The resorts along the sandy **Lidi di Comacchio** begin at the **Lido di Volano** on the other side of the wetlands of the Valle Bertuzzi, where the setting sun ignites the waters in a thousand colours. Of the resorts the **Lido delle Nazioni** and **Porto Garibaldi** are

Trepponti Bridge, Comacchio

the most interesting and best equipped. The most important town in the area is **Comacchio**, with its famous monumental triple bridge, the **Trepponti**, spanning three of the town's many canals. Comacchio is famed for its eels, farmed in the Valli di Comacchio—if you're in the area between September and December, you can watch the fishermen scoop them up on their way to the sea. Just west of Comacchio stood the ancient Etruscan port of **Spina**—now over four miles from the sea. Its rich necropolis produced the prize exhibits in Ferrara's archaeology museum.

RAVENNA

Innocently tucked away among the art towns of Emilia-Romagna, there is one famous city that has nothing to do with Renaissance popes and potentates, Guelphs or Ghibellines, sports cars or socialists. Little, in fact, has been heard from Ravenna in the last thousand years. Before that time, however, this little city's career was simply astounding—heir to Rome itself, and the leading city of western Europe for centuries. For anyone interested in Italy's shadowy progress through the Dark Ages, this is the place to visit.

There's a certain magic in three-digit years; history guards their secrets closely, giving us only occasional glimpses of battling barbarians, careful monks 'keeping alive the flame of knowledge' and local Byzantine dukes and counts doing their best to hold things together. In Italy, the Dark Ages were never quite so dark, never the vacuum most people think. This can be seen in Rome, but much more clearly here, in the only Italian city that not only survived, but prospered all through those troubled times. In Ravenna's churches, adorned with the finest mosaics ever made, such an interruption as the Dark Ages seems to disappear, and you will experience the development of Italian history and art from ancient to medieval times as a continuous and logical process.

History

Ravenna first became a prominent Roman town during the reign of Augustus. With its port of Classis, the city lay along an important trade and conquest route to Dalmatia and the Danube. With their nearly impregnable setting, surrounded by broad marshes, the military advantage was clear, and Classis became Rome's biggest naval base on the Adriatic. As conditions in Italy became unsettled in the 5th century, the relative safety of Ravenna began to look very inviting to frightened emperors. Honorius moved the capital of the Western Empire here in 402—just in time, with Alaric's sack of Rome coming eight years later. Honorius' sister, a grand Roman lady named Galla Placidia, ruled the city in the emperor's absence, and began to embellish it with churches and monuments befitting its new status. When the Goths attacked Ravenna, Galla Placidia saved the city from the threat by marrying the Gothic king Ataulf. They got on well together, and before his assassination she rode at his side everywhere, even in battle. She returned eventually to Ravenna, and ruled it until her death in 450.

By the 6th century, with sheep grazing in the Roman Forum and cooling off in the ruins of Diocletian's baths, Ravenna had become the accustomed metropolis of Italy. Odoacer and Theodoric made it their capital; under the latter the last flowering of Latin letters took place, influenced by the Gothic king's three famous councillors: Boethius, Symmachus, and Cassiodorus. Boethius, one of the Fathers of the Church, wrote his *Consolation of Philosophy* in Theodoric's dungeon, where the Goths had consigned him after suspecting the philosopher of intrigues with Constantinople. The terrible wars between the Goths and the Eastern Emperor for control of Italy were beginning. In them Ravenna was spared the destruction which the Byzantine generals Belisarius and Narses spread through the rest of Italy; after the Byzantine victory, the city became the seat of the *Exarchs*, the Byzantine viceroys who were to rule increasingly smaller bits of Italy over the next 500 years.

The Greek Exarchs, never popular among their new subjects, nevertheless performed the occasional service of obtaining Constantinople's aid in keeping the Lombards at bay throughout their period of rule. While tolerating the Exarch's presence, the Ravennans were coming to rely increasingly on their own resources; when help from the east failed to appear it was their own citizen militia that defended the city against invaders. So, in the worst times, the city survived as a sort of cultural time capsule, protected by its own efforts—and its surrounding swamps—still maintaining trade and cultural relations with the east, and carrying on the best traditions of classical culture single-handedly.

In 751, the Lombards finally succeeded in taking Ravenna, chasing out the last Exarch and erasing Constantinople's last sure foothold in Italy. Only six years later, however, Pepin the Short's Frankish army snatched it back, and the city was placed under the rule of the popes. Ravenna declined slowly and gracefully in the following centuries. Venice took over its role as leading port of the Adriatic as Classis silted up, eventually becoming completely abandoned. The newer cities of the Romagna, such as Ferrara and Faenza, assumed a larger role in the region's economy, and even Ravenna's ancient school of Roman law was transferred to Bologna, there to become the foundation of Europe's first university.

Despite its declining fortunes, Ravenna still managed to rouse itself in 1177, becoming a free *comune* like so many other towns in the Romagna. During the 13th century, government fell into the hands of the da Polenta family, famous for offering refuge to Dante when a change in Florentine politics made the poet an exile. Dante finished the *Divine Comedy* and died in Ravenna in 1321. In 1441, Ravenna came under the rule of Venice, and enjoyed a brief period of renewed prosperity, lasting until the popes came back in 1509; the economic decadence ensured by papal rule has been reversed only since the 1940s. With the construction of a ship channel and new port, the discovery of offshore gas deposits and the introduction of large chemical industries, Ravenna has now become a booming modern city—just coincidentally one with a medieval centre full of Byzantine mosaics.

The Mosaics

> Either light was born here,
> Or reigns here imprisoned.
> *—Latin inscription in the Sant'Andrea chapel*

In Byzantine times, the greatest gift an emperor could bestow on any dependent town was a few tons of gold and enamel tesserae and an artist. Before Christianity, mosaics were a favourite Roman medium, but not always taken too seriously. They were usually reserved for the decoration of villas. Some reached the level of fine art (see the Naples museum, or the great villa at Piazza Armerina, Sicily), but more often the productions were on the level of the famous 'Beware of the dog' mosaic in Pompeii, or prophylactic images of Priapus. It was the early Christians, with a desire to build for the ages and a body of scriptures that could best be related pictorially, who made mosaics the new medium of public art in the 6th century. Mostly it was an affair of the Greeks, who still had the talent and the resources for it; we cannot say with absolute certainty, but most likely Greek artists from the court of Constantinople created the celebrated mosaics in the churches and baptistries of Ravenna.

Mosaics in Ravenna

Western Christian art was born here, developing from the simple images—the Good Shepherd and the Cross and Stars—to the iconic Christ in Sant'Apollinare Nuovo and the beautiful scriptural scenes in San Vitale. Never, though, did the early mosaicists turn their back on the idea of art; with the ideals of the ancient world still in their minds, they naturally thought of art and religion as going hand in hand, and found no problem in serving the cause of both. Using a new vocabulary of images, and the new techniques of mosaic art, they strove to duplicate, and surpass, the sense of awe and mystery still half-remembered from the interiors of the pagan temples. Try to imagine a church like San Vitale in its original state, with candles—lots of candles—flickering below the gold ground and gorgeous colours. You may see that same light that enchanted the Byzantines—the light of the Gospels, the light from beyond the stars.

GETTING AROUND

Ravenna is not on the main Adriatic railway line, but there are several trains a day from Florence, Venice, Ancona and Bologna (change at Faenza or Ferrara from other cities). The station is on the eastern edge of the old town, next to the ship channel, a short walk from the centre. City buses from the train station or from Piazza del Popolo will take you to Classe or any of Ravenna's nearby lidos. The No 2 bus, from the station, goes past Theodoric's Mausoleum, otherwise a half-hour walk from the centre on a busy highway.

TOURIST INFORMATION

Via Salaria 8/12, tel (0544) 35 404

San Vitale

Bring a bag of 100 and 200 lire coins for the light machines. At first this dark old church may not seem much, but as soon as you pop a coin in the box, the floodlights ignite the 1400-year-old mosaics into an explosion of colour. The mosaics of San Vitale, Ravenna's best, are one of the last great works of art of the ancient world, and one of Christianity's first. The octagonal church, begun in 525 during the reign of Theodoric, is itself a fine example of the surprisingly sophisticated architecture from that troubled age. By the time it was finished, in 548, the city was in the hands of Belisarius' Byzantine army; the famous mosaic portraits of Justinian and Theodora can be taken as the traditional imperial style of political propaganda.

Outside Ravenna, nothing like this church was built, or could have been built, in the 6th century. Far from being the sorry recapitulation of old building forms and styles you might expect, San Vitale was a breathtakingly original departure in architecture—not the last work of the Romans, but the first of the Romanesque. Take some time to admire the exterior, with its beautiful interplay of octagons, arches, gables, and exedrae, pure proportional geometry done in plain solid brick. Inside, the curious double capitals on the columns are no design conceit, but an important 5th-century invention; the trapezoidal *impost block* on top is a capital specially designed to support the weight of arches. Holding up the second-floor galleries and large octagonal cupola was an unusual design problem; these capitals and the eight stout piers around the dome were the solution. We do not know the name of San Vitale's architects, or whether they were Latins or Greeks,

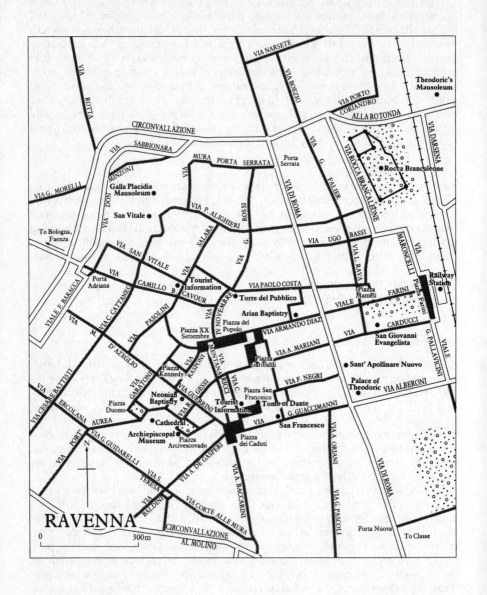

RAVENNA

0   300m

but the year after it was begun, work commenced on the very similar church of SS. Sergius and Bacchus in Constantinople, the prototype for the Hagia Sophia ten years later.

In its structure, the great dome in Constantinople owes everything to the little dome of Ravenna: the innovation of the galleries, for example, to which the women were segregated during services, and the elongated apse cleverly combining the central plan favoured by eastern Christians, and the basilica form needed for a court's religious ceremony. Nowhere in Constantinople, however, or anywhere else in the east will you find anything as brilliant as San Vitale's **mosaics**. Much of the best was undoubtedly lost during the iconoclastic troubles of the 8th century; iconoclasm was fiercely resisted in Italy—indeed it was one of the first causes of the rupture between the Roman and Greek churches—and most of Ravenna's art was fortunately left in peace.

The colours are startling. Almost all the other surviving Byzantine mosaics, in Sicily, Greece and Turkey, are simple figures on a bright gold ground, dazzling at first but somewhat monotonous. There is plenty of gold on the walls of San Vitale, but the best mosaics, in the **choir**, have deep blue skies and rich green meadows for backgrounds, highlighted by brightly coloured birds and flowers. (The usual nomenclature is misleading; the 'choir' was and is the site of the main altar, while the clergy actually sat on the bench around the apse.) The two **lunettes** over the arches flanking the choir, each a masterpiece, show the hospitality of Abraham and the sacrifice of Isaac, and the offerings of Abel and Melchizedek, set under fiery clouds with hands of benediction extended from Heaven. These sacrifices are the two events in the Old Testament that prefigure the Transfiguration of Christ. Around the two lunettes are scenes of Moses and Jeremiah; note the delicately posed pairs of angels holding golden crosses above the lunettes—almost identical to the fanciful figures from earlier Roman art displaying the civic crown of the Caesars. At the front of the choir, the **triumphal arch** has excellent mosaic portraits of the Apostles supported by a pair of dolphins. Look up at the galleries, and you will see more fine portraits of the four evangelists.

The **apse** is dominated by portraits of Justinian and Theodora—mostly, of course, of Theodora, the Constantinople dancing girl who used her many talents to become an empress, eventually coming to wear poor Justinian like a charm on her bracelet. Here she is wearing a rich crown, with long strings of fat diamonds and real pearls. Justinian, like Theodora, appears among his retinue offering a gift to the new church; here he has the air of a hung-over saxophone player, badly in need of a shave and a cup of coffee. His cute daisy slipper steps on the foot (a convention of Byzantine art to show who's boss) of his General Belisarius, to his left. The likenesses are good—very like those in Constantinople, suggesting that the artist may have come from there, or at least have copied closely imperial portraits on display at Ravenna.

It can easily be imagined how expensive it was in the 5th century to make mosaics like these. It is said that the Hagia Sophia in Constantinople originally had over 2 hectares of them, and even the treasury of Justinian and Theodora was not bottomless; consequently most of San Vitale remained undecorated until the 17th-century bishops did the dome and the other parts in a not too discordant Baroque. Recently, the new floor they laid has been pulled up to reveal the original, a beautiful inlaid marble pavement in floral and geometric patterns that is a direct ancestor of medieval pavements in the churches of Tuscany and the south.

Mausoleum of Galla Placidia

This small chapel, set in the grounds of San Vitale and originally attached to the neighbouring church of Santa Croce, never really held the tomb of Ravenna's great patroness—she is buried near St Peter's in Rome. Nobody has peeked into the three huge stone sarcophagi, traditionally the resting places of Galla Placidia and two emperors, her second husband Constantius III and her son Valentinian, and it's anyone's guess who is really inside. Galla Placidia did construct the chapel, a small, gabled and cross-shaped building that is almost 2 m shorter than when built; the ground level has risen that much in 1400 years.

The simplicity of the brick exterior, as in San Vitale, makes the brilliant mosaics within that much more a surprise. Save some coins for the light box; the only natural light inside comes from a few tiny slits of windows, made of thin sheets of alabaster. The two important mosaics, on lunettes at opposite ends of the chapel, are coloured as richly as San Vitale. One represents St Lawrence, with his flaming grid-iron; the other is a beautiful and typical early Christian portrait of Jesus as the Good Shepherd, a beardless, classical-looking figure in a fine cloak and sandals, stroking one of the flock. On the lunettes of the cross-axis, pairs of stags come to drink at the fountain of life; around all four lunettes, floral arabesques and maze patterns in bright colours cover the arches and ceilings. Everything in the design betrays as much of the classical Roman style as of the nascent Christian, and the unusual figures on the arches holding up the central vault seem hardly out of place. They are SS. Peter and Paul, dressed in togas and standing with outstretched hands in the conventional pose of Roman senators.

The vault itself, a deep blue firmament glowing with hundreds of dazzling golden stars set in concentric circles, is the mausoleum's most remarkable feature. In the centre, at the top of the vault, a golden cross represents the unimaginable, transcendent God above the heavens. At the corners, symbols of the four evangelists provide an interesting insight into the origins of Christian iconography. Mark's lion, Luke's ox, and Matthew's man occupy the places in this sky where you would expect the constellations of the lion, the bull, and Aquarius, 90 degrees apart along the zodiac. For the fourth corner, instead of the objectionable scorpion (or serpent, as it often appeared in ancient times) the early Christians substituted the eagle of St John.

The National Museum

The medieval and Baroque cloisters attached to San Vitale now house this large collection of antiquities found in Ravenna and Classis. There's a little bit of everything: lead pipes and other bits of good Roman plumbing, a boy's linen shirt that has somehow survived from the 6th century, and no end of coins and broken pots (daily 8:30–1:30, Sat 8:30–5; adm). The detailed and well-labelled coin collection is interesting, even to the non-specialist, providing a picture history of Italy from Classical times into the early Middle Ages. This is a museum worth spending some time in, for exceptional works of art like the beautiful 6th-century Byzantine carved screens, and a possibly unique sculpture of Hercules capturing the Cerynean hind. This, too, is from the 6th century, perhaps the last art made in ancient times with a classical subject, possibly a copy of an earlier Greek work.

Not all of the exhibits are ancient; lovely, intricately carved ivory chests and plaques from the Middle Ages and Renaissance fill an entire room. Most are from France, with charming tableaux of medieval scenes such as tournaments and banquets. Cinquecento Italy is represented by a lavishly fancy intarsia cabinet. To understand Ravenna and its buildings better, be sure to see the fascinating architectural models of the Neonian baptistry (see below), the work of a modern Ravenna architect named Raffaello Trinci. Glass cross-sections elaborate the proportions and geometrical theory behind the Byzantines' new architecture of the 6th century, a recasting of ancient sacred geometry that was to have a great influence on the cathedral builders of the Middle Ages.

Ravenna's Centre

The **Piazza del Popolo**, at the centre of Ravenna, has a Venetian feel to it; the Venetians built it during their brief period of rule, and added the twin columns bearing statues of Ravenna's two patrons, San Vitale and Sant'Apollinare. Two blocks south, off the colonnaded **Piazza San Francesco**, a modest neoclassical pavilion was built in the 18th century over the **Tomb of Dante**. Ravenna is especially proud of having sheltered the storm-tossed poet in his last years, and the city will gently remind you of it in its street names, its tourist brochures, its Teatro Aligheri, and its frequent artistic competitions, based on themes from the *Divina Commedia*. Coming here may help explain just what Dante means to Italy; in all the country's wars, for example, groups of soldiers come here for little rituals to 'dedicate their sacrifice' to the poet's memory. Today there are always wreaths and bouquets, from organizations of all kinds and private citizens across Italy. **San Francesco** Church, behind the tomb, was founded in the 5th century but rebuilt in the 11th and then thoroughly Baroqued in the 1700s. Greek marble columns and a fine 4th-century altar survive, and in the church itself and the adjacent 'Braccioforte' oratory (behind the iron gate, next to Dante's tomb) there are some fine early Christian sarcophagi, one familiarly called the 'Tomb of Elijah'.

North of Piazza del Popolo, Ravenna has a fine example of a medieval leaning tower, the tall, 12th-century **Torre Pubblico**. This one seems good evidence for those who believe such things to be intentional. The tower leans more than Pisa's, but the windows near the top were built perfectly level. Nearby, on a little square off Via Paolo Costa, the **Arian Baptistry** recalls church struggles of the 6th century. Theodoric and his Goths, like most of the Germanic peoples, adhered to the Arian heresy, a doctrine condemned by the orthodox as denying the absolute divinity of Christ. Like all heresies, this one is really the story of a political struggle, between the Gothic kings and the emperor in Constantinople. Unlike Justinian, a great persecutor, the Goths usually tolerated both faiths; the baptistry belonged to the adjacent Santo Spirito church (rebuilt in the 16th century), once the Arians' cathedral, while the Athanasians (orthodox) worshipped at what is now Ravenna's cathedral. The Arian baptistry preserves a fine mosaic ceiling, with the Twelve Apostles arranged around a scene of the baptism of Jesus. The old man with the palm branch, across from John the Baptist, represents the River Jordan (open 9–12 and 2–6).

There is another leaning tower—an even tipsier one—nearby on Viale Farini, two blocks from the railway station. It is the 12th-century campanile of **San Giovanni Evangelista**, a much-altered church that was begun by Galla Placidia in 425. Bombings in the last War destroyed the apse, with its original mosaics, but some parts of the

13th-century mosaic floor, with scenes of the Fourth Crusade and some fantastical monsters, can be seen in the aisles.

Sant'Apollinare Nuovo

After those of San Vitale, the mosaics of this 6th-century church are the finest in Ravenna. Theodoric built it, and after the Byzantine conquest and the suppression of Arianism it was re-dedicated to St Martin, another famous persecutor of heretics. The present name comes from the 9th century, when the remains of Sant'Apollinare were moved here from the old Sant'Apollinare in Classe. The tall, circular campanile, a style that is a trademark of Ravenna's churches, was added in the 10th century.

Unlike San Vitale, Sant'Apollinare was built in the basilican form, with a long nave and side aisles. The two rows of Greek marble columns were probably recycled from an ancient temple. Above them are the mosaics, on panels that stretch the length of the church. On the left, by the door, you see the city of Classe, with ships in the protected harbour, between twin beacons, and the monuments of the city rearing up behind its walls. On the right, among the monuments of Ravenna, is the Palatium, Theodoric's royal palace. The curtains in the archways of the palace cover painted-over Gothic notables and probably Theodoric himself, effaced by the Byzantines. Beyond these two urban scenes are processions of martyrs bearing crowns: 22 ladies on the left side, 26 men on the right. The female procession is led by colourful, remarkable portraits of the Magi (officially enrolled as Saints of the Church, according to the inscription above), offering their gifts to the enthroned Virgin Mary.

Above these panels, more mosaics on both sides portray Old Testament prophets and doctors of the Church, as well as a series of scenes from the life of Jesus. These mosaics, smaller and not as well executed, are from Theodoric's time. Next to Sant'Apollinare, a brick façade with some marble columns is all that remains of the 6th-century building traditionally called the **Palace of Theodoric**. More likely this was a later governmental building of some sort; it may have been the palace of the Byzantine exarchs.

Neonian Baptistry and the Archiepiscopal Museum

An earthquake in 1733 wrecked Ravenna's **Cathedral**, west of the Piazza del Popolo, and there's little to see in the replacement but another round medieval tower. Somehow the disaster spared the 'Orthodox' or **Neonian Baptistry**, named after the 5th-century bishop Neone who commissioned the splendid mosaics. Unlike the Arian baptistry, here almost the entire decoration has survived: a scene of the Baptism of Jesus and fine portraits of the Twelve Apostles on the ceiling under the dome. Below, the eight walls bear four altars and four empty thrones. The *etoimasia*, the 'preparing of the Throne' for Jesus for the Last Judgement, is an odd bit of Byzantine mysticism; interestingly enough, classical Greek art often depicts an empty throne as a symbol for Zeus, but only with a pair of thunderbolts instead of a cross.

In the 1500 years since its construction, the ground level here has risen over 3 m—so has the baptistry's floor, and recent excavations have uncovered marble supporting columns down to the bottom. In the side niches, there is a 6th-century Byzantine altar and a huge, thoroughly pagan marble vase. The marble font, big enough for immersion baptisms of adults, is from the 1200s.

The **Archiepiscopal Museum**, behind the Cathedral, comes as a real surprise. Few ever visit, and the little old woman who watches over the place will be surprised to see you, but there are some treasures inside: the ivory throne of Bishop Maximian, a masterpiece of 6th-century sculpture, thought to have been perhaps a gift from Emperor Justinian, and an 11th-century reliquary, the silver 'Cross of Sant' Agnello'. Among the fragments of sculpture and mosaics are works saved from the original cathedral. The large marble disc by the wall, divided into 19 sections, is an episcopal calendar, regulated to the 19-year Julian cycle to allow Ravenna's medieval bishops to calculate the date of Easter and other holy days.

The biggest surprise, however, is finding that the nondescript Archbishop's Palace, in which the museum is located, is in parts as old as anything in Ravenna. A little door at the back leads to a small chapel called the **Oratorio di Sant'Andrea**, built around 500 during the reign of Theodoric. The mosaics on the vaults are among Ravenna's best: the antechamber has a fanciful scene of multicoloured birds and flowers, and an unusual warrior Christ, in full Roman armour and wielding the cross like a sword, treading a lion and snake underfoot. In the chapel itself, four angels and the four evangelists' symbols surround Christ's monogram on the dome, and the apse bears a beautiful starry sky around a golden cross, like the one at the Galla Placidia mausoleum. The finest works, however, are the portraits of saints decorating the arches. Early Christian representations of the saints are often much more than the pale, conventional figures of later art. These portraits betray an enduring fascination with the personalities and the psychology of saints; such figures as St Felicitas or St Ursicinus may be forgotten now, but to the early Christians they were not mere holy myths, but near-contemporaries, the spiritual heroes and heroines responsible for the miraculous growth of Christianity, the exemplars of a new age and a new way of life. (Museum and chapel open daily 9–12, 2:30–6; Sun, 9–1; adm.)

Theodoric's Mausoleum

For the real flavour of the days of the Roman twilight, nothing can beat this compellingly strange, sophisticated yet half-barbaric building outside the old city. To reach it, walk north from the railway station, past the new port and the Venetian fortress called the **Rocca di Brancaleone**, which now has a city park inside. Theodoric's tomb is in another small park on Via Cimitero, near the industrial zone. Perhaps the only regular 10-sided building in Italy, the Mausoleum has two floors. Downstairs, there is a cross-shaped chamber of unknown purpose. The second storey, also decagonal though slightly smaller, contains the porphyry sarcophagus, now empty. It is a comment on the times that scholars believe this originally to have been a recycled bathtub from a Roman palace. Theodoric was hardly broke, though; he could afford to bring the stone for his tomb over from what is now Yugoslavia. And note the roof, a single slab of Istrian stone, weighing over 300 tons. No one has yet explained how the Goths brought it here and raised it—or why (open daily 8:30–12, 2–7).

Classe

If you have the time, there is another important monument to Ravenna's golden age to be seen at the ruins of Classe, 5 km from town; any local train towards Rimini, or the regular

Sant'Apollinare, Classe

bus service can take you there. **Sant'Apollinare in Classe**, in fact, is literally all that remains of what was once the leading port of the northern Adriatic. The little River Uniti began to silt up Classe's harbour in classical times; when the port ceased to be a Roman military base and the funds for yearly dredging were no longer there, the city's fate was sealed. By the 9th century Classe was abandoned. The people of Ravenna presumably carted away most of the stone, and encroaching forests and swamps erased the last traces. Today the former port is good farmland, 6 km from the sea.

Sant'Apollinare, a huge basilican church completed in 549, survives only because of its importance as the burial place of Ravenna's patron. The exterior, in plain brick, is another finely proportioned example of Ravenna's pre-Romanesque, with another tall cylindrical campanile. Inside it's almost empty, with only a few early-Christian sarcophagi lining the walls. The beautiful Greek marble columns have well-carved capitals in a unique style. Above them are 18th-century portraits of all Ravenna's bishops—important to this city, where for centuries the bishops defended local autonomy against emperors, exarchs, and popes. The real attraction, however, is the mosaics in the apse, an impressive green-and-gold-ground allegorical vision of the **Transfiguration of Christ**, with Sant'Apollinare in attendance and three sheep, in a flower-strewn Mediterranean landscape, that represent Peter, James, and John (they were with Christ on Mount Tabor). As at San Vitale, there are scenes of the sacrifices of Abel, Melchizedek, and Abraham, opposite a mosaic of the Byzantine Emperor Constantine IV bestowing privileges on Ravenna's independent church. Archangels Gabriel and Michael appear in Byzantine court dress, under a pair of palm trees, the 'tree of life'.

Elsewhere around Classe, there's little to see; bits of Roman road, pine groves, some foundations. Excavations began only in 1961, and continue today. Sant'Apollinare is near the centre of an immense necropolis with some half-million burials. Some interesting things could turn up here in coming years (visiting hours at the excavations, daily 9–12).

WHERE TO STAY AND EATING OUT (tel prefix 0544)

Ravenna is well supplied with rooms in all categories. At the top of the list, and on a quiet street two blocks from San Vitale, is the ****Bisanzio, modern, luxurious and serene—only 36 rooms (Via Salaria 30, tel 27 111, all air-conditioned; L110–150 000). An older favourite, ageing gracefully at Via IV Novembre 14 off the Piazza del Popolo, is the ***Centrale Byron—also air-conditioned, with some very nice rooms and some very plain ones (tel 33 479; L58–70 000; some cheaper without bath).

Ravenna has plenty of budget accommodation, but most of it is around the port, a long walk from the centre, along Via delle Industrie. A very good one close to the railway station, with a friendly new owner, is *Al Giaciglio, at Via Rocca Brancaleone 42 (tel 39 403; L30 000 without bath). If you wish to loll on the beach after a day perusing the mosaics, there is one good bargain along the Lido at Classe: the ***Adler with a pool and private beach, at Viale Caboto 121 (tel 939 216; L50–60 000). Marina Romea, a little farther from the city, is a somewhat nicer spot; the ***Columbia is a beautiful modern hotel—but like all the places here it's a 10-minute walk to the beach (Viale Italia 70, tel 446 038; L54–60 000). In all the various 'lidos' around Ravenna there is an infinity of hotels in the L30–40 000 range.

The city does not seem to have many restaurants, but those they've got are choice. One you should not miss is **Tre Spade**, on Via G. Rasponi 37 west of the Piazzo del Popolo, tel 32 382 where they like to innovate and never put a foot wrong. Most of Ravenna comes for the seafood, but you can be adventurous and try the vegetable pastry concoctions, stuffed pigeon or some pasta combinations never seen before on this planet (L45 000; closed Mon and 20 July–25 Aug). At Via Mentana 31, **Da Renato** is a cosy first floor, where you might try the *scallopine alla Madera* (tel 23 684; about L18 000), and the restaurant of the Albergo Al Giaciglio (see above) has good home cooking, and a policy of only fresh ingredients, on the L12 000 daily menu.

The Adriatic Riviera

From Ravenna and Classe, the long stretch of small resorts that began at Comacchio straggles on towards the beach-Babylon of Rimini. The various tiny lidos are slow-paced, though packed with Bolognese families in the summer. Those nearest Ravenna suffer somewhat from industrial pollution, but there has been a big effort to keep the beaches clean. **Marina Romea**, a spit of land with a broad beach and a pine forest behind it, is perhaps the nicest. None are really good picks for a long stay, though quite convenient for a day on the beach if you're passing through; any of them would be an easy day trip from Ravenna. The first big centre on the coast is **Cervia-Milano Marittima**, the next, **Cesenatico**, built around a pretty, canal-like harbour designed for Cesare Borgia in 1502 by Leonardo da Vinci. In it, the **Museo della Mariniera** is a floating maritime museum, a display of the traditional types of fishing and trading boats in the northern Adriatic.

Rimini

At first glance, the Mediterranean's biggest resort may strike you as strictly cold potatoes, a full 15 km of peeling skin and pizza, serenaded by the portable radios of ten thousand teenagers and the eternal whines and giggles of their little brothers and sisters. To many Italians, however, Rimini means pure sweaty-palmed excitement. For decades now, following the grand old Italian pastime of *caccia alle svedese*, a staple of the national film industry has been the Rimini holiday seduction movie, in which a bumbling protagonist with glasses is swept off his feet by some incredible spicy tomato, who is as bouncy as she is adventurous. After many complications, embarrassing both for the audience and the actors, it all may just lead to true love. For the bumbling protagonists of real life, whether from Milano, Manchester, or München, all this may only be wishful thinking, but still they come in their millions each year. As a resort, Rimini has its advantages. Noisy as it is, it's a respectable, family place, relatively cheap for northern Italy, convenient and well organized. Also, tucked away behind the beachfront is a genuine old city, dishevelled but inviting, and offering one first-rate Renaissance attraction.

GETTING AROUND
On this stretch of coast, the FS Adriatic coast line works almost like a tram service, with lots of trains and stops near the beaches in all the resorts. In summer, there are regular flights from Milano and lots of foreign charters to Rimini's little airport, behind the beaches at Miramare. Rimini city buses run regularly in summer, carrying holiday-makers up and down the long beach strip. From the railway station, on Piazzale Cesare Battisti, there are buses to most nearby towns, and 5 buses a day to San Marino—more in summer. Cultural day-trippers who shudder at the thought of Rimini's beach madness can dip in easily—the Tempio Malatesta is only a 5-minute walk from the station.

TOURIST INFORMATION
In summer, at least, it's positively difficult to remain uninformed; Rimini and its suburbs have more information offices than any place in this solar system—even more than ice cream stands:
Rimini: Piazzale C. Battisti, next to the station (tel 51 480, 51 331). Next door is an information office for San Marino (tel 56 333). There is also an office by the beach, on Parco dell'Indipendenza (tel 55 051, 55 267, 55 056) as well as six other offices along the 15-km beach:
Cesenatico: Via Roma 112, tel (0547) 80 091
Gatteo a Mare: Piazza della Libertà 5, tel (0547) 86 083
Bellaria: Via Leonardo da Vinci 3, tel (0541) 44 574
Riccione: Piazzale Ceccarini 10, tel (0541) 43 361, 605 627
Misano Adriatico: Viale Platani 22 tel (0541) 615 520
Cattolica: Piazza Nettuno 1, tel (0541) 963 341

The Malatesta Temple
Sigismundo Malatesta ('Headache'), tyrant of Rimini, went into the books as one bad hombre. According to Jacob Burckhardt, 'the verdict of history ... convicts him of murder, rape, adultery, incest, sacrilege, perjury, and treason, committed not once, but often.' The historian adds that his frequent attempts on the virtue of his children, both male and female, may have resulted from 'some astrological superstition'. Pope Pius II, in 1462, accorded him a unique honour—a canonization to Hell. The Pope, who was

behind most of the accusations, can be excused a little exaggeration. He wanted Sigismundo's land, and resorted to invoking supernatural aid when he couldn't beat him at war.

Modern historians give Sigismundo better reviews, finding him on the whole no more pagan and perverse than the average Renaissance duke, and less so than many popes. The family had ruled at Rimini since the 1300s—ironically it was a pope who first put them in business. Early dukes, like Malatesta 'Guastafamiglia' ('Destroyer of Families') were hard men, and good role models for Sigismundo, but they succeeded for a time in spreading their rule as far as Cesena and Fano. By Sigismundo's time, money and allies were suddenly lacking, and the family was deposed by the unspeakable Alexander VI in 1500.

The shortage of funds was also responsible for the abandonment in 1461 of Sigismundo's personal monument, the eclectic and thoroughly mysterious work that has come to be known as the **Malatesta Temple.** Whatever Sigismundo's personal habits, he was a learned man and a good judge of art. To transform the unfinished 13th-century Franciscan church into his Temple, he called in Leon Alberti to redesign the exterior and Agostino di Duccio for the reliefs inside. Scholars have been puzzling for centuries over Sigismundo's intentions. Though the temple has been Rimini's cathedral since 1809, it is hardly a Christian building, full of undecipherable sculptural allegories with everywhere the entwined monograms of Sigismundo and his wife Isotta degli Atti; in part it seems a tribute to this famous lady, who is buried here along with Sigismundo.

Alberti's unfinished exterior, grafting Roman arcades and pilasters onto the plain Francescan building, grievously feels the lack of the planned cupola that might have tied the composition together. The big arches on the sides were meant to hold sarcophagi of Rimini's notable men; only a few were ever used. Inside these arches, four pairs of chapels hold the Temple's major feature, the **sculptural reliefs** made by Agostino, among the greatest works of the Renaissance. These low reliefs, on blue backgrounds like a della Robbia cameo, depict angels and child musicians, The Arts and The Sciences, St Michael, various putti, Sigismundo himself, and the Triumph of Scipio. Some of the best are the allegorical panels of the planets and signs of the zodiac; note especially the enchanting *Moon*: Cynthia in her silver car, and a scene of 14th-century Rimini under the claws of the Crab.

Among the other famous works in the Temple are a fresco by Piero della Francesca of Sigismundo and his patron, St Sigismund of Burgundy, and a painted crucifix by Giotto. The tombs of Sigismundo and Isotta, with their strange device (the omnipresent monograms S and I together like a dollar sign) and elephants (the Malatesta heraldic symbol) are also fine works (daily 7–12, 3:30–7, less frequently in winter).

Old Rimini is the home town of Federico Fellini, and you may recognize some of the street scenes from *Amarcord*. Some ruins survive as reminders of Roman *Arminium*, a thriving Adriatic port and a rival to Classe: the foundation of an amphitheatre near the southern walls, and the well-preserved **Arch of Augustus**, in the southern gate near the post office. This arch marked the crossing of the Via Aemilia and the Via Flaminia. The Roman high street, the *cardo*, is now called Corso di Augusto; it passes from here through the central **Piazza Tre Martiri** (which retains some arcades in the shop fronts from the days when it was the Roman forum) and continues on to the north gate and the five-arched **Bridge of Augustus** of AD21, a fine work badly patched after damage in the

Greek-Gothic wars. A few blocks over the bridge, the church of **San Giuliano** contains a painting of that saint's martyrdom, the last work of Paolo Veronese. From here towards the sea, along the riverbank, stretches Rimini's colourful fishing port. Back at the centre, on Piazza Cavour, the **Palazzo del'Arengo** has been Rimini's town hall since 1207; it faces the bulky castle of the Malatestas, the **Rocca Sigismundo**. Two blocks away at Via Gambalunga 27, the **Museo Comunale** has Roman mosaics and earlier archaeological items, and paintings by Ghirlandaio and Giovanni Bellini (daily, 8–1; adm).

Some Beach Statistics

> Rimini is not the place for those who want to be alone.
> *Tourist brochure*

The subject makes Rimini's holiday barons and the hotel consortium mildly uneasy. 'There's room for everybody,' they say, and in a way they're right. The Mediterranean's biggest resort has 15 km of broad beaches, and about 1600 hotels with some 55,000 rooms. At the usual resort ratio, that means about 85,000 beds. It could be a problem in the really busy season. If all the beds are full—adding another 25,000 day-trippers, campers, and holiday apartment tenants—that makes 110,000 souls, or 7333 per kilometre of beach front. There's plenty of other things to do in Rimini, fortunately, but with only 13.6 cm of shore per bum, if everyone tries to hit the water at the same time the results could be catastrophic.

This really need never happen. Many of these people at any given time will be in Rimini's 751 bars, 343 restaurants, 70 dance halls and discos, 49 cinemas, or three miniature golf courses. There's something for everybody—plenty of sailing schools and wind-surfing schools, a dolphin show (on the beach near the port). Other attractions include **Fiabilandia**, an amusement park for the little ones with a Mississippi riverboat, a Fort Apache, coloured fountains, the genuine King Kong (on SS16 south of Rimini; buses 8 and 9 go there); another dolphin show, at Riccione; **Aquafan**, also in Riccione, an aquatic amusement park with long water slides, bumper boats, wave pools and noisy discos; and **Italia in Miniatura**, which besides mouse-sized cathedrals and castles, offers you performing bears, go-karts, and more bumper boats (on the coast road, north towards Viserba).

More Beaches

Holiday madness continues in a big way through the string of resorts south of Rimini. **Riccione**, **Misano Adriatico**, **Cattolica**, and **Gabicce Mare** are all huge places, and in the summer they can be as crowded and intense as Rimini itself. Admittedly it's hard to tell one from the other. The Adriatic Riviera begins to fade when the wide beaches of the Romagna give way to the more rugged coast of the Marches, but soon picks up again when the hills recede.

WHERE TO STAY   (tel prefix 0541)

A vacation in Rimini means a standard package, and it's unlikely there will be any surprises—good or bad. Expect a modern room with a balcony, pleasant enough but rather unimaginatively furnished; in the high season you'll probably be stuck on half-board, which is unfortunate. You may as well take pot luck by ringing up the

Promozione Alberghiera (Piazzale Indipendenza 1; tel 52 459, in the railway station; tel 51 194, and four other well-marked offices around town) and let them find you a vacancy. Expect nothing really distinctive or interesting; people do not come to Rimini for scenery, charming inns, or fine cuisine, but to join the oceanic crowd and seek out the endless possibilities for diversion that go with it. If that sounds good, make sure to get a place in the crowded centre where the action is—don't let the PA stick you out in Torre Pedrera or Miramare.

An old-fashioned Grand Hotel might seem terribly out of place in Rimini, but that's exactly what you'll find right in the centre, on Parco dell'Indipendenza at Marina Centro—the *****Grand Hotel**, Via Ramusio 1, tel 56 000. This imposing turn-of-the-century palace helped make Rimini what it is today. Nowadays the place hasn't slipped at all, with rooms that are almost indecently luxurious, all the brass well polished and the enormous crystal chandeliers well dusted. It's the only hotel in Rimini with its own dance orchestra; also pool and private beach, and nice gardens; L265–380 000, cheaper rooms in the *Residenza* when the main building is full. The ****Ambasciatori**, a block from the sea at Viale Amerigo Vespucci 22, tel 55 561, has a splashy modern building designed to attract the fast crowd, also air conditioning and TV (which the Grand Hotel lacks) as well as a private beach (L125–280 000). Where Viale Vespucci changes its name to Viale Regina Elena, you will find the ***Admiral**, another sharp ultra-modern palace with a rooftop terrace and spacious balconies for most rooms (Via R. Elena 67, tel 381 771; L56–84 000). There's no end of less expensive establishments in the L25–45 000 range. Some of the better ones: ***Apogeo**, Via Oriani 11, tel 384 552, L40–80 000; small swimming-pool. **Primavera**, Via Lagomaggio 113, tel 380 206; few amenities but very nice just the same; L28–60 000; *Pensione Primula**, Via Trento 12, tel 23 712; L25–48 000. All of the above are central and a block or two from the beach. *Pensione Urbinati**, Via Fiume 7, tel 26 558, is an excellent pensione whose friendly owner hails from Umbria; delicious Emilia-Romagnan specialities in the kitchen (L40–50 000 full board per person, open 25 May–25 Sept).

EATING OUT

There's nothing to complain about as regards Rimini's restaurants (this is still Emilia-Romagna, after all). The **Taverna degli Artisti**, Viale Vespucci 1, tel 28 519, is the best-known spot for seafood, along with some imaginative light pasta openers and something unexpected—a little *degustazione* of whisky; they have almost every brand from around the world (L35–45 000). Nearby on Lungomare Tintori 7, near the Grand Hotel, **Lo Squero**, tel 27 676, has an outdoor terrace overlooking the sea; you can have a formidable full dinner (shellfish are a speciality—try the *bruschetta alle vongole*) or just a pizza (L35–40 000; closed Tues). In the old town, **Dallo Zio**, Via S. Chiara 16, tel 786 160, is an excellent seafood palace—marine lasagne, fishy vol-au-vent and other surprises. Very popular with locals and vacationers alike (L30–35 000).

Near the market, on Piazza Malatesta, there's the **Osteria di Santa Colomba**, tel 780 048, an old favourite (they say Napoleon slept here), with simple traditional fare—the best possible antidote to the cosmopolitanism of beach Rimini may be a plate of pasta with chick peas (about L25 000). At the other extreme, a dubious establishment that owes everything to cosmopolitanism: the **Ristorante Pic-Nic**, Via Tempio Malatestiano 30, tel 21 916, has many different kinds of pizza—*noisy* pizza, *atomic* pizza, or perhaps pizza with radishes, not to mention roast beef *all'inglese*, and mystery goulash—not a bad place, really (L7 000 for pizza and beer, full dinners L18 000). If your mood leans more to romance rather than the casual, one-night pizza, **C'era una Volta**, Via Consolare 91, tel 751 318 offers little candle-lit nooks to match its imaginative light meals—try crêpes with porcini mushrooms, or stuffed veal baked in wood oven (L35 000, closed Mon and 20 Dec–20 Jan).

None of the other nearby resorts—Cesenatico, Misano, Cattolica, and the rest—have any particular charm. Think of them as suburban extensions of Rimini; there's no reason to go out of your way. Avoid the worst of them, ugly and overpriced **Riccione**.

San Marino

As a perfect counterpart to the sand-strewn fun-fair of Rimini, just 23 km inland you may visit the world's only sovereign and independent roadside attraction. Before Rimini became the Italian Miami Beach, the 50,000 citizens of San Marino had to make a living peddling postage stamps. Now, with their medieval streets crowded with day-trippers, the San Marinese have been unable to resist the temptation to order some bright medieval costumes, polish up their picturesque mountain towns, and open up some souvenir stands and 'duty-free' shops. Their famous stamps, though nothing like the exquisitely engraved numbers of forty years ago, are still prized by collectors, and recently the country has begun to mint its own coins again after a lapse of thirty-nine years; nevertheless, the citizens of San Marino, who may just have the highest national average income in Europe, are making their living almost entirely from tourism.

TOURIST INFORMATION
In San Marino, there is one tourist office for each 7 sq. m.
San Marino town: Contrada del Collegio, tel (0549) 992 059.
Dogana: Piazza Tini, tel 905 414.
Tavolucci: Via XXVIII Luglio, tel 902 701.

The World's Smallest Republic
Also the oldest republic. According to legend, San Marino was founded as a Christian settlement on the easily defensible slopes of Monte Titano by a stonecutter named Marinus, fleeing from the persecutions of Diocletian in the early 4th century. 'Overlooked', as the San Marinese charmingly put it, by the empire and various states that followed it, the little community had the peace and quiet to evolve its medieval democratic institutions; its constitution in its present form dates from 1243, when the first pair of 'consuls' was elected by a popular assembly. The consuls are now called Captains Regent, but little else has changed in 700 years. Twice, in 1503 and 1739, the Republic was invaded by papal forces, and independence was preserved only by a little good luck. Napoleon, passing through in 1797, found San Marino amusing, and half-seriously offered to enlarge its boundaries, a proposal that was politely declined. The republic felt secure enough to offer refuge to Garibaldi, fleeing from Venice after the end of the Roman revolt of 1849, and as an island of peace during World War II, it distinguished itself by taking in thousands of refugees.

San Marino last made the world news in the 70s, when the Communists were threatening to win the elections. The San Marino government decided that even emigrants were still citizens, with the right to vote. Of course the government felt obliged to assist them; thousands of San Marinese descendants in places like New Jersey were given free holidays at government expense to help tip the election.

Entering San Marino from Rimini at the hamlet called Dogana (though there are no border formalities now), you see a green and pretty countryside. The main road passes through a string of villages. San Marino, no midget like the Vatican City, is all of 12 km long at its widest extent. At the foot of Monte Titano, rising dramatically above the plain, is **Borgomaggiore**, the largest town, with a cable car up to the capital and citadel of the republic, also called **San Marino**. Here, among medieval streets and squares, there are wonderful views over Rimini and the coast. Nothing is really as old as it looks; the **Palazzo del Governo**, full of Ruritanian guardsmen in brass buttons and epaulettes, is a reconstruction of 1894. Here the Grand Council meets, and the Captains Regent have their offices. Some new museums have been conjured up for the tourists—a Stamp and Coin Museum, Garibaldi Museum, and a Museum of Weaponry, but the best thing to do is walk the paths through Monte Titano's forests to the three (rebuilt) medieval **tower fortresses** on the three peaks that give San Marino its famous silhouette—famous to philatelists anyhow, and long the symbol of the republic.

Two other mountain towns, near the borders of San Marino, are most easily visited from Rimini: **Verucchio**, a pleasant medieval village that retains some of its gates and churches, also the 10th-century fortress that later became the stronghold of the tyrants of Rimini, the **Rocca Malatesta**. There is a small **Archaeology Museum** at the lower end of town, with unusual ceramics of the 1400 BC Villanova culture. **San Leo**, on the other side of San Marino in the Marches, was founded by a companion of Marinus, according to legend, but lost its independence long ago. The rough-walled, 9th-century church called the **Pieve** is worth a look, but San Leo's real attraction is the **castle**, built for the Montefeltro dukes of Urbino in the 15th century. Like their palace at Urbino itself, this fortress is a perfect representative building of the Renaissance, balanced, finely proportioned in its lines, a building of intelligence and style. It is also impregnable, hung on a breathtakingly sheer cliff. Once this mount held a temple of Jupiter; as *Mons Feretrius* (referring to Jove's lightning) it gave its name to the Montefeltro family. A later fortress on this site was briefly 'capital of Italy' in the 960s, during the reign of King Berengar II. Now there is a small picture gallery in the castle—it's a stiff climb up if you don't have a car.

WHERE TO STAY AND EATING OUT (tel prefix 0541)

San Marino has become accustomed to entertaining tourists in the last twenty years; being so close to Rimini has turned out to be an unexpected windfall. Italian currency is valid everywhere, but make sure you don't get too many San Marino coins in change; they are only good for souvenirs once you get back to Italy. It isn't a bad place to stop over if you can resist the charms of the Rimini lido; there are two fine old hotels up on San Marino's citadel, in the middle of the old town. One is the *****Titano**, at Contrada del Collegio 21, tel 991 375, a restored century-old building where half the rooms have great views over the countryside (L47–56 000); not far away, *****La Rocca,** Via delle Penne on Salita alla Rocca, tel 991 166, has a pool, and a TV in every room, and balconies with a view (L44–55 000). You won't find anything much cheaper—price-fixing is an old tradition of the republic.

The best restaurant in the centre, and a very pretty place it is, can be found at Piazzetta Placito Feretrano, nearthe Hotel Titano. **Buca San Francesco**, tel 991 462, has nothing out of the ordinary, but its soups, tortellini, and *scallopine alla sanmarinese* are good (L30 000). In good weather, the outdoor terrace of the **Trattoria Panoramica** on Salita alla Rocca, tel 991 378, is a fine spot to contemplate San Marino, but the view isn't the only attraction; there's good simple cuisine at an honest price (L20–30 000). One of the oldest restaurants in the historic centre of San Marino is **La Fratta**, Via Salita della Rocca 14, tel 991 594; among the homecooked specialities, try the *tris* and grilled lamb with a carafe of *vino della casa* for L23 000.

ARCHITECTURAL, ARTISTIC AND HISTORICAL TERMS

Ambones: twin pulpits in some southern churches (singular: *ambo*), often elaborately decorated.

Atrium: entrance court of a Roman house or early church.

Badia: *abbazia*, an abbey or abbey church.

Baldacchino: baldachin, a columned stone canopy above the altar of a church.

Basilica: a rectangular building, usually divided into three aisles by rows of columns. In Rome this was the common form for lawcourts and other public buildings, and Roman Christians adapted it for their early churches.

Broletto: a medieval town hall.

Calvary chapels: a series of outdoor chapels, usually on a hillside, that commemorate the stages of the Passion of Christ.

Campanile: a bell-tower.

Campanilismo: local patriotism; the Italians' own word for their historic tendency to be more faithful to their home towns than to the abstract idea of 'Italy'.

Cardo: transverse street of a Roman *castrum*-shaped city.

Carroccio: a wagon carrying the banners of a medieval city and an altar; it served as the rallying point in battles.

Cartoon: the preliminary sketch for a fresco or tapestry.

Caryatid: supporting pillar or column carved into a standing female form; male versions are called *telamons*.

Castrum: a Roman military camp, always neatly rectangular, with straight streets and gates at the cardinal points. Later the Romans founded or refounded cities in this form, hundreds of which survive today (Verona, Padua, Parma, and Piacenza are clear examples).

Cavea: the semicircle of seats in a classical theatre.

Cenacolo: fresco of the Last Supper, often on the wall of a monastery refectory.

Ciborium: a tabernacle; the word is often used for large, freestanding tabernacles, or in the sense of a baldacchino.

Chiaroscuro: the arrangement or treatment of light and dark in a painting.

Comune: commune, or commonwealth, referring to the governments of the free cities of the Middle Ages. Today it denotes any local government, from the Comune di Roma down to the smallest village.

Condottiere: the leader of a band of mercenaries in late medieval and Renaissance times.

Confraternity: a religious lay brotherhood, often serving as a neighbourhood mutual-aid and burial society, or following some specific charitable work (Michelangelo, for example, belonged to one that cared for condemned prisoners in Rome).

Cupola: a dome.

303

Decumanus: street of a Roman *castrum*-shaped city parallel to the longer axis, the central, main avenue called the Decumanus Major.

Duomo: cathedral.

Forum: the central square of a Roman town, with its most important temples and public buildings. The word means 'outside', as the original Roman Forum was outside the first city walls.

Fresco: wall painting, the most important Italian medium of art since Etruscan times. It isn't easy; first the artist draws the *sinopia* (q.v.) on the wall. This is covered with plaster, but only a little at a time, as the paint must be on the plaster before it dries. Leonardo da Vinci's endless attempts to find clever shortcuts ensured that little of his work would survive.

Ghibellines: one of the two great medieval parties, the supporters of the Holy Roman Emperors.

Gonfalon: the banner of a medieval free city; the *gonfaloniere*, or flag-bearer was often the most important public official.

Grotesques: carved or painted faces used in Etruscan and later Roman decoration; Raphael and other artists rediscovered them in the 'grotto' of Nero's Golden House in Rome.

Guelphs (see *Ghibellines*): the other great political faction of medieval Italy, supporters of the Pope.

Intarsia: work in inlaid wood or marble.

Lozenge: the diamond shape—along with stripes, one of the trademarks of Pisan architecture.

Narthex: the enclosed porch of a church.

Palazzo: not just a palace, but any large, important building (though the word comes from the Imperial *palatium* on Rome's Palatine Hill).

Palio: a banner, and the horse race in which city neighbourhoods contend for it in their annual festivals.

Pantocrator: Christ 'ruler of all', a common subject for apse paintings and mosaics in areas influenced by Byzantine art.

Pieve: a parish church, especially in the north.

Polyptych: an altarpiece composed of more than three panels.

Predella: smaller paintings on panels below the main subject of a painted altarpiece.

Presepio: a Christmas crib.

Pulvin: stone, often trapezoidal, that supports or replaces the capital of a column; decoratively carved examples can be seen in many medieval cloisters.

Putti: flocks of plaster cherubs with rosy cheeks and bums that infested much of Italy in the Baroque era.

Quadriga: chariot pulled by four horses.

Quattrocento: the 1400s—the Italian way of referring to centuries (*duecento, trecento, quattrocento, cinquecento*, etc.).

Rocca: a citadel.

Scuola: the headquarters of a confraternity or guild.

Sinopia: the layout of a fresco (q.v.), etched by the artist on the wall before the plaster is applied. Often these are works of art in their own right.

Stigmata: a miraculous simulation of the bleeding wounds of Christ, appearing in holy men like St Francis in the 12th century.

Telamon: see *caryatid*.

Thermae: Roman baths.

Tondo: round relief, painting or terracotta.

Transenna: marble screen separating the altar area from the rest of an early Christian church.

Triclinium: the main hall of a Roman house, used for dining and entertaining.

Triptych: a painting, especially an altarpiece, in three sections.

Trompe l'oeil: art that uses perspective effects to deceive the eye—for example, to create the illusion of depth on a flat surface, or to make columns and arches painted on a wall seem real.

Tympanum: the semicircular space, often bearing a painting or relief, above the portal of a church.

CHRONOLOGY

Date

BC

*c.*5000	Neolithic culture and technology reach Italy
*c.*1800	Celto–Ligurians begin to occupy the north
*c.*1600	Terramare culture
1185	Legendary date of Padua's founding by Antenor of Troy
*c.*900	Arrival of Etruscans in Italy
753	Legendary date of Rome's founding
530	Etruscans found port of Spina
390	Rome sacked by Gauls
268	Rimini becomes a Roman colony
264–238	First Punic War
236–222	Romans capture Po Valley from Gauls; conquest complete up to the Rubicon
218–201	Second Punic War
187	M. Aemilius Lepidus constructs Via Aemilia as a military road to guard new conquests of Cisalpine Gaul
181	Romans found Aquileia
151–146	Third Punic War and the destruction of Carthage
115–102	Last Celtic raids on Italy
100	Birth of Julius Caesar
89	Verona becomes a Roman colony
87	Catullus born near Verona
82–78	Dictatorship of Sulla
60–50	First Triumvirate: Caesar, Pompey, and Crassus
59	Livy born near Padua
51	Caesar conquers Transalpine Gaul
50	Caesar crosses the Rubicon and seizes Rome
45	Padua becomes a Roman municipium
44	Caesar done in by friends
42–32	Second Triumvirate: Octavian, Mark Antony, and Lepidus
31	Battle of Actium leaves Octavian sole ruler of the Empire
27 BC–AD 14	Octavian (now Augustus Caesar) rules Romes as Princeps
AD42	St Peter comes to Rome
100	Building of Verona's Arena
300	Founding of San Marino by Marinus of Dalmatia, fleeing Diocletian's second persecution
305	Diocletian's reforms turn the Empire into a bureaucratized despotism
313	Basilica founded at Aquileia
330	Pagan temples closed by orders of Emperor Constantine

364	Final division of the Empire into eastern and western halves
402	Ravenna becomes capital of Western Empire
408	General Stilicho murdered at Emperor Honorius' orders
421	First settlement on the Rivoalto (Rialto)
452	Attila the Hun destroys the great city of Aquileia and plunders Venetia; people seek safety in the lagoon
466	The twelve lagoon communities elect their own tribunes
476	Western Empire ends when Goth Odoacer is crowned King of Italy
493–514	Theodoric rules west, mostly from Ravenna
540	Byzantines capture Ravenna and rule it through their Exarchs
568	Lombards invade and make Cividale del Friuli their first duchy; inhabitants of *Altinum* flee to Torcello
573	Lombard Queen Rosamunda murders King Alboin in Verona, after he made her drink from her father's skull
590	Lombards become orthodox Christians
600s	Benedictines found Abbey of Pomposa
612	Irish saint Colombanus founds monastery at Bobbio
639	People of Altinum build cathedral on Torcello island
726	Orso Ipato, first Venetian to take title of Dux, or Doge, in a show of independence from Byzantium
737	Patriarchate of Aquileia moves to Cividale del Friuli
757	Romagna comes under the suzerainty of the popes—until 1860
774	Pepin, defeating the Lombards and claiming the kingdom of Italy, leads his Franks against the Venetians gathered on the Rialto but is defeated by the lagoon
810	Charlemagne and Byzantine Emperor Nicephorus sign a treaty recognizing Venice as subject to Constantinople but enjoying special trading concessions in Italy
829	St Mark's body stolen by Venetian merchants and welcomed with tremendous pomp in Venice; building of the original St Mark's to house it
888	Berengar I of Cividale del Friuli becomes king of Italy
900s	Emperors grant special privileges to the bishops of Trent, which they hold until 1796
960	Dalmatians raid Venice
962	Otto the Great occupies north Italy, and is crowned emperor at Rome
976	Basilica of San Marco destroyed by fire
1000	Doge Pietro Orseolo II leads Venice's fleet in crushing the pirates of Dalmatia, beginning conquest of the Adriatic
1019	Reconciliation of rival Patriarchates in Friuli; rebuilding of Aquileia's basilica
c.1060	Founding of the University of Bologna
1075	Beginning of Investiture conflict between popes and emperors
1077	Emperor Henry IV's 'penance at Canossa'.
1082	In gratitude for Venice's aid against the Normans, Emperor Alexius Comnenus signs the *Crisbolo*, absolving the merchants of Venice of all taxes and tolls in the Byzantine Empire

1097	First Crusade begins
1099	Modena begins its Cathedral
1104	Founding of the Arsenal
1107	*Comuni* of Verona, Padua, Treviso, and Vicenza form Veronese League to combat Imperial threats
1109	The Republic joins the Crusades; commercial rivalry with Genoa intensifies in the east
1116	Bologna becomes an independent *comune*
1167	To combat Emperor Barbarossa, cities in the north form Lombard League
1171	Venice's trading colony in Constantinople, 200,000 strong, is arrested and its goods confiscated by the Emperor, at the instigation of the Genoese. Doge declares war on empire, and leads Venice into one of its most humiliating defeats. The six *sestieri* are established to facilitate tax collections.
1177	Barbarossa apologizes to Pope Alexander III in Venice, earning the city a rare papal brownie point
1183	Treaty of Constance between Barbarossa and Lombard League
1196	Antelami begins Parma Baptistry
1204	Taking charge of the Fourth Crusade, 90 year-old Doge Dandolo subdues Dalmatia, Zara, and captures Constantinople. Venice now controls the Adriatic, the Aegean, the Sea of Marmora, the Black Sea, and seaports of Syria and the major East-West trade routes
1212	Birth of Malatesta di Verucchio, founder of Rimini dynasty of lords
1208	Da Camino family rules Treviso until 1312
1220	St Francis visits Venice
1220s	Manfredi family takes control of Faenza
1222	Founding of the University of Padua
1231	St Anthony of Padua dies and is canonized the next year
1237–54	Ezzelino da Romano terrorizes the Veneto
1238	Patriarchate of Aquileia moves from Cividale del Friuli to Udine
1258	Francesca da Rimini slain
1260	Mastino della Scala takes control of Verona
1261	Charles of Anjou invades Italy at behest of the Pope
1266	Charles defeats the last of the Hohenstaufens
1267	Este family takes control of Ferrara
1278	Papal states chartered in deal with Emperor Rudolf
1288	Este family takes Modena
1291	Glass furnaces moved to Murano
1297	Venice becomes an oligarchy with the *Serrata*, or closing, of the Consiglio Maggiore, limiting membership to patricians
1298	Genoa defeats Venice at Curzola, sinking 65 out of the total fleet of 95 ships; publication of Marco Polo's *Description of the World*, written in a Genoese prison
1300	The disenfranchised people of Venice rebel; ringleaders are beheaded to discourage others

1301–04	Dante takes refuge in Verona
1304	Giotto begins painting Padua's Cappella degli Scrovegni
1309	French Pope Clement V moves papacy to Avignon
1310	Nobles led by Tiepolo conspire to seize power in Venice; Council of Ten established to arrest rebels
1314	Dante completes the *Commedia*
1318	Da Carrara family begins its dominant role in Padua
1321	Dante dies and is buried in Ravenna
1325	Names of Venetian patricians inscribed in the Golden Book
1335	Venice's Council of Ten becomes a permanent institution
1337	Taddeo Pépoli takes power in Bologna over papal legates; succeeded by the Visconti and Bentivoglio families
1348	The Black Death cuts the population in half
1355	Doge Marin Falier plots to take real power in Venice and is beheaded
1364	Cardinal Albornoz conquers much of Romagna for the pope; founds Collegio di Spagna at University of Bologna
1373	Arrival of Jews in Venice
1374	Petrarch dies in Arquà, in the Euganean Hills
1377	Papacy moves back to Rome once and for all
1380	Venice's arch-rival Genoa defeated at Chioggia
1400	Birth of Jacopo Bellini
1402	Death of Milan boss Gian Galeazzo Visconti leaves most of northern Italy up for grabs
1405	Venice eliminates the Carrara lordlings of Padua and picks up its first mainland possessions: Padua, Verona, Bassano and Belluno
1416	Venice victorious in its first battle against the Turks at Negroponte (Euboea) and conquers Rovereto, rallying the Tridentines around their bishop
1420	Venice wrests Udine and the Friuli from the King of Hungary
1421	Birth of Gentile Bellini
1426	Birth of Giovanni Bellini
1432	Venice executes the *condottiere* Carmagnola for losing a battle; he is replaced by the luckier captain, Gattamelata
1438	Earthquake wrecks Aquileia
1441	Venice captures Ravenna
1447	Birth of Ariosto in Reggio Emilia
1450	Birth of Carpaccio
1451	Patriarchate moved from Aquileia and Udine to Venice
1452	Duchy of Modena created for Borso d'Este
1453	Mahomet II captures Constantinople; Venice quickly signs trade agreement with Sultan and sends Gentile Bellini to paint his portrait
1454	Venetian expansion on the mainland includes Treviso, Bergamo, Friuli, and Ravenna; Venice signs a peace treaty with Milan
1462	Pope Pius II canonizes Sigismondo Malatesta of Rimini to hell
1469	First books printed in Venice, soon to become the printing capital of Europe

1471	Ercole I becomes lord of Ferrara and makes it 'the first modern city in Europe'
1474	Birth of Ariosto
1476	Giovanni Caboto (John Cabot) granted Venetian citizenship
1478	Birth of Giorgione
1484	Venice wins Rovigo and the Polésine from Ferrara, completing a *terra firma* empire that was to last until Napoleon
1485	Titian born in Pieve di Cadore (sometime between 1480 and 1490)
1487	Counts of Tyrol defeat Venice
1489	Caterina Cornaro 'cedes' Cyprus to Venice
1494	Italy invaded by Charles VIII of France; Venice allies with other states to fight the French and pick up a little more real estate
1495	Indecisive Battle of Fornovo: Italian armies, led by Venice, try to stop the French army of Charles VIII
1498	Vasco da Gama's voyage around the Horn to India spells the end of Venice's old trade monopolies with the east
1499	Cesare Borgia captures Imola, Forlì, and Cesena
1500	Aldus founds Greek Academy in Venice; Cesare Borgia captures Rimini, Pesaro, and Faenza
1501	Alfonso I d'Este weds Lucrezia Borgia; Manfredi family loses control of Faenza to Cesare Borgia
1505	Bembo publishes the *Asolani*
1506	Pope Julius II reconquers Bologna from the last of the Bentivoglio family
1508	League of Cambrai formed against Venice by jealous rivals Emperor Maximilian, Pope Julius II, Louis XII, and Ferdinand of Aragon; birth of Palladio
1509	League of Cambrai defeats Venice at Agnadello but mutual jealousies prevent members from holding her mainland possessions; Julius II picks up Cesare Borgia's territories; Austria gains Gorizia
1511	Austria establishes protectorate over Trentino
1512	Birth of Tintoretto; Ravenna sacked after battle between troops of Louis XII and the Holy League; Julius II bestows Pésaro on his Della Rovere relatives
1516	Venetian Jews confined to the Ghetto
1519	Charles V elected Holy Roman Emperor
1527	With the Sack of Rome artists, architects, and scholars flee to the Veneto, bringing the High Renaissance in tow. New arrivals include Sansovino and Aretino
1528	Birth of Veronese; Castiglione publishes *The Courtier*
1529	Charles V crowned Emperor by Clement VII in Bologna
1530	Girolamo Fracastoro, a physician of Verona, publishes *Syphilis sive morbus gallicus* ('Syphilis or the French disease'), giving a name to a new epidemic
1532	Ariosto publishes *Orlando Furioso*

1534	Founding of the Jesuits
1539	Council of Three established in Venice
1545	Pope Paul III sets up his son Pierluigi Farnese as Duke of Parma and Piacenza; Paduan botanist plants Europe's first botanical garden
1545–63	Council of Trent initiates reforms in the Catholic Church
1559	Treaty of Câteau-Cambrésis confirms Spanish control of Italy
1570	Turks take Cyprus from Venice and skin captain Bragadino alive
1571	Battle of Lepanto, great naval victory over the Turks in the Gulf of Corinth, won by the Holy League led by Venice
1576	A vicious outbreak of plague in Venice carries off 60,000, including Titian
1580	Birth of Longhena
1592	Galileo obtains mathematics chair at Padua University
1593	Venice builds new ideal military town of Palmanova as a bulwark against Austria
1597	The last Este, Cesare, obliged by the pope to leave Ferrara for a new duchy in Modena; Ferrara stagnates under papal rule
1606	The Great Interdict: Pope Paul V excommunicates Venice, but thanks to Paolo Sarpi the Republic stands strong
1630	Venice decimated by the most deadly plague of its history
1669	After holding out against a siege of 21 years, the Venetians surrender Candia (Herakleon), Crete, to the Turks
1678	Venetian Elena Lucrezia Corner-Piscopia becomes the first woman to receive a university degree (at Padua, in philosophy)
1685	Francesco Morosini reconquers the Morea for Venice, but blows the roof off the Parthenon in the process
1693	Birth of Giambattista Tiepolo
1697	Birth of Canaletto
1700–13	War of the Spanish Succession
1712	Birth of Guardi
1718	With the Congress of Passarowitz, Venice loses the Morea, its last possession in the eastern Mediterranean, to the Turks
1719	Austria makes Trieste a Free Port
1720	Piedmont becomes the Kingdom of Piedmont-Sardinia
1752	Venice completes the Murazzi, the great sea walls
1792	'La Fenice' opera house built in Venice
1797	Napoleon abolishes Venetian Republic: Venetian apathy is replaced by anger when he sells it to the Austrians; Verona rebels against the French, and is partially destroyed in revenge
1800	Papal conclave held in Venice
1805	Veneto annexed to Napoleon's Cisalpine kingdom, with its capital in Milan; the French steal as much art as they can
1809	Pro-Austria insurrection of Andreas Hofer in Trentino/South Tyrol
1814	Northeast thrown back into the detested Austro-Hungarian empire

1815	Congress of Vienna bestows Duchy of Parma on Napoleon's former Empress, Marie Louise, and Venice goes to Austria
1816	Byron swims up the Grand Canal and learns Armenian
1821	Byron lives with his mistress and her husband in Ravenna, and finishes *Don Juan*
1836	Merano's radioactive springs begin to attract visitors
1846	Railway bridge ends for ever Venice's unique isolation
1848	Daniele Manin's heroic uprising against the Austrians, foiled in part by another cholera epidemic
1849	Roman Republic falls to the French; Garibaldi hides out in the pine forests of Ravenna, where his wife Anita dies from the hardship
1859	Duchy of Parma joins new Kingdom of Italy
1866	Veneto joins Italy; Prussia refuses to let Trentino leave Austria
1869	Opening of Suez Canal improves trade at Trieste
1882	Triple Alliance of Germany, Austria, and Italy confirms Austria's rule of Trentino and South Tyrol
1883	Mussolini born at Predappio, near Forlì
1902	Collapse of S. Marco campanile on 14 July
1905–14	James Joyce lives in Trieste
1910–14	Rainer Maria Rilke stays at Duino
1915	Italy enters World War I
1917	Military disaster at Caporetto
1918	Victory over Austria at Vittorio Veneto; Trentino and South Tyrol join Italy; Italians occupy Trieste; Hemingway, in the Red Cross, wounded by the Piave
1919	Gabriele D'Annunzio occupies Fiume
1920	Treaty of Rapallo returns Trieste to Austria; Fellini born in Rimini
1925	Conversion of Italy to a Fascist dictatorship
1931	Mussolini builds road causeway to Venice
1934	Hitler and Mussolini meet for the first time at the Villa Pisani on the Brenta Canal
1935	War against Ethiopia
1940	Italy enters World War II
1943	Nazis set Mussolini up in puppet government at Salò, on Lake Garda
1944	Half of Treviso destroyed in a few minutes in air bombardments on Good Friday
1945	Udine the last Italian city to be liberated; General Tito occupies Trieste, and it becomes a neutral zone until 1954
1946	National referendum makes Italy a republic
1956	Italy becomes a charter member of the EC; Winter Olympics held at Cortina d'Ampezzo
1950s	Continuing 'economic miracle' integrates Italy more closely into Western Europe
1959	Patriarch Roncalli of Venice elected Pope John XXIII

1963	Friuli-Venezia Giulia granted regional autonomy
1966	On 4 November, the worst flood in modern times sets off international alarms for Venice's safety
1976	Major earthquake in Friuli kills 1000 people
1978	Ten-mile free zone set up around Italian and Yugoslavian halves of Gorizia
1980	Rightwing extremists plant bomb in Bologna train station, killing 85 people
1990	Italian Communist Party changes its name in Bologna

LANGUAGE

The fathers of modern Italian were Dante, Manzoni, and television. Each did his part in creating a national language from an infinity of regional and local dialects; the Florentine Dante, the first 'immortal' to write in the vernacular, did much to put the Tuscan dialect in the foreground of Italian literature. Manzoni's revolutionary novel, *I promessi sposi* (The Betrothed), heightened national consciousness by using an everyday language all could understand in the 19th century. Television in the last few decades is performing an even more spectacular linguistic unification; although the majority of Italians still speak a dialect at home, school, and work, their TV idols insist on proper Italian.

Perhaps because they are so busy learning their own beautiful but grammatically complex language, Italians are not especially apt at learning others. English lessons, however, have been the rage for years, and at most hotels and restaurants there will be someone who speaks some English. In small towns and out of the way places, finding an Anglophone may prove more difficult. The words and phrases below should help you out in most situations, but the ideal way to come to Italy is with some Italian under your belt; your visit will be richer, and you're much more likely to make some Italian friends.

Italian words are pronounced phonetically. Every vowel and consonant (except 'h') is sounded. Consonants are the same as in English, except the *c* which, when followed by an 'e' or 'i', is pronounced like the English 'ch' (*cinque* thus becomes cheenquay). Italian *g* is also soft before 'i' or 'e' as in *gira*, pronounced jee-ra. *H* is never sounded; *z* is pronounced like 'ts'. The consonants *sc* before the vowels 'i' or 'e' become like the English 'sh' as in *sci*, pronounced shee; *ch* is pronouced like a 'k' as in *Chianti*, kee-an-tee; *gn* as 'ny' in English (*bagno*, pronounced ban-yo; while *gli* is pronounced like the middle of the word million (*Castiglione*, pronounced Ca-steely-oh-nay).

Vowel pronunciation is: *a* as in English father; *e* when unstressed is pronounced like 'a' in fate as in *mele*, when stressed can be the same or like the 'e' in pet (*bello*); *i* is like the i in machine; *o* like 'e', has two sounds, 'o' as in hope when unstressed (*tacchino*), and usually 'o' as in rock when stressed (*morte*); *u* is pronounced like the 'u' in June.

The accent usually (but not always!) falls on the penultimate syllable. Also note that in the big northern cities, the informal way of addressing someone as you, *tu*, is widely used; the more formal *lei* or *voi* is commonly used in provincial districts.

Useful words and phrases

yes/no/maybe	si/no/forse
I don't know	Non lo so
I don't understand (Italian)	Non capisco (italiano)
Does someone here	C'è qualcuno qui
speak English?	chi parla inglese?
Speak slowly	Parla lentamente
Could you assist me?	Potrebbe aiutarmi?

314

Help!	Aiuto!
Please	Per favore
Thank you (very much)	(Molto) grazie
You're welcome	Prego
It doesn't matter	Non importa
All right	Va bene
Excuse me	Scusi
Be careful!	Attenzione!
Nothing	Niente
It is urgent!	E urgente!
How are you?	Come sta?
Well, and you?	Bene, e lei?
What is your name?	Come si chiama?
Hello	Salve *or* ciao (both informal)
Good morning	Buongiorno (formal hello)
Good afternoon, evening	Buona sera (also formal hello)
Good night	Buona notte
Goodbye	Arrivederla (formal), arrivederci, ciao (informal)
What do you call this in Italian	Come si chiama questo in italiano?
What	Che
Who	Chi
Where	Dove
When	Quando
Why	Perchè
How	Come
How much	Quanto
I am lost	Mi sono smarrito
I am hungry	Ho fame
I am thirsty	Ho sede
I am sorry	Mi dispiace
I am tired	Sono stanco
I am sleepy	Ho sonno
I am ill	Mi sento male
Leave me alone	Lasciami in pace
good	buono/bravo
bad	male/cattivo
It's all the same	Fa lo stesso
slow	piano
fast	rapido
big	grande
small	piccolo
hot	caldo
cold	freddo
up	su

down	giù
here	qui
there	lì

Shopping, service, sightseeing

I would like...	Vorrei...
Where is/are...	Dov'è/Dove sono...
How much is it?	Quanto viene questo?/Quante'è/Quanto costa questo?
open	aperto
closed	chiuso
cheap/expensive	a buon prezzo/caro
bank	banca
beach	spiaggia
bed	letto
church	chiesa
entrance	entrata
exit	uscita
hospital	ospedale
money	soldi
museum	museo
newspaper (foreign)	giornale (straniero)
pharmacy	farmacia
police station	commissariato
policeman	poliziotto
post office	ufficio postale
sea	mare
shop	negozio
room	camera
telephone	telefono
tobacco shop	tabaccaio
WC	toilette/bagno
men	Signori/Uomini
women	Signore/Donne

TIME

What time is it?	Che ore sono?
month	mese
week	settimana
day	giorno
morning	mattina
afternoon	pomeriggio
evening	sera
today	oggi
yesterday	ieri

316

tomorrow	domani
soon	presto
later	dopo/più tarde
It is too early	E troppo presto
It is too late	E troppo tarde

DAYS

Monday	lunedì
Tuesday	martedì
Wednesday	mercoledì
Thursday	giovedì
Friday	venerdì
Saturday	sabato
Sunday	domenica

NUMBERS

one	uno/una
two	due
three	tre
four	quattro
five	cinque
six	sei
seven	sette
eight	otto
nine	nove
ten	dieci
eleven	undici
twelve	dodici
thirteen	tredici
fourteen	quattordici
fifteen	quindici
sixteen	sedici
seventeen	diciassette
eighteen	diciotto
nineteen	diciannove
twenty	venti
twenty-one	ventuno
twenty-two	ventidue
thirty	trenta
thirty-one	trentuno
forty	quaranta
fifty	cinquanta
sixty	sessanta
seventy	settanta
eighty	ottanta
ninety	novanta

hundred	cento
one hundred and one	cento uno
two hundred	duecento
thousand	mille
two thousand	due mila
million	milione
a thousand million	miliardo

TRANSPORT

airport	aeroporto
bus stop	fermata
bus/coach	auto/pulmino
railway station	stazione ferroviaria
train	treno
platform	binario
port	porto
port station	stazione marittima
ship	nave
automobile	macchina
taxi	tassi
ticket	biglietto
customs	dogana
seat (reserved)	posto (prenotato)

TRAVEL DIRECTIONS

I want to go to...	Desidero andare a...
How can I get to...?	Come posso andare a...?
Do you stop at...?	Ferma a...?
Where is...?	Dov'è...?
How far is it to...?	Quanto siamo lontani da...?
When does the... leave?	A che ora parte...?
What is the name of this station?	Come si chiama questa stazione?
When does the next ... leave?	Quando parte il prossimo...?
From where does it leave?	Da dove parte?
How long does the trip take...?	Quanto tempo dura il viaggio?
How much is the fare?	Quant'è il biglietto?
Good trip!	Buon viaggio!
near	vicino
far	lontano
left	sinistra
right	destra
straight ahead	sempre diritto
forward	avanti
backward	in dietro
north	nord/settentrionale
south	sud/mezzogiorno

east	est/oriente
west	ovest/occidente
around the corner	dietro l'angolo
crossroads	bivio
street/road	strada
square	piazza

DRIVING

car hire	noleggio macchina
motorbike/scooter	motocicletta/Vespa
bicycle	bicicletta
petrol/diesel	benzina/gasolio
garage	garage
This doesn't work	Questo non funziona
mechanic	meccanico
map/town plan	carta/pianta
Where is the road to...?	Dov'è la strada per...?
breakdown	guasto *or* panna
driving licence	patente di guida
driver	guidatore
speed	velocità
danger	pericolo
parking	parcheggio
no parking	sosta vietato
narrow	stretto
bridge	ponte
toll	pedaggio
slow down	rallentare

Italian menu vocabulary

Antipasti
These before-meal treats can include almost anything; among the most common are:

Antipasto misto	mixed antipasto
Bruschetto	garlic toast
Carciofi (sott'olio)	artichokes (in oil)
Crostini	liver pâté on toast
Frutta di mare	seafood
Funghi (trifolati)	mushrooms (with anchovies, garlic, and lemon)
Gamberi al fagioli	prawns (shrimps) with white beans
Mozzarella (in carrozza)	buffalo cheese (fried with bread in batter)
Olive	olives
Prosciutto (con melone)	raw ham (with melon)
Salame	cured pork
Salsicce	dry sausage

Minestre e Pasta

These dishes are the principal typical first courses (*primo*) served throughout Italy.

Agnolotti	ravioli with meat
Cacciucco	spiced fish soup
Cannelloni	meat and cheese rolled in pasta tubes
Cappelletti	small ravioli, often in broth
Crespelle	crepes
Fettuccine	long strips of pasta
Frittata	omelette
Gnocchi	potato dumplings
Lasagne	sheets of pasta baked with meat and cheese sauce
Minestra di verdura	thick vegetable soup
Minestrone	soup with meat, vegetables, and pasta
Orecchiette	ear-shaped pasta, usually served with turnip greens
Panzerotti	ravioli filled with mozzarella, anchovies, and egg
Pappardelle alla lepre	pasta with hare sauce
Pasta e fagioli	soup with beans, bacon, and tomatoes
Pastina in brodo	tiny pasta in broth
Penne all'arrabbiata	quill shaped pasta in hot spicy sauce
Polenta	cake or pudding of corn semolina, prepared with meat or tomato sauce
Risotto (alla Milanese)	Italian rice (with saffron and wine)
Spaghetti all'Amatriciana	with spicy sauce of salt pork, tomatoes, onions, and chilli pepper
Spaghetti alla Bolognese	with ground meat, ham, mushrooms, etc.
Spaghetti alla carbonara	with bacon, eggs, and black pepper
Spaghetti al pomodoro	with tomato sauce
Spaghetti al sugo/ragu	with meat sauce
Spaghetti alle vongole	with clam sauce
Stracciatella	broth with eggs and cheese
Tagliatelle	flat egg noodles
Tortellini al pomodoro/panna/ in brodo	pasta caps filled with meat and cheese, served with tomato sauce/with cream/in broth
Vermicelli	very thin spaghetti

Second courses–Carne (Meat)

Abbacchio	milk-fed lamb
Agnello	lamb
Animelle	sweetbreads
Anatra	duck
Arista	pork loin

Arrosto misto	mixed roast meats
Bistecca alla fiorentina	Florentine beef steak
Bocconcini	veal mixed with ham and cheese and fried
Bollito misto	stew of boiled meats
Braciola	pork chop
Brasato di manzo	braised meat with vegetables
Bresaola	dried raw meat similar to ham
Capretto	kid
Capriolo	roe deer
Carne di castrato/suino	mutton/pork
Carpaccio	thin slices of raw beef in piquant sauce
Cassoeula	winter stew with pork and cabbage
Cervello (al burro nero)	brains (in black butter sauce)
Cervo	venison
Cinghiale	boar
Coniglio	rabbit
Cotoletta (alla Milanese/alla Bolognese)	veal cutlet (fried in breadcrumbs/with ham and cheese)
Fagiano	pheasant
Faraono (alla creta)	guinea fowl (in earthenware pot)
Fegato alla veneziana	liver and onions
Involtini	rolls (usually of veal) with filling
Lepre (in salmi)	hare (marinated in wine)
Lombo di maiale	pork loin
Lumache	snails
Maiale (al latte)	pork (cooked in milk)
Manzo	beef
Osso buco	braised veal knuckle with herbs
Pancetta	rolled pork
Pernice	partridge
Petto di pollo (alla fiorentina/bolognese/sorpresa)	boned chicken breast (fried in butter/with ham and cheese/stuffed and deep fried)
Piccione	pigeon
Pizzaiola	beef steak with tomato and oregano sauce
Pollo (alla cacciatora/alla diavola/alla Marengo)	chicken (with tomatoes and mushrooms cooked in wine/grilled/fried with tomatoes, garlic and wine)
Polpette	meatballs
Quaglie	quails
Rane	frogs
Rognoni	kidneys
Saltimbocca	veal scallop with prosciutto and sage, cooked in wine and butter

Scaloppine	thin slices of veal sautéed in butter
Spezzatino	pieces of beef or veal, usually stewed
Spiedino	meat on a skewer or stick
Stufato	beef braised in white wine with vegetables
Tacchino	turkey
Trippa	tripe
Uccelletti	small birds on a skewer
Vitello	veal

Pesce (Fish)

Acciughe or Alici	anchovies
Anguilla	eel
Aragosta	lobster
Aringa	herring
Baccalà	dried cod
Bonito	small tuna
Branzino	sea bass
Calamari	squid
Cappe sante	scallops
Cefalo	grey mullet
Coda di rospo	angler fish
Cozze	mussels
Datteri di mare	razor (or date) mussels
Dentice	dentex (perch-like fish)
Dorato	gilt head
Fritto misto	mixed fried delicacies, usually fish
Gamberetto	shrimp
Gamberi (di fiume)	prawns (crayfish)
Granchio	crab
Insalata di mare	seafood salad
Lampreda	lamprey
Merluzzo	cod
Nasello	hake
Orata	bream
Ostriche	oysters
Pesce spada	swordfish
Polipi/polpi	octopus
Pesce azzurro	various types of small fish
Pesce di San Pietro	John Dory
Rombo	turbot
Sarde	sardines
Seppie	cuttlefish
Sgombro	mackerel
Sogliola	sole
Squadro	monkfish
Tonno	tuna

Triglia	red mullet (rouget)
Trota	trout
Trota salmonata	salmon trout
Vongole	small clams
Zuppa di pesce	mixed fish in sauce or stew

Contorni (side dishes, vegetables)

Asparagi (alla fiorentina)	asparagus (with fried eggs)
Broccoli (calabrese, romana)	broccoli (green, spiral)
Carciofi (alla giudia)	artichokes (deep fried)
Cardi	cardoons, thistles
Carote	carrots
Cavolfiore	cauliflower
Cavolo	cabbage
Ceci	chickpeas
Cetriolo	cucumber
Cipolla	onion
Fagioli	white beans
Fagiolini	French (green) beans
Fave	broad beans
Finocchio	fennel
Funghi (porcini)	mushroom (boletus)
Insalata (mista, verde)	salad (mixed, green)
Lattuga	lettuce
Lenticchie	lentils
Melanzana (al forno)	aubergine/eggplant (filled and baked)
Mirtilli	bilberries
Patate (fritte)	potatoes (fried)
Peperoni	sweet peppers
Peperonata	stewed peppers, onions, etc. similar to ratatouille
Piselli (al prosciutto)	peas (with ham)
Pomodoro	tomato(es)
Porri	leeks
Radicchio	red chicory
Radice	radishes
Rapa	turnip
Sedano	celery
Spinaci	spinach
Verdure	greens
Zucca	pumpkin
Zucchini	zucchini (courgettes)

Formaggio (Cheese)

Bel Paese	a soft white cow's cheese
Cascio/Casciocavallo	pale yellow, often sharp cheese
Fontina	rich cow's milk cheese

Groviera	mild cheese (gruyère)
Gorgonzola	soft blue cheese
Parmigiano	Parmesan cheese
Pecorino	sharp sheep's cheese
Provalone	sharp, tangy cheese; *dolce* is more mild
Stracchino	soft white cheese

Frutta (Fruit, nuts)

Albicocche	apricots
Ananas	pineapple
Arance	oranges
Banane	banana
Cachi	persimmon
Ciliege	cherries
Cocomero	watermelon
Composta di frutta	stewed fruit
Dattero	date
Fichi	figs
Fragole (con panna)	strawberries (with cream)
Frutta di stagione	fruit in season
Lamponi	raspberries
Macedonia di frutta	fruit salad
Mandarino	tangerine
Melagrana	pomegranate
Mele	apples
Melone	melon
More	blackberries
Nespola	medlar fruit
Pera	pear
Pesca	peach
Pesca noce	nectarine
Pompelmo	grapefruit
Prugna/susina	plum
Uve	grapes

Dolci (Desserts)

Amaretti	macaroons
Cannoli	crisp pastry tubes filled with ricotta, cream, chocolate or fruit
Coppa gelato	assorted ice cream
Crema caramella	caramel topped custard
Crostata	fruit flan
Gelato (produzione propria)	ice cream (homemade)
Granita	flavoured ice, usually lemon or coffee
Monte Bianco	chestnut pudding with whipped cream
Panettone	sponge cake with candied fruit and raisins

Panforte	dense cake of chocolate, almonds, and preserved fruit
Saint Honoré	meringue cake
Semifreddo	refrigerated cake
Sorbetto	sorbet/sherbet
Spumone	a soft ice cream
Tiramisù	cream, coffee, and chocolate dessert
Torrone	nougat
Torta	cake, tart
Torta millefoglie	layered pastry with custard cream
Zabaglione	whipped eggs and Marsala wine, served hot
Zuppa inglese	trifle

Bevande/beverages

Acqua minerale con/senza gas	mineral water with/without fizz
Aranciata	orange soda
Birra (alla spina)	beer (draught)
Caffè (freddo)	coffee (iced)
Cioccolata (con panna)	chocolate (with cream)
Gassosa	lemon flavoured soda
Latte	milk
Limonata	lemon soda
Succo di frutta	fruit juice
Tè	tea
Vino (red, white, rosé)	wine (rosso, bianco, rosato)

Cooking terms, miscellaneous

Aceto (balsamico)	vinegar (balsamic)
Affumicato	smoked
Aglio	garlic
Alla brace	on embers
Bicchiere	glass
Burro	butter
Caccia	game
Conto	bill
Costoletta/Cotoletta	chop
Coltello	knife
Cotto adagio	braised
Cucchiaio	spoon
Filetto	fillet
Forchetta	fork
Forno	oven
Fritto	fried
Ghiaccio	ice
Griglia	grill
Limone	lemon

Magro	lean meat/or pasta without meat
Mandorle	almonds
Marmellata	jam
Menta	mint
Miele	honey
Mostarda	candied mustard sauce
Nocciole	hazelnuts
Noce	walnut
Olio	oil
Pane (tostato)	bread (toasted)
Panini	sandwiches
Panna	fresh cream
Pepe	pepper
Peperoncini	hot chilli peppers
Piatto	plate
Pignoli/pinoli	pine nuts
Prezzemolo	parsley
Ripieno	stuffed
Rosmarino	rosemary
Sale	salt
Salmi	wine marinade
Salsa	sauce
Salvia	sage
Senape	mustard
Tartufi	truffles
Tazza	cup
Tavola	table
Tovagliolo	napkin
Tramezzini	finger sandwiches
Umido	cooked in sauce
Uovo	egg
Zucchero	sugar

FURTHER READING

General and Travel

Barzini, Luigi, *The Italians* (Hamish Hamilton, 1964). A perhaps too clever account of the Italians by an Italian jounalist living in London, but one of the classics.

Goethe, J. W., *Italian Journey* (Penguin Classics, 1982). An excellent example of a genius turned to mush by Italy; brilliant insights and big, big mistakes.

Haycraft, John, *Italian Labyrinth* (Penguin, 1987). One of the latest attempts to unravel the Italian mess.

Morton, H. V., *A Traveller in Italy* (Methuen, 1957). Among the most readable and delightful accounts of Italy in print. Morton is a sincere scholar, and a true gentleman. Also a good friend to cats.

Nichols, Peter, *Italia, Italia* (Macmillan, 1973). An account of modern Italy by an old Italy hand.

History

Burckhardt, Jacob, *The Civilization of the Renaissance in Italy* (Harper & Row, 1975). The classic on the subject (first published 1860), the mark against which scholars still level their poison arrows of revisionism.

Clark, Martin, *Modern Italy: 1871 to the Present Day* (Longman 1983).

Hale, J. R., editor, *A Concise Encyclopaedia of the Italian Renaissance* (Thames and Hudson, 1981). An excellent reference guide, with many concise, well-written essays.

Herder, Harry, *Italy in the Age of the Risorgimento 1790–1870* (Longman, 1983). Light shed on a very confusing period, where most of the action happens in the northwest.

Hibbert, Christopher, *Benito Mussolini* (Penguin, 1965, 1979).

Joll, James, *Gramsci* (Fontana, 1977). A look at the father of modern Italian Communism, someone we all should get to know better.

Procacci, Giuliano, *History of the Italian People* (Penguin, 1973). An in-depth view from the year 1000 to the present—also an introduction to the wit and subtlety of the best Italian scholarship.

Rand, Edward Kennard, *Founders of the Middle Ages* (Dover reprint, New York). A little-known, but incandescently brilliant work that can explain Jerome, Augustine, Boethius and other intellectual currents of the decaying classical world.

Art and Literature

Boccaccio, Giovanni, *The Decameron* (Penguin, 1972). The ever-young classic by one of the fathers of Italian literature. Its irreverent worldliness still provides a salutary antidote to whatever dubious ideas persist in your mental baggage.

327

Calvino, Italo, *Invisible Cities, If Upon a Winter's Night a Traveller* (Picador). Provocative fantasies that could only have been written by an Italian. Something even better is his recent compilation of *Italian Folktales*, a little bit Brothers Grimm and a little bit Fellini.

Cellini, *Autobiography of Benvenuto Cellini* (Penguin, trans. by George Bull). Fun reading by a swashbuckling braggart and world-class liar.

Dante Aligheri, *The Divine Comedy* (plenty of equally good translations). Few poems have ever had such a mythical significance for a nation. Anyone serious about understanding Italy and the Italian world view will need more than a passing acquaintance with Dante.

Levy, Michael, *Early Renaissance* (1967) and *High Renaissance* (1975), both by Penguin. Old-fashioned accounts of the period, with a breathless reverence for the 1500s—but still full of intriguing interpretations.

Murray, Linda, *The High Renaissance* and *The Late Renaissance and Mannerism* (Thames and Hudson, 1977). Excellent introduction to the period; also Peter and Linda Murray, *The Art of the Renaissance* (Thames and Hudson, 1963).

Petrarch, Franceso, *Canzionere and Other Works* (Oxford, 1985). The most famous poems by 'the First Modern Man'.

Vasari, Giorgio, *Lives of the Artists* (Penguin, 1985). Readable, anecdotal accounts of the Renaissance greats by the father of art history, also the first professional Philistine.

Wittkower, Rudolf, *Art and Architecture in Italy 1600–1750* (Pelican, 1986). The classic on Italian Baroque.

Venice

Lane, Frederic C., *Venice, A Maritime Republic* (Johns Hopkins, 1973). The most thorough history in English.

Lauritzen, Peter and Wolf, Reinhart, *Villas of the Veneto* (Pavilion, 1988). Lush pictures and light descriptions.

McCarthy, Mary, *The Stones of Florence* and *Venice Observed* (Penguin 1986). Brilliant evocations of Italy's two greatest art cities, with an understanding that makes many other works on the subject seem sluggish and pedantic.

Morris, James/Jan, *Venice* (Faber & Faber, 1960). Another classic on the 'World's most beautiful city'; *The Venetian Empire* (Faber & Faber, 1980).

Norwich, John Julius, *A History of Venice* (Penguin 1983). A classic, wittily-written account of the Serenissima.

Steer, John, *A Concise History of Venetian Painting* (Thames and Hudson, 1984). A good, well-illustrated introduction.

Zorzi, Alvise, *Venice: City-Republic-Empire* (Sidgwick & Jackson, 1980). Beautifully illustrated, with a large section on Venice's dealings in the Veneto and eastern Mediterranean.

GENERAL INDEX

Note: Page references in *italics* indicate illustrations, references in **bold** indicate maps.

329

INDEX OF ARTISTS AND CRAFTSMEN

Other Cadogan Guides available from your local bookstore or from the UK or the USA direct:

From the UK: Cadogan Books, 16 Lower Marsh, London SE1.
From the US: The Globe Pequot Press, 138 West Main Street, Chester, Connecticut 06412.

Title

Australia	☐
Bali	☐
The Caribbean (available November 1990)	☐
Greek Islands (Update)	☐
India (Update)	☐
Ireland (Update available September 1990)	☐
Italian Islands (Update)	☐
Italy	☐
Morocco	☐
New York	☐
Northeast Italy	☐
Northwest Italy	☐
Portugal	☐
Rome	☐
Scotland (Update)	☐
South Italy	☐
Spain (Update)	☐
Thailand & Burma	☐
Turkey (Update)	☐
Tuscany & Umbria	☐
Venice (available September 1990)	☐

Name ....

Address ....

.... Post Code ....

Date .... Order Number ....

Special Instructions ....

....

Please use this form to tell us about the hotels or restaurants you consider to be special and worthy of inclusion in our next edition, as well as to give any general comments on existing entries. Please include your name and address on the order form on the reverse of this page.

Hotels

Name ....

Address ....

Tel.. Price of double room ....

Description/Comments ....

....

....

Name ....

Address ....

Tel.. Price of double room ....

Description/Comments ....

....

....

Restaurants

Name ....

Address ....

Tel.. Price per person ....

Description/Comments ....

....

....

Name ....

Address ....

Tel.. Price per person ....

Description/Comments ....

....

....